Strengths-Based
Batterer Intervention

Peter Lehmann, PhD, LCSW, is an Associate Professor of Social Work at the School of Social Work of the University of Texas at Arlington. His research interests revolve around the assessment needs of men and women adjudicated for batterer intervention programming. In particular, he is interested in developing protocols that address a strengths perspective in the assessment process. Dr. Lehmann teaches in the direct practice stream and is Co-Director of the Community Service Center, a community mental health center associated with the School of Social Work. In addition to seeing clients, Dr. Lehmann trains and supervises graduate clinical interns.

Catherine A. Simmons, PhD, LCSW, is an Assistant Professor at the College of Social Work of the University of Tennessee. Her research interests revolve around trauma and violence with a focus on family violence, offenders, and strengths-based interventions. Dr. Simmons has over 15 years of social work practice experience with family violence, trauma, and mental health populations. Currently, Dr. Simmons teaches direct practice and leadership courses in the graduate program.

Strengths-Based Batterer Intervention

A New Paradigm in Ending Family Violence

PETER LEHMANN, PhD, LCSW
CATHERINE A. SIMMONS, PhD, LCSW

EDITORS

SPRINGER PUBLISHING COMPANY

New York

Springer Publishing Company, LLC
11 West 42nd Street
New York, NY 10036
www.springerpub.com

Acquisitions Editor: *Jennifer Perillo*
Production Manager: *Kelly J. Applegate*
Cover design: *TG Design*
Composition: *Publication Services, Inc.*

09 10 11 12/5 4 3 2 1

Library of Congress Cataloging-in-Publication Data

Lehman, Peter, 1950—
Simmons, Catherine A, 1970—
   Strengths-based batterer intervention: a new paradigm in ending family violence/Peter Lehman, Catherine Simmons.
      p. cm.
   ISBN 978-0-8261-1081-7
   1. Family violence.   2. Marital violence.   3. Family violence—Treatment.
4. Marital violence—Treatment.   5. Abusive men—Rehabilitation.   I. Simmons,
Catherine.   II. Title.
   HV6626.L444 2009
   362.82'9286–dc22   2008055617

Printed in the United States of America by Bang Printing

This book is dedicated to all those committed to ending family violence. We are particularly grateful to the tireless work of Judge Jamie Cummings, Criminal Court 5, Fort Worth, Texas, and her staff, Sally Smith, Jennifer Staples, Maria Aguilar, and Debra Bezner. They have been ongoing advocates of ending relationship violence, are role models, and inspiration for building collaborative community partnerships.

—**Peter Lehmann**
—**Catherine A. Simmons**

Contents

**4   Motivational Interviewing for Perpetrators of Intimate
Partner Violence   87**

David A. Dia, Catherine A. Simmons, Mark A. Oliver, and R. Lyle Cooper

**5   Narrative Therapy: Addressing Masculinity in Conversations
with Men who Perpetrate Violence   113**

Tod Augusta-Scott

6   Cognitive Behavioral Interventions for Partner-Abusive Men   137

Christopher I. Eckhardt and Jacqueline Schram

Contributors

Tod Augusta-Scott, MSW, RSW
Program Coordinator
Bridges (a domestic violence counseling, research, and training institute)
Truro, Nova Scotia

R. Lyle Cooper, PhD, LCSW
Assistant Professor, College of Social Work
The University of Tennessee
Nashville, TN

David A. Dia, PhD, LCSW, CCBT
Assistant Professor, College of Social Work
The University of Tennessee
Memphis, TN

Christoper I. Eckhardt, PhD
Associate Professor, Psychological Sciences
Purdue University
West Lafayette, Indiana

Barbara L. Fredrickson, PhD
Kenan Distinguished Professor of Psychology
Principal Investigator, Positive Emotions and Psychophysiology Lab
University of North Carolina - Chapel Hill
Chapel Hill, NC

Eric L. Garland, MSW, LCSW
NIH Predoctoral Fellow in Complementary and Alternative Medicine
School of Social Work
University of North Carolina - Chapel Hill
Chapel Hill, NC

Elizabeth Gilchrist, MA, MPhil, PhD
Professor and Chartered Forensic Psychologist
Department of Psychology
Glasgow Caledonian University
Glasgow, Scotland

Robyn L. Langlands, BA, MA
Postgraduate Student and PhD Candidate, Clinical Psychology
Victoria University of Wellington
Wellington, New Zealand

Mo Yee Lee, PhD
Professor, College of Social Work
The Ohio State University
Columbus, Ohio

Mark A. Oliver, MSW, LISW
PhD Program, College of Social Work
The University of Tennessee
Knoxville, TN

Joy D. Patton, MSSW, PhD (Cand.)
School of Social Work
The University of Texas at Arlington
Arlington, Texas

Jacqueline Schram, PhD
Program Clinical Psychology
Purdue University
West Lafayette, Indiana

John Sebold, LCSW
Director, Plumas County Mental Health
Meadow Valley, California

Julie A. Sutter, BA, MSSW
PhD Program, College of Social Work
The University of Tennessee
Knoxville, TN

Adriana Uken, LCSW
Trainer and Consultant
Chester, California

Tony Ward, MA, PhD, DipClinPsyc
Professor of Clinical Psychology
Victoria University of Wellington
Wellington, New Zealand

Forewords

The field of intimate partner violence (IPV) is at an impasse. We have created an industry of IPV intervention whereby most men arrested for domestic violence are routinely mandated to attend a battering intervention and prevention program. Despite declarations that arrest followed by court-ordered treatment offers "great hope and potential for breaking the destructive cycle of violence" (U.S. Attorney General's Task Force on Family Violence, 1994, p. 48), there is little evidence that our current interventions are very effective in stopping the recurrence of family violence (Babcock, Green & Robie, 2004). Current interventions, when studied appropriately with rigorous experiments, appear to be relatively ineffective at stopping domestic violence. So what do we do now? Dismantle the system? Ignore the data and proceed with "treatment as usual"? Develop new interventions? If we are going to create new IPV interventions should we modify existing interventions? Or should we chuck it all and start from scratch? What should future IPV interventions look like?

This book addresses these questions. Until quite recently, the Duluth-type model and feminist philosophy have had a stranglehold on the field. Some states mandate that only Duluth-model battering intervention programs receive funding, regardless of the fact that they are largely ineffective. Entrenched political and philosophical dogmas have thwarted the exploration of alternative theories, dismissed empirical findings, and discouraged rigorous study of the causes of intimate partner violence. This book unabashedly presents possible solutions to move the field forward. It presents alternative models of IPV interventions that will help the IPV field get "unstuck."

While the strengths-based approaches detailed in this book consider the problem of IPV from different angles, all converge on several points:

- IPV interventions should take a helping, therapeutic position rather than a didactic, educational, or authoritarian stance.

- The therapist should be empathic, as opposed to confrontational, and develop an alliance with clients.
- The therapy should adopt an idiographic approach rather than a "one size fits all" treatment package and should embrace the complexity of IPV and the diversity among perpetrators.
- The therapist should be respectful of the client—rather than pejorative, moralizing, or punitive.
- The therapy should "meet the client where he is" and strive to increase his motivation to pursue behavior change.
- The therapy should attend to and address the client's emotions.
- The therapist should help the client to modify and articulate positive and functional self-statements, which in turn will modify his emotions and behavior.
- The therapist should play to the client's strengths and foster self-compassion, as opposed to focusing on the client's weakness or past mistakes, impugning his character, and fostering shame.

All of these points are, as we know from the general clinical psychology research literature, empirically supported therapeutic principles or techniques of behavior change (Babcock, Canady, Graham & Schart, 2007). They have proven to be effective with a variety of populations. They are not radical approaches, yet they are in radical contrast with the predominant battering intervention models.

With increasing dissatisfaction with the status quo and theories that do not address the complexity of IPV, our field is poised to enter the evidence-based practice movement. This work presents novel treatments based on empirically supported techniques rather than ideology and dogma. The next step is to submit these interventions to rigorous randomized clinical trials, discarding those that prove to be ineffective and widely disseminating those that decrease IPV.

No longer will family violence research and intervention remain isolated from general standards of practice in social welfare, criminal justice, psychology, and behavioral intervention. This book harkens a new era of intimate partner violence intervention, one in which we are free to experiment with alternative ways to end intimate partner abuse.

—Julia Babcock, PhD

REFERENCES

Babcock, J. C., Canady, B., Graham, K. H., & Schart, L. (2007). The evolution of battering interventions: From the Dark Ages into the Scientific Age. In J. Hamel &

T. Nicholls (Eds). *Family Therapy for Domestic Violence: A Practitioner's Guide To Gender-Inclusive Research and Treatment* (pp. 215-244). NY: Springer.

Babcock, J. C., Green, C. E., & Robie, C. (2004). Does batterers' treatment work?: A meta-analytic review of domestic violence treatment outcome research. *Clinical Psychology Review, 23*, 1023–1053.

U.S. Attorney General (1994). *Task Force on Family Violence: Final report.* U.S. Department of Justice.

Domestic violence offenders are typically thought of as persons who are physically or verbally or psychologically abusive and controlling. What is sometimes overlooked and/or misunderstood is that a variety of other qualities may also be present in the abusive person that may further contribute to an abusive and oppressive environment in the home. These qualities can include an intolerance of opinions that differ from his, a tendency to assume that other family members are "against" him, an absence of compassion and empathy for others—particularly during abusive episodes, and a tendency to be punishing and retaliatory.

Ironically, some of the people who work with abusive men can display some of the same or similar qualities that abusive men do in the home—inflexible rules; limited compassion for the men they work with; an intolerance of opinions that differ from or challenge the program approach; viewing the men as being against them (and then responding in kind); and willfully striving to be punitive so that the men choose not to be abusive again in order to avoid having to suffer through another such program. The irony of our attempts to recreate the system that they themselves are seeking to change appears to be lost on most of them. They are also the ones who will be most likely to object to the contents of this book, beginning with its title.

"Strengths-Based Batterer Intervention" sounds like it could be terrifying. Don't abusive men have enough strength and power already? Isn't the idea to "cut them down to size"? Actually, no, it's not. The problem is not that abusive men have power or strength, but how they use their power to overpower others. The key isn't to take away any power they might have, but rather, to help them to act more appropriately with that power.

The book you hold in your hands offers a variety of approaches intended to help abusive men change by utilizing of the strengths and assets they already possess. It is intended to build upon and enhance the work that is already being done with this population. Key themes that are emphasized throughout by the various authors include the exercise of respect, compassion, collaboration, and faith, on the part of those who work with abusive men. The underlying belief is that accountability can be pursued, collusion avoided, and safety maintained while exercising these virtues in the work. The qualities that those who work with abusive men are being encouraged to practice are the very same ones we are seeking to instill in the abusive men with whom we work. As Martin Luther King, Jr., so eloquently stated: "Returning violence for violence multiplies violence, adding deeper darkness to a night already devoid of stars. Darkness cannot drive out darkness; only light can do that. Hate cannot drive out hate; only love can do that."

—Chris Huffine, PsyD

Preface

Imagination is the highest kite one can fly. —*Lauren Bacall*

In the United States and Canada, acts of physical violence against a person's intimate partner is a serious criminal act and against the law. Over the years, systems of justice have been implemented so that when an assault and arrest occurs, the offender begins a process that generally moves through the criminal justice system. For many who enter this system, participation in batterer intervention programs (BIPs) is mandated.

The most common form of mandated BIP treatment is based on the Domestic Abuse Intervention Project, founded in Duluth, Minnesota (e.g., Gondolf, 2002; Jackson et al., 2003). Commonly referred to as the Duluth model, this BIP approach was developed by a dedicated group of community feminist activists who declared that (a) violence must be brought out of the shadows of secrecy, (b) women and children must be safe, and (c) men must be fully accountable for their violent and abusive behaviors. What started as a grassroots group intervention movement through shelters for battered women has mushroomed into the primary mode of intimate partner violence (IPV) intervention, delivered in curriculum form, with a strong educative component (e.g., Gondolf, 2002; Jackson et al., 2003).

A number of critical issues have brought the tradition of the Duluth model to a turning point. The first of these is increasing dissatisfaction with the feminist ideals incorporated into political and philosophical messages about ending violence against women (e.g., Gelles, 2007; Mills, 2008). A second is growing agreement that there are limitations to the currently used approaches (e.g., Babcock, Green & Robie, 2004; Feder & Wilson, 2005; Levesque & Gelles, 1998). However, this is controversial, leading to open disagreements between professionals in the field, such as that between Edward Gondolf and Donald Dutton (please see Gondolf, 2007; Dutton & Corvo, 2007).

It goes without saying that society does not consider people who commit acts of violence against their partners in a kindly manner. Within the professional field, and particularly within batterer intervention, they have been described as generally pathological, defiant, and in a constant state of denial. They are also characterized as resistant, are vilified for their behaviors, seen as absent, irrelevant, inherently needing to exercise power and control over others, and just plain "bad people." To change their abusive behavior, many believe IPV offenders must be confronted, challenged, educated, and resocialized. They must acknowledge their wrongdoing, account for their abuse/violence, and be willing to change. In some ways, these ideals have become part of the *regimes of truth* (Foucault, 1980) about batterer intervention; however, these explanations too have come into question.

Within the family violence community, multiple controversies exist, with all sides having the same purpose: to protect people by stopping family violence. However, regardless of the arguments, empirical literature demonstrates the poor effectiveness of current approaches (e.g., Babcock, Green & Robie, 2004: Feder & Wilson, 2005; Levesque & Gelles, 1998). What we are currently doing simply does not work.

What, then, are we to do about all this? The purpose of this text is to consider other possibilities. Imagine it is possible to shift our customary thinking about people who perpetrate violence from hopeless to hopeful. Imagine it is possible that these same people who have demonstrated significant deficits by committing acts of violence actually have positive qualities. Imagine it is possible to help IPV offenders change their future behavior by incorporating their strengths, competencies, attributes, and resources into the treatment regimen.

In the smallest manner, this text opens a dialogue toward examining a paradigm shift within the field of batterer intervention. The intent is not wholesale dismantling of the good that has been accomplished, but rather a small move away from deficits, toward strengths. Thus, the objective is to provide an argument for and a means to move the field in a manner that incorporates strengths into batterer treatment practices.

The idea of using strengths is not new. Over 50 years ago Carl Rogers (1951) addressed the utility of strengths as essential to human growth and change. It is also important to say that focusing on strengths does not discount the need for IPV offenders to be responsible for their behaviors. People who have harmed their partners should be held accountable for the damage they have done. However, they also need help to change their behavior. The contents of this text pursue this change through a different route, one that is not currently a focus of the field.

To some of our colleagues, bringing strengths into work with people who are perpetrators of violence is common, rational, and makes sense. For many of our colleagues, however, it is controversial, divisive, dismissive, simplistic, risky, and perhaps even unethical. We recognize not every reader will support the contents of this text and we are realistic that there are limitations when it comes to building competencies, resources, and strengths with people who have been and may still be dangerous. Thus, at the outset let us be clear: this text supports and endorses the need for the safety of partners and children. Every man, woman, and child deserves to be safe from violence and at no time does this text endorse minimizing the need for safety.

Additionally, this text is not meant to be a multidimensional response to ending IPV, and we are cognizant the contents herein are only a small part of what has been accumulated from the professional field. We are sensitive to what this text does not cover. As a cursory example, we are aware of the burgeoning literature on the gender symmetry of violence (e.g., Dutton, 2006; Hamel & Nichols, 2007), the serious role alcohol and drugs play in the lives of men who are abusive (e.g., Stuart, 2005; van Wormer, 2007), the broad theory base (e.g., psychological, sociological, feminist), same-sex violence (Jackson, 2007), the role of parenting in relationship violence (e.g., Edleson & Williams, 2006; Scott, Francis, Crooks & Kelly, 2006), and the value of broadening the scope of treatment beyond traditional batterer intervention (e.g., Hamel, 2005; Stith, Rosen, McCollum & Thomsen, 2004; Stosny, 1995). In providing this acknowledgement, we argue that each issue has previously been detailed and presented in a balanced form by numerous authors. Clearly the field is dynamic and we recognize that practitioners are mindful of the controversies. With this in mind, this text offers a small forum to integrate another side of human nature into the treatment of people who have been violent toward their intimate partner. The side that is positive, competency driven, and strengths-based.

CONTENTS OF THIS BOOK

The contents of this book are divided into three parts. Part I forms the foundation for changing the paradigm. Chapter 1 provides an analytic discussion about the current state of batterer intervention programs. In chapter 1 the need for something different in the field of IPV intervention and the reasons for movement toward strengths-based BIP approaches are highlighted. Designed to introduce the need for "something different" and give a general overview of this new direction, Part I provides a foundation for subsequent chapters, supports the need for changing the way IPV intervention is conceptualized, and gives a general overview of what strengths-based batterer intervention is and what it is not. Chapter 2 introduces the overarching components of strengths-based batterer intervention, contrasting this approach with traditional models, and providing the groundwork for the theoretical models included in this text.

After this foundation, Part II introduces six theoretical models that can be utilized by family violence professionals when working with IPV offending populations. The first four are currently being empirically examined within the family violence field: solution-focused, motivational interviewing, narrative therapy, and strengths focused cognitive behavioral therapy (CBT).

The first theoretical model, solution-focused treatment of domestic violence offenders, is a solution-based, goal-directed, domestic violence group treatment program developed through the Plumas Project (Uken, Lee & Sebold, 2007), first described by Lee, Greene, and Rheinscheld (1999) and further elaborated by Lee, Sebold, and Uken (2003a). In addition to these descriptive works, multiple studies have demonstrated the effectiveness of the solution-focused theoretical approach with IPV offenders (please see Lee, Sebold & Uken, 2003b; Lee, Uken & Sebold, 2004, 2007; Uken, Lee & Sebold, 2007).

The second theoretical model, motivational interviewing, is a focused, client-centered, and goal-directed approach to intervention designed to help clients explore and resolve their ambivalence to change (Rollnick & Miller, 1995). Theoretically based on the transtheoretical model (TTM) of change (Prochaska & DiClemete, 1983, 1984; Prochaska, DiClemente & Norcross, 1992), aspects of motivational interviewing are proving to be effective with the IPV offender population (please see Easton, Swan & Sinha, 2000; Kistenmacher & Weiss, 2008; Musser, Semiantin, Taft & Murphy, 2008; Taft, Murphy, Elliott & Morrel, 2001).

The third theoretical model, narrative therapy, utilizes language in a collaborative therapeutic engagement with IPV offending clients (Augusta-Scott, 2008; Augusta-Scott & Dankwort, 2002). Adapted for IPV offenders at a program called "Bridges" in Nova Scotia, Canada, narrative therapy is a promising conversational approach to intervention.

The fourth theoretical model is a strengths-focused CBT. Although traditional CBT is evident throughout the family violence field, the presented approach shifts the paradigm to strengths building.

In addition to the four theoretical models addressed above, two additional methods that are not currently used with IPV offenders but have shown promise are also presented: broaden-and-build and the Good Lives Model. Although no agencies are currently utilizing these two promising approaches with the IPV offender populations, they have proven effective with other populations traditionally considered "challenging," such as sexual offenders, serious violent offenders, and prison populations (e.g., Maruna, 2001; Ward & Marshall, 2004; Whitehead, Ward & Collie, 2007). Thus, both broaden-and-build and the Good Lives Model have exciting potential to become helpful with batterer intervention. In addition to the four theoretical models discussed above, this text provides six promising and useful theoretical approaches that family violence professionals can incorporate into their work with IPV offending clients.

The third and final part of this text provides practical applications and a look toward the future. Grounded in the idea that reducing negative behaviors is dependent on building the positive side of the person's potential, chapter 9 discusses assessment and treatment of IPV offenders from a strengths-based perspective. It also includes 20 examples of practical "tools" that can be used in the domestic violence treatment setting. The included instruments, exercises, questions, and assessment strategies build on strengths and competencies, with an emphasis on promoting safety. In addition to the tools provided, this part also includes an annotated bibliography of additional resources family violence professionals may find helpful. The final chapter closes the book with a look forward that summarizes the strengths-based models presented, then discusses future theoretical, empirical, and practical directions for expanding strengths-based approaches within IPV offender intervention.

THE HOPE

In closing the preface, we want to say that we believe the future of batterer intervention is hopeful. The field of batterer intervention, grounded in the strides made by the feminist movements, can now be moved forward in a positive way. The ideas, constructs, and concepts included in this text are intended to facilitate this move by incorporating strengths into intervention with domestic violence offenders. It is not our intent to diminish the work of others, but instead to build on this foundation in a way that improves the field. Our hope is to change lives by providing family violence professionals with ideas, resources, and tools that can positively affect intervention with people who have been violent with their partner. We hope this text is helpful to those who imagine a different, positive way to approach batterer intervention. To this end, if even one family violence professional changes the paradigm in which they view their IPV offending clients, then we believe we have succeeded in this task.

REFERENCES

Augusta-Scott, T. (2008). *Narrative therapy abuse intervention program: A program to foster respectful relationships. A group facilitator's manual.* Nova Scotia: Bridges, a domestic violence counseling, research, and training institute.

Augusta-Scott, T. & Dankwort, J. (2002). Partner abuse group intervention: Lessons from education and narrative therapy approaches. *Journal of Interpersonal Violence, 17,* 783–805.

Babcock, J.C., Green, C.E., & Robie, C. (2004). Does batterers' treatment work? A meta-analytic review of domestic violence treatment. *Clinical Psychology Review, 23,* 1023–1053.

Barker, R.L. (2003). *The social work dictionary.* Washington DC: NASW Press.

Dutton, (2006). *Rethinking domestic violence.* (2nd ed.). Vancouver: University of British Columbia Press.

Dutton, D.G., & Corvo, K. (2007). The Duluth model: A data-impervious paradigm and a failed strategy. *Aggression and Violent Behavior, 12,* 658–667.

Easton, C., Swan, S., & Sinha, R. (2000). Motivation to change substance use among offenders of domestic violence. *Journal of Substance Abuse Treatment, 19,* 1–5.

Edleson, J.L., & Williams, O.J. (2006). *Parenting by men who batter: New directions for assessment and intervention.* New York: Oxford University Press.

Feder, L., & Wilson, D.B. (2005). A meta-analytic review of court-mandated batterer intervention programs: Can courts affect abusers' behavior? *Journal of Experimental Criminology, 1,* 239–262.

Foucault, M. (1980). *Power/Knowledge: Selected interviews and other writings 1972–1977.* New York: Pantheon.

Gelles, R.J. (2007). The politics of research: The use, abuse, and misuse of social science data—the cases of intimate partner violence. *Family Court Review, 45,* 42–51.

Gondolf, E.W. (2002). *Batterer Intervention Systems: Issues Outcomes and Recommendations.* Thousand Oaks California: Sage.

Gondolf, E.W. (2007). Theoretical and research support for the Duluth model: A reply to Dutton and Corvo. *Aggression &Violent Behavior, 12,* 644–657.

Hamel, J. (2005). *Gender inclusive treatment of intimate partner abuse: A comprehensive approach.* New York: Springer.

Hamel, J., & Nicholls, T.L. (Eds.). (2007). *Family interventions in domestic violence: A handbook of gender-inclusive theory and treatment.* New York: Springer.

Jackson, N.A. (2007). Same-sex domestic violence: Myths, facts, correlates, treatment, and prevention strategies. In A.R. Roberts (Ed.). *Battered women and their families: Intervention strategies and treatment programs* (3rd ed.) (pp. 451–470). New York: Springer.

Jackson, S., Feder, L., Forde, D.R., Davis, R.C., Maxwell, C.D., & Taylor, B.G. (June 2003). Batterer intervention programs: Where do we go from here? *Special NIJ Report*, Washington DC; National Institute of Justice, U.S. Department of Justice.

Kistenmacher, B.R., & Weiss, R.L. (2008). Motivational interviewing as a mechanism for change in men who batter: A randomized control trial. *Violence and Victims, 5*, 558–570.

Levesque, D.A., & Gelles, R.J. (1998, July). *Does treatment reduce recidivism in men who batter: A meta-analytic evaluation of treatment outcome.* Paper presented at the Program Evaluation and Family Violence Research: An International Conference: Durham, NH.

Lee, M.Y., Greene, G.J., & Rheinscheld, J. (1999). A model for short-term solution-focused group treatment of male domestic violence offenders. *Journal of Family Social Work, 3*, 39–57.

Lee, M.Y., Sebold, J., & Uken, A. (2003a). *Solution-focused treatment of domestic violence offenders: Accountability for change.* New York: Oxford University Press.

Lee, M.Y., Sebold, J., & Uken, A. (2003b). Brief solution-focused group treatment with domestic violence offenders: Listen to the narratives of participants and their partners. *Journal of Brief Therapy, 2*, 3–26.

Lee, M.Y., Uken, A., & Sebold, J. (2004). Accountability for solutions: Solution-focused treatment with domestic violence offenders. *Families in Society, 85*, 463–476.

Lee, M.Y., Uken, A., & Sebold, J. (2007). Role of self-determined goals in predicting recidivism in domestic violence offenders. *Research on Social Work Practice, 17*, 30–41.

Maruna, S. (2001). *Making good: How ex-convicts reform and rebuild their lives.* Washington, DC: American Psychological Association.

Mills, L.G. (2008) *Violent partners: A breakthrough plan for ending the cycle of abuse.* New York: Basic Books.

Musser, P.H., Semiantin, J.N., Taft, C.T., & Murphy, C.M. (2008). Motivational interviewing as a pregroup intervention for partner violent men. *Violence and Victims, 23*, 539–557.

Prochaska, J.O., & DiClemete, C.C. (1983) Stages and processes of self-change of smoking: Toward an integrative model of change. *Journal of Consulting and Clinical Psychology, 51*, 390–395.

Prochaska, J.O., & DiClemete, C.C. (1984). *The transtheoretical approach: Crossing the traditional boundaries of therapy.* Malabar, FL: Krieger.

Rogers, C. (1951). Client-centered therapy: *Its current practice, theory, and implications.* Chicago, IL: Houghton Mifflin.

Rollnick, S., & Miller, W.R. (1995). What is motivational interviewing? *Behavioural and Cognitive Psychotherapy, 23*, 325–334.

Scott, K., Francis, K., Crooks, C., & Kelly, T. (2006). *Caring Dads: Helping fathers value their children.* Victoria, BC: Trafford.

Stith, S.M., Rosen, K.H., McCollum, E.E., & Thomsen, C.J. (2004). Treating intimate partner violence within intact couple relationships: Outcomes of multi-couple versus individual couple therapy. *Journal of Marital and Family Therapy, 30*, 305–318.

Stosny, S. (1995). *Treating attachment abuse: A compassionate approach.* New York: Springer.

Stuart, G.L., (2005). Improving violence intervention outcomes by integrating alcohol treatment. *Journal of Interpersonal Violence, 20*, 388–393.

Taft, C.T., Murphy, C.M., Elliott, J.D., & Morrel, T.M. (2001). Attendance enhancing procedures in group counseling for domestic abusers. *Journal of Counseling Psychology, 48,* 51–60.

Uken, A., Lee, M.Y., & Sebold, J. (2007). The Plumas project: Solution-Focused treatment of domestic violence offenders. In P. DeJong & I.K. Berg, *Interviewing for solutions* (3rd ed.) (pp. 313–323). Pacific Cove, CA: Brooks/Cole.

van Wormer, K.S. (2007). Domestic violence and substance abuse: An integrated approach. In A.R. Roberts (Ed.). *Battered women and their families: Intervention strategies and treatment programs.* (3rd ed.) (pp. 399–422). New York: Springer.

Ward, T., & Marshall, W.L. (2004). Good lives, aetiology, and the rehabilitation of sex offenders: A bridging theory. *Journal of Sexual Aggression, 10,* 153–169.

Whitehead, P.R., Ward, T., & Collie, R.M (2007). Time for a change: Applying the Good Lives Model of rehabilitation to a high-risk violent offender. *International Journal of Offender Therapy and Comparative Criminology, 51,* 578–598.

Acknowledgments

I want to acknowledge the people who are most important to me and who made this book possible, including my husband Matt, my mother Dolly, my brother Harold, my sister Ramona, and my aunts and uncles. I also want to thank the colleagues I've worked with through the years who have helped me develop the ideas included in this text.

—Catherine A. Simmons, PhD, LCSW

To Delphine; to Daley and Rory; to Insoo and Steve.

—Peter Lehmann, PhD, LCSW

A Changing Paradigm

PART
I

1

The State of Batterer Intervention Programs: An Analytical Discussion

PETER LEHMANN
CATHERINE A. SIMMONS

Re-examine all you have been told . . . dismiss whatever insults your soul.
                                                                    —*Walt Whitman*

The impact of violence on intimate partner relationships has tragically continued to be part of the North American fabric of life. The thought that people who have committed to love each other become violent, occasionally resulting in injury or death, seems anathema to a common sense way of thinking and behaving. The public is appalled by the sheer brutality and horror of those cases that reach media attention. Yet, as a society we have been unable to stem the tide of pain that is inflicted by intimate partner violence (IPV). All too often we are left to wonder "why," "how could anyone do such terrible things," and "how could this happen?"

Such questions have led to open and frank discussions about violence, particularly violence against women by their male partners. Consequentially, in the last three decades, the problems surrounding IPV have become recognized as an important and critical social issue that

---

It is recognized that intimate partner violence is perpetrated by both men and women, and within the context of both heterosexual and homosexual relationships. However, the pronouns used in this chapter often reflect the typical case that is seen in batterer intervention: a male offender and a female survivor/victim.

deserves attention. A collective response from the professional field has emerged as the criminal justice response system, the battered women's shelter movement, and an increasing number of community responders, educators, researchers, policy makers, and batterer treatment providers work to develop programs designed to end IPV.

Of further relevance to IPV professionals has been the adoption of mandatory arrest laws (also called pro arrest laws) that began in the 1980s. These laws require legal intervention in cases where evidence of probable cause exists. A natural consequence of these laws was a dramatic increase in the number of IPV offenders who were arrested, and subsequent pressure on the courts to deal with them (Ford & Regoli, 1993). From this, the growth of mandatory programming for male IPV offenders expanded.

Since their grass-roots beginnings in the early 1970s, batterer intervention programs (BIPs) for men have evolved into the most prominent and visible form of intervention aimed at ending IPV (Gondolf, 2002; Jackson et al., 2003). At present, every state in the United States and every province and territory in Canada have adopted some form of mandated batterer intervention programming (Austin & Danwort, 1999; Dankwort & Austin, 1999). Current estimates suggest that at least 80% of all BIP participation is mandated (Healey, Smith & O'Sullivan, 1998) and that most of the programs these men attend are based on the tenets of the Domestic Abuse Intervention Project (DAIP) (e.g., Gondolf, 2002; Jackson et al., 2003), commonly referred to as the Duluth model.

To their credit, those involved with the Duluth model have helped raise awareness with respect to violence against women, created an infrastructure dedicated to helping victims/survivors, contributed to the development of the professional field, and produced a new generation of professional practitioners and researchers devoted to eliminating this significant social problem. At the same time, Mills (2008) correctly stated that a point has been reached where "the enormous gains we've made must give us the courage to confront our weaknesses and expand our horizons" (p. 252). Consequently, questions are being raised such as "What else can be done to improve batterer intervention?" and "Are there other ways of responding to IPV that are potentially helpful?" The purpose of this chapter, then, is to address these questions by way of an analytical discussion of the current trends affecting batterer intervention. In this discussion, a cursory summary of the two most prominent models is presented first. Next, a section reviewing outcome effectiveness and ideological polarities highlights the emerging changes that are now influencing the family violence field. Finally, an overview of the rationale for shifting the paradigm used to approach batterer intervention is developed with an introduction to strengths-based approaches.

PROMINENT APPROACHES

The following section reviews the Duluth and cognitive-behavioral models of batterer intervention. While the psychodynamic/trauma method might also be considered prominent in some areas, we agree with Hamberger (2008b), who stated that the approach actually represents three separate treatment approaches: attachment, trauma, and shame. Thus, an outline of the psychodynamic/trauma method is not included in the present discussion.

Duluth Model of Batterer Intervention

An analytical discussion about the state of batterer intervention must start with an overview of the most prominent approaches, the first of which is the Duluth model. It was founded in 1981 in Duluth, Minnesota, as a means to (a) change the privacy and secrecy which often surrounded IPV, and instead make it public, (b) make communities safer for victims and (c) hold offenders accountable for their behavior (Pence & Paymar, 1993). The Duluth Model is regarded as a hybrid of feminist and cognitive behavioral principles (see also chapter 2) in that accountability for one's actions, challenging and changing beliefs/attitudes, and education are central to changing the violent behavior of men who batter (e.g., Edleson & Tolman, 1992; Gondolf, 2007; Healey, Smith & O'Sullivan, 1989; Schmidt et al., 2007; Shepard & Pence, 1989; Vincent & Jouriles, 2000). The Duluth model is grounded in the belief that arrest and prosecution coupled with court-mandated intervention, primarily in the form of group work, is crucial for change. Because the Duluth model views IPV as learned behavior, treating psychological problems and/or changing personalities is not considered part of the process. Group facilitators typically avoid the *Diagnostic and Statistical Manual of Mental Disorders* (DSM) or other psychiatric-type diagnoses and do not consider their work to be "therapy." Instead, peer group formats are viewed as the best vehicle for re-learning gender sensitive, non-violent behaviors (Caesar & Hamberger, 1989; Edleson & Tolman, 1992).

Critical to the Duluth model is the belief that male-only groups are the safest and most ethical means of helping men take responsibility for changing their behaviors. Administered over a period of 6 months (or more) in weekly 1½ to 2 hour group sessions, the Duluth curriculum is a manualized educative mixture of feminist principles integrated with cognitive-behavioral interventions (e.g., Pence & Paymar, 1985, 1993). A working premise of this approach is the belief that domestic violence is a learned pattern of intimidation, coercive control, and socially sanctioned behavior against women (e.g., Pence & Paymar, 1985, 1993). Thus, the work of men-only groups is to reeducate participants in a structured manner by confronting (a) their sense of gendered entitlement and sexist attitudes towards women and (b) their minimization and denial of abusive behavior (e.g., Minnesota Program Development, Inc., 2007; Paymar, 2000; Pence & Paymar, 1993; Shepard & Pence, 1999), and challenging each man to be fully accountable and take responsibility for his behavior. As part of the Duluth approach participants sign a release-of-information form and a program contract agreement with the understanding that acts of violence and violation of court orders will be reported to the court, and that noncompliance with program rules will likely result in suspension from the group (Paymar, 2000). In this model of intervention, volunteers are treated in the same manner as those who are court-mandated and program staff may testify at revocation or review hearings regarding violations of the program contract (Minnesota Program Development, Inc., 2007; Paymar, 2000).

CBT–Cognitive Behavioral Interventions

While the majority of batterer intervention programs base much of their curricula and policies on the feminist cognitive behavioral principles outlined in the Duluth curriculum (e.g., Gondolf, 2002; Jackson et al., 2003), a few alternatives exist. Of those, in the last two decades, cognitive behavioral therapy (CBT) in the form of CBT based men's groups are the most prominent (e.g., Hamberger, 1997, 2002; Jennings, 1987; Sonkin & Durphy, 1997; Wexler, 2000). In contrast to the Duluth model, a CBT approach conceptualizes IPV as a consequence of problems with the person's thoughts, assumptions, beliefs, and behaviors (Murphy & Eckhardt, 2005). The underlying idea of those operating from a CBT paradigm is that violence is used because it is functional for the person using it. That is, the batterer uses violence against his partner to reduce his inner tension, to achieve victim compliance, to end an uncomfortable situation, and/or to give the batterer a feeling of power and control over a situation (Sonkin, Martin & Walker, 1985). Therefore, CBT approaches to batterer intervention focus on behavioral skill building/role playing with the intent of reducing anger, conflict management, and increasing positive interaction (such as active listening and/or nonviolent assertiveness).

On the surface these groups sound promising, however it has been pointed out that some CBT labels are often misleading, as most of these groups also address emotional components such as empathy and jealousy (Babcock, Green & Robie, 2004; Dunford, 2000). Further, it is widely known that most CBT groups adhere to a combination of educational methods; they focus more on cognitive information, but less on cognitive or emotional processing (see Eckhardt & Schramm, this volume). Additionally, Babcock, Green, and Robie (2004) observed that

> Most modern cognitive-behavioral groups also usually address perpetrator attitudes and values regarding women and the use of violence toward women. To the extent that CBT groups address patriarchal attitudes, and Duluth model groups address the learned and reinforced aspects of violence, any distinction between CBT and Duluth model groups becomes increasingly unclear. (p. 1026)

Eckhardt and Schram (see chapter 6) provide greater detail with respect to the underlying components of this model and examine some of this criticism in the evolving field. At the same time, it would seem the current state of batterer intervention is one of similarities across systems that have resulted in manualized singular approaches. This cross fertilization has been integrated with what has become known as the traditional BIP approach to batterer intervention.

EMERGING CHANGES

As the Duluth model has gained influence in the intervention field it has been held up as "one of the most successful community-based projects for violent men anywhere in the world" (Dobash, Dobash, Cavanagh & Lewis, 2000, p. 48). Consequently, for more than two decades the basic assumptions and ideals of the model (see chapter 2) have remained effects ranging from minimal (Feder & Wilson, 2005) to small (Babcock, Green & Robie, 2004), it is logical that academics and practitioners have begun to seriously consider other forms of batterer intervention/treatment.

Ideological Polarities

A second area of divergence with traditional BIP models centers on an ideological polarity within the field. The development of this polarity was evident over a decade ago in the work of Eisikovits and Buchbinder (1996). At the time, the authors predicted that the rise and fall of ideologies, pressure groups, and modes of intervention would grow as the field of domestic violence became more professionalized. Eisikovits and Buchbinder believed that the idea of "who owns the problem" (p. 186) would create tensions between pressure groups, claims makers, and interest groups. In a spirit of optimism, it was felt that these tensions would create opportunities to enhance interventions. Unfortunately, evidence of a convergence among professionals on behalf of understanding the complexity of domestic violence and what might be done to intervene is yet to be seen.

More recently, Dutton (2008) has referred to the polarity of thinking as the "gender analysis" (p. 20) while Hamel and Nicholls (2007) described it as the "gender camp" (p. xii). Essentially, these views have divided the field of batterer intervention into two groups. The first group represents those who ascribe to the view that (a) patriarchy, male privilege, and male acceptance of violence is, was, and continues to be the root cause of IPV, (b) that men, for the most part, are the only so-called real IPV perpetrators, and (c) operating from a different paradigm compromises safety. The second group argues that (a) patriarchy has little to do with changing behavior, (b) men and women can be both perpetrators and victims, and (c) it is entirely possible to think outside of the box (Dutton, 2007, 2008), develop innovative interventions, and not compromise safety. As will be pointed out below, these ideological polarities are currently at their height; however, a forecast of change is developing throughout the field.

An Array of Differences

Grounded in the view that patriarchy is tied to IPV, the first side of the ideological split can be traced to a number of feminist clinicians/authors, including Bograd (1984, 1988), Chornesky (2000), MacKinnon and Miller (1984), Pressman (1989), Shepard and Pence (1999), and Walker (1989), to name a few. These prominent authors argued that although non-feminist models of IPV intervention attempted to remain neutral, they actually often blamed women. Many argued that non-feminist models ignored the real effects of violence, dismissed the unequal power imbalances in relationships, and were less willing to acknowledge that male domination and oppression of women existed at almost every level of society. Further, these views supported the idea that batterer intervention should focus on reducing the male batterer's need for power and control over his female partners. Although the outcome of these arguments provided a foundation for both increasing awareness about IPV and the need for intervention, they also provided a one dimensional perspective of violence, excluding the possibility of alternative models of batterer intervention. In effect, the literature and political argument created by this philosophical perspective set the stage for BIP approaches, such as the Duluth model, to be the sole mode of change.

The nature of ideological polarities may be the result of passionate pro-feminist authors who, while meaning to draw attention to the problem of IPV, seem to both discount existing evidence and simplify the complexity of relationship violence to a single variable. For example, in responding to intimate partner homicide, Serran and Firestone (2004) suggested "the law and the patriarchal hierarchy have legitimized wife beating and control, resulting in unequal power relationships between men and women" (p. 12). Likewise, in their discussion about battering, Pence and Das Dasgupta (2006) state:

> . . . historically, groups of people have established and sustained supremacy over other groups of people by the use of violence that includes ongoing and systematic patterns of intimidation, coercion, as well as other tactics of control to physically, morally, spiritually, and economically devastate them. This is the kind of violence that has been used by whites over people of color; traffickers over prostituted women; the economically powerful over the poor; slave owners over slaves; and feudal landlords over subjects. At its extreme, it is manifested as witch hunt, ethnic cleansing, genocide, slave trading, and holocaust. The analogy is easily extended to the battering of women in marriage (Mies, Bennholdt-Thomsen & Von Werlhof, 1988) and intimate relationships. It is manifested as the murder of thousands of women and their children every year in the U.S. (p. 6)

Finally, in arguing that "husband abuse" is a continuing myth which may be perceived as a backlash against women, Minaker and Snider (2006) concluded, "The invention and celebration of husband abuse makes it more difficult to deal with power imbalances between male and female partners and easier to ignore or explain away empirical evidence showing that family violence usually means wife abuse" (p. 770). The above comments reflect a narrow and misleading perspective of IPV, making it akin to ethnic cleansing and genocide, while ignoring both the complex nature of intimate partner relationships and the idea that there could be other plausible explanations. It is entirely possible that such post-Duluth writings have come to represent what has been seen as biased assimilation (Lord, Ross & Lepper, 1979) and groupthink (Dutton & Nicholls, 2005; Janis, 1982). The perception could be that strongly held beliefs about patriarchy and male violence have led writers to ignore contradictory evidence, setting the stage for social groups to sustain the status quo by also ignoring other support.

Although such activist writing has generated much attention within the field, over time divisions have developed among IPV professionals. Rather than pooling expertise and collaborating on how to better understand and treat batterer populations, it appears that sides have been drawn that leave little room for the field to advance. For example, Gelles (2007) argued that the many pro-feminist "facts" presented about why men's violence is so common have little to do with existing evidence. In effect, Gelles argues, information has been published about the prevalence, seriousness, and risk of men's violence that has yet to be measured or collected. He further cautions that undertaking such research has the potential to reduce "the credibility of the advocates" (p. 44). What is missing is an opportunity to create openings for dialogue around feminist ideas, not by disposing of gender, but by assimilating gender in a manner consistent with the growth of the field. One exception stands out as a meeting ground for theory and practice. As a result of a focus group study with front line workers, McPhail, Busch, Kulkarni, and Rice (2007) proposed an integrated feminist model (IFM). The authors' model rests on two feminist practice positions: (a) it is behavior, not the person (male/female), that should be the focus, and (b) empathy and accountability for all involved. In effect, the authors took worker practice experiences and combined them with an expanded theoretical/knowledge base of the field while keeping certain feminist principles as guides.

One final exemplar of the ongoing ideological split are the series of essays from Gondolf (2007) and Dutton and Corvo (2007), in which both engage in a lively yet tense debate about the merits of the Duluth model. Both openly criticize each other's work, devoting a great deal of space to advancing what appears to be the objective truth of their evidence and the falsehoods of the other. Clearly, the end result seems to have eliminated much hope for collegial dialogue between the esteemed researchers about where the field is headed. Both accuse the other of falling into ideological, false positions yet neither offer constructive steps for moving toward the center. Gondolf ends by inviting the dialogue to broaden (p. 11) while in the same breathe accusing Dutton and Corvo of circumventing the field. Likewise, Dutton and Corvo suggest broader treatments may work but not without ending their essay by disdainfully asking how arrested women fit in a model (Duluth) when they are themselves are "slaves to patriarchy" (p. 8). If anything, these debates are essentially an ongoing culmination of a polarized field where ownership of the problem has become politicized to an extreme.

What has become increasingly clear is that something different is needed for the field of batterer intervention to move forward. The purpose of this discussion is not to advocate for the dismantling of what already exists. Instead, the purpose of this analysis is to (a) create a partnership and collaboration between science and practice, (b) promote reasonable, progressive thinking about effective and new program development, (c) support continued research into what works, and (d) seek to develop coordinated respect for differences (McNamee, 2004). The argument is simply for a small move forward, a shift away from "more of the same" and toward a strategy that is not risky, dangerous, or completely foreign. The purpose of this text is to encourage a paradigm shift from the current understanding of batterer intervention as the "only correct approach" to a model that is open to incorporating new ideas, ideas that integrate strengths into the equation.

A PARADIGM SHIFT

Any discussion with respect to a paradigm shift in batterer intervention is not intended to be a sweeping scientific revolution like that prescribed by Kuhn (1962). Instead small incremental changes are needed in the way professionals conceptualize IPV. A small paradigm shift will allow the field of batterer intervention to broaden, hopefully resulting in an expanded set of new ideas and methods about what is (or could be) helpful. From this, a strengths-based paradigm is introduced below, further elaborated in chapter two, and incorporated throughout this book. A strengths-based perspective has the potential to create new variations in IPV assessment and intervention.

The move toward a paradigm shift in the professional field has been in progress for some time as articulated by a small group of authors. For example, in moving beyond the parameters of traditional feminism with respect to batterers, Grauwiler and Mills (2004) endorsed a paradigm change incorporating restorative justice with men. In their work, Grauwiler and Mills introduced the concept of *Intimate Abuse Circles* that address violence but also create a continuum of community support, which may or may not include a criminal justice response. Mills (2003) earlier called for social policy changes in the arrest of batterers and the response to domestic violence based on the ideas that violence is not always one sided, and treatment should focus on healing rather than shame and punishment. Likewise, Stuart (2005) suggested that the treatment of batterer populations should find ways to move from a universal singular approach to a range of interventions based on the need for a balance between (a) assessment and treatment and (b) individual and conjoint work. These ideas were summarized in a review of current "systemic" models of practice, which include various treatment options (for a review, see Hamel, 2007). Additionally, waning allegiance to the dominant model has created a host of conceptually diverse and broad treatment regimens. Beyond CBT interventions, additional models have included dialectical behavior therapy (e.g., Fruzzetti & Levensky, 2000; Waltz, 2003), feminist-cognitive behavioral therapy (Saunders, 1996a) as well as psychodynamic models of BIPs, aimed at modifying underlying behaviors that are associated with traumatic experiences and/or personality deficits by targeting attachment, dependency (Browne, Saunders & Staecker, 1997; Sonkin & Dutton, 2003) and shame (Stosny, 1995). More recently, a solution-focused model (Lee, Seebold & Uken, 2003; Milner & Jessop 2003; Milner & Singleton, 2008), and a narrative model (Augusta–Scott, 2008) have been developed. As the argument for a paradigm shift continues to develop in the batterer intervention literature, a number of issues emerge that may also be considered. The following 6 issues are addressed in this narrative below: (a) the question of heterogeneity, (b) manualization, (c) the process to outcome dilemma, (d) group confrontation, (e) creating behavior change, and (f) safety. It is important to note that these issues are not finite ones for the field but instead represent a beginning step.

The Question of Heterogeneity

The question of heterogeneity represents the first argument for a paradigm shift for moving the field beyond traditional BIP approaches. Although these traditional approaches view batterers as similar, there appears to be growing consensus within the professional field that the batterer population is heterogeneous. That is, there are vast differences, both large and small, that may be found in and between men who perpetrate IPV.

The importance of heterogeneity may be traced to the clinical and empirical work with batterer typologies. Typology research attempts to narrow the vast dissimilarities between IPV offenders into workable profiles so that treatment can target identified characteristics, decrease recidivism, and find better ways to increase partner safety. The idea of typologies first developed with Elbow's (1977) summary of four personality syndromes in wife abusers: the controller, the defender, the approval seeker, and the incorporator. Gondolf (1988) followed suit with his theory of three primary typologies: sociopathic, antisocial, and nondisordered men. Nevertheless, the idea of profiling a "batterer typology" came to fruition with Holtzworth-Munroe's and Stuart's (1994) documentation of 3 batterer typologies: family only, borderline-dysphoric, and generally violent-antisocial. Cavanaugh and Gelles (2005) recently categorized offenders into low-, medium-, and high-risk types that are further sub-divided into severity and frequency of violence, criminal history, and psychopathology. The evolution and summary of these ideas is exemplified in the recent work of Bender and Roberts (2007), which synchronizes the conceptual and empirical typology literature. In this body of work, the authors create a template for use, an informative horizontal (level of risk by offender typology) by vertical (level of risk to survivor) axis that integrates the potential impact on female partners.

The problem with the current understanding of offender "types" is that they appear to follow the risk-need-responsivity models of offender rehabilitation (Andrews & Bonta, 2003). Such models are specifically aimed at reducing and changing offender (in this case, batterer) risk factors (e.g., sexist beliefs/attitudes, power/control issues, mental illness issues, substance issues, psychopathy, and childhood maltreatment issues) as found with BIP work. At the same time, no consensus exists concerning which typology is the most helpful for assessment or which risk-reducing interventions fit best with which type of profile (Healey & Smith, 1998). While it is important that attention is given to batterer risk so as to reduce harm, it is not sufficient for effective treatment and long-lasting change (Yates & Ward, 2008). Further, the current typology models do not seem to acknowledge one's wellbeing, mental health, capabilities, or competencies (Whitehead, Ward & Collie, 2007), which are seen as necessary to reduce dangerous behavior.

A second issue with heterogeneity is that over the last 20 years, innovative treatment programs that might develop from typology models have not kept pace with the large numbers of men adjudicated by the courts. As a result, most communities have continued to use a singular form of batterer intervention instead of seeking ways to build typologies into treatment. It is likely that this trend may be a function of a combination of variables including but not limited to: (a) an unwillingness to accept novel approaches that do not include patriarchy as the central cause of IPV (Dutton & Corvo, 2007); (b) a rejection on the part of jurisdictions of programming that is not based on Duluth model type principles (Gelles, 2002); (c) a sustained preference for arrest and mandated programming (beyond typologies and treatment) held by the community (e.g., Pence & Paymar, 1993); (d) a continual interest in understanding the history, roots, and dynamics associated with IPV (Lee, Seebold & Uken, 2003) to the exclusion of all other behaviors; (e) a lack of significant exposure to typology training used to identify accurate profiles (Lohr et al., 2005); and (f) a gap between the practice and research fields. Specifically, there are questions about whether empirically derived subtypes (research) will be useful in clinically-driven (practice) settings. In attempting to address some of these questions, Langhinrichsen-Rohling, Huss, and Ramsey, (2000) found that a small cohort (n = 5) of advanced clinical psychology graduate students could not reliably sort out profiles into subtypes using standardized measures and police reports These findings suggest that individual variation could limit clinical/practical usefulness of empirical subtypes. It should be noted, though, that there are challenges beyond keeping men in offender treatment (e.g., those identified by their psychopathy) (Langhinrichsen-Rohling, Huss & Ramsey, 2000). The complexities of integrating research with the human side of therapy are challenges still being explored (such as discussed by Lambert & Ogles, 2004).

Based on the literature noted, a paradigm shift in conceptualizing what might work with batterer populations is needed. In particular, and departing from the interest in typology, others (Chang & Saunders, 2002; Dalton, 2007) acknowledged that program development should be tied to cultural competency where ethnicity, gender, and/or sexual orientation are included in the focus. Indeed, some authors are arguing that batterer programming for African American men will be negative without culturally-sensitive interventions (Bennett & Williams, 2001; Williams, 1992, 2000). The same may be said of programming for Hispanic men (Aldarondo & Mederos, 2002; Welland & Ribner, 2008). The challenge, it seems, is overcoming state standardized batterer programming while accounting for one's diverse cultural context (Buttell & Mohr Carney, 2007; Gelles, 2002).

Indeed, a paradigm shift toward heterogeneity has the potential to make room for programming that is not reductionist or narrow in design. Heterogeneity need not simply rely on current knowledge of typologies to produce the necessary behavior change but instead should be flexible and open to integrating other parts of men's experiences into the intervention process. Consequently, this can leave room for considering human agency (Bandura, 1977, 1997; Magyar-Moe & Lopez, 2008), the idea that men can be intentional (forming action plans to change), future-minded (goal setters), self-regulated (capable of monitoring behaviors), and self-reflective (observant of their thoughts/actions). It is entirely possible that IPV perpetrators may possess characteristics and/or exhibit behaviors that are in fact redeeming. Typologies that shift from male profiles of risk and/or psychopathology (Gondolf & White, 2001), or mental disorder (Lohr, Hamberger, Witte & Parker 2006), to profiles addressing variables as mentioned above have hardly been considered for this population. Consequently, the idea of human agency can challenge us to examine the batterer beyond current thinking that men's abusive/violent behaviors solely revolve around narrow characteristics that include power, control, oppression, and so forth.

Manualization of Batterer Intervention Programs

A second argument for a paradigm shift is related to the widespread manualization of BIPs as peer-educative group work. The primary reason for the similarity across all BIPs is a result of the need to develop treatment standards. Hamberger (2001) stated these standards have

been designed to (a) ensure treatment accountability, (b) support victim safety, (c) promote offender accountability, and (d) end controversial
practices with this population. The intent of standards is certainly laud-
able in that manualization helps set minimum standards of practice that
should include practitioner/facilitator competence where the community can be confident it resembles a best practice (Hamburger, 2008a,
2008b). Further, treatment standards following a manualized process
provide a systematic way of training and replication (Lambert & Ogles,
2004). On the other hand, manualization may also be what Levitt (1975)
long ago referred to as "an orientation toward the product rather than
the people who consume it" (p. 27). Thus, there are some limitations to
the current process that may lend itself to a paradigm shift within batterer programming.

The first limitation is that manualized approaches can be narrowly
construed as technical eclecticism. Coady (2007) sees technical eclecticism as (a) using knowledge about what works with clients who have
similar characteristics/problems with clients who are dissimilar and
(b) drawing on techniques from therapy models without necessarily
subscribing to those theories. The problem with technical eclecticism
is that the end results, especially in the case of batterer intervention
programs, are meant to be based on a singular accepted protocol of batterer intervention. What may be missing in this manualized approach is
the ability to move beyond the "dodo bird" effect (Luborsky, Singer &
Luborsky, 1975; Rosenzweig, 1936; Shadish, 2002) that suggests specific
approaches do not show specific differing effects when comparing treatment. Here, comparison studies on batterer treatment programs have
failed to find one approach better than another (Murphy & Eckhardt,
2005; O'Leary, Heyman & Neidig, 1999; Saunders, 1996a; Witte, Parker,
Lohr & Hamberger, 2007). In fact, Murphy and Eckhardt (2005) identified three specific points worth noting; (a) no specific treatment group
has been more effective in reducing violence in head to head comparison, (b) recidivism rates are slightly lower on average when compared
to control groups with little to no counseling (Babcock, Green & Robie,
2004), and (c) individuals with co-occurring problems (such as substance
abuse) are less responsive to intervention. Thus, it is plausible that the
"technical operations" associated with manualized approaches have little effect. In addition to Coady's technical eclecticism, there are some
arguments that manualized batterer intervention programming lacks the
cognitive-behavioral consistency it proclaims (Dutton & Corvo, 2007)
and that many BIPs do not exactly follow curricula—nor do programs

appear to be consistently applying the curriculum (e.g., Gondolf, 2002; Hamberger, 2008a, 2008b).

The second drawback is that the present manualized approach for a "one sized" population moves practice and research in the wrong direction (Duncan & Miller, 2006). Duncan and Miller argue that manuals can provide a "map of the territory" (p. 3), but that they have yet to show how specific technical operations are responsible for client change. Clearly, one of the unanswered questions with regard to manualization is transferability from research to clinical practice (Duncan & Miller, 2006). Maiuro, Hagar, Lin, and Olson (2001) called this the "woozle effect" (p. 25) or the continuous copying and replication of manualization (from county to county, from state to state), which creates an illusion of clinical fact, when in reality there is little basis for it. As a result, Hamberger (2008a) stated some standards exist having little value and poor empirical support. However, he does recommend standards be flexible and open to change as evidence to new theories and approaches gain ground. Thus, the technical "how to" approach of current manualization efforts may not represent the "best practice" approach in how to support client change with BIP groups. Following the thinking of Duncan and Miller, a critical missing piece is how to put relevance back into the relationship between the client and the facilitator/therapist. Given what is already known about the outcomes of batterer intervention programming, this could be a new link to different and potentially effective work with batterer populations.

The Process To Outcome Dilemma

An additional paradigm shift argument relates to process as a mainstay of batterer intervention effectiveness. In other words, there is an emphasis on the process (e.g., specific BIP group protocol) of intervening, where technique-driven, specific step-by step modules are central to part of the work done with changing men. Hence, the Duluth model of BIP. The problem with process as it exists in BIP-like programming is the creation of a "dummy proof" (Duncan, Miller & Sparks, 2007, p. 38) methodology. What is missing and taken less into account is the connection between facilitator and group member that might contribute to needed change.

At this point one can wonder whether current batterer intervention designed to reduce violence might be better served by considering what other process factors are known to improve outcomes. Interest in process-to-outcome thinking of this kind is related to the very active litera-ture that attempts to answer the question, *what do we know about what leads to change?* To answer this question and provide an argument for a shift in thinking about what could work better with batterer populations, it is important to consider an area of research, to date not found in this field: that of the common factors of change.

A common factors perspective is not the same as a one-size-fits-all approach found in manualization. Instead, common factors seek to iden-tify commonalities that predict good outcomes beyond a standardized approach. Thus, focusing on common factors considers a spectrum of possibilities related to how change occurs, instead of a singular vision, which currently exists in the BIP field. The interest in common factors dates back to the seminal work of Rosenzweig (1936, 1940) and Frank (1961), and was recently articulated by Duncan (2002). Essentially, Duncan traces the historical evolution of the common factors of change and con-cluded there are "pantheoretical factors in operation that overshadow any perceived or assumed differences among (intervention) approaches" (pp. 40–41).

The pantheoretical factors of change have been summarized and simplified to the common factors perspective. Miller, Duncan, and Hubble (1997, 2004) centered in on four common features of outcome research that makes for successful and predictable change. These fea-tures are found in many other analyses of outcome studies, including those of Lambert and Ogles (2004) and Lambert and Barley (2001). Pantheoretical summaries attribute 40% of the change variance to the client's extra-therapeutic factors (such as strengths, resources, coping skills, motivations, where they live, social support, and so forth); 30% to the client/therapist therapeutic relationship (this includes the quality of the client's participation in the therapeutic relationship); and 15% to the therapist's attitude in conveying a sense of hope to the client. Only the remaining 15% is attributed to the technique and/or model used in the change process.

In sum, the process associated with common factors could be another pathway to shift batterer intervention in a different direction. For example, if the technique or model, or in this case batterer inter-vention programming, accounts for the variance in change as stated above, then perhaps what leads to good outcomes might come from what remains extra-therapeutic, the facilitator/client relationship, and/or client hope. Wampold (2001) has long noted that the "relation-ship accounts for dramatically more of the variability in outcomes than does the totality of specific ingredients" (p. 158). To date, this issue is beginning to be considered in batterer intervention programming. One can see the common factors of change embedded in the IPV literature that identify individual and personal strengths (Bennett, Stoops, Call & Flett., 2007), therapeutic alliance (Brown & O'Leary, 2000), working alliance (Taft, Murphy, Musser & Remington., 2004), relationship building (Dutton, 2003), therapeutic bond (Dutton & Corvo, 2007), compassion (Stosny, 1995), and so forth. The construction of an alternative language and practice with respect to the process to outcome dilemma represents an opportunity to identify treatment contexts beyond what currently exists. Forging ahead of current batterer programming in this manner may be a small move in answering some of the questions that have to do with, for example, decreasing treatment dropout (Augusta-Scott & Dankwort, 2002), increasing men's interest in the change process (Eckhardt & Utschig, 2007), and stepping beyond the education approach (Milner & Singleton, 2008).

Group Confrontation

An additional explanation for shifting paradigms can be found in the confrontational approach that guides much of the traditional batterer intervention. The idea of confrontation is viewed by these traditional models as essential to break down men's denial, minimization, and resistance (Pence & Paymar, 1993). In some ways, confrontation has been portrayed as akin to "gender shaming" (Dutton & Corvo, 2007, p. 660) and as taking an adversarial stance in relation to men (based on the belied sex-role conditioning as a function of IPV) (Dutton, 2003), ideas that have yet to demonstrate a relationship that promotes change.

The notion of challenging and confronting men's behavior in practice has long been considered the "tour de force" of batterer intervention, to the extent that Milner (2004) labeled it a "mantra" (p. 84). Milner also suggests that there is a circular nature to this kind of thinking. That is, the more a BIP professional challenges past behavior that the client denies, the more likely the professional will predispose men to deny and deceive, thus confirming the untruthfulness of the client's behavior. Further, Milner makes the point that such an approach leads to problem-focused thinking and a problem-focused conversational stance. The difficulty is that the information at hand can become seen as "the only focal point" of a person's circumstances. Thus, one becomes more vulnerable to generalizing, labeling, and/or constructing male behavior as one of dysfunction. The problem with this vulnerability is that it can lead to the BIP professional evaluating the situation inaccurately, thereby excluding some or all information that does not conform or fit with the intent of the assessment.

Clearly, Milner's ideas are not unique, as others have articulated similar objections to the importance of challenging and confrontation. Dominelli (1992) believed confrontation supported male stereotyping of women needing men, whereas Senior (1992) drew attention to the masculinity and power of the word "confrontation" in the hands of male professionals with male clients. Similarly, Edleson (1996) and Murphy and Baxter (1997) suggested confrontation can come to represent coercive behavior modeling, and Wexler (2000) recommended one avoid confronting resistance altogether. Likewise, Mankowski, Haaken, and Silvergild (2002) described confrontation as a "law and order approach" (p. 174), having the potential to mirror the coercion and power-and-control found in abusive relationships. Finally, in a recent essay, Milner & Singleton (2008) wrote that confrontation can force the therapeutic relationship into an adversarial position because of the push to help offenders see the errors of their ways.

One final reason for shifting away from a confrontation approach may stem from the changes in the field of positive psychology and its view of broadening the human experience—that is, finding a balance between what is wrong and what is right. In the last decade, positive psychology has attempted to change mainstream psychology's fixation on psychopathology (or what is wrong), mental illness, and the medicalization of behaviors and instead focus on positive human qualities (or what's right), such as one's strengths, virtues, wellbeing, and happiness (e.g., Aspinwall & Staudinger, 2003; Joseph & Linley, 2005, 2008; Keyes & Haidt, 2003; Peterson & Seligman, 2004; Seligman, Steen & Nansook, 2005; Seligman, 1999, 2003; Snyder & Lopez, 2007).

The emergence of something positive (e.g., human qualities) should not be seen as just the absence of something negative; if that were the case, changing one's behavior would only need to include removing the negative (Duckworth, Steen & Seligman, 2005). Instead, the authors argue that the emergence of positives states such as emotions or good feelings are seen as a separate psychological process (neurological and cognitive) having its own course of action (see the chapter on Broaden-and-Build Theory). Put another way, ending one's violence and taking responsibility is an accomplishment of self that is more likely to occur through other means/actions that do not include confrontation. Thus, programming that might harness attributes such as wellbeing and personal strengths provides an opportunity for bolstering existing BIP curricula and/or interventions. As the field evolves, it may reach the point where professionals working with batterer populations can address nonviolent behavior through strengths and/or competency based interventions with the same urgency found in the function of confrontation.

Creating Behavior Change

The introduction of a transtheoretical model (TTM; Prochaska & DiClemente, 1984) in the addiction literature has been shown to be an alternative perspective for addressing change in batterer populations, thus providing a continuing rationale for a shift in paradigms. A transtheoretical approach relies on five distinct but interrelated processes to explain how behaviors change. These processes are seen to build on one another from beginning to end with individuals utilizing different processes of change depending on which specific stage of change they are in at the time of intervention. The processes of precontemplation, contemplation, preparation, action, and maintenance have been slowly adapted in the batterer intervention literature.

A number of authors (Begun et al., 2003; Eckhardt, Babcock & Homack, 2004; Eckhardt, Holtzworth-Munroe, Norlander, Sibley & Cahill, 2008; Levesque, Gelles & Velicer, 2000; Levesque, Velicer, Castle & Greene, 2008; Scott & Wolfe, 2003; Simmons, Lehmann & Cobb, 2008) have generally come to similar conclusions about what is involved with changing behavior. Murphy and Eckhardt (2005) summarized these conclusions into two main threads. The first states that batterers have widely ranging attitudes about the need for change (Murphy & Eckhardt, 2005). Thus, working with the respective stages of change represents a focus for developing interventions that are aimed at self-appraising behaviors and self-motivated changes. The second thread states that there are two distinct batterer "self presentation styles" (Murphy & Eckhardt, 2005, p. 146). Early-stage men do not identify any problem behavior, generally deny any wrongdoing, and tend to blame their partners or the judicial system for their misfortunes. Conversely, later-stage clients acknowledge what they have done, and convey guilt or accept responsibility for their behavior.

Considering a TTM within batterer intervention programming has significant advantages for shifting the paradigm toward strengths. While introducing their tool for measuring resistance based on TTM principles,

Levesque, Velicer, Castle, and Greene (2008) highlight three key components inherent to the TTM that are useful for facilitating change: decisional balance, processes of change, and self-efficacy. Decisional balance is the process in which clients consider the pros and cons associated with given behaviors (Janis & Mann, 1977; Velicer, DiClemente, Prochaska & Brandenberg, 1985). Processes of change include cognitive, affective, and behavioral activities that assist progress though the stages of change (Prochaska, Velicer, DiClemente & Fava, 1988; Prochaska, DeClemente & Norcross, 1992). Self-efficacy is the client's inner belief that he can (a) make changes in his life, (b) sustain these changes, and (c) resist the natural temptation to slip back into previous behavior once change has occurred (Bandura, 1977; Velicer, DiClemente, Rossi & Prochaska, 1990). By understanding change through these TTM constructs, shifting the paradigm for batterer intervention is a bit easier to understand.

Of particular relevance in this shifting paradigm are four important TTM concepts. First, rather than employing an umbrella approach, TTM indicates that interventions can (and should) be tailored for the individual and his particular stage of change. Second, the TTM model contends that batterer intervention should not be thought of as an "all or nothing" approach. Instead, considering the idea that batterers gradually move through stages of change in a manner that can be aided by both the content of the material and the approach used by group facilitators, the TTM strategy is likely to reduce resistance, facilitate progress, and improve engagement with the ultimate effect of producing behavior change. Third, an organizing assumption of integrating a TTM approach is the belief that most clients have the potential to change. Translating this into practice lies in the manner of how one engages with the batterer population in working toward nonviolent behavior. Fourth, a TTM model of intervention is a template (or map) for change and it should be evident that the development of good professional relationships is a key strategy in facilitating these changes. In sum, the most effective manner for creating behavior change is a fluid process that is dependent on the stage the client is in at time of intervention. For a BIP to be effective, this process must be understood, respected, and incorporated.

SAFETY

All batterer intervention practices placed the safety of women and children at the core of their work with men. Nevertheless, the safety of all family members does not preclude the possibility that models of practice can vary, nor does it rule out the idea that men can also be in charge of addressing their own safety behaviors. Therefore, the final line of reasoning toward a paradigm shift within the field of batterer intervention programming lies in the argument that the safety of the victim/survivor *will not* be compromised by moving beyond traditional batterer intervention models.

The question of safety in practice has historically been a stumbling block for considering alternative models of intervention (see, for example, Bograd, 1984; Minaker & Snider, 2006); however, safety focused reasons for shifting to a new direction are certainly relevant. First and foremost, the discussion of safety has become a universal part of the lexicon found in relationship violence literature. Compared to a decade ago, it is now virtually impossible to participate in professional discussions without acknowledging the importance of partner/child safety. Further, within the area of batterer intervention, the priority given to safety is a critical focus of virtually every working professional associated with this issue (e.g., nurses, criminal justice employees, child care workers, police officers, family violence professionals, etc.). Likewise, in almost every jurisdiction in North America it is common to find coordinated community responses where safety is emphasized at every level of professional involvement. The field is in a position where safety is always part of the discussion; it is never ignored or minimized. Thus, expanding the intervention context of batterer intervention can and will continue this focus.

Second, the field of family violence has made enormous advances in identifying the threats to safety via instruments and survey tools that recognize markers of possible harm. Currently, general level risk tools have been developed that capture a model of predictive variables that lead to future risk (Murphy & Eckhardt, 2005). Some of these tools include the Historical, Clinical, Risk-20 (HCR-20) (Douglas & Webster, 1999), the Violence Risk Appraisal Guide (VRAG) (Harris, Rice & Quinsey, 1993), and the Danger Assessment Instrument (DAI) (Campbell, 1995). A second, more current level of risk tools relates to capturing the frequency, intensity, and variability of abusive behaviors. Here, a list of paper and pencil tools includes but is not limited to the Conflict Tactics Scale (CTS2) (Straus, Hamby, Boney-McCoy & Sugerman, 1996); the Severity of Violence against Women Scales (Marshall, 1992), the Abusive Behavior Inventory (Shepard & Campbell, 1992), the Measure of Wife Abuse (Rodenburg & Fantuzzo, 1993), the Psychological Maltreatment of Women Inventory (Tolman, 1989), and the Checklist of Controlling Behaviors (Lehmann, Simmons & Pillai, 2007). Although not scientifically fail-proof, these tools allow the practitioner to move in a direction guided by safety issues.

Third and last, a paradigm shift that involves safety recognizes a man's potential contribution toward his own safekeeping. Although programming focuses on the safety of women and children, there is little if any discussion about "male safety" in this process. If IPV can be conceptualized on a high- to low-risk continuum, men can and should be able to demonstrate any number of behaviors that parallel a high to low personal safety factor. For example, B. Moore's focus on skill building in which the client demonstrates specific behavior on a proactive, rather than a reactive, continuum is one response toward keeping men safe from resorting to violence (personal communication, June 7, 2008). Similarly, an interest in integrating the alliance building literature within batterer intervention has the potential to increase men's nonviolent behavior. In this vein, proactive safety nets occur because of engagement in which men define and agree on goals and intervention tasks that will connect to new behavior (Miller, Duncan & Hubble, 1997). These ideas assume men can be active participants in designing strategies around personal accountability and responsibility.

MOVING BEYOND

As outlined in our analytic discussion, some answers to the questions "what else?" and "is there more?" have been considered. At this point the batterer intervention field can begin to move in a new and thoughtful direction, one that advances, contributes to, and constructively changes what currently exists. To this end, the remainder of this text moves the field to strengths-based BIP approaches. Conceptually, strengths-based BIPs are alternative methods of approaching intervention with batterer populations, the environments they live in, and/or their current circumstances. More so, the approaches considered in this text are an attempt to "mobilize strengths (talents, knowledge, capacities, resources) in the service of achieving their (the client's) goals and visions" (Saleebey, 2006, p. 1). Grounded in the helping profession's changing paradigm of focusing on how people achieve health and wellbeing, and not simply an effort to thwart problems and illness (e.g., Linley & Joseph, 2004; Saleebey, 2006), strengths-based approaches place a greater emphasis on finding what is right, effective, and commendable about individuals who have been violent toward their partners.

The shift toward a paradigm of strength building takes into account heterogeneity, individualization of approaches, and a focus on the outcome. Including a strengths perspective involves the notion of finding a balance between the very real risks men pose, but also finding "what else," the idea that competencies and resources exist, but need to be discovered and/or accessed. Last, shifting the paradigm to a strengths perspective is intended to reduce the idea of "polar thinking" (Eisikovits & Buchbinder, 1996, p. 187). In the place of such thinking, it is proposed that the field of batterer intervention can move closer to the middle, allowing for an expansion of ideas and new forms of practice that will be helpful in ending partner violence.

REFERENCES

Aldarondo, E., & Mederos, F., (Eds.). (2002). *Programs for men who batter: Intervention and prevention strategies in a diverse society.* Kingston, NJ: Civic Research Institute.

Andrews, D.A., & Bonta, J. (2003). *The psychology of criminal conduct* (3rd ed.). Cincinnati, OH: Anderson.

Archer, J. (2000). Sex differences in aggression between heterosexual partners: A meta-analytic review. *Psychological Bulletin, 126,* 651–680.

Aspinwall, L.G., & Staudinger, U.M. (2003). A psychology of human strengths: Some central issues of an emerging field. In L.G. Aspinwall & U.M. Staudinger, (Eds.), *A psychology of human strengths: Fundamental questions and future directions for a positive psychology* (pp. 9–22). Washington, DC: American Psychological Association.

Augusta-Scott, T. (2008). *Narrative therapy: Abuse intervention program.* Nova Scotia, Canada: Bridges.

Augusta-Scott, T., & Dankwort, J. (2002). Partner abuse group intervention: Lessons from education and narrative therapy approaches. *Journal of Interpersonal Violence, 17,* 783–805.

Austin, J.B., & Dankwort , J. (1999). Standard for batterer programs: A review and analysis. *Journal of Interpersonal Violence, 14,* 152–168.

Babcock, J.C., Canady, B., Graham, K., & Schart, L. (2007). The evolution of batterer intervention: From the dark ages into the scientific age. In J. Hamel & T.L. Nicholls (Eds.). *Family Interventions in Domestic Violence* (pp. 215–246). New York, Springer.

Babcock, J.C., Green, C.E. & Robie, C. (2004). Does batterers' treatment work? A meta-analytic review of domestic violence treatment. *Clinical Psychology Review, 23,* 1023–1053.

Babcock, J.C. & LaTaillade, J. (2000). Evaluating interventions for men who batter. In J.P. Vincent & E.N. Jouriles (Eds.), *Domestic violence: Guidelines for research informed practice* (pp. 37–77). Philadelphia: Jessica Kingsley.

Bandura, A. (1977). Self-efficacy: Toward a unifying theory of behavioral change. *Psychological Review, 84,* 191–215.

Bandura, A. (1997). *Self-efficacy: The exercise of control.* New York: Freeman.

Begun, A.L., Murphy, C., Bolt, D., Weinstein, B., Strodthoff, T., Short, L., & Shelley, G. (2003). Characteristics of the Safe at Home instrument for assessing readiness to change intimate partner violence. *Research on Social Work Practice,* 13, 80–107.

Bender, K., & Roberts, A.R. (2007). Battered women versus male batterer typologies: Same or difference based on evidence-based studies. *Aggression and Violent Behavior,* 12, 519–530.

Bennett, L., & Williams, O. (2001). Intervention programs for men who batter. In C. Renzetti & J. Edleson (Eds.). *Sourcebook on violence against women* (pp. 261–277). Thousand Oaks, CA: Sage.

Bennett, L.W., Stoops, C., Call, C., & Flett, H. (2007). Program completion and re-arrest in a batterer intervention system. *Research on Social Work Practice,* 17, 42–54.

Bograd, M. (1984). Family systems approaches to wife battering: A feminist critique. *American Journal of Orthopsychiatry,* 54, 558–568.

Bograd, M. (1988). How battered women and abusive men account for domestic violence: Excuses, justifications, or explanations. In G.T. Hotaling, D. Finkelhor, J.T. Kirkpatrick, & M.A. Straus (Eds.), *Coping with family violence: Research and policy perspectives* (pp. 60–77). Thousand Oaks, CA: Sage.

Bordin,E.S., (1979). The generalizability of the psychoanalytic concept of the working alliance. *Psychotherapy: Theory, Research & Practice,* 16, 252–260.

Boyle, D.J., O'Leary, K.D., Rosenbaum, A., & Hassett-Walker, C. (2008). Differentiating between generally and partner-only violent subgroups: Lifetime antisocial behavior, family of origin violence, and impulsivity. *Journal of Family Violence,* 23, 47–55.

Brown, P.D. & O'Leary, K.D. (2000). Therapeutic alliance: Predicting continuance and success in group treatment for spouse abuse. *Journal of Consulting and Clinical Psychology,* 68, 340–345.

Browne, K.O., Saunders, D.G., & Staecker, K.M. (1997). Process-psychodynamic groups for men who batter: A brief treatment model. *Families in Society,* 78, 265–271.

Buttell, F., & Mohr Carney, M. (2007). Emerging trends in batterer intervention programming: Equipping forensic workers for effective practice. In D.W. Springer & A.R. Roberts (Eds.). *Handbook of forensic mental health with victims and offenders: Assessment, treatment, and research* (pp. 151–169). New York: Springer.

Campbell, J.C. (Ed.). (1995). *Assessing dangerousness: Violence by sexual offenders, batterers, and child abusers.* Thousand Oaks, CA: Sage.

Cavanaugh, M.M., & Gelles, R.J. (2005). The utility of male domestic offender typologies: New Directions for Research, Policy, and Practice. *Journal of Interpersonal Violence,* 20, 155–166.

Ceasar, P.L., & Hamberger, L.K. (1989). *Treating men who batter: Theory, practice, and programs.* New York: Springer.

Carlson, B.E. (2005). The most important things learned about violence and trauma in the past 20 years. *Journal of Interpersonal Violence,* 20, 119–126.

Chang, H., & Saunders, D.G. (2002). Predictors of attrition in two types of group programs for men who batter. *Journal of Family Violence,* 17, 273–292.

Chornesky, A. (2000). The dynamics of battering revisited. *Affilia: Journal of Women and Social Work.* 15, 480–501.

Coady, N. (2007). The science and art of direct practice: An overview of theory and an intuitive-inductive approach to practice. In N. Coady & P. Lehmann, (Eds.), *Theoretical perspectives for direct social work practice: A generalist-eclectic approach* (pp. 41–66). New York: Springer.

Crowell, N.A., & Burgess, A.W. (1996). *Understanding violence against women.* Washington, DC: National Academy Press.

Dalton, B. (2007). What's going on out there? A survey of batterer intervention programs. *Journal of Aggression, Maltreatment & Trauma*, 15, 59–74.

Dankwort J., & Austin, J.B. (1999). Standards for batterer intervention programs in Canada: A history and review. *Journal of Community Mental Health*, 18, 19–38.

Davis, R.C., & Taylor, B.C. (1999). Does batterer treatment reduce violence: A review of the literature. *Women and Criminal Justice*, 10, 69–93.

Dobash, R.P., Dobash, R.E., Cavanagh, K., & Lewis, R. (1995). Evaluating criminal justice programs for men who are violent. In R.E. Dobash, R.P. Dobash, & L. Noah. (Eds.). *Gender and Crime.* (pp. 13–22). Cardiff, Wales: University of Wales Press.

Dobash, R.P., Dobash, R.E., Cavanagh, K., & Lewis, R. (2000). *Changing violent men.* London: Sage.

Dominelli, L. (1992). Masculinity, sex offenders and probation practice. In P. Senior and D. Woodhill (Eds.). *Gender, crime and probation practice.* (pp. 13–22). Sheffield: PAVIC.

Douglas, K.S., & Webster, C.D. (1999). The HRC-20 violence risk assessment scheme: concurrent validity in a sample of incarcerated offenders. *Criminal Justice and Behavior*, 26, 3–19.

Duckworth, A.L., Steen, T.A., & Seligman, M.E.P. (2005). Positive psychology in clinical practice. *Annual Review of Clinical Psychology*, 1, 629–651.

Duncan, B.L. (2002). The legacy of Saul Rosenzweig: The profundity of the dodo bird. *Journal of Psychotherapy Integration*, 12, 32–57.

Duncan, B.L., & Miller, S.D. (2006). Treatment manuals do not improve outcomes. In J.C. Norcross, R.F. Levant, & L.E. Beutler (Eds.), *Evidence-based practices in mental health: Debate and dialogue on the fundamental questions* (pp. 140–149). Washington, DC: APA.

Duncan, B.L., Miller, S.D., & Sparks, S. (2007). Common factors and the uncommon heroism of youth. *Psychotherapy in Australia*, 13, 34–43.

Dunford, F.W. (2000). The San Diego Navy experiment: An assessment of interventions for men who assault their wives. *Journal of Consulting and Clinical Psychology*, 68, 468–476.

Dutton, D.G. (1987). The criminal justice response to wife assault. *Law and Human Behavior*, 11, 189–206.

Dutton, D.G. (1988). *The domestic assault of women: Psychological and criminal justice perspectives.* Boston, MA; Allyn & Bacon.

Dutton, D.G. (1995). *The domestic assault of women: Psychological and criminal justice perspectives.* Vancouver: UBC Press.

Dutton, D.G. (2003). Treatment of assaultiveness. In D.G. Dutton & D.L. Sonkin (Eds.) *Intimate violence: Contemporary treatment approaches.*

Dutton, D.G. (2007). Thinking outside the box: Gender and court-mandated therapy. In J. Hamel & T.L. Nicholls (Eds.), *Family Interventions in Domestic Violence* (pp. 27–58) New York: Springer.

Dutton, D.G. (2008). My back pages: reflections on thirty years of domestic violence research. *Trauma, Violence, and Abuse,* 9, 131–143.

Dutton, D.G., & Corvo, K. (2006). Transforming a flawed policy: A call to revive psychology and science in domestic violence research and practice. *Aggression and Violent Behavior,* 11, 457–483.

Dutton, D.G., & Corvo, K. (2007). The Duluth model: A data-impervious paradigm and a failed strategy. *Aggression and Violent Behavior,* 12, 658–667.

Dutton, D.G. & Nicholls, T.L. (2005). The gender paradigm in domestic violence research and theory: Part 1 the conflict of theory and data. *Aggression and Violent Behavior,* 10, 680–714.

Eckhardt, C.I., Babcock, J., & Homack, S. (2004). Partner assaultive men and the stages and processes of change. *Journal of Family Violence,* 19, 81–93.

Eckhardt, C.I., Holtzworth-Munroe, A., Norlander, B., Sibley, A., & Cahill, M. (2008). Readiness to change, partner violence subtypes, and treatment outcomes among men in treatment for partner assault. *Violence and Victims,* 23, 446–475.

Eckhardt, C.I., & Utschig, A.C. (2007). Assessing readiness to change among perpetrators of intimate partner violence: Analysis of two self-report measures. *Journal of Family Violence,* 22, 319–330.

Edleson, J.L., (1996). Controversy and change in batterers' programs. In J.L. Edleson & Z.C. Eisikovits (Eds.), *Future interventions with battered women and their families* (pp. 154–169). Thousand Oaks, CA, US: Sage.

Edleson, J., & Tolman, R. (1992). *Interventions for men who batter: An ecological approach.* Newbury Park, CA: Sage.

Eisikovits, Z.C., & Buchbinder, E. (1996). Toward a phenomenological intervention with violence in intimate relationships. In J.L. Edleson & Z.C. Eisikovits (Eds.), *Future interventions with battered women and their families* (pp. 186–200). Thousand Oaks, CA, US: Sage.

Eisikovits, Z.C., & Edelson, J.L. (1989). Intervening with men who batter: A critical review of the literature. *Social Service Review,* 37, 384–414.

Elbow, M. (1977). Theoretical considerations of violent marriages. *Social Casework,* 58, 515–526.

Feder, L., & Wilson, D.B. (2005). A meta-analytic review of court-mandated batterer intervention programs: Can courts affect abusers' behavior? *Journal of Experimental Criminology,* 1, 239–262.

Ford, D., & Regoli, M.J. (1993). The criminal prosecution of wife assaulters. In Z. Hilton (Ed.). *Legal responses to wife assault: Current trends and evaluation* (pp. 188–229). Newbury Park, CA: Sage.

Frank, J.D. (1961). *Persuasion and healing: A comparative study of psychotherapy.* Baltimore, MD: Johns Hopkins.

Fruzzetti, A.E., & Levensky, E.R. (2000). Dialectical behavior therapy for domestic violence: Rationale and procedure. *Cognitive and Behavioral Practice,* 7, 435–447.

Geffner, R., & Mantooth, C. (1999). *Ending spouse/partner abuse: A Psychoeducational approach for individuals and couples.* New York: Springer.

Gelles, R.J. (2002). Standards for programs for men who batter? Not yet. *Journal of Aggression, Maltreatment, and Trauma,* 5, 11–20.

Gelles, R.J. (2007). The politics of research: The use, abuse, and misuse of social science data-the cases of intimate partner violence. *Family Court Review,* 45, 42–51.

Gondolf, E.W. (1988). Who are these guys? Toward a behavioral typology of batterers. *Violence and Victims*, 3, 187–203.

Gondolf, E.W. (1991). A victim-based assessment of court-mandated counseling for batterers. *Criminal Justice Review*, 16, 213–226.

Gondolf, E.W. (1995). Batterer intervention: What we know and need to know. Paper presented at the National Institute of Justice Violence Against Women Strategic Planning Meeting. Washington, DC. March 31, 1995.

Gondolf, E.W. (2002). *Batterer Intervention Systems: Issues Outcomes and Recommendations*. Thousand Oaks, California: Sage.

Gondolf, E.W. (2004). Evaluating batterer counseling programs: A difficult task showing some effects and implications. *Aggression and Violent Behavior*, 9, 606–631.

Gondolf, E.W. (2007). Theoretical and research support for the Duluth model: A reply to Dutton and Corvo. *Aggression &Violent Behavior*, 12, 644–657.

Gondolf, E.W., & White, R.J. (2001). Batterer program participants who repeatedly reassault: Psychopathic tendencies and other disorders. *Journal of Interpersonal Violence*, 16, 361–380.

Grauwiler, P., & Mills, L.G. (2004). Moving beyond the criminal justice paradigm: A radical restorative justice approach to intimate abuse. *Journal of Sociology and Social Welfare*, XXI, 49–69.

Hamberger, L.K. (1997). Cognitive behavioral treatment of men who batter their partners. *Cognitive and Behavioral Practice*, 4, 147–169.

Hamberger, L.K. (2001). Musings of a state standards committee chair. *Journal of Aggression, Maltreatment, & Trauma*, 5, 265–287.

Hamberger, L.K., (2002). The men's group program: A community-based cognitive-behavioral, profeminist intervention program. In E. Aldarondo & F. Mederos (Eds.). *Batterer intervention programs: A handbook for clinicians, practitioners, and advocates* (pp. 7.1–7.43). Kingston, NJ: Civic Research Institute.

Hamberger, L.K. (2008a). Twenty-five years of change in working with partner abusers-part 1: Observations from the trenches about community and system-level changes. *Journal of Aggression, Maltreatment, & Trauma*, 16, 355–375.

Hamberger, L.K. (2008b). Twenty-five years of change in working with partner abusers-part II: Observations from the trenches about changes in understanding of abusers and abuser treatment. *Journal of Aggression, Maltreatment, & Trauma*, 17, 1–22.

Hamberger, L.K., & Hastings, J.E. (1990). Recidivism following spouse abuse abatement counseling: Treatment program implications. *Victims and Violence*, 5, 157–170.

Hamberger, L.K., & Hastings, J.E. (1993). Court mandated treatment of men who assault their partners: Issues, controversies, and outcomes. In N.Z. Hilton (Ed.) *Legal responses to wife assault* (pp. 188–229). Thousand Oaks, CA: Sage.

Hamel, J. (2007). Gender-inclusive family interventions in domestic violence: An overview. In I.J. Hamel & T.L. Nicholls (Eds.), *Family Interventions in Domestic Violence* (pp. 247–273). New York: Springer

Hamel, J., & Nicholls, T.L. (Eds.). (2007). *Family interventions in domestic violence*. New York: Springer.

Harris, G.T., Rice, M.E., & Quinsey, V.L. (1993). Violent recidivism of mentally disordered offenders: The development of a statistical prediction instrument. *Criminal Justice and Behavior*, 20, 315–335.

Healey, K.M., & Smith, C. (1998). *Batterer programs: What criminal justice agencies need to know.* National Institute of Justice Research in Action Report. Washington, DC: Department of Justice. Retrieved October 23, 2008 from http://www.ncjrs.gov/txtfiles/171683.txt.

Healey, K.M., Smith, C., & O'Sullivan, C. (1998). *Batterer intervention: Program approaches and criminal justice strategies.* Washington, DC: Department of Justice. Retrieved October 23, 2008 from http://www.ncjrs.gov/pdffiles/168638.pdf.

Holtzworth-Munroe, A., & Stuart, G.L. (1994). Typologies of male batterers: Three subtypes and the differences among them. *Psychological Bulletin, 116,* 476–497.

Jackson, S., Feder, L., Forde, D.R., Davis, R.C., Maxwell, C.D., & Taylor, B.G. (June 2003). Batterer intervention programs: Where do we go from here? *Special NIJ Report,* Washington DC; National Institute of Justice, U.S. Department of Justice.

Janis, I.L. (1982). *Groupthink.* (2nd ed.). Boston: Houghton Mifflin.

Janis, I.L., & Mann, L. (1977). *Decision making: A psychological analysis of conflict, choice and commitment.* New York: Free Press.

Jennings, J.L. (1987). History and issues in the treatment of battering men: A case for unstructured group therapy. *Journal of Family Violence, 2,* 193–214.

Joseph, S., & Linley, A.P. (2005). Positive psychological approaches to therapy. *Counseling and Psychotherapy Research, 5,* 5–10.

Joseph, S., & Linley, A.P. (Eds.). (2008). *Trauma recovery and growth: Positive psychological perspectives on posttraumatic stress.* Hoboken, NJ: John Wiley & Sons.

Keyes, C.L.M., & Haidt, J. (2003). *Flourishing: Positive psychology and the life well lived.* Washington, DC: APA.

Kuhn, T.S. (1962). *The structure of scientific revolutions.* Chicago, IL: University of Chicago Press.

Labriola, M., Rempel, M., & Davis, R.C. (2005). *Testing the effectiveness of batterer programs and judicial monitoring.* Washington, DC: National Institute of Justice.

Langhinrichsen-Rohling, J, Huss, M.T., & Ramsey, S. (2000). The clinical utility of batterer typologies. *Journal of Family Violence, 15,* 37–53.

Lambert, M.J., & Barley, D.E. (2001). Research summary on the therapeutic relationship and psychotherapy outcome. *Psychotherapy: Theory, Research, Practice, Training, 38,* 357–361.

Lambert, M.J., & Ogles, B.M. (2004). The efficacy and effectiveness of psychotherapy. In M.J. Lambert (Ed.), *Bergin and Garfield's handbook of psychotherapy and behavior change.* (5th ed., pp. 139–193). New York: John Wiley & Sons.

Lee M.Y., Sebold, J., & Uken A. (2003). *Solution-focused treatment of domestic violence offenders: Accountability for change.* New York: Oxford.

Lehmann, P., Simmons, C., & Pillai, V.J. (2007). The checklist of controlling behaviors. Unpublished documents. Arlington, TX: University of Texas at Arlington.

Levesque, D.A., Gelles, R.J. (1998, July). *Does treatment reduce recidivism in men who batter: A meta-analytic evaluation of treatment outcome.* Paper presented at the Program Evaluation and Family Violence Research: An International Conference: Durham, NH.

Levesque, D.A., Gelles, R.J., & Velicer, W.F. (2000). Development and validation of a stages of change measure for men in batterer treatment. *Cognitive Therapy and Research, 24,* 175–199.

Levesque, D.A., Velicer, W.F., Castle, P.H., & Greene, R.N. (2008). Resistance among domestic violence offenders: Measurement, development and initial validation. *Violence Against Women, 14,* 158–184.

Levitt, T. (September-October, 1975). Marketing myopia. Harvard Business Review, 53, 19–31.

Linley, P.A. & Joseph, S. (Eds.). (2004). *Positive psychology in practice,* Hoboken, NJ: John Wiley & Sons.

Lohr, J.M., Bonge, D., Witte, T.H., Hamberger, L.K., & Langhinrichsen-Rohling, J. (2005). Consistency and accuracy of batterer typology identification. *Journal of Family Violence, 20,* 253–258.

Lohr, J.M., Hamberger, L.K., Witte, T.H., & Parker, L.M. (2006). Scientific evidence for domestic violence treatment. In J.E. Fisher & W.T. O'Donohue (Eds.), *Practitioners guide to evidence-based psychotherapy* (pp. 258–265). New York, Springer.

Lord, C.G., Ross, L., & Lepper, M.R. (1979). Biased assimilation and attitude polarization: The effects of prior theories and subsequently considered evidence. *Journal of Personality and Social Psychology, 37,* 2098–2109.

Luborsky, L., Singer, B., & Luborsky, L. (1975). Comparative studies of psychotherapies: Is it true that 'everyone has won and all must have prizes'? *Archives of General Psychiatry, 32,* 995–1008.

Magyar-Moe, J.L., & Lopez, S.J. (2008). Human agency, strengths-based development and well being. In W.B. Walsh (Ed.), *Biennial review of counseling psychology* (pp. 157–177). New York: Routledge Psychology Press.

MacKinnon, L., & Miller, D. (1984). The sexual component in family therapy: A feminist critique. *Journal of Social Work and Human Sexuality, 3,* 81–101.

Mankowski, E.S., Haaken, J., & Silverglid, C.S. (2002). Collateral damage: An analysis of the achievements and unintended consequences of batterer intervention programs and discourse. *Journal of Family Violence, 17,* 167–184.

Marshall, L.L., (1992). Development of the severity of violence against women scales. *Journal of Family Violence, 7,* 103–121.

Maiuro, R.D., Hagar, T.S., Lin, H.H., & Olson, N. (2001). Are current state standards for domestic violence perpetrator treatment adequately informed by research? A question of questions. *Journal of Aggression, Maltreatment and Trauma, 5,* 21–44.

McNamee, S. (2004). Therapy as social construction: Back to basics and forward toward challenging issues. In T. Strong & D. Pare (Eds.), *Furthering talk: Advances in discursive therapies* (pp. 253–270). New York: Kluwer Academic/Plenum Press.

McPhail, B.A., Busch, N.B., Kulkarni, S., & Rice, G. (2007). An integrative feminist model: The evolving feminist perspective on intimate partner violence. *Violence Against Women, 13,* 817–841.

Mies,M., Bennholdt-Thomsen, V., & Von Werlhof, C.(1988). *Women: The last colony.* Highland, NJ: Zed Books.

Miller S.D., Duncan, B.L., & Hubble, M.A. (1997). *Escape from Babel: Toward a unifying language for psychotherapy practice.* New York: Norton.

Miller S.D., Duncan, B.L., & Hubble, M.A. (2004). Beyond integration: The triumph of outcome over process in clinical practice. *Psychotherapy in Australia, 10,* 2–19.

Mills, L.G. (2003). *Insult to injury; Rethinking our responses to intimate abuse.* Princeton: Princeton University Press.

Mills, L.G. (2008) *Violent partners: A breakthrough plan for ending the cycle of abuse.* New York: Basic Books.

Milner, J. (2004). From 'disappearing' to 'demonized': The effects on men and women of professional interventions based on challenging men who are violent. *Critical Social Policy,* 24, 79–101.

Milner, J., & Jessop, D. (2003). Domestic violence: Narratives and solutions. *Probation Journal,* 50, 127–141.

Milner, J., & Singleton, T. (2008). Domestic violence: Solution-focused practice with men and women who are violent. *Journal of Family Therapy,* 30, 29–53.

Minaker, J.C. & Snider, L. (2006). Husband abuse: Equality with a vengeance? *Canadian Journal of Criminology and Criminal Justice,* 48, 753–780.

Minnesota Program Development, Inc. (2007). The Duluth Model web site downloaded from http://www.duluth-model.org/ on August 30, 2008.

Murphy, C.M., & Baxter, V.A. (1997). Motivating batterers to change in the treatment context. *Journal of Interpersonal Violence,* 12, 607–619.

Murphy, C.M., & Eckhardt, C.I. (2005). *Treating the abusive partner: An individualized cognitive-behavioral approach.* New York: Guilford.

O'Leary, K.D., Barling, J., Arias, I., Rosenbaum, A., Malone, J., & Tyree, A. (1989). Prevalence and stability of physical aggression between spouses: A longitudinal analysis. *Journal of Consulting and Clinical Psychology,* 57, 263–268.

O'Leary, K.D., Heyman, R.E., & Neidig, P.H. (1999). Treatment of wife abuse: A comparison of gender-specific and couples approaches. *Behavior Therapy,* 30, 475–505.

Paymar, M. (2000). *Violence no more: Helping men end domestic abuse.* Alameda, CA: Hunter House.

Pence, E., & Das Dasgupta, S. (2006). *Re-examining 'battering': Are all acts of violence against intimate partners the same?* Duluth, MN: Praxis International.

Pence, E., & Paymar, M. (1985). *Power and control: Tactics of men who batter.* Duluth, MN: Domestic Abuse Intervention Project.

Pence, E., & Paymar, M. (1993). *Education groups for men who batter: The Duluth model.* New York: Springer.

Perry, P.D. (1997). Realities of the effect size calculation process: Considerations for beginning meta-analysts. In W.J. Bukoski (Ed.), *Meta-analysis of drug abuse prevention programs.* NIDA: Report No. 170 (pp. 120–128). Rockville, MD: NIDA.

Peterson, C., & Seligman, M.E.P. (2004). *Character strengths and virtues: A handbook and classification.* Washington, DC: American Psychological Association.

Pressman, B. (1989). Power and ideological issues in intervening with assaulted women. In B. Pressman, G. Cameron, & M. Rothery. (Eds.). *Intervening with assaulted women: Current theory, research, and practice* (pp. 21–46). Hillsdale, NJ: Lawrence Erlbaum.

Prochaska, J.O., & DiClemente, C.C. (1984). *The transtheoretical approach: Crossing the traditional boundaries of therapy.* Homewood, IL: Dow Jones Irwin.

Prochaska, J.O., DiClemente, C.C., & Norcross, J.C. (1992). In search of how people change: Applications to addictive behaviors. *American Psychologist,* 47, 1102–1114.

Prochaska, J.O., Velicer, W.F., DiClemente, C.C., & Fava, J. (1988). Measuring processes of change: Applications to the cessation of smoking. *Journal of Consulting and Clinical Psychology,* 56, 520–528.

Rosenbaum, A., & O'Leary, K. (1986). The treatment of marital violence. In N.S. Jacobson & A.S. Gurman. (Eds.). *Clinical handbook of marital therapy.* (pp. 385–406). New York: Guilford.

Rodenburg, F.A., & Fantuzzo, J.W. (1993). The measure of wife abuse: Steps toward the development of a comprehensive assessment technique. *Journal of Family Violence,* 8, 203–228.

Rosenfeld, B.D. (1992). Court-ordered treatment of spouse abuse. *Clinical Psychology Review,* 12, 205–226.

Rosenzweig, S. (1936). Some implicit common factors in diverse methods of psycho-therapy. *American Journal of Orthopsychiatry,* 6, 412–415.

Rosenzweig, S. (1940). Areas of agreement in psychotherapy. *American Journal of Orthopsychiatry,* 6, 412–415.

Saleeby, D. (2006). *The strengths perspective in social work practice,* (4th ed.) Boston, MA: Pearson Education.

Saunders, D.G. (1996a). Interventions with men who batter: Do we know what works? *Psychotherapy in Practice,* 2, 81–93.

Saunders, D.G. (1996b). Feminist-cognitive-behavioral and process-psychodynamic treatments for men who batter: Interaction of abuser traits and treatment models. *Violence and Victims,* 11, 393–414.

Saunders, D.G., & Azar, S.T. (1989). Treatment programs for family violence. In L. Ohlin & M. Tonry. (Eds.). *Family violence: Crime and justice, a review of research* (pp. 481–546). Chicago, IL: University of Chicago Press.

Schmidt, M.C., Kolodinsky, J.M., & Carsten, G., Schmidt, F.E., Larson, M., & MacLachlan, C. (2007). Short term change in attitude and motivating factors to change abusive behavior of male behaviors after participating in a group intervention program based on a pro-feminist and cognitive behavioral approach. *Journal of Family Violence,* 22, 91–100.

Scott, K.L., & Wolfe, D.A. (2003). Readiness to change as a predictor of outcome in batterer treatment. *Journal of Consulting and Clinical Psychology,* 71, 879–889.

Seligman, M.E.P. (1999). Positive Psychology, In J. Gillham. *The science of optimism and hope: Research Essays in honor of M.E.P. Seligman* (pp. 415–429). West Conshohocken, PA: Templeton Foundation.

Seligman, M.E.P., & Csikszentmihalyi, M. (2000). Positive psychology: An introduction. *American Psychologist,* 55, 5–14.

Seligman, M.E.P. (2003). Positive psychology: Fundamental assumptions. *The Psychologist,* 16, 126–127.

Seligman, M.E.P., Steen, T.A., & Nansook, P. (2005). Positive psychology progress: Empirical validation of interventions. *American Psychologist,* 60, 410–421.

Senior, P. (1992). Gender-conscious service delivery: Implications for staff development. In P. Senior and D. Woodhill (Eds.). *Gender, crime, and probation practice* (pp. 47–58). Sheffield: PAVIC.

Serran, G., & Firestone, P. (2004). Intimate partner homicide: A review of the male proprietariness and the self defense theories. *Aggression and Violent Behavior,* 9, 1–15.

Shadish, W.R. (2002). Revisiting field experiments: Notes for the future. *Psychological Methods,* 7, 3–18.

Sheldon, K., Frederickson, B., Rathunde, K, Csikszentmihalyi, M., & Haidt, J. (1999). Akumal Manifesto. Retrieved July 18, 2008 from http://www.ppc.sas.upenn.edu/akumalmanifesto.htm.

Shepard, M.F., & Campbell, J.A. (1992). The abusive behavior inventory: A measure of psychological and physical abuse. *Journal of Interpersonal Violence, 7,* 291–305.

Shepard, M.F., & Pence, E.L. (Eds.). (1999). *Coordinating community responses to domestic violence: Lessons from Duluth and beyond.* Thousand Oaks, CA: Sage.

Simmons, C.A., Lehmann, P., & Cobb, N. (2008). A comparison of women versus men charged with intimate partner violence: General risk factors, attitudes regarding using violence, and readiness to change. *Violence and Victims, 23,* 571–585.

Snyder, C.R., & Lopez, S.J. (2007). *Positive psychology: The scientific and practical explorations of human strengths.* Thousand Oaks, CA: Sage.

Sonkin, D.J., & Durphy, M. (1997). *Learning to live without violence: A handbook for men* (4th ed.), Volcano, CA: Volcano Press.

Sonkin, D.J., & Dutton, D.G. (2003). Treating assaultive men from an attachment perspective. In D.J. Sonkin & D.G. Dutton (Eds.). *Intimate violence: Contemporary treatment innovations* (pp. 105–134). New York: Haworth.

Sonkin, D.J., Martin, D., & Walker, L.E.A. (1985). *The male batterer: A treatment approach.* New York: Springer-Verlag.

Stosny, S. (1995). *Treating attachment abuse: A compassionate approach.* New York: Springer.

Straus, M.A., Hamby, S.L., Boney-McCoy, S., & Sugarman, D.B. (1996). The revised conflict tactics scale (CTS2). *Journal of Family Issues, 17,* 283–316.

Stuart, R.B. (2005). Treatment for partner abuse: Time for a paradigm shift. *Professional Psychology: Research and Practice, 36,* 254–263.

Taft, C.T., Murphy, C.M., Musser, P.H., & Remington, N.A., (2004). Personality, interpersonal, and motivational predictors of the working alliance in group cognitive-behavioral therapy for partner violent men. *Journal of Consulting and Clinical Psychology, 72,* 349–354.

Tolman, R.M. (1989). The development of a measure of psychological maltreatment of women by their male partners. *Violence & Victims, 4,* 150–177.

Tolman, R.M., & Bennett, L.W. (1990). A review of quantitative research on men who batter. *Journal of Interpersonal Violence, 5,* 87–118.

Tolman, R.M., & Edleson, J.L. (1995). Interventions for men who batter: A review of research. In S.M. Stith & M.A. Straus, (Eds.). *Understanding partner violence: Prevalence, Causes, Consequences, and Solution* (pp. 262–273). Minneapolis, MN: National Council on Family Relations.

Velicer, W.F., DiClemente, C.C., Prochaska, J.O., & Brandenburg, N. (1985). Decisional balance measure for assessing and predicting smoking status. *Journal of Personality and Social Psychology, 48,* 1279–1289.

Velicer, W.F., DiClemente, C.C., Rossi, J.S., & Prochaska, J.O. (1990). Relapse situations and self efficacy: An integrative model. *Addictive Behaviors, 15,* 271–283.

Vincent, J.P. & Jouriles EN. (2000). (Eds.), *Domestic violence: Guidelines for research informed practice* Philadelphia: Jessica Kingsley.

Walker, L.E., (1989). Psychology and violence against women. *American Psychologist, 44,* 695–702.

Waltz, J. (2003). Dialectical behavior therapy in the treatment of abusive behavior. *Journal of Aggression, Maltreatment, & Trauma, 7,* 75–103.

Wampold, B.E. (2001). *The great psychotherapy debate: Models, methods, and findings.* Mahwah, NJ: Lawrence Erlbaum.

Ward, T. (2002). Good lives and the rehabilitation of offenders: Promises and problems. *Aggression and Violent Behavior, 7,* 513–528.

Ward, T., Mann, R.E., & Gannon, T.A. (2007). The good lives model of offender rehabilitation: Clinical implications. *Aggression and Violent Behavior, 12,* 87–107.

Welland, C., & Ribner, N. (2008). *Healing from violence: Latino men's journey to a new masculinity.* New York: Springer.

Wexler, D.B. (2000). *Domestic violence 2000: An integrated skills program for men. Group leaders manual.* New York: Norton.

Whitehead P.R., Ward, T., & Collie, R.M. (2007). Time for a change: Applying the good lives model of rehabilitation to a high-risk violent offender. *International Journal of Offender Therapy and Comparative Criminology, 51,* 578–598.

Williams, O. (1992). Ethnically sensitive practice to enhance treatment participation of African men who batter. *Families in Society, 73,* 588–595

Williams, O. (2000). The public health and social consequences of Black male violence. *Journal of African-American Men, 5,* 71.

Witte, T., Parker, L.M., Lohr, J.M., & Hamberger, L.K. (2007). Research evidence for the efficacy of psychosocial interventions for intimate partner violence: A critical review of the literature. *Scientific Review of Mental Health Practice, 5,* 8–20.

Yates, P.M., & Ward, T. (2008). Good lives, self-regulation, and risk management: An integrated model of sexual offender assessment and treatment. *Sexual abuse in Australia and New Zealand, 1,* 3–20.

2

Strengths-Based Batterer Intervention: A New Direction with a Different Paradigm

CATHERINE A. SIMMONS
PETER LEHMANN

Little progress can be made by merely attempting to repress what is evil; our great hope lies in developing what is good. *—Calvin Coolidge*

Strengths-based intervention with intimate partner violence (IPV) offenders is a new direction for batterer intervention programs (BIPs) that is based on the profession's changing paradigm of focusing on how people achieve health and wellbeing, not simply thwarting problems and illness (e.g., Linley & Joseph, 2004; Saleebey, 2006; Sheldon, Frederickson, Rathunde, Csikszentmihalyi & Haidt, 1999). Different from traditional approaches grounded in deficits and punishment, such as the Duluth model (e.g., Minnesota Program Development, Inc., 2007; Paymar, 2000; Pence & Paymar, 1993) and many cognitive behavioral men's group approaches (e.g., Adams, 1988; Sonkin, Martin & Walker, 1985), strengths-based batterer intervention builds on individual strengths to help IPV offenders[*] end their abusive/violent lifestyle. Not a "one-size-fits all" approach, strengths-based batterer intervention recognizes that each IPV offender uses

---

[*]NOTE: Although most literature uses the term "batterers" to refer to men arrested for partner violence, for consistency this chapter uses the term "IPV offenders" to refer to such individuals and the term "batterers" within the context of BIPs.

violence differently and for different reasons. Thus, different methods are needed to help change the life of each IPV offender so that he can live (and wants to live) a nonabusive and nonviolent lifestyle. This means that although some aspects of intervention can and will be similar, it is recognized that not every intervention will work with every IPV offender. As was discussed in chapter 1 of this text, traditional models of intervention have proven relatively ineffective in helping IPV offenders stop their abusive and violent behaviors, or in protecting the partners who are abused (e.g. Babcock, Green & Robie, 2004; Babcock & LaTaillade, 2000; Davis & Taylor, 1999; Jackson et al., 2003). Clearly, different approaches to intervening with IPV offenders are needed.

The six different approaches discussed in this text share a common foundation: each builds on the strengths that clients bring with them to the intervention process. To some readers, even the idea that IPV offenders have strengths may seem misguided. Haven't those IPV offenders who present to intervention programs been adjudicated for horrific crimes against their intimate partner—the one person to whom they have committed to protect and love? Doesn't this make them essentially bad and deserving of punishment? To these questions we state a resounding "YES." IPV offenders have done bad things and deserve punishment for their crimes, through the criminal justice system.

However, it is the contention of the editors of this book that BIPs should not be considered a form of punishment. Instead, BIPs should be considered an opportunity for change based on the truism that just as no human being is entirely good, so too, no human being is entirely bad or evil. All human beings have strengths of character: skills, desires, hopes, aspirations, loves, and dreams. It is from these strengths that the chapters in this text ground intervention aimed at instilling the skills, knowledge, and resources IPV offenders need to change the factors related to their offending behavior. Just as Alfred Adler stated about teachers: *"the educator must believe in the potential power of his pupil, and he must employ all his art in seeking to bring his pupil to experience this power,"* so it is true that family violence professionals must both recognize and utilize the potential power that each of their offending clients has to utilize his individual strengths, values, and interests in a manner that will change his behavior from abusive and violent to nonabusive and nonviolent.

CORE CONSTRUCTS OF STRENGTHS-BASED BATTERER INTERVENTION

Strengths-based batterer intervention encompasses approaches to intervention with IPV offenders that focus on building individuals' strengths, not simply eliminating their weaknesses. Approaches that are strengths-based operate under ideologies and processes that (a) facilitate client-directed change, (b) focus on strengths and resources, not deficits and problems, (c) are fair and respectful of clients regardless of the harm they have inflicted on others, (d) put values of respect and social justice into action, (e) enable clients to identify and embrace their unique personal, social, and cultural strengths and abilities, and (f) assist clients in making changes that are meaningful, significant, and reflect how they want their lives to be. To address these important issues and to provide a framework for subsequent chapters, a discussion is needed to clarify the core assumptions from which all strengths-based IPV intervention is based. It is also important to address how strengths-based batterer intervention is different from those approaches currently driving the BIP field.

Assumptions of Strengths-Based Batterer Intervention

Translating strengths-based ideas into batterer intervention is predicated on seven assumptions about IPV offenders and the process of intervention, illustrated in Exhibit 2.1

Exhibit 2.1

ASSUMPTIONS OF STRENGTHS-BASED BATTERER INTERVENTION

1. Abusive behavior is injurious and must be ended
2. Everyone has strengths, regardless of current and past behavior
3. The key to ending violent behavior is tapping into the person's strengths
4. All environments have positive resources
5. BIPs are not an extension of the punishment, but an opportunity for positive change
6. Positive working and therapeutic relationships produce promising outcomes
7. No one method of intervention will end violence for all people

Straightforward and congruent across all IPV offender intervention, regardless of theoretical approach, is the first assumption that abusive behaviors are injurious and must be ended. The reason IPV offenders are referred to treatment is to help them stop their abusive behaviors and live nonviolent lifestyles.

Emerging from this first and primary assumption, the second assumption is that every human being has strengths. Regardless of current and past behavior, every person presenting to batterer intervention has a reservoir of positive features, including talents, skills, assets, abilities, internal resources, and capacities.

This axiom provides the foundation for the third assumption, that the key to ending violent behavior is tapping into the individual's strengths. Ending violence is predicated on IPV offenders discovering skills they can use in their steps toward changing their lives from abusive and violent to nonabusive and nonviolent.

In an effort to facilitate these changes, the fourth assumption is that regardless of the situation that surrounds the individual, each person who presents for treatment after using violence against his intimate partner lives in an environment that has positive resources. Identifying and tapping into these resources is an important component in the change process.

The fifth assumption is that even though it is rare for an IPV offender to present to the treatment environment without first being court mandated, BIPs should not be considered an extension of punishment. Instead, intervention should be considered an opportunity for the person to make positive changes in his life; the catalyst to begin a nonabusive and nonviolent life style.

Part of this assumption is inherent in the sixth assumption, that positive working and therapeutic relationships produce promising outcomes. Unlike intervention that is based on shame and punishment, strengths-based intervention is grounded in the premise that processes based on mutual respect and positive interpersonal relationships will elicit real and lasting change.

The seventh and final assumption is that no one method of intervention will end violence for all people. Strengths-based BIP approaches are not manualized to fit every situation, every offender, or every need. There is no one-size-fits-all approach. Instead, although some aspects of intervention will be the similar (or even the same), each intervention should be tailored to the individual's needs, based on the findings of a comprehensive bio-psycho-social assessment.

The core constructs and assumptions inherent to all strengths-based intervention with IPV offenders may seem simplistic and idealistic at first. Indeed, many may believe they already operate from the strengths perspective. However, in describing strengths-based social work practice, Saleebey (2006) articulately stated:

> Many of us believe (or have at one time believed) that we are building on clients' strengths. But sometimes we fall short. To really practice from a strengths perspective demands a different way of seeing clients, their environments, and their current situation. Rather than focusing exclusively or dominantly on problems, your eye turns toward possibilities. In the thicket of trauma, pain, and trouble you can see blooms of hope and transformation." (p. 1)

Operating from strengths is not simply putting a happy face on otherwise terrible circumstances. Nor is it about ignoring real and important problems. Instead, it is about focusing every aspect of intervention in such a way as to help clients to discover, enhance, build, and otherwise grow their capacities, achieve their goals, and change their lives. Although these ideas are being translated into other areas of the helping professions (e.g., Linley & Joseph, 2004; Saleebey, 2006; Sheldon, Frederickson, Rathunde, Csikszentmihalyi & Haidt, 1999), they are dramatically different from those of the traditional batterer intervention approaches used throughout the United States and Canada (e.g., Gondolf, 2002; Minnesota Program Development, Inc., 2007; Paymar, 2000; Pence & Paymar, 1993; Healy, Smith & O'Sullivan, 1998). To understand these differences, it is helpful to compare and contrast the core assumptions of each.

CONTRASTING STRENGTHS-BASED BATTERER INTERVENTION WITH TRADITIONAL APPROACHES

Strengths-based batterer intervention is dramatically different from traditional BIP approaches in the way intimate partner abuse is interpreted, the view of what causes intimate partner abuse, and the way the IPV offender is regarded. Traditional BIP approaches interpret IPV as an extension of the universal power men have over women, and of men's gender-based acceptance that they have a "right" to use violence against women (e.g., Gondolf, 2002; Minnesota Program Development, Inc., 2007; Paymar, 2000). Most, but not all, of the traditional BIP approaches view IPV as one-directional, where the man is the aggressor and the women is the victim (e.g., Minnesota Program Development, Inc., 2007; Paymar, 2000). Conversely, strengths-based BIP approaches interpret

IPV as a complex problem involving a host of emotions, such as anger, jealousy, fear, and shame, with no one cause and no one pattern that fits all situations of violence or all couples. Strengths-based BIP approaches recognize research indicating that sometimes the violence is one-directional, sometimes the violence is asymmetrical, and sometimes the violence is mutual (please see Archer, 2000; Fiebert, 2004; Straus, 2006).

Traditional BIP approaches postulate that IPV is caused by a society that reinforces patriarchal beliefs (e.g., Gondolf, 2002; Minnesota Program Development, Inc., 2007; Paymar, 2000). With this approach, socialization, cultural variables, and various other mediums both teach and support men's dominance over women, which includes using various forms of abuse to control the man's partner (e.g., Gondolf, 2002; Minnesota Program Development, Inc., 2007; Paymar, 2000). Conversely, strengths-based batterer intervention avoids imposing a universal explanation for violence, instead arguing that social learning is important to understanding what causes one partner to be violent against the other. However, no "one-size-fits-all approach" predominates, as both interpersonal and intrapersonal variables also play a role in abuse and violence.

Traditional BIP approaches regard IPV offenders (i.e., batterers) as all being the same, or at least very similar. The relationship between IPV offenders' behaviors and their use of violence towards women is solely about control, power, privilege, and the entitlement of men over women (e.g., Gondolf, 2002; Minnesota Program Development, Inc., 2007; Paymar, 2000). Conversely, strengths-based batterer intervention contends that different types of IPV offenders exist, and that no one theory describes all people who use violence against their partners. A single explanation does not exist for every violent incident within a violent relationship. The relationship between the IPV offender's behavior and his use of violence can only be explained by understanding an infinite combination of relationship factors, including but not exclusive to power and control.

The key interpretive differences between traditional and strengths-based approaches are outlined in Table 2.1.

Strengths-based batterer intervention also differs from traditional approaches in relation to views and focus of intervention, treatment approaches, and the theories of change. Traditional BIP approaches view intervention as purely educational. The dominant assumption for the BIP professional is that the IPV offender's behavior is culturally and socially determined. Therefore, re-education of these beliefs is critical to the change process (e.g., Gondolf, 2002; Minnesota Program Development, Inc., 2007; Paymar, 2000). Conversely, strengths-based BIP approaches

Table 2.1

INTERPRETATION AND CAUSE CONTRASTS BETWEEN TRADITIONAL AND STRENGTHS-BASED APPROACHES

Area	Traditional Approaches	Strengths-Based Approaches
Violence against women is interpreted as	An extension of men's universal power & control	A complex phenomenon
Causes of violence	Society that reinforces patriarchal beliefs	Avoids imposing a universal explanation
Reason violence is used by batterer	To exert power & control over victim	Varies with individual—usually some imbalance in batterer's life
View of batterer	All are similar/same	Different types

view intervention as therapeutic and restorative. Because the strengths-based BIP professional views causes of violence as multidimensional, it is also recognized that the needs, competencies, and potential for healing must be considered if violence is to end. For traditional approaches the focus of micro-level intervention is on the individual's violence, creating a context of safety first with an education base where accountability and challenging gendered beliefs and behaviors are the priority, while skill-building is an intermediate concern (e.g., Gondolf, 2002; Minnesota Program Development, Inc., 2007; Paymar, 2000).

Conversely, strengths-based approaches focus on the whole person, creating a context of safety first that can be educative but also therapeutic. The IPV offender's strengths are recognized as a motivating factor as he focuses on skill building through an alliance process. On the macro-level of intervention, traditional approaches work on changing community systems that are inherently patriarchal and support violence against women (e.g., Gondolf, 2002; Minnesota Program Development, Inc., 2007; Paymar, 2000). Intervention with IPV offenders must be coordinated with the criminal justice response, which was in part shaped by these traditional approaches (e.g., Gondolf, 2002; Minnesota Program Development, Inc., 2007; Paymar, 2000). Alternately, strengths-based BIP approaches focus macro-intervention on the person's interaction with his environment. Strengths-based intervention works with the positive aspects of one's environment in partnership with the criminal justice system; however, strengths-based batterer intervention is not an extension of punishment.

Table 2.2

VIEW AND FOCUS CONTRASTS BETWEEN TRADITIONAL AND STRENGTHS-BASED BIP APPROACHES

Area	Traditional Approaches	Strengths-Based Approaches
View of intervention	Educational	Therapeutic
Micro focus of intervention	Individual's violence	Whole person
Macro focus of intervention	Community system	Person's interaction with environment
Needs of the victim or survivor	To be protected from his or her batterer, even when he or she may not wish to be protected	To be included in the process in whatever manner he or she desires

Traditional BIP approaches view the victim/survivor as a person in need of protection from her abuser, even when she may not wish to be protected (Mills, 2003). Indeed, although the focus of traditional batterer intervention is designed to keep the victim/survivor safe, she is rarely included in the change process (Mills, 2003). Conversely, strengths-based approaches focus on safety while allowing the victim/survivor to be included in the process in whatever manner she desires, recognizing her right to either participate in the process or not.

The view and focus contrasts between traditional and strengths-based approaches are outlined in Table 2.2.

Strengths-based BIP approaches also differ from traditional approaches in various aspects of intervention, including theories of change, role of the professional, modality, and views of resistance and defensiveness. The theory of change utilized by most traditional BIP approaches is educative, focusing on changing the male IPV offender's view of women (Gondolf, 2002). These intervention models are gender specific, feminist informed, and often incorporate a strong educative component (Gondolf, 2002). Inversely, strengths-based IPV approaches are therapeutic, focusing on building strengths and skills. These intervention models are non-gender specific, and the models of practice are seen as therapeutic and based on identified needs.

Traditional BIP approaches believe that to change an individual's behaviors, that person's beliefs must be confronted and challenged (e.g., Gondolf, 2002; Minnesota Program Development, Inc., 2007; Paymar, 2000). Strengths-based IPV approaches believe that to change an individual's behaviors, that person's beliefs must be the starting point for intervention and be worked with, not against. The role of the BIP professional in traditional BIP approaches is the respectful educator, expert, and teacher (e.g., Gondolf, 2002; Minnesota Program Development, Inc., 2007; Paymar, 2000), whereas the role of the BIP professional in strengths-based IPV approaches is that of the helper, facilitator, and collaborating therapist.

The intervention method that facilitates change in traditional BIP approaches is almost always a men's group (e.g., Gondolf, 2002; Minnesota Program Development, Inc., 2007; Paymar, 2000). Usually, the group format is based on a manualized approach aimed at reeducation and is not intended to be therapy (e.g., Gondolf, 2002; Minnesota Program Development, Inc., 2007; Paymar, 2000). Strengths-based IPV approaches use a variety of modalities including, but not limited to, group counseling, individual counseling, psychoeducational classes, and restorative activities. The focus of these methods is change within a therapeutic context that always includes an emphasis on building the IPV offender's resources and capacities.

Finally, traditional BIP approaches view resistance and defensiveness as a problem blocking the change process in IPV offenders (e.g., Gondolf, 2002; Minnesota Program Development, Inc., 2007; Paymar, 2000). Only through challenging and confronting this resistance and defensiveness can ingrained gendered beliefs and abusive behaviors be changed (e.g., Gondolf, 2002; Minnesota Program Development, Inc., 2007; Paymar, 2000). Inversely, strengths-based IPV approaches view resistance and defensiveness as a natural part of the change process. Working with the resistance through relationship building and understanding can reduce the resistance and defensiveness; thus it is an important step.

The differences in intervention approaches are outlined in Table 2.3.

Reasons for Not Using Strengths-Based Batterer Intervention

The core constructs inherent in strengths-based approaches are simple, yet understanding why they have not been integrated into batterer intervention may be a result of theoretical and practical concerns.

One possible theoretical concern is that, as previously described, strengths-based approaches contradict many of the core constructs inherent to the traditional approaches. These constructs have dominated the field for the past three decades, serving as a guide for much of the

Table 2.3

INTERVENTION CONTRASTS BETWEEN TRADITIONAL AND STRENGTHS-BASED APPROACHES

Area	Traditional Approaches	Strengths-Based Approaches
Theory of change	Educating—focusing on changing views of women	Therapeutic—focusing on strengths and skills
To change behaviors, beliefs need to be . . .	Challenged & confronted	A place to start and worked with throughout the intervention
Role of the BIP professional	Expert and teacher	Helper and facilitator
Treatment	Same method for everyone	Different people need different methods of intervention
Intervention method	Always in a group	Sometimes group, sometimes individual
View of resistance and defensiveness	Problem that blocks change	Natural stage of change

governmentally mandated intervention currently in place (such as Austin & Dankwort, 1999; Gondolf, 2002; Healy, Smith & O'Sullivan, 1998; Jackson et al., 2003; Mankowski, Haaken & Silvergild, 2002; Minnesota Program Development, Inc., 2007; Paymar, 2000; Pence & Paymar, 1993). In discussing strengths-based batterer intervention it is important not to negate the pioneering work that went into creating the traditional approaches to batterer intervention, as they form the foundation for the entire family violence field. Some of the important contributions include generating an awareness of the prevalence of IPV, creating an understanding that IPV is a social problem, developing services to protect victims and survivors, and constructing the fundamental need for intervention with IPV offenders (e.g., Gondolf, 2002; Mankowski, Haaken & Silvergild, 2002). However, it appears that those working in this area have sold the idea that their approach is the only one that works, when in fact, evidence supports the contrary (please see Babcock, Green & Robie, 2004; Babcock & LaTaillade, 2000; Davis & Taylor, 1999; Jackson et al., 2003). Indeed, all IPV offender intervention is grounded in a manner that makes the promotion of other options risky for fear of retaliation (e.g. Mills, 2003; Dutton, 2007). Additionally, there appears to be a belief that in saying that batterers have strengths, one demeans the victims and survivors, negates the punishment aspect of intervention, and causes the batterers to justify their behaviors. These theoretical obstructions are unfortunate, as the result appears to be stagnation of a very important aspect of the family violence field.

In addition to theoretical reasons for not pursuing strengths-based approaches within the BIP field, practical concerns also exist. First and foremost, concerns regarding safety of the victim influence all family violence literature, as they should. Safety of the victim should always be the first concern of family violence and criminal justice professionals. However, the currently used approaches are not decreasing recidivism (please see Babcock, Green & Robie, 2004; Babcock & LaTaillade, 2000; Davis & Taylor, 1999; Jackson et al., 2003). Many victims stay with their partner, and most IPV offenders will continue having relationships with someone, regardless of whether the current partner decides to leave or stay. Therefore, safety is a priority with all of the approaches described in this text.

A second practical reason is that taking a strengths-based approach to batterer intervention is a much more difficult process than educating and punishing the offender through manualized efforts. Strengths-based approaches focus on changing the IPV offender's behavior through individualized plans; no one-size-fits-all approach is condoned. This process is time-consuming, difficult, and does not promise success in every situation. Strengths-based approaches do not consider intervention with people who have chosen to harm their intimate partners as a simple recipe where failure can be blamed on the client's resistance and defensiveness. Instead, strengths-based approaches acknowledge that change is a challenge and that the work will be hard for both the client and family violence practitioners. Resistance and defensiveness are a part of the change process; thus, those clients who demonstrate such behaviors must be acknowledged, worked with, accepted, supported, and most certainly not considered failures. These ideas are radical, challenging, and create practical hurdles that family violence professionals must overcome to help their IPV offending clients change their behaviors from abusive and violent to nonabusive and nonviolent.

Despite the practical and theoretical hurdles present in implementing strengths-based BIP approaches, it is important for the field to progress beyond business as usual and search for a way to improve. What is known about human behavior is that people enter the change process at various stages of readiness to change (e.g., Eckhardt, Babcock & Homack,

2004; Levesque, Gelles & Velicer, 2000; Prochaska, DiClemente & Norcross, 1992) and business as usual is doing little to help IPV offenders make these changes (please see Babcock, Green & Robie, 2004; Babcock & LaTaillade, 2000; Davis & Taylor, 1999; Jackson et al., 2003; Klein & Tobin, 2008). However, positive interactions are likely to help produce the desire to change. As stated in chapter 1, the editors of this book are not advocating a radical and evolutionary shift such as that discussed by Kuhn (1962). Instead, this text advocates small foundational changes in thinking about interventions designed to end family violence. The key components inherent in these foundational changes make it important that strengths-based BIP approaches be discussed, explored, researched, and implemented. The six theoretical approaches included in this text are grounded in the strengths-based constructs discussed in this chapter.

As previously stated, strengths-based intervention with IPV offending clients is a new direction for the family violence profession. Underlying strengths-based approaches is the idea that intervention is not designed to simply thwart problems and punish the IPV offender. Instead, strengths-based intervention is designed to help IPV offenders end their abusive and violent behavior by changing their lives so they can (and want to) live a nonabusive and nonviolent life. The strengths-based ideas, theories, approaches, and techniques included in this text can help the family violence practitioner and researcher not simply to repress what is evil or wrong with the IPV offending client, but instead to develop what is good within him. Although these ideas are radical and controversial, they are nothing new. Emerging throughout the helping professions is a changing paradigm focusing on how people achieve health and wellbeing, not simply on thwarting problems and illness (e.g., Linley & Joseph, 2004; Saleebey, 2006; Sheldon, Frederickson, Rathunde, Csikszentmihalyi & Haidt, 1999). From these ideas, the field of intervention with IPV offenders can shift toward a paradigm of strength building, allowing for an expansion of ideas and new forms of practice that will be helpful in ending partner violence.

REFERENCES

Adams, D. (1988). Treatment models of men who batter: A profeminist analysis. In K. Yllo & M. Bograd (Eds.), *Feminist perspectives on wife abuse* (pp. 176–199). Thousand Oaks, CA: Sage.

Archer, J. (2000). Sex differences in aggression between heterosexual partners; A meta-analytic review. *Psychological Bulletin, 126,* 651–680.

Austin, J.B., & Dankwort, J. (1999). Standards of batterer programs: A review and analysis. *Journal of Interpersonal Violence*, 14, 152–168.

Babcock, J.C., Green, C.E., & Robie, C. (2004). Does batterers' treatment work? A meta-analytic review of domestic violence treatment. *Clinical Psychology Review*, 23, 1023–1053.

Babcock, J.C. & LaTaillade, J. (2000). Evaluating interventions for men who batter. In J.P. Vincent, E.N. Jouriles (Eds.), *Domestic Violence: Guidelines for research informed practice* (pp. 37–77). Philadelphia: Jessica Kingsley.

Davis, R.C. & Taylor, B.G. (1999). Does batterer treatment reduce violence? A synthesis of the literature. *Women and Criminal Justice*, 10, 69–93.

Dutton, D.G. (2007). *Rethinking domestic violence*. Vancouver, British Columbia; UBC Press.

Eckhardt, C.I., Babcock, J., & Homack, S. (2004). Partner assaultive men and the stages and processes of change. *Journal of Family Violence*, 19, 81–93.

Fiebert, M.S. (2004). References examining assaults by women on their spouses or male partners: An annotated bibliography. *Sexuality and Culture: An Interdisciplinary Quarterly*, 8, 140–176.

Gondolf, E.W. (2002). *Batterer intervention systems: Issues outcomes and recommendations*. Thousand Oaks, CA: Sage.

Healy, K., Smith C., & O'Sullivan, C. (1998). *Batterer intervention: Program approaches and criminal justice strategies*. Report to the National Institute of Justice, Washington, DC.

Jackson, S., Feder, L., Forde, D.R., Davis, R.C., Maxwell, C.D., & Taylor, B.G. (June 2003). Batterer intervention programs: Where do we go from here? *Special NIJ Report*, Washington DC; National Institute of Justice, U.S. Department of Justice.

Klein, A.R., & Tobin, T. (2008). A longitudinal study of arrested batterers, 1995–2005: Career criminals. *Violence Against Women*, 14, 136–157.

Kuhn, T.S. (1962). *The structure of scientific revolutions*. Chicago, IL: University of Chicago Press.

Levesque, D.A., Gelles, R.J., & Velicer, W.F., (2000). Development and validation of a stages of change measure for men in batterer treatment. *Cognitive Therapy and Research*, 24, 175–199.

Linley, P.A. & Joseph, S. (Eds.) (2004). *Positive psychology in practice*, Hoboken, NJ: John Wiley & Sons.

Mankowski, E.S., Haaken, J., & Silvergild, C.S. (2002). Collateral damage: An analysis of the achievements and unintended consequences of batterer intervention programs and discourse. *Journal of Family Violence*, 17, 167–184.

Mills, L.G. (2003). *Insult to injury: Rethinking our responses to intimate abuse*. Princeton: Princeton University Press.

Minnesota Program Development, Inc. (2007). The Duluth model web site downloaded from http://www.duluth-model.org/ on August 30, 2007.

Paymar, M. (2000). *Violence no more: Helping men end domestic abuse* (2nd ed.) Alameda, CA: Hunter House.

Pence, E., & Paymar, M. (1993). *Education groups for men who batter: The Duluth model*. New York: Springer.

Prochaska, J.O., DiClemente, C.C., & Norcross, J.C. (1992). In search of how people change: Applications to addictive behaviors. *American Psychologist*, 47, 1102–1114.

Saleebey, D. (2006). *The strengths perspective in social work practice*, (4th ed.) Boston, MA: Pearson Education, Inc.

Sheldon, K., Frederickson, B., Rathunde, K, Csikszentmihalyi, M., & Haidt, J. (1999). Akumal Manifesto. Downloaded from http://www.ppc.sas.upenn.edu/akumalmanifesto.htm on December 21, 2007.

Sonkin, D.J. Martin, D., & Walker, L.E.A. (1985). *The male batterer: A treatment approach*. New York: Springer-Verlag.

Straus, M.A. (2006). Future research on gender symmetry in physical assaults on partners. *Violence Against Women, 12,* 1086–1097.

Theoretical Models for Strengths-Based Batterer Intervention

PART II

3

Accountability for Change: Solution-Focused Treatment of Domestic Violence Offenders[1]

MO YEE LEE
ADRIANA UKEN
JOHN SEBOLD

Too often people who want to learn SFBT fall into the trap of not being able to see that the difficulty is to stay on the surface when the temptation to look behind and beneath is at its strongest.

> *— Author correspondence with Steve de Shazer, September 5, 2001*

What is noticed becomes reality and what is unnoticed does not exist.

> *— From a work by the authors of this chapter*

This chapter introduces and discusses solution-focused treatment of domestic violence offenders. We briefly introduce the history and research of the model; followed by a detailed description of our assumptions of a solution-focused approach for treating domestic violence offenders. This chapter also outlines a pragmatic, step-by-step, how-to description of what helping professionals can do in treatment to create positive changes in domestic violence offenders. We also provide case illustrations and examples to elucidate how to capitalize on participants' strengths and goal accomplishments, in order to encourage and assist their efforts toward ending violence in their relationships.

---

[1]Acknowledgment: The study was partly supported by the Lois and Samuel Silberman Fund, the New York Community Trust, Social Work Faculty Awards Program, 1999–2000.

HISTORY OF SOLUTION-FOCUSED TREATMENT OF DOMESTIC VIOLENCE OFFENDERS

In 1989, a local superior court judge approached the authors (John Sebold and Adriana Uken) at the Plumas County Mental Health Department in Quincey, California, to ask if they could provide a treatment program for domestic violence offenders. They searched for applicable models for treatment and found a widely adopted psycho-educational model, requested the materials, and began implementing the program. The adopted model was heavily influenced by a cognitive-behavioral-feminist perspective and included materials depicting different types of domestic violence, control logs, and videotapes of couples fighting. The resulting program focused on confronting participants to assure that they recognized and admitted their violent behaviors, took full responsibility for their problems (Lindsey, McBride & Platt, 1993; Pence & Paymar, 1993; Russell, 1995), learned new ways to manage their anger, and communicated effectively with their spouses (Geffner & Mantooth, 1999; Sonkin, 1995; Wexler, 1999).

After implementing this program for one year, Uken and Sebold were disheartened with the results. Using this traditional model they had difficulty engaging offenders in treatment and convincing offenders to take responsibility for their past behaviors. Although both were experienced practitioners, they found that their attempts to convince offenders to admit and assume responsibility for their dysfunctional behavior often served only to push offenders into responding with pseudo-compliance, resulting in a dysfunctional, non-therapeutic relationship.

Most domestic violence offenders are involuntary clients who are court-ordered or forced by their partners to receive treatment. Their perceptions of their problems (and whether or not they even believe they have problems) are oftentimes at odds with the perceptions of their referral sources or service providers. At the time Uken and Sebold became involved in treating offenders, cognitive and feminist approaches set the standard by which treatment programs were measured. However, the authors' poor treatment results using these approaches indicated that such approaches might not be the best match for this population.

They were particularly concerned that a focus on confronting participants and forcing them to recognize and admit their violent behaviors appeared to only aggravate and create distance between offenders and the treatment process. The traditional approach seemed to create a contest of wills between offenders and the program. This apparent mismatch between offenders' perception of their problems and the cognitive-behavioral-feminist treatment approaches seemed to result in the creation of roadblocks to change, as opposed to creating a bridge to more effective behaviors. These roadblocks were apparent in participants' constant evasiveness, silence, phony agreement, and vociferous counter-arguments when confronted with their problems of violence (Murphy & Baxter, 1997). We began to believe that the mismatch between how programs viewed offenders and how offenders viewed themselves was at the core of why we were unsuccessful with traditional approaches. Offenders clearly saw their lives differently and in a more complex manner then the traditional programs allowed for.

A significant negative outcome of this disparity between treatment philosophy and participant problem perception is that many treatment programs have high drop-out rates, high rates of continuance of violent behaviors, and significantly high rates of failure to pay for services (Uken, Lee & Sebold, 2007). Program non-completion rates have been high in both short-term and long-term traditional treatment programs. Approximately 60% of men attending the first session of short-term batterer programs (usually 10–20 weeks) completed the program; program completion was usually defined as having missed no more than two to four sessions (Cadsky et al., 1996; Chang & Saunders, 2002; DeMaris, 1989; Edleson & Syers, 1990). Other studies have found similarly high rates. Gondolf and Foster (1991) studied the attrition rates of a 32-session batterer program. Of the 27 participants who attended the first session, only 7.4% (2) completed all 32 of the sessions. The recidivism rate of the Duluth Domestic Abuse Intervention Program, which is based on the Duluth model, was 40% (Shepard, 1992). Saunders (1996) also reported a recidivism rate of 45.9% for the feminist-cognitive-behavioral treatment models. Two experimental evaluations have found batterer treatment programs to be largely ineffective in that there were no significant differences, between those who received group treatment and those who did not in terms of their attitudes, beliefs, and behaviors (Feder & Forde, 2000), or victims' reports of new violent incidents (Davis, Taylor & Maxwell, 2000).

In addition to the problem of attrition and recidivism, the relationship between group facilitators and the members seemed to be part of the problem. The authors' (Sebold and Uken's) initial attempts to use traditional treatment models convinced them that such models actually aggravate participants' problems regarding power and control; and as a result, treatment is less likely to have a positive outcome. Specifically, Uken and Sebold noted that the more they attempted to force participants to admit to problems, the more participants resisted engaging with treatment. (In some cases, participants would admit to problems but fail to assume any responsibility for real change.) Such responses to treatment have consistently been described as *resistance* or as part of the offender profile. Sebold and Uken, however, have come to view these responses as typical, if not normal, responses by offenders to treatments that attempt to force an unaccustomed worldview on offenders.

The authors' work and research suggests that offenders are not resistant to treatment per se, but are resistant to treatments that frame them in a manner they find disrespectful. The authors believe that successful treatment must be delivered in a tone and structure that invites offenders to engage in developing a collaborative treatment goal that the offenders themselves define as potentially helpful to them. Such an approach is likely to result in better treatment and also higher completion rates, lower recidivism, and higher levels of efficacy. Attempting to force anyone to define himself in a preconceived negative manner creates a conflictual and frustrating dynamic in which great energy and power must be exerted to gain treatment compliance. To some degree it can be argued this process mirrors the problem that brings the offender into treatment in that one entity is attempting to force its will on to another.

As we questioned the effectiveness of historical assumptions and traditional models that attempted to hold individuals accountable for admitting to and talking about past behaviors, we began to search for alternatives. Around this same time we had been reading and applying some of Steve de Shazer's work on solution-focused therapy and were beginning to have success using solution-focused treatments with other problem presentations. From this work we began to conceptualize an experiment to assess its application to the treatment of domestic violence offenders. Our work is grounded in the basic solution-focused principle, *if something doesn't work—don't keep doing more of it—do something different.*

Our original attempt at applying a solution-focused approach included shortening the time frames for treatment. This was in dramatic contrast to other approaches that had consistently expanded time frames in attempts to improve outcomes. Studies that have examined the relationship between time and therapeutic change indicate that change occurs as a linear function of the logarithm of the number of sessions, with the greatest gains produced early in treatment and diminishing returns thereafter (Howard, Kopta, Krause & Orlinsky, 1986); most therapeutic gains occurring within the first eight sessions (Garfield, 1989). We shortened our treatment program to eight sessions.

We were interested in how the solution-focused *miracle question* (de Shazer, 1994) and the concept of well-formed goals could be applied to the offender problem and wondered if group members might be more focused and committed if they were required to work on a goal. We decided the goal must offer the group members considerable opportunity to determine what would be most helpful to them to work on, while at the same time holding them accountable for improving their ability to interact effectively with others. For this reason the goal was required to include a specific focus on improving a relationship in their lives. Our approach also defined a list of rules that in part required participants to explore, discover, and define a relationship they wanted to make better; including the specific behavioral details of what they would need to do to accomplish their relationship goals. The therapeutic tasks in this model focus mainly on asking helpful questions that elicit the search for what might work and what might not work for group participants. Once participants discovered what is likely to be helpful to them, the facilitators' work becomes one of complimenting successes, encouraging participants to do more of the same, and helping group members discover what differences these changes are making in their lives (Uken et al., 2007).

Our initial work included only first-time offenders, but after gradually seeing how effective the program was, the court began to expand its referrals to include all domestic violence offenders, including repeat offenders, those coming out of prison, and both men and women. We believe that one of the striking differences between the solution-focused treatment program and other approaches in the field of domestic violence is that we chose not to receive information about the nature or details of various group members' offences. Knowing about previous offences might lead to bias and preconceptions, and limit our ability to be open to group members' strengths. While many in the field might doubt the wisdom of this decision, the authors' previous experience had taught them that focusing on problems did nothing to help offenders figure out what to do differently in their lives and, until they figured that out, nothing could change (Lee, Sebold & Uken, 2003b; Uken et al., 2007).

In sum, this is a solution-based, goal-directed, domestic violence group treatment program. It is an accumulation of practice experience, wisdom, and learning from errors since 1991. The program is inspired by the work of Insoo Kim Berg, Steve de Shazer, and their associates at the Brief Family Therapy Center in Milwaukee (Berg, 1994; de Jong & Berg; 2007; de Shazer, 1985; 1991). Our program uses a treatment approach that holds domestic violence offenders accountable for solutions rather than responsible for problems. Building on a strengths perspective and using a time-limited approach, solution-focused treatment for domestic violence offenders postulates that positive and long-lasting change can occur in a relatively brief period of time by focusing on *"solution-talk"* instead of *"problem-talk."* Focusing on and emphasizing solutions, competencies, and strengths in offenders must never be equated with a minimization of the destructiveness of their violent behaviors. A solution-focused group treatment model does not deny or minimize aggressive and violent behaviors. Similar to other treatment programs, such an approach recognizes the role of offenders in instigating violence against the victims and that treatment programs are a part of the coordinated community response to domestic violence. In addition, the effectiveness of a solution-focused treatment program is contingent on the support of the legal system that provides a strong sanction against violent behaviors. Different from the cognitive-behavioral-feminist approaches, however, a solution-focused approach uses the language and symbols of "solution and strengths" and does not go into the history of problems in the treatment process. (Lee, Sebold & Uken, 2003a)

RESEARCH ON SOLUTION-FOCUSED TREATMENT OF DOMESTIC VIOLENCE OFFENDERS

For a treatment to be based on an informed position (Gingerich & Eisengart, 2000), it is important to evaluate the effectiveness of a particular treatment program and examine the process of change that contributes to its effectiveness. We have conducted three studies to evaluate the effectiveness and understand the impact of the program on domestic violence offenders.

Study 1

The first was an outcome study that used a one-group pre- and post-test design with a 6-month follow-up to evaluate the effectiveness of a solution-focused group treatment program for 90 domestic violence offenders who were court-ordered to receive treatment. Details of the study can be found in Lee, Uken, and Sebold (2004). As a summary, the study explored the following research questions:

1. How did the behaviors of program participants in a relational context change following program completion as evaluated by their partners/spouses using Solution Identification Scale (Goldman & Baydanan, 1990)?
2. How did participants' self-assessment of their self-esteem change following program completion using Index of Self Esteem (Hudson, 1992)?
3. What were the recidivism rates of program participants as based on official arrest records from the victim witness office, the probation office, and the district attorney's office, and self-reports of participants and their partners/spouses?
4. What were the program completion rates of those participants who were admitted to the program?
5. What are the relationships between participants' profiles and recidivism rates as based on official arrest records?

Data analyses were based on data of participants of 14 groups that were conducted between October 1996 and January 2002. Respondents consisted of 90 program participants: 77 males (85.6%) and 13 females (14.4%). The age of the program participants ranged from 19 to 61 years (mean = 37.2, SD = 9). Program participants were predominantly Caucasian (84.1%), with 10.2 % African Americans, 3.4% Native Americans, and 2.3% Hispanic Americans. Participants had attained an average of 12.6 years of education (SD = 1.5; range = 9–19). Regarding the marital status of program participants, 46.7% were currently married or lived with a partner, 42.2% were divorced or separated, and 11.1% had never married. Over half of the participants self-identified as laborers (55.1%), 7.9% were professionals, 6.7% were service workers, 5.6% were students, 2.2% were on welfare or disability, 1.1% owned a business, 1.1% were homemakers, and 20.2% were unemployed. Using DSM IV criteria, 18.8% of the program participants had an Axis I diagnosis and 25.5% had personality characteristics that suggested an Axis II diagnosis of personality disorder. The Global Assessment Function (GAF) scores of participants ranged from 50 to 74 (mean = 61.6; SD = 4.1) meaning that an average program participant was able to function in social, occupational, or school settings with only mild symptoms.

The study also collected information about the participants regarding their involvement in criminal offenses and childhood experiences. Of the 90 participants, 61.4% had substance and/or alcohol abuse problems, and 23.3% had involvement with criminal offenses other than domestic violence. In addition, 39.5% of program participants experienced parental divorce or separation, 56.9% were children of alcoholics, and 44.3% had experienced abuse as children. This profile is consistent with what is being suggested by existing literature regarding characteristics of domestic violence offenders; in that a sizable number of offenders have problems with substance abuse, and/or experienced abuse as children.

Findings of the study provided initial empirical evidence of the effectiveness of a solution-focused approach for treating domestic violence offenders. Using official arrest records and including all reoffending cases that were reported by the victim witness office, the probation office, and the district attorney's office, the recidivism rate of 16.7% of this program is considerably lower than that of most other conventional treatment programs. The recidivism rate based on official arrest records is comparable to the recidivism rate of 13.5% reported by spouses and partners at the 6-month follow-up interviews. In addition, participants and their spouses and partners perceived a significant decrease in participants' verbally and physically violent behavior 6 months after participants' completion of the program.

The program completion rate of 92.8% was impressive compared with rates for most other batterer treatment programs based on feminist-cognitive-behavioral or process-psychodynamic approaches, including short-term programs, whose program completion rate is approximately 60% (Cadsky et al., 1996; Chang & Saunders, 2002, DeMaris, 1989; Edleson & Syers, 1991).

Among program participants who were currently involved in intimate relationships, which was around half of the original sample, findings indicated a significant improvement in their relational skills in intimate relationships as evaluated by their spouses and partners. The improvement in participants' relational skills from pretreatment to posttreatment was maintained 6 months after completion of the program. Based on self-reports of participants, findings indicated a significant increase in their self-esteem from pretreatment to posttreatment. The increase in participants' self-esteem was maintained 6 months after their completion of the treatment program. In addition, participants' recidivism as based on official arrest records was only related to experiencing abuse as a child, but not to other profiles, including psychiatric diagnoses, substance and/or alcohol abuse problems, involvement with criminal offenses, experience of parental divorce, or coming from a family with a history of parental alcoholism.

Study 2

The purpose of the study was to investigate the role of self-determined goals in predicting recidivism in treating domestic violence offenders. Details of the study are reported in Lee, Uken, and Sebold (2007). The study hypothesized that *goal specificity* and *goal agreement* would predict *recidivism* as mediated by *confidence* to work on goal. Data was collected from 88 court-mandated batterers who were offered the opportunity to avoid prosecution by completing the Plumas Program between October 1996 and February 2004.

Research participants included 70 males and 18 females with their ages ranging from 19 to 74 years (mean = 37.5, SD = 9.8). Predictor variables of the model were: (1) *Goal specificity* that was measured by a 3-point Likert scale completed by the facilitators at termination that evaluated participants' self-determined treatment goals as behaviorally described, positively stated, and stated as small steps and in process form. (2) *Goal agreement* that was measured by a 3-point Likert scale completed by facilitators at termination that evaluated the extent to which the goal was mutually agreed upon by the participant and the facilitator. The mediating variable *confidence* was measured by participants' self-reported level of confidence to continue working on their goals upon completion of treatment program. The dependent variable *recidivism* measured participants' reoffending behaviors after attending the treatment program, based on accumulative statistics provided by the victim witness office, probation office, and district attorney's office between 1997 and 2004. Brain injury and experience of child abuse were entered as controlled variables in the model because of significant association between these variables and recidivism.

The study used the M-plus structural equation modeling program 2.12 (Muthén & Muthén, 2001) to test the relationships between predictor, mediator, and dependent variables. M-plus allows for the specification of categorical endogenous variables (recidivism). The recidivism rate for participants who completed the Plumas Program was 10.2%. Findings indicated that the hypothesized model was a good fit to the data, χ^2 (5, n = 88) = 4.72, p = .45, CFI = 1.0, RMSEA = 0. This model accounted for 58% of variance in recidivism. *Goal specificity* and *goal agreement*

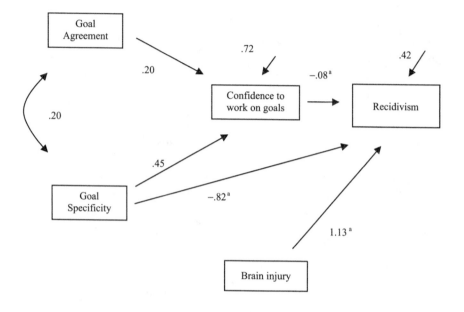

χ^2 $(df = 9, N = 88) = 7.966, p = .538, CFI = 1.0, RMSEA = 0.0$

[a] parameters represent the probit estimates for recidivism as a categorical variable

Figure 3.1 Final Model of Goal Setting and Recidivism

significantly predicted *recidivism*. There was a direct path from *goal specificity* to *recidivism* (Beta = −.43) and an indirect path through *confidence*. *Goal agreement* had an indirect path to *recidivism* mediated through *confidence*. The controlled variables, brain injury and experience of childhood abuse, significantly predicted *recidivism* (Figure 3.1).

Study 3

This study utilized qualitative methodology to understand the experiences of domestic violence offenders and their spouses in a solution-focused treatment program. Data analyses were based on the responses of 90 participants of 14 groups that were conducted between October 1996 and January 2002, and their spouses and partners from the following sources: an assignment completed by participants at the end of the group that asked them to write down one page of what they have learned from the group. In addition, analyses were conducted on answers to five open-ended questions asked in the 6-month follow-up phone interviews. Three questions were addressed to participants: (1) What were the things in the group that you found most helpful or unhelpful to you? (2) What did the group facilitators say or do that you find helpful or unhelpful? (3) Two questions were addressed to spouses and partners: (1) In your own words, can you tell me any positive changes in your spouse/partner after s/he participated in the diversion program? (2) What things about the program *did* you find helpful or unhelpful to your spouse/partner?

Details of the study are reported in Lee, Sebold, and Uken (2003b). In summary, content analysis was used to understand program participants' perception of their experience in the treatment program. An emergent design based on the constant comparison method was used to explore the qualitative data (Glaser & Strauss, 1967; Lincoln & Guba, 1985; Charmaz, 2000). Consumers' narratives described helpful and unhelpful treatment components, beneficial therapeutic and relational behaviors of facilitators that contributed to positive changes in offenders, and learning generated from attending the treatment program.

The ultimate purpose of intervention research is the development and advancement of effective treatment models for the benefit of clients. Intervention research and practice are intimately related, mutually informing, and inseparable. The primary purpose of these studies is to examine the utility of a solution-focused, goal-directed approach for treating domestic violence offenders so that findings of the study can inform further development and refinement of practice. Findings of this study provided initial empirical evidence regarding the positive impact of the program on domestic violence offenders.

However, limitations of these studies must be acknowledged. First, the sample size was limited and it was a purposive sample. In addition, there was no control or comparison group with randomized assignment procedures to compare the effectiveness of this approach with other established models of treatment. Another limitation of these studies was the use of self-reports to measure studied variables. These findings could be affected by the problem of reporting bias. Third, findings of the studies can be affected by the problem of attrition. For instance, study 2 only included 88 participants out of 127 because of the incomplete data presented by 39 participants. Although there were no significant differences between the two groups in all demographic variables, childhood experiences, and DSM IV diagnoses, findings could still be influenced by the problem of measurement attrition (Fraser, 2004).

These limitations pose challenges to and raise suggestions for future research regarding domestic violence treatment programs. Specific recommendations for future investigations include: (1) use a larger sample size that uses representative samples, (2) include control or comparison groups using randomized assignment procedures, (3) use multiple reporting sources to avoid reporting bias, (4) use multiple reporting sources to measure recidivism rates, and (5) monitor the data collection process carefully to reduce problems in measurement attrition.

IMPLICATIONS FOR USE OF SOLUTION-FOCUSED TREATMENT WITH DOMESTIC VIOLENCE OFFENDERS

Assumptions of Practice

The structure of solution-focused group treatment with domestic violence offenders is guided by the following assumptions of practice (Lee, Uken & Sebold, 2004):

1. *A focus on solutions and strengths:* Instead of discussing or exploring clients' problems of violence or deficiencies, the focus is on the successes of participants in dealing with their problems of violence, and how to notice and use these abilities more often (Lee, Greene & Rheinscheld, 1999). Focusing on solutions is neither a consequence of "naive" beliefs regarding strengths in group participants nor simplistic "positive thinking." The focus on solution-talk to achieve change is supported by a systems perspective (Bateson, 1979). One basic assumption of a systems perspective is that change is constant. Every problem pattern includes some sort of exception to the rule (de Shazer, 1985). Despite the multi-deficiencies and/or problems participants may perceive that they have, there are always times when they handle their life situations in a more satisfying way or in a different manner; there must be times when he or she is not aggressive or violent and uses other means to resolve conflicts and differences with people (Lee et. al, 1999). These exceptions provide the clues for solutions (de Shazer, 1985), and represent the participant's "unnoticed" strengths and resources to address the problem of violence. The task for the therapist is to assist group participants in noticing, amplifying, sustaining, and reinforcing

these exceptions, regardless of how small or infrequent they may be (Berg, 1994).

2. *Utilizing language of strengths and successes:* Influenced by social constructivism, solution-focused therapists view language as the medium through which personal meaning and understanding are expressed and socially constructed in conversation (de Shazer, 1994). Further, the meaning of dialogue/conversation is always contingent on the contexts and the language within which it is described, categorized, and constructed by participants (Wittgenstein, 1958). Because the limits of reality that can be known and experienced by an individual are framed by the language available to him or her to describe it, and these meanings are inherently unstable and shifting, a major therapeutic challenge for solution-focused therapists is to initiate a "conversation of change" that assists participants in constructing meanings and solutions by describing goals, observable behaviors, and progressive lives in new and beneficial ways (Miller, 1997). In our program, we did not drill participants on problems of violence or its history. It has been our contention that pathology or problem-talk may sustain a problem reality through self-fulfilling prophecies, further disempowering participants, and distracting group participants' and facilitators' attention from developing solutions (de Shazer, 1994; Miller, 1997).

3. *Accountability for solutions:* Not focusing on participants' responsibility for problems or deficits is an important way for treatment providers to direct all therapeutic energy toward supporting offenders' responsibility for building solutions. In this program, the "solution" is established in the form of a goal that is to be determined and attained by individual participants, within parameters set by the facilitators. Participants are required to develop a goal by the third session and report on their goal efforts every session. They are held accountable for goal accomplishments that require hard work, discipline, and effort (Berg & Kelly, 2000).

4. *Participants define their own goals and solutions:* Influenced by social constructivism, solution-focused facilitators view "solutions" as private, local, meaning-making activities by individual participants (Miller, 1997). In working with domestic violence offenders, the facilitator refrains from suggesting goals or making assumptions regarding the appropriateness or helpfulness

Intervention Protocol: Utilizing Goals to Create a Context for Change in Domestic Violence Offenders

A solution-focused approach for treating domestic violence offenders primarily utilizes goals to create a context for participants to identify, notice, rediscover, and reconnect with their strengths and resources in addressing problems with domestic violence. Goals are a mandatory part of group involvement and serve as a major focus of group activity where change is expected to occur. For discussion purposes, we can roughly divide the group process into five phases, even though the process is more cyclical and continuous rather than discrete and linear. The following describes the primary tasks to be accomplished in each phase (Lee, Sebold & Uken, 2003a).

Phase One: Solution-Focused Intake Interview (Prior to the Beginning of the Treatment Group)
- Initiate a collaborative relationship
- Build initiative for change
- Plant seeds for immediate and future change efforts
- Define the expectations for the group
- Search for strengths

Phase Two: Introduction (Session 1)
- Establish group rules and structure
- Establish collaborative relationship
- Give the goal task

Phase Three: Developing Useful Goals (Sessions 2 and 3)
- Assist participants in developing a useful and well-formed goal
- Assist participants in focusing on solutions, changes, exceptions, and past successes
- Assist participants who "get stuck" in developing a useful goal

Phase Four: Goal Utilization: Expanding the Solution Picture (Sessions 4, 5, 6)
- Review positive changes
- Assist participants in expanding, amplifying, and reinforcing their solution behaviors in their real life context
- Assist participants in making connection between their behavior and positive outcomes
- Reinforce and compliment participants' positive changes

Phase Five: Consolidation and Celebration of Changes (Sessions 7, 8)
- Review goals, evaluate progress and make future plans
- Consolidate personally meaningful change descriptions and/or "new" identity
- Develop connection between participants' actions and positive outcomes
- Acknowledge and compliment goal accomplishments
- Celebrate changes: Ownership of goal accomplishments

BRIEF EXAMPLES OF SOLUTION-FOCUSED TREATMENT OF DOMESTIC VIOLENCE OFFENDERS

Phase 1: Solution-Focused Intake Interview. All participants were given an individual assessment prior to starting the group (Lee, Sebold & Uken, 2003a, 2003b; Lee, Uken & Sebold, 2004; Uken, Lee & Sebold, 2007). Instead of focusing on assessing problems of violence, we did two things. First, we explained the group's requirements, including coming up with a goal to improve a relationship. While it is up to the person to choose whether to join the group or not, there was no choice about working on a goal. We encouraged potential members to begin thinking about a goal because we were going to ask about their ideas for a goal at the first session. We believed this suggestion created the seeds for change at our initial contact. We also explained other group rules such as there being eight sessions with only one excused absence permitted, dismissal from the group if a member arrives at group under the influence of alcohol or drugs, completion of written assignments, participation in group discussions, no blaming talk, and required attendance reported by us to participants' probation officers. We believe that explaining what the requirements of the group are and what members can expect helps to resolve fears about how they might be treated. We knew from past experience that many offenders were intimidated by the prospect of being in a treatment group. Giving them as much information as we can helps to allay some of their concerns (Uken et al., 2007).

The second part of the individual assessment involved us asking questions about participants' strengths and resources. The solution-building process began with the intake process when the facilitator asked specific questions related to client strengths: "What are some of your recent successes? What have you done that you are proud of? What have you done that took a lot of hard work? Have you ever broken a habit that was hard to break? What kinds of things do people compliment you on?" These questions allowed the potential participant and the facilitator an opportunity to begin assessing potential strengths and resources in offenders (Lee et al., 2004; Uken et al., 2007). There was no exploration of the history of the problem of violence at intake or during treatment. We also did not screen and/or exclude potential participants based on severity of violence, substance use, or DSM IV diagnoses. From a solution-focused perspective, facilitators are more interested in assessing the observable, "surface" behaviors of individual participants that are relevant in their search for and accomplishment of personally meaningful goals than using diagnoses for determining treatment (de Shazer, 1994). Because participants have problems with violence, it is also important to help potential participants assess their ability to cooperate, develop solutions, and manage their anger and frustrations in the treatment process (Lee et al., 2004).

Phase 2: Introduction (Session 1). In the first session, we asked group participants to take turns reading and discussing group rules, which set important parameters for effective treatment within a relatively brief period of time. Each participant was given an opportunity to ask questions or express disagreement about the rules. Utilizing this time to talk about group rules prevents problems about the rules coming up later. We had eight group rules that pertain to: attendance, violence, confidentiality, alcohol and drugs, group assignments, group discussion and participation, no blaming-talk, and goal requirement (Lee, Sebold & Uken, 2003a, p. 43–45).

We then focused on giving the goal task and described the parameters of a useful goal in the following manner:

- "We want *you* to create a goal for *yourself* that will be *useful* to *you* in improving your life." (Self-determined goal to enhance commitment)
- "The goal should be one that is *interpersonal* in nature, that is to say that when you work on the goal, another person will be able to *notice* the changes you've made and potentially they could be affected by the change in how you behave." (Interpersonally related, observable, and specific)
- "Another way to think about this is that if you brought us a videotape of yourself working on your goal, you would be able to point

out the different things you were *doing* and maybe even note how these changes affected the other people on the tape." (Goal being specific and observable)

■ "The goal needs to be something *different*, a behavior that you have not generally done before." (Different and new)

■ "The goal doesn't need to be something big. In fact, it is better to keep it small and doable" (Self-efficacy to enhance confidence to work on goal)

■ "Keep in mind that because you will be expected to *report* on your goal work every time we meet so that we can keep track of the progress, it is important that your goal be a behavior you can do at least a few times a week." (Feedback)

Phase 3: Developing Useful Goals. The treatment program's primary purpose of treatment is creating a context for clients to engage in a change process that will benefit them personally and interpersonally, which in turn helps them successfully address the problem of violence. Helping clients to develop useful goals, therefore, constitutes a major therapeutic task. Consequently, individual goals were always varied, reflecting their unique and diverse life circumstances. We did not educate participants or require them to set particular treatment goals related to the problem of violence. Externally imposed goals would only serve to dampen motivation of change, make the treatment process irrelevant, and block creativity to change (Bohm & Peat, 2000).

The focus of treatment was not so much on determining the goal content but on facilitating the process of goal development and goal accomplishment in participants. Our task was to ask solution-focused questions that helped participants begin to choose what they could do in a behavioral way (so that it can be seen or heard by others) that might improve a relationship. Useful goals do not come easily or effortlessly, so we devoted the first three sessions to goal formulation. Some helpful questions that we have used are (Lee, Sebold & Uken, 2003a; Uken, Lee & Sebold, 2007):

■ What do you think someone who knows you well might advise you to work on?

■ If you were to work on _____ what would you actually be doing that someone would notice?

■ What is the first small thing that you could do that would help with that?

- Have you done that before and has it been helpful?
- On a scale of 1 to 10, how confident are you that you could actually do that?
- On a scale of 1 to 10, how confident are you that this will be helpful?
- When will be the first time that you will do this?
- How often will you do this between now and the next time we meet?
- Who do you think might notice that you're doing this?

While there were times when clients developed well-formed, clear, and specific goals, more often participants struggled in the process of developing personal, meaningful, and useful goals. In our work, we often experience the following scenarios of goal development: (1) clients who had vague goals; (2) clients who had complex, undefined goals; (3) clients who had goals that were too big; (4) the "I'm fine" client (client with no goals); (5) clients who had "politically correct" but personally unhelpful goals and (6) clients who had difficulties coming up with goals. It is beyond the scope of this chapter to discuss therapeutically helpful ways to address each scenario, although interested readers can refer to the book *"Solution-focused treatment of domestic violence offenders: Accountability for solutions"* (Lee, Uken & Sebold, 2003a). The general principles for facilitators are to (a) remain persistent and patient, (b) offer choices as much as possible, (c) ask clients what might help them in developing an useful goal, and (d) look for ways that clients are cooperating.

Participant goals were diverse and reflected three major themes. First, goals focused on the self. A second theme of goals focused on relationships, followed by a third theme of goals that focused on developing. (Lee, Uken & Sebold, 2003a).

Phase 4: Noticing and Amplifying Goal Efforts and Changes. For beneficial change to occur, clients should be able to fully envision the positive benefits of the goal behaviors, experiment with goal behaviors, and notice differences between the new goal behaviors and their previous behaviors. Clients also need the ability to *observe* and *evaluate* beneficial consequences of their goal efforts. In this program, we used therapeutic dialogues to facilitate a process that provided feedback to participants regarding their goal efforts. The facilitator used a great number of solution-focused, evaluative questions that helped participants provide self-initiated feedback (for detailed description of these questions, please

refer to Lee, Sebold & Uken, 2003a). These questions required participants to self-evaluate the feasibility, helpfulness, effect, and limitations
of their goal behaviors on other people and their personal situation. We
believed that this was a better way to facilitate feedback; that is, instead
of providing feedback for participants regarding their efforts and behaviors, it was more helpful for them to carefully evaluate and think about
their situation to come up with ideas and perceptions of their own. They
were more likely to have ownership of these perceptions because these
thoughts were not externally imposed, and these perceptions were more
likely to be viable and appropriate in their own context. The facilitators also provided feedback via listening responses, affirming responses,
restating responses, expanding responses, and complimentary responses
(Lee, Uken & Sebold, 2003a).

In terms of the treatment process, once participants established a
workable goal, they were expected to work on the goal between sessions
and report on their efforts during each group session. As participants
began to behave in a way that was consistent with their goal, the group
facilitators engaged them in a feedback process that helped them to see
all the possible benefits of their goal behavior.

When clients reported positive changes in response to goal efforts,
we routinely engaged in the following tasks: (1) helped the client notice
all the benefits of the goal behavior; (2) complimented the efforts;
(3) offered the client the opportunity to draw conclusions about what
the change meant, and (4) helped the client assess whether or not the
goal was comprehensive and helpful. We did not overlook small changes.
In order to make exceptions meaningful and help participants develop a
sense of personal agency, we asked questions such as:

- How do you account for your ability to do this?
- How did you decide to do this?
- Was this easy for you to do or was it difficult?
- How have your mistakes and errors made you a better person?
- How have you managed to decrease or increase _____ since
  last session?

Amplifying positive changes

- What are you continuing to do this week to keep up this change?
- Let's assume you are able to _____ (desired change), what
  will be different for you, for your family?

■ What do you need to focus on doing this week to keep the problem from coming back?

Some participants reported goals as not being helpful or they had not worked on the goals. We did not blame participants as resistant or see the treatment as failure. Instead, we viewed these response as feedback that guided us to the next step in treatment. Here, we listened to how specific goal setting had not been helpful but also gave them an opportunity to re-state their goals. Our intent was to help clients detail future goals by asking specific questions about exceptions of goal-related behavior and/or how they might notice small changes occurring (Lee, Sebold & Uken, 2003a). Some helpful questions were:

■ Was part of the work on your goal helpful?
■ Did you discover any clues about what would be more helpful?
■ What do you think you will need to do different to be more successful?
■ Are there some adjustments that you would make?

The focus of the treatment process in this phase was to: (1) help participants evaluate and notice what was useful, (2) observe the broader impact that their efforts have had on themselves and others, (3) amplify how their goal-related efforts have affected their interpersonal relationships, even if the changes seemed insignificant or small, (4) encourage and compliment all goal efforts, and (5) optimize treatment by helping participants attach as much meaning as possible to their goal work. The purpose was to "make the ordinary extraordinary" so the resulting behaviors are noticed, expanded, amplified, and experienced as being of great benefit and importance to participants (Lee, Sebold & Uken, 2003a).

Phase 5: Consolidating Change. As a result of developing and accomplishing self-initiated, personally meaningful goals, participants usually have a positive outlook about themselves and their life toward the end of treatment. There was a significant increase in participants' self-esteem from pretreatment to post-treatment (Lee, Uken & Sebold, 2004). The pertinent question, however, is whether they will be able to maintain or follow the path that they have already started. A major challenge in the field of treatment of domestic violence offenders is the reduction of reoccurrence of violent behaviors after completion of treatment. In our experience, we have found that change will be more long-lasting when participants begin to describe themselves differently (Lee, Sebold & Uken, 2003b). This process of ascribing a new description of self is the antithesis of diagnosing problems. Instead of using problem "labels" to describe themselves, such as "domestic violence offenders" or "being bad tempered," the participants solidify descriptions that match the solutions that they create as a result of their goal efforts. From a therapeutic point of view, it is important to help participants: (1) evaluate and increase awareness of the positive changes, (2) consolidate change descriptions into "phrases" (such as an honest man, a caring mother, a good parent, a loving husband) that encapsulate the overall change so that participants develop "the language of success" in place of the "language of problem" in describing the self, and (3) connect participants' goal work to the future by developing a road map that identifies indicators of progress (Lee, Sebold & Uken 2003a).

In summary, the program utilizes personalized goal setting to create a context for participants to identify, notice, rediscover, and reconnect with their strengths and resources. Participants are required to develop a personally meaningful outcome that is interpersonal, can be practiced on a regular basis, and is a behavior that is new (Lee, Sebold & Uken, 2003a). They are required to share their steps toward meeting goals in each session. Therapeutic interventions revolve around assisting participants to develop useful and well-formed goals; utilizing accomplishment to expand, amplify, and reinforce solution behaviors in real-life context; and consolidating new descriptions of self that do not contain violence.

CASE STUDY: DEVELOPING USEFUL GOALS

Moving from a Big Goal to a Useful Goal

Tom, the client, begins by describing a big goal that is too vague and broad to be helpful. The following excerpt illustrates the use of focusing and clarifying questions in helping participants to move from a big goal to develop a sense of the proper parameters of an acceptable goal (Lee, Sebold & Uken, 2003a). "T" indicates Tom, "F1" indicates the first facilitator, and "F2" indicates the second facilitator.

T: I'm gonna try stress management cause I don't handle stress well. It doesn't work. I want to burn it, break it, or destroy it.

F1: So how are you gonna do that?

T: Take a break just, instead of jumping forward I think I'll try to just sit back and take a deep breath and cool off for a minute and reappraise my situation, day by day.

F1: Have you done that already?

T: No.

F1: You haven't ever done that?

T: Well I said I had, but I haven't really.

F1: So, did you have any ideas about what could set you off and then what you're going to do instead?

T: That is the hard part, is stress. Sometimes it slowly builds and sometimes it's (Snaps his fingers) right there in front of you. You have to, I'm gonna try, I won't say I'm gonna succeed. I'm gonna try to not be such a, what do you call it? Oh, an asshole. (Another participant laughs)

F2: How would you know that you're successful, Tom? What would tell you that?

T: How I felt. If the stress, if the anger didn't come out. If the belligerence wasn't there. If the, even if it's a lot, for four years now I've been hoping, but it's still been here (points to self) a lot of times. Like a volcano, wanting to explode.

F1: So how will you know when you're being successful? What will be there instead?

T: My reaction, my attitude. I can change that. Then I'll know I'm successful.

F1: OK, so what will, what will be, what will be there instead of the volcano?

T: I don't know. I'll have to experience that and then I'll tell you.

F1: OK, can you have some ideas between now and next time we meet of how you're going to implement this?

T: Yes, cause I live under a very stressful situation. I have a wife that's had six back surgeries. They're telling her she's gonna have to have another six and it'll take her back, financial stress cause I just went back to work.

Tom mentioned a big goal of stress management, although he does not seem to have a clear idea of the steps or of past successes in dealing with his temper. While F1 attempts to use the "how would you know" questions to help Tom describe the envisioned behavioral changes, F2 steps in to help Tom evaluate the "size" of his goal.

F2: It seems too big?

T: No, what's too big?

F2: The goal.

  T: No, why is it too big, explain it. Are you saying you don't feel I can handle it?

F2: No.

  T: Okay.

F2: I think maybe I was saying that. . . . because it's hard for me to see what you're gonna do that's going to get you from this place to where you want to go. I can't see the step yet.

  T: You can't see the step?

F2: No.

  T: The step is to rather than run away, a lot of times the stress happens you run away and hide and get away from it. You know, if there's a problem there's only two things to do, you solve it or get rid of it. Most the time I ignore it. So now I'm trying mainly to solve it, or to get rid of it, the problem that causes me the stress.

F1: Has ignoring it helped?

  T: No.

F1: It doesn't help?

  T: No, running away never does, does it?

F1: Sometimes.

  T: (Laughs) Unless he's got a big enough gun but no, it's not that kind.

F1: Sometimes things change, sometimes when you leave and then come back it's better.

  T: I ran away five times, that's enough.

F1: Okay, so that doesn't work for you.

  T: No.

F2: I think what F1's trying to get at is he can't see a clear picture of what you're going to do that's different? Of what it is you're going to do specifically that will be different.

  T: I'm specifically going to handle the situations that I'm involved in differently than I have been handling them.

F1: Yeah, I hear that, but if I had a camera in your house?

  T: I'd shoot you. (He laughs)

F1: If we had a camera in your house what would we see you doing now that would be different, that we wouldn't see a week before? What would we see different on that camera?

  T: What I would try, try to have you see?

F1: Yeah.

  T: The, the lack of irritation and aggravation on my face almost constantly.

F1: Okay, so what would we see on your face?

  T: Passiveness I hope.

This is the first description Tom has created that begins to describe a doing versus not doing change in observable behavior. The team continues to help Tom create clear descriptions of change behavior that are different or new for him. This is a difficult but helpful exercise for Tom.

F1: Passiveness?

 T: More understanding, maybe.

F1: So on this camera, what would we see on your face?

 T: More understanding.

F1: How would we see more understanding?

 T: Because you would see verbal reactions even though they wouldn't be, wouldn't be, I don't swear but still I can use words with more than one syllable to get my point across to aggravate those who are aggravating me.

F1: So we would hear something different?

 T: You would hear, I would be different. You would hear words coming out of my mouth different. I've already

F1: You've already what?

 T: I've already started.

F1: You have?

F2: Great! Can you give us an example?

 T: Oh I started what was it, last weekend, when a situation came up that normally I would have said something like, "I told you so." Now and my face would get as red as his tee-shirt, "I told you." So I just said, "Well, you know, that's one thing about a mistake, you'll recognize it the second time a lot more than you do the first. Just try not to do it again." and she said, "huh?" (Tom laughs) Because she expected me to really rebuke her. Because I had warned her of the situation, "don't get involved, don't get in it. It's gonna be trouble."

F1: So how were you able to say something instead of "I told you so," which is what you really wanted to say?

 T: Well, I'll tell you what I did. I went in the bathroom, took a deep breath, washed my face and came out and then I expressed myself. Rather than (smacks his hands together) shooting my mouth off like that.

F1: Okay, so that's what we'd see on the camera. We'd see you going into the bathroom, washing your face.

 T: I just put cool water on my face because I knew I was getting ready to blow.

F1: Okay, so you put cold water on your face and you took a deep breath. We'd see you taking a deep breath and then we would hear you say?

T: I just, I said, "the thing about making a mistake is you'll recognize it real good the second time, but let's not try it again."

F2: Well, how did you decide to say that, because that's amazing.

T: It just came out. It wasn't pre-thought or pre-planned. I didn't have a script, I just, and it came out that way.

F2: That's great.

F1: Was it helpful?

T: Yeah, I felt better.

F1: You felt better.

T: Yeah, because I didn't start arguing.

F1: OK, that's exactly what we're looking for.

Tom started with a broad, vague goal of stress management that did not offer specific direction as to how he was going to handle his negative feelings. By sharing with Tom that his goal is "too big," assisting him to look at the small steps, focusing on what he would be doing that was different, Tom arrived at a much more specific and concrete description of "stress management." He moved from "Take a break instead of jumping forward, I think I'll try to just sit back and take a deep breath and cool off for a minute and reappraise my situation, day by day" to "I went in the bathroom, took a deep breath, washed my face and came out and then I expressed myself. Rather than shooting my mouth off like that." The latter description offers a more helpful and specific behavioral guide to facilitate a change in Tom's reaction (Lee et al., 2003).

Also noted is the subtlety of the process. Tom was able to arrive at a concrete description of "stress management" only after much probing and questioning. At one point, he got visibly upset in reaction to the facilitator's comment that the goal is too big, "No, why is it too big, explain it. Are you saying you don't feel I can handle it?" Helping the participant to visualize a well-formed goal requires a lot of patience and consistency on both parts.

CONCLUSION

There are great differences and much diversity in how the problem of domestic violence should be approached. Helping professionals are constantly in search of effective ways to provide treatment for domestic

Charmaz, K. (2000). Grounded theory: Objectivist and constructivist methods. In N.K. Denzin & Y.S. Lincoln (2nd Eds.), *Handbook of qualitative research.* (pp. 509–535). Thousand Oaks, CA: Sage.

Davis, R.C., Taylor, B.G., & Maxwell, C.D. (2000 January). *Does batterer treatment reduce violence? A randomized experiment in Brooklyn.* New York: Victim Services.

DeJong, P., & Berg, I.K. (2007). *Interviewing for solutions (2nd ed.).* Pacific Grove, CA: Brooks/Cole.

DeMaris, A. (1989). Attrition in batterer counseling: The role of social and demographic factors. *Social Service Review, 63,* 142–154.

de Shazer, S. (1994). *Words were originally magic.* New York: W. W. Norton.

de Shazer, S. (1991). *Putting difference to work.* New York: W. W. Norton.

de Shazer, S (1985). *Keys to solutions in brief therapy.* New York: W. W. Norton.

Edleson, J.L. & Syers, M. (1990). Relative effectiveness of group treatments for men who batter. *Social Work Research Abstracts, 26,* 10–17.

Feder, L., & Forde, D.R. (2000, June). *A test of the efficacy of court-mandated counseling for domestic violence offenders: The Broward Experiment.* Executive summary of final report. Washington, DC: National Institute of Justice.

Fraser, M. (2004). Intervention research in social work: Recent advances and continuing challenges, *Research on Social Work Practice, 14,* 210–222.

Garfield, S.L. (1989). *The practice of brief psychotherapy.* New York: Pergamon.

Geffner, R., & Mantooth, C. (1999) *Ending spouse/partner abuse; A psychoeducational approach for individuals and couples.* New York: Springer Publishing Company.

Gingerich, W.J., & Eisengart, S. (2000). Solution-focused brief therapy: A review of the outcome research. *Family Process, 39,* 477–498.

Glaser, B. & Strauss, A.L. (1967). *The discovery of Grounded Theory: Strategies for qualitative research.* Chicago: Aldine.

Goldman, J., & Baydanan, M. (1990). *Solution identification scale.* Denver, CO: Peaceful Alternatives in the Home.

Gondolf, E.W., & Foster, R.A. (1991). Pre-program attrition in batterers programs. *Journal of Family Violence, 6,* 337–349.

Howard, K.I., Kopta, S.M., Krause, M.J., & Orlinsky, D.E. (1986). The dose-effect relationship in psychotherapy. *American Psychologist, 41,* 17–22.

Hudson, W.W. (1992). *The WALMYR assessment scales scoring manual.* Tempe, AZ: WALMYR Publishing Co.

Lee, M.Y., Greene, G.J., & Rheinscheld, J. (1999). A model for short-term solution-focused group treatment of male domestic violence offenders. *Journal of Family Social Work, 3,* 39-57.

Lee, M.Y., Sebold, J., & Uken, A. (2003a). *Solution-focused treatment with domestic violence offenders: Accountability for change.* New York: Oxford University Press.

Lee, M.Y., Sebold, J., & Uken, A. (2003b). Brief solution-focused group treatment with domestic violence offenders: Listen to the narratives of participants and their partners. *Journal of Brief Therapy, 2,* 3–26.

Lee. M.Y., Uken. A., Sebold, J. (2004). Accountability for solutions: Solution-focused treatment with domestic violence offenders. *Families in Society, 85,* 463–476.

Lee, M.Y., Uken. A., Sebold, J. (2007). Role of self-determined goals in predicting recidivism in domestic violence offenders. *Research on Social Work Practice, 17,* 30–41.

Lincoln, Y.S. & Guba, E.G. (1985). *Naturalistic inquiry.* Thousand Oaks, CA: Sage.

Lindsey, M., McBride, R.W., & Platt, C.M. (1993). *AMEND: Philosophy and curriculum for treating batterers*. CO: Gylantic Publishing Company.

Miller, G. (1997). *Becoming miracle workers: Language and meaning in brief therapy*. New York: Aldine de Gruyter.

Murphy, C.M., & Baxter, V.A. (1997). Motivating batterers to change in the treatment context. *Journal of Interpersonal Violence, 12*, 607–619.

Muthén, B.O. & Muthén, L.K. (2005). *Mplus® statistical analysis with latent variables; User guide*. Los Angeles, CA: Muthén & Muthén.

Pence, E. & Paymar, M. (1993). *Education groups for men who batter: The Duluth model*. New York: Springer.

Russell, M.N. (1995). *Confronting abusive beliefs; Group treatment for abusive men*. Thousand Oaks, CA: Sage.

Saunders, D.G. (1996). Feminist-cognitive-behavioral and process-psychodynamic treatments for men who batter: Interaction of abuser traits and treatment models. *Violence and Victims, 11*, 393–413.

Shepard, M. (1992). Predicting batterer recidivism five years after community intervention. *Journal of Family Violence, 7*, 167–178.

Sonkin, D.J. (1995). *The counselor's guide to learning to live without violence*. Volcano, CA: Volcano.

Wexler, D.B. (1999). *Domestic violence 2000: An integrated skills program for men, group leader's manual and resources for men*. New York: W. W. Norton.

Wittgenstein, L. (1958). *Philosophical investigation*, Translated by G. E. M. Anscombe. New York. Macmillan.

Uken, A., Lee, M.Y., Sebold, J. (2007). The Plumas Project: Solution-Focused Treatment of Domestic Violence Offenders In P. DeJong & I.K. Berg, *Interviewing for solutions (3rd ed)* (pp. 313–323). Pacific Cove, CA: Brooks/Cole.

Motivational Interviewing for Perpetrators of Intimate Partner Violence

4

DAVID A. DIA
CATHERINE A. SIMMONS
MARK A. OLIVER
R. LYLE COOPER

Question: How many therapists does it take to change a light bulb?
Answer: Only one, but the light bulb has to want to change.

—Therapist's Joke

It is fairly well known that intimate partner violence (IPV) rarely occurs in isolation. Substance abuse, mental illness, financial issues, child abuse, and pet abuse often compound IPV, creating a complicated mix of problems. Unfortunately, currently used approaches to intervention with IPV offenders show little to no effect (e.g., Babcock, Green & Robie, 2004; Babcock & LaTaillade, 2000; Davis & Taylor, 1999; Jackson et al., 2003). Thus, new avenues of research and intervention need to be strongly pursued to address this serious public health concern. Among those potentially helpful approaches, it has been suggested that motivational interviewing may be an innovative move forward (Murphy & Baxter, 1997; Stuart, Temple & Moore, 2007), as it has shown to be effective in helping other "challenging" populations both want to change problematic behavior and actually make those changes (for reviews please see Burke, Arkowitz & Menchola, 2003; Burke, Dunn, Atkins & Phelps, 2004; Hettema, Steele & Miller, 2005; Rubak, Sandboek, Lauritzen & Christensen, 2005; Vasilaki, Hosier & Cox, 2006). The goal of this chapter, then, is to help family violence clinicians and researchers to move in that direction by examining how the motivational interviewing style can be useful when working with the IPV offender population (Murphy & Baxter, 1997; Stuart, Temple & Moore, 2007). To this end, a history of motivational interviewing with its empirical foundation and techniques is discussed, followed by a case example demonstrating application with an IPV offending client.

HISTORY OF MOTIVATIONAL INTERVIEWING

Motivational interviewing is a therapeutic style that was developed to enhance the intrinsic motivation of individuals with substance related problems (Miller, 1983). Prior to the inception of motivational interviewing, the widespread belief was that substance abusing or dependant clients could not be helped unless they first admitted they had a problem with substances. The client needed to "self-diagnose" as an alcoholic and/or addict, thus labeling himself/herself before change could occur. Because very few clients present to treatment ready to make this "self-diagnosis," clinicians relied heavily on confrontation to facilitate the change process.

The problem with this approach to treatment of addictions is twofold. First, many clients with substance related concerns are unable to self-diagnose early in treatment. Second, many get "turned-off" by confrontation. Thus, clients who were unable to label themselves as alcoholics, abusers, or addicts are labeled as "treatment failures" by clinicians and others in the intervention setting. Motivational interviewing developed as a contrast to this prevailing view of how to help individuals with substance problems (e.g., Miller, 1985; Miller & Rolnick, 2002; Miller, Zweben, DiClemente & Rychtarik, 1992; Rollnick, Miller & Butler, 2007), which is rather similar to the current view of how to help IPV offenders (e.g., Minnesota Program Development, Inc. 2007; Paymar, 2002; Pence & Paymar, 1985, 1993; Shepard & Pence, 1999).

Motivational interviewing differs greatly from the confrontation and labeling techniques traditionally used in addiction treatment approaches and programs. First, motivational interviewing borrows heavily from the client-centered psychotherapy ideas, including demonstrating (a) genuine positive regard, (b) acceptance, and (c) empathy for the client (Miller, 1983). In addition, motivational interviewing draws from the practical group supervision experiences of the founder William R. Miller. From his experience, ideas related to self-efficacy, attribution, cognitive dissonance, and individual responsibility were incorporated into what is now referred to as the motivational interviewing style (Miller, 1983). In this approach, motivation is considered an interpersonal process, not a personality trait. A heavy emphasis is placed on individual responsibility and internal attribution of change, while deemphasizing confrontation and labeling. These radically new ideas were first published in a concept paper that outlined the model, linked it to the change process (described below), and presented a 6-step sequence for implementation (Miller, 1983).

The interest generated by his first paper introducing motivational interviewing encouraged Miller to expand the approach and develop its empirical foundation. The culmination of this work lead to collaboration with Stephen Rollnick and a number of other professionals resulting in multiple published works (e.g., Miller, 1985; Miller & Rolnick, 1991, 2002; Miller, Zweben, DiClemente & Rychtarik, 1992; Rollnick, Miller & Butler, 2007). As excitement about motivational interviewing grew, countless addictions practitioners and researchers adopted the motivational interviewing style, further developing its empirical foundation (for reviews please see Burke, Arkowitz & Menchola, 2003; Burke, Dunn, Atkins & Phelps, 2004; Hettema, Steele & Miller, 2005; Rubak, Sandboek, Lauritzen & Christensen, 2005; Vasilaki, Hosier & Cox, 2006). Indeed, a movement toward motivational interviewing can be seen throughout the helping professions and continues to spread to new and interesting applications.

CORE CONSTRUCTS

Before broadened application of motivational interviewing can be addressed, the core constructs of the style must be explained. Simply defined: *"Motivational interviewing is a directive, client-centered counseling style for eliciting behavior change by helping clients to explore and resolve ambivalence"* (Rollnick & Miller, 1995, p. 325). This approach is focused, goal-directed, and theoretically based on the transtheoretical model (TTM) of change (Prochaska & DiClemete, 1983, 1984).

The TTM encompasses the idea that people who engage in problematic behaviors are typically in one of the five stages of change outlined in Exhibit 4.1. It is important to understand that the order of these stages is variant, as people move through them at different rates, often

Exhibit 4.1

FIVE STAGES OF CHANGE

1. Precontemplation: Unaware of problem or unwilling to change behavior.
2. Contemplation: The problem is acknowledged, and there is serious thought put into solving it.
3. Preparation: On the verge of taking action to change, forming plans for that change.
4. Action: Action is taken on plans formed in the previous stage.
5. Maintenance, relapse and recycling: Work is focused on sustaining change; return to problematic use may take place (relapse), as well as a return to non-problematic use (recycling).

(DiClemente & Velasquez, 2002)

returning to an earlier stage, then progressing to the following stage numerous times before actual behavior change occurs (DiClemente & Velasquez, 2002). Motivational interviewing is grounded in the idea that intervention needs to adapt to the stage that the person is in by working directly with them to move through the precontemplation, contemplation, and preparation phases of change in an effort to finally reach a point of action, followed by maintenance (Miller & Rollnick, 2002).

Motivational interviewing is an overarching approach to intervention. In fact, it is wrong to think of motivational interviewing as a set of techniques "applied to" or "used on" people (Miller, 1994). Rather, it is a combination of directive and client-centered components shaped by a guiding philosophy on what triggers change (Miller, 1994). A few of the behaviors that clinicians with a motivational interviewing style demonstrate are (a) seeking to understand the client's frame of reference, (b) reflective listening, (c) clinician expression of acceptance and affirmation, (d) ensuring that resistance is not generated by jumping ahead of the client, (e) monitoring the client's degree of readiness to change, (f) affirming the client's freedom of choice and self-direction, and (g) eliciting and reinforcing the client's self motivational statements, expressions, problem recognition, concerns, desires, intentions, and abilities to change (e.g., Miller, 1994; Miller & Rollnick, 2002; Rollnick & Miller, 1995). Rollnick and Miller (1995) discussed the need for clinicians and researchers to keep the *"spirit"* of motivational interviewing in mind because techniques and clinical encounters vary across client situations. In their discussion they state:

> We believe it is vital to distinguish between the spirit of motivational interviewing and techniques that we have recommended to manifest that spirit. Clinicians and trainers who become too focused on matters of technique can lose sight of the spirit and style that are central to the approach. (Rollnick & Miller, 1995, p. 326)

Based on the idea that the essence of motivational interviewing is lost if it becomes a trick or a manipulative technique, Rollnick and Miller (1995) highlighted seven key points that characterize the spirit of motivational interviewing.

First, *"motivation to change is elicited from the client, and not imposed from without"* (p. 326). Although coercion, persuasion, confrontation, and external contingencies can be motivating, the spirit of motivational interviewing relies on identifying and mobilizing the client's intrinsic values and goals to elicit change in his behavior.

Second, *"it is the client's task, not the counselor's, to articulate and resolve his or her ambivalence"* (p. 326). Ambivalence takes the form of two conflicting courses of action that the counselor helps the client to express. The counselor guides the client toward an acceptable resolution that triggers change.

Third, *"direct persuasion is not an effective method for resolving ambivalence"* (p. 326). Although it is tempting to persuade the client by using (a) the urgency of the problem and (b) the benefits of change, these tactics generally increase resistance and diminish the likelihood that change will occur (Miller, Benefield & Tonigan, 1993).

Fourth, *"the counseling style is generally a quiet and eliciting one"* (p. 326). It is incongruent with the motivational interviewing approach to use aggressive strategies such as confrontation, persuasion, arguing, and pushing clients to make changes for which they are not ready.

Fifth, *"the counselor is directive in helping the client to examine and resolve ambivalence"* (p. 327). Motivational interviewing is not designed to build the clients behavioral coping skills but instead to elicit, clarify, and resolve ambivalence. Once this ambivalence is resolved, further intervention, such as skill training or anger management may or may not be needed, but it is simply not the point of motivational interviewing.

Sixth, *"readiness to change is not a client trait, but a fluctuating product of interpersonal interaction"* (p. 327). Client "resistance" and "denial" are not labels or traits, but instead a part of the process and a result of interpersonal interaction.

Seventh and finally, *"the therapeutic relationship is more like a partnership or companionship than expert/recipient roles"* (p. 327). At all times, the therapeutic relationship is respectful of the client's autonomy, freedom of behavioral choice, and freedom to experience the consequences of his own behavior.

In addition to the key concepts outlined in motivational interviewing texts (e.g., Miller, 1985; Miller & Rolnick, 2002; Miller, Zweben, DiClemente & Rychtarik, 1992; Rollnick, Miller & Butler, 2007), a number of additional intervention methods have been derived from this style. Among the most salient for the IPV offending population include the check-up (Miller & Sovereign, 1989; Schippers, Brokken & Otten, 1994), Motivational Enhancement Therapy (Miller, Zweben, DiClemente & Rychtarik, 1992), and brief motivational interviewing (Rollnick, Heather & Bell, 1992; Stott, Rollnick, Rees and Pill, 1995). Most of these approaches have significant overlap with the conceptual framework of motivational interviewing, but differ slightly in their approach (Miller & Rollnick, 2002). The difference between motivational interviewing and these methods is that motivational interviewing is the *style* in which intervention is delivered, while the methods are structured intervention approaches (Rollnick & Miller, 1995). As both the original motivational interviewing style and the related offshoots mentioned gain empirical support, application across a variety of client populations has become evident.

APPLICATION ACROSS DISCIPLINES

With the growing numbers of researchers and practitioners adopting the motivational interviewing style, new and interesting applications of the approach continue to emerge. Among these applications has been the adoption of motivational interviewing to address other non-addiction-related problem areas such as anxiety, depression, diabetes management, diet and exercise, smoking cessation, HIV risk behaviors, cardiovascular rehabilitation, family preservation, pain management, and public health interventions, just to name a few (for reviews please see Burke, Arkowitz & Menchola, 2003; Burke, Dunn, Atkins & Phelps, 2004; Hettema, Steele & Miller, 2005; Rubak, Sandboek, Lauritzen & Christensen, 2005; Vasilaki, Hosier & Cox, 2006). Interestingly, increased excitement about motivational interviewing has also grown within the criminal justice system. When discussing what is possible with offenders, Miller (1999a) first highlighted the addiction field's move away from a punitive, moralistic, and arrogant stance to a more respectful and collaborative approach. He then called on the criminal justice system to do the same:

> Is it too much to hope, then, that the field of corrections could see a similarly major change in the next twenty years? Offenders are the last major group in our society whom it is generally acceptable to abuse because they "need" and "deserve" it – because it is good for them and for society, and is "the only language they can understand." All evidence to the contrary, we collectively imagine somehow that it makes them better, and makes us a safer and more just society. (Miller, 1999a, p. 3)

Although not yet widely accepted in the field of family violence, motivational interviewing is starting to make headway. Murphy and Baxter (1997) first proposed using a motivational interviewing style to increase offender motivation in their conceptual paper discussing ways to better motivate IPV offenders to change. In this work, they directly linked the motivational interviewing approaches to family violence intervention by highlighting (a) the adverse effects of therapeutic confrontation, (b) the importance of developing a collaborative working alliance, and (c) the process of change based on the TTM (Murphy & Baxter, 1997). A few others have followed suit by both conceptually supporting the use of a motivational interviewing style with IPV offenders (e.g., Stuart, Temple & Moore, 2007) or by utilizing various aspects of motivational interviewing and its offshoots (e.g., Easton, Swan & Sinha, 2000; Eckhardt, Babcock & Homack, 2004; Taft, Murphy, Musser & Remington, 2004; Taft, Murphy, Elliott & Morrel, 2001).

RESEARCH SUPPORTING MOTIVATIONAL INTERVIEWING

The motivational interviewing style has strong empirical support across a range of client population areas, including addictions, anxiety, depression, diabetes management, diet, and exercise. Indeed, meta-analytic studies generally find a medium and occasionally large effect size (please see Burke, Arkowitz & Menchola, 2003; Burke, Dunn, Atkins & Phelps, 2004; Hettema, Steele & Miller, 2005; Rubak, Sandboek, Lauritzen &

Christensen, 2005; Vasilaki, Hosier & Cox, 2006). For example, motivational interviewing has been shown to increase attendance and compliance across a variety of client populations (e.g., Aubrey, 1998; Nielson, Nielson & Wraae, 1998; Reid, Teesson, Sannibale, Matsuda & Haber, 2006). Additionally, motivational interviewing is generally effective as a prelude or an adjunct to treatment, and with individuals who can be viewed as resistant and angry (Burke, Arkowitz & Menchola, 2003; Chanut, Brown & Dongier, 2005; Knight, McGowan, Diskens & Bundy, 2006). Both areas of effectiveness are particularly relevant to the IPV offender population.

IPV Offender Research

At this time, no published studies investigate effectiveness of motivational interviewing with IPV offenders throughout the treatment process. However, a few studies have applied the TTM to the IPV offending population (e.g., Eckhardt, Babcock & Homack, 2004; Levesque, Gelles & Velicer, 2000; Simmons, Lehmann & Cobb, 2008), and one investigated the relationship between motivation for change and working alliance formation in a sample of IPV offenders (Taft, Murphy, Musser & Remington, 2004). Additionally, two studies have investigated the use of motivational interviewing during the intake assessment/pre-group stage (Kistenmacher & Weiss, 2008; Musser, Semiantin, Taft & Murphy, 2008), while two other studies have looked at the effect of motivational enhancement techniques (MET) on (a) the improvement of attendance at domestic violence group counseling (Taft, Murphy, Elliott & Morrel, 2001), and (b) IPV offender readiness to change substance use (Easton, Swan & Sinha, 2000). From understanding these studies, further insight concerning the applicability of the motivational interviewing style with IPV offenders can be ascertained.

Transtheoretical Model (TTM). As stated previously, the TTM encompasses the idea that people who engage in problematic behaviors are typically in one of five stages of change. Although the order of the stages is invariant, individuals move through them at varying rates, often returning to an earlier stage, then progressing to the following stage numerous times before actual behavior change occurs. Studies investigating the TTM with IPV offending populations suggest that offering stage-matched interventions has a greater effect than a one-size-fits-all type of programming (Levesque, Gelles & Velicer, 2000). For example, IPV offenders in the contemplative stage might start treatment by attending orientation and information sessions, while individuals in the preparation or action stage might benefit from going right into traditional mixed groups.

The TTM-based University of Rhode Island Change Assessment-Domestic Violence (URICA-DV) was devised for and has successfully been used with the IPV offender population for just such reasons (e.g., Eckhardt, Babcock & Homack, 2004; Levesque, Gelles & Velicer, 2000). In the first study validating the URICA-DV, 258 men enrolled in two different batterer intervention programs completed the instrument, yielding 7 stage clusters: reluctant, immotive, nonreflective action, unprepared action, preparticipation, decision-making, and participation. Findings indicated that participants in the most advanced stage clusters were (a) more likely to have used strategies to end the violence in the last year, (b) engaged in less partner blame, and (c) valued the benefits of changing more than counterparts in the earlier stage clusters. Thus, the URICA-DV is an important tool that can be used with the IPV offending population.

Using the URICA-DV and a developed process of change scale, Eckhardt, Babcock, and Homack (2004) identified three clusters of men who were court-ordered to treatment. "Immotive men who are in the Precontemplative stage; Unprepared Action males, who may be 'going through the motions' of behavior change; Preparticipation men, who are moderately aware of the problem and making some attempts to change" (Eckhardt et al., p. 91). Likewise, Bowen & Gilchrest (2004) found that men self-referred to batterer intervention programs exhibited higher levels of motivation to change, an internal locus of control, and greater anger than men who were court-referred to such programs. In addition, Babcock, Green, and Robie (2004) and Simmons, Lehmann, and Cobb (2008) found the TTM to be relevant for both men and women IPV offenders, and that both groups present to treatment programs at similar stages of readiness for change. This information is helpful in gearing treatment to the appropriate stage of change and choosing which motivational interviewing strategy will help move the IPV offending client into the next stage. It also suggests one reason why traditionally used confrontational and labeling approaches of batterer intervention programming have shown to be ineffective.

In addition to research supporting readiness to change, Taft, Murphy, Musser, and Remington (2004) examined the influence of (a) personality and interpersonal characteristics, (b) motivational readiness to change, and (c) demographic factors on working alliance formation among men (N = 107) participating in a group IPV offender treatment program. Building on prior research demonstrating that quality of the working alliance is a predictor of positive outcome with men who engage in IPV (Taft, Murphy, King, Musser & DeDeyn, 2003), results of this study indicate motivational readiness to change is the strongest predictor of the working alliance (Taft, Murphy, Musser & Remington, 2004). Other predictors of a working alliance included low psychopathic personality traits, low borderline personality traits, fewer total hostile-dominant interpersonal problems, self-referred status, married status, and higher age and income. Thus, the study suggests that motivation is an important treatment target for IPV offenders (Taft Murphy, Musser & Remington, 2004). Because IPV offenders who enter treatment involuntarily are less likely to agree with the treatment goals and are also less likely to develop a positive working alliance, findings indicate the motivational interviewing style can be elicited to improve motivation congruent with the stage of change the client presents at the time of the intervention.

Motivational Interviewing During Intake Process. In addition to studies investigating aspects of the stages of change, two studies have utilized the motivational interviewing style during the intake assessment with IPV offenders. In the first study Musser, Semiantin, Taft, and Murphy, (2008) unsystematically (but not technically randomly) assigned IPV offenders presenting for court-mandated intervention to either a two-session intake using the techniques of motivational interviewing (N=55) or a standardized structured intake control (N=53). Following the intake process, all participants attended similar 12-week cognitive behavioral treatment groups with cohorts homogeneous to intake condition (Musser, Semiantin, Taft & Murphy, 2008). Findings of this study indicated the men who received the motivational interviewing-based intake procedures demonstrated (a) more constructive behaviors in the early stage of treatment, (b) greater compliance with homework assignments, (c) higher working alliance ratings in later stages of treatment, and (d) more outside help-seeking behavior (Musser, Semiantin, Taft & Murphy, 2008). In a similar second study, Kistenmacher and Weiss (2008) randomly assigned IPV offenders court-mandated to attend group treatment into experimental and control groups. The experimental group (a) completed a battery of tests, followed by a 50–60 minute interview using motivational interviewing techniques and (b) returned two weeks later for a second 50-60 minute interview, followed by a similar battery of tests

(Kistenmacher & Weiss, 2008). The control group received the same tests but did not receive an interview. Following the intake process, both groups attended group treatment, which was not included in the results. Findings of this study indicated that members of the group who received the motivational interviewing sessions demonstrated pre- and post-test (a) contemplation and action toward changing their behavior, and (b) increased responsibility for their behavior (Kistenmacher & Weiss, 2008). Findings of both studies highlight the promise motivational interviewing has with the IPV offender population.

Motivational Enhancement Techniques. Family violence professionals can also employ the relatively straightforward motivational enhancement technique (MET) of sending a personalized note or making a telephone call to the client between treatment sessions to express concern, summarize recent progress, and communicate interest in working together. Taft, Murphy, Elliott, and Morrel (2001) used a quasi-experimental design to investigate the effectiveness of this straightforward and easily implemented retention technique with a sample of IPV offending clients (106 control and 83 treatment). Prior to beginning the group, the clinician sent a handwritten note to participants in the treatment cohort expressing an interest in working with the client, followed by a telephone call reiterating what was stated in the letter. Once the group started, the clinician called treatment group clients who missed a session to express concern, inquire about the reason for missing, encourage the client to attend the next session, problem solve with the client if necessary, and remind them of the requirements for completing group. This call was then followed up by a handwritten note expressing sorrow that the person missed the session and hope that they would return to the next session. Results indicated that participants in the treatment group (average = 12.89 sessions) attended 10 percent more frequently than the control group (average = 11.22 sessions) with a small to medium effect size (*Cohen's d* = .35) (Taft, Murphy, Elliott & Morrel, 2001).

In a similar smaller study, Easton, Swan, and Sinha (2000) used a quasi-experimental design to evaluate the effectiveness of a single MET session on readiness to change substance use in a sample of IPV offenders (N=41). Results of this study indicate (a) a high percentage of IPV offenders were either dependent on or abusing substances and (b) their pre- to post-session motivation to change their substance use behaviors increased in the group that received MET (Easton, Swan & Sinha, 2000). These findings highlight the importance of assessing and treating IPV offenders for addictions, while also indicating the relevance of MET and the motivational interviewing style with IPV offending clients. Indeed, additional research into the effectiveness of motivational interviewing with IPV offenders is certainly needed.

Further Empirical Support

In addition to the empirical support mentioned above, three general areas of motivational interviewing research indicate potential effectiveness with IPV offending clients. First, dropout rates in batterer intervention programs average between 40% and 60% (e.g., Cadsky, Hanson, Crawford & Lalonde, 1996; Edleson & Syers, 1991; Pirog-Good & Stets, 1986), and significant evidence indicates that those who drop out have higher violence recidivism and risk than those who complete treatment (Chen, Bersani, Myers & Denton, 1989; Dutton, Bodnarchuk, Kropp, Hart & Ogloff, 1997; Hamberger & Hastings, 1989). Because motivational interviewing has repeatedly shown to improve retention in addiction treatment (Dailey & Zuckoff, 1998, 1999; Dench & Bennett, 2000; Donovan, Rosengren, Downey, Cox & Sloan, 2001; Mattson, DelBoca, Cooney, DiClemente, Donovan, Rice & Zweben, 1998; Saunders, Wilkinson & Phillips, 1995), it is logical to expect similar approaches will increase retention rates with IPV offenders as well. Second, IPV offenders are often assumed to be "resistant" and "angry." Motivational interviewing has shown to be effective with such clients (e.g., Britt, Blampied & Hudson, 2003; Chanut, Brown & Dongier, 2005; Knight, McGowan, Diskens & Bundy, 2006). Finally, as noted previously, a high co-occurrence of battering behaviors and addictions exists (Bennett, Tolman, Rogalski & Srinivasaraghavan, 1994; Brookoff, O'Brien, Cook, Thompson & Williams, 1997; Holzworth-Munrow & Stuart, 1994; Rivera et al, 1997). Because motivational interviewing was founded on and has consistently demonstrated effectiveness within the addictions field, it is logical that it would also be effective with IPV offending populations.

IMPLICATIONS FOR USE WITH THE IPV OFFENDER POPULATION

All too often family violence professionals use words like "non-compliant," "resistant," "treatment-failure," and "difficult" to describe IPV offending clients and the IPV offender population as a whole. In essence, these labels do little to increase understanding of individual clients or to enhance responsiveness to the IPV offending population. Although the following quote was not directed at the use of labels within the family violence community, it is certainly applicable.

> . . . labels do little to enhance our understanding or our responsiveness to the people we're serving. If we're truthful, we'd recognize that these labels are another way of saying to our clients, "Look, we haven't been able to help you. We've had enough of banging our head against the wall. We are exasperated, we're frustrated, and come back and see us some time if you can get your act together because there must be something defective about you that's causing this. (Winarski, Silver & Kraybill, 2003)

Motivational interviewing can help family violence professionals change the focus from labeling and confrontation to understanding that "resistance" is a part of the change process. By doing so, it is possible that the family violence profession can move forward, better help IPV offenders want to change, and prevent additional incidents of family violence. To do this, the motivational interviewing style proposes four general principles essential to the therapeutic encounter that are applicable to the IPV offender population.

General Principles

From a motivational interviewing perspective, all persons considering a behavior change experience an internal conflict regarding the pros and cons of change. This internal conflict, or ambivalence, must be resolved in order for a client to make the decision to change his or her behavior. It is the role of the motivational interviewing clinician to help clients overcome their negative perceptions of change in favor of positively recognizing the benefits of such changes. With the goal of ambivalence resolution, and linked to the core assumptions previously addressed, four general principles apply to clinicians following a motivational interviewing style: express empathy, support self-efficacy, roll with resistance, and develop discrepancy. These strategies are all employed to enable the practitioner to engage the client in "*change talk*." Change talk is the client's verbal expression of the positive impacts of engaging in behavioral change (Miller & Rollnick, 2002). Although the following was originally designed for clients in treatment for addictions (e.g., Miller & Rollnick, 1991, 2002; Miller, Zweben, DiClemente

& Rychtarik, 1992), these four general principles are also relevant with IPV offender clients.

Express Empathy.[1] The first motivational interviewing principle is to express empathy. Empathy "is a specifiable and learnable skill for understanding another's meaning through the use of reflective listening" (Miller & Rollnick, 1991, p. 20). Expressing empathy requires skillful, reflective listening to understand a person's feelings and perspectives without judging, criticizing, or blaming. It also "requires sharp attention to each new client statement, and the continual generation of hypotheses as to the underlying meaning" (Miller & Rollnick, 1991, p. 20). All too often, the confrontational approach advocated by traditional BIP models fails to convey the expression of empathy for the client. However, empathy is critical to the motivational interviewing approach (Miller & Rollnick, 2002).

Underlying this need for empathy is the core belief that when clients feel they are understood, they are (a) more able to be open and share their experiences, (b) more able to examine their ambivalence about change, (c) less likely to defend unhealthy ideas, such as denying they use violence, attempt to control, etc., (d) more open to gently challenging beliefs about using violence, and (e) more likely to make the changes needed to live a violence-free lifestyle (Miller, Zweben, DiClemente, & Rychtarik, 1992). Additionally, empathy can help the client feel comfortable in sharing his experiences, making it easier for the IPV professional to assess needs, potential pitfalls, changes needed, and safety concerns (Miller, Zweben, DiClemente, & Rychtarik, 1992). In short, the family violence professional's accurate understanding of the client's experience can help facilitate change.

Support Self-Efficacy.[2] The second motivational interviewing principle is to support self-efficacy. Self-efficacy is defined as "people's beliefs about their capabilities to produce designated levels of performance that exercise influence over events that affect their lives" (Bandura, 1994, p. 71). A powerful concept in client behavior, self-efficacy determines how clients think, feel, behave, motivate themselves, and believe they

---

[1] Express Empathy is adapted from Miller & Rollnick, 1991, 2002; Miller, Zweben, DiClemente, & Rychtarik, 1992
[2] Support Self-Efficacy is adapted from Miller & Rollnick, 1991, 2002; Miller, Zweben, DiClemente, & Rychtarik, 1992

can do what they need/want to do in all aspects of their lives. Effectiveness of the motivational interviewing style is based on the client's belief that change is possible, thus, self-efficacy is an important motivator to making successful changes. Included in this is the idea that IPV offending clients need to be held responsible for choosing and carrying out actions to live a violence-free lifestyle. Through this process, family violence professionals should focus their efforts on helping the clients stay motivated by supporting their sense of self-efficacy. A key component of supporting self-efficacy is the idea that there is no "right way" to change. If a given plan for change does not work, clients are only limited by their own creativity as to the number of other plans that might be tried. (Miller, Zweben, DiClemente & Rychtarik, 1992)

With MI, it is the family violence professional's job to help clients develop beliefs that they can change. In this process, skills that clients already have can be highlighted by asking them about other changes they have made in their lives, or about times they did not choose to be violent. Similarly, sharing how other clients successfully chose to not use violence is also helpful. This is particularly relevant in the group setting, as most batterer intervention programs are designed. The power of having other people discuss how they made similar changes in their lives can provide enormous assistance in showing that people can and do change (Miller, Zweben, DiClemente, & Rychtarik, 1992).

Roll with Resistance.[3] The third motivational interviewing principle is to not fight the client's natural resistance, but instead "roll with it." Viewing "resistance" as a natural part of the change process that should not be confronted but used instead as "momentum" to further explore the client's views is a dramatically different approach to intervention. By so doing, the client's need for "resistance" tends to be decreased rather than increased, as the client is not reinforced for becoming argumentative and playing "devil's advocate" to the counselor's suggestions. Clients are encouraged to develop their own solutions to the problems they have defined, thus eliminating the obstacle clients usually fight against. Client concerns are explored and family violence professionals may invite clients to examine new perspectives. However, counselors do not impose new ways of thinking on them. Instead, they develop it themselves (Miller, Zweben, DiClemente, & Rychtarik, 1992).

---

[3] Roll with Resistance is adapted from Miller & Rollnick, 1991, 2002; Miller, Zweben, DiClemente, & Rychtarik, 1992.

Develop Discrepancy.[4] The fourth motivational interviewing principle is to develop discrepancy. Developing discrepancy refers to helping clients recognize dissonance between their current behavior and their desired life goals. "Motivation for change occurs when people perceive a discrepancy between where they are and where they want to be" (Miller, Zweben, DiClemente & Rychtarik, 1992, p. 8). Family violence professionals can help clients examine the discrepancies between their current behavior and future goals. By understanding that their current behaviors are not leading toward these goals, clients can become more motivated to make important life changes. It is important to note that this is a gentle and gradual process of helping clients see how some of their current behaviors may lead them away from, rather than toward, their eventual goals. Among other techniques, Miller and Rollnick (2002) defined two types of reflection used to develop discrepancy: amplified and double-sided reflections. Amplified reflection refers to reflecting back client statements supporting the status quo in a slightly exaggerated form. This encourages the client to provide the opposite side of the statement he or she made, thus engaging him or her in change talk. Double-sided reflections, on the other hand, are used to reflect both sides of the ambivalence back to the client, literally bringing the internal conflict associated with behavior change to the surface.

Therapeutic Encounter

In motivational interviewing, the therapeutic encounter is considered an opportunity to either push clients toward change or further entrench them in the status quo. Avoiding argumentation helps prevent situations in which clients feel the need to defend their desire to maintain problematic behaviors. Such defense serves to reinforce, rather than weaken, client's resolve to maintain the problem behavior. Miller and Rollnick (2002) posit that change only takes place when clients can express their desire, capability, or intention to change. "Resistance" is a key element in that it is a barometer of the client-worker interaction; it is not intrapersonal but interpersonal. When resistance arises in the counseling relationship it is seen as an indication that the therapist must change the tactic that he or she is taking with the client. To effectively help clients, therapists should avoid direct confrontation, offer alternatives

---

[4] Develop Discrepancy is adapted from Miller & Rollnick, 1991, 2002; Miller, Zweben, DiClemente, & Rychtarik, 1992

but not impose them, and change their approach when resistance arises. Although a number of counseling strategies can be used in this process, the following three may be beneficial to get started: (a) review the typical day, (b) discuss the stages of change, and (c) value exploration. As is the case with all motivational interviewing strategies, if the client constantly argues, disagrees with, or ignores the practitioner, then the strategy is not working, and a different approach should be used.

Review a Typical Day.[5] The first recommended motivational interviewing strategy family violence professionals can use is to review a typical day with a client. The purpose of this strategy is to build rapport while gathering information. Doing so will help avoid focusing solely on violence and other problematic behaviors. In applying this approach, Rollnick, Heather, and Bell (1992) suggest starting with questions such as, *"Can we spend the next 5–10 minutes going through a day from beginning to end?" "What happened, how did you feel"* and *"Let's start at the beginning"* (p. 30). Building on the four general principles previously described, this process allows practitioners to help the client tell a story of his or her day, focusing on feelings and behaviors. From this the relationship is strengthened, valuable insight into helpful behaviors and harmful behaviors can be ascertained, and the client can start to understand what is and what is not working in his or her own life.

Explain the Stages of Change.[6] A third motivational interviewing strategy family violence professionals can use is to explain the stages of change to their clients. After an explanation, the practitioner can ask the client to (a) react to the explanation about the stages of change, (b) think about things he or she has changed in the past, and (c) give examples of his or her movement through the various stages of change during this process. Understanding the stages of change can reduce defensiveness about changing violent behavior and help teach clients how choosing to live a nonviolent lifestyle is similar to other changes offenders have made in their lives.

Values Exploration.[7] A third motivational interviewing strategy family violence professionals can use is to help the client to define his or her

---

[5] Review a Typical Day was adapted from Rollnick, Heather, & Bell, 1992

[6] Explain the Stages of Changes was adapted from Ingersoll, Wagner & Gharib, 2000; Rosengren & Wagner, 2001

[7] Values Exploration was adapted from Ingersoll, Wagner & Gharib, 2000; Rosengren & Wagner, 2001

"ideal self" by exploring his or her values. Sometimes, clients have forgotten their values or have simply rejected them as unachievable. Focusing on what the client values and identifying discrepancies between his or her stated values and the things that brought the client to the intervention setting may (a) induce a desire to "recalibrate" daily behaviors to be more congruent with deeply held beliefs, (b) help the client become increasingly aware that violence does not lead to fulfillment of higher values or long-term satisfaction, and (c) shift the intervention toward a focus on a lifestyle that can be pursued and enjoyed.

In addition to a general discussion about values, family violence professionals can create a set of *"values cards"* with topics relevant to family, violence, and lifestyle. By asking IPV offending clients to sort through these cards and order them in accordance with their priorities, they can discover what is important to them and identify those things that are incongruent with these values. The discussion that follows can include (a) the meaning of the values statements, (b) consistency between values and behavior, (c) perceived barriers to and opportunities for increasing value-behavior, and (d) evaluation of the extent to which violence plays a role in achieving these valued behaviors.

CASE EXAMPLE

Following is a case example of the use of motivational interviewing techniques within the context of batterer intervention. The client was an African-American male who had been court-ordered into a batterers' group and individual therapy due to a domestic violence incident with his wife. The client was a Vietnam veteran in his early sixties and was employed as a long-haul truck driver. His wife, whom he met during the war, was Vietnamese. The couple had no children. The client reported having problems with alcohol use when he was younger (i.e., twenties) and stopped drinking on his own. He also indicated a history of anger problems prior to the referral incident.

In the first session of individual therapy, the client was angry and defensive at being ordered by the court into treatment through a domestic violence shelter. The clinician deliberately took a very nondirective approach. In fact, the client spoke mostly about his job as a trucker rather than the referral incident or his anger. While the client did the majority of the talking, the clinician periodically used techniques such as open-ended questions and reflective listening to facilitate the client's expression. The initial session provides examples of the clinician's use of several of the five methods that Miller and Rollnick (2002) state can be very helpful in the beginning stages of therapy, as well as throughout treatment. These methods are open questions, reflective listening, affirming statements, summarizing, and eliciting change talk.

Very early in the session, the clinician affirmed the client's attendance by stating, "I know it's hard for you to come in for this today." This simple, sincere statement acknowledged the client's obvious discomfort. Such affirming statements can quickly lay the groundwork for improved rapport between clinician and client (Miller & Rollnick, 2002).

The clinician also made frequent use of reflection. For example, simple reflections such as "You're pretty unhappy about being here" encouraged further expression related to the client's anger at being court-ordered. As this expression continued, the clinician used more complex reflections: "You hope that by choosing to attend the required therapy sessions, things will go better for you with the judge in court." This reflection was used to place emphasis on the personal choices that remained for the client despite feeling "forced" into treatment.

The clinician summarized the early portions of the session in order to emphasize the client's ambivalence. After listening to the client's expression about his treatment circumstances for some time, the clinician stated, "Sounds like on the one hand you are very frustrated at being in therapy. You don't appreciate being forced into something you don't think you need. On the other hand, you want to participate in a way that will put you in the best position you can be in when you next go before the judge. What about your current situation concerns you?" The double-sided reflection within the summary played up the client's ambivalence. Then, the open-ended question at the end of the summary was used to attempt to evoke increased change talk (Miller & Rollnick, 2002). This question led to the client talking about how his court-ordered sessions hindered his work schedule.

When the client arrived for the second individual session, his mood was more somber than in the first session. The client appeared more resigned to the therapy process and less resistant to the clinician. Judging that the client might be exhibiting early signs that he was ready for change, the clinician attempted to elicit change talk. As the client talked about things that were important to him, such as his roles as a husband and a member of his church, the clinician used reflection to encourage this line of discussion. Eventually, the client began to speak about the type of husband he wanted to be. The clinician used the following double-sided reflection to develop discrepancy (Miller & Rollnick, 2002) between the client's behavior and his personal ideals: "You love your wife and want to be a caring husband. At the same time, you've been ordered into counseling for violent behavior toward her. It's tough to fit together."

The client responded by talking about how lack of sleep from truck-driving contributed to his abusive behavior. The clinician followed-up by amplifying the client's choices in such situations. Sensing that the session was perhaps moving too quickly toward change for this client, the clinician then elected to indulge the client's shift to a tangential, less-weighty subject about the client's truck-driving schedule.

After only a few minutes of following the tangent, the client became silent. He broke the pause with, "She's never going to trust me again." The client then began to describe what he had done to his wife during the referral incident. With minimal reflection on the part of the clinician, the client took responsibility for his behavior and professed that he loved his wife and wanted to make the relationship better.

For the clinician, these direct-change statements constituted a turning point in the therapy. The clinician now shifted to working with the client to set goals for change (Miller & Rollnick, 2002). Again using open-ended questions and reflections to guide the discussion, the clinician helped the client identify two broad, initial goals: Building trust with his wife and managing his anger. After an emotional session, the clinician reinforced the client's attendance and hard work.

The third session was spent breaking down the client's broad goals into manageable, attainable steps. In the remaining therapy sessions, the clinician shifted his approach to cognitive-behavioral therapy in order to help the client meet his goals.

LIMITATIONS

Although motivational interviewing has exciting potential to improve intervention with IPV offenders, significant limitations exist. The primary and most significant limitation is that there is little empirical-based evidence for this treatment approach with this population. Even though both of the studies reviewed utilized Motivational Enhancement Therapy, each intervention was described very differently. Taft et al. (2001) utilized techniques between the treatment sessions to encourage attendance, such as phone calls and handwritten notes. Easton et al. (2000)

describe a treatment approach more similar to motivational interviewing as described by Miller and Rollnick (2002). However, for both treatment studies, there was no mention of how treatment integrity was monitored. A second limitation is that although the theoretical insights of motivational interviewing grew from clinical experience, it has been suggested that it may lack conceptual refinement (Miller, 1999b; Vansteenkiste & Sheldon, 2006). Although there is a likelihood the theoretical foundation will grow with time and empirical investigation, it is an important limitation to note. Indeed, it is equally important to add that the interventions and ideas discussed in this chapter are not guaranteed to work with IPV offenders. Motivational interviewing is an exciting idea, but significant work is yet to be done.

CONCLUSION

For many years now, clinical attention has been focused on individuals who engage in IPV. What seems fairly clear is that our interventions, in their current form, are not meeting the needs of these individuals. As the chapter began, the therapist's joke tells us that to change, the light bulb has to want it. Despite the empirical and theoretical limitations noted above, motivational interviewing has the potential to help family violence professionals work with clients in a way that can help them understand the need to change, develop a desire to want to change, and take the steps needed to make change. The final hope is that this chapter has motivated the reader to consider using and empirically examining the motivational interviewing approach with the IPV offender population.

REFERENCES

Aubrey, L.L. (1998). Motivational interviewing with adolescents presenting for outpatient substance abuse treatment. Doctoral Dissertation, University of New Mexico.

Babcock, J.C., Green, C.E., & Robie, C. (2004). Does batterers' treatment work?: A meta-analytic review of domestic violence treatment outcome research. *Clinical Psychology Review*, 23, 1023–1053.

Babcock, J.C., & LaTaillade, J. (2000). Evaluating interventions for men who batter. In J. Vincent, E. Jouriles (Eds.), *Domestic violence: Guidelines for research informed practice* (pp. 37–77). Philadelphia: Jessica Kingsley.

Bandura, A. (1994). Self-efficacy. In V.S. Ramachaudran (Ed.), *Encyclopedia of human behavior* (Vol. 4, pp. 71–81). New York: Academic Press. (Reprinted in H. Friedman [Ed.], *Encyclopedia of mental health*. San Diego: Academic Press, 1998).

Bennett, L.W., Tolman, R.M., Rogalski, C.J., & Srinivasaraghavan, J. (1994). Domestic abuse by male alcohol and drug addicts. *Violence and Victims, 9*, 359–368.

Bowen, E.I., & Gilchrest, E. (2004). Do court- and self-referred domestic violence offenders share the same characteristics? A preliminary comparison of motivation to change, locus of control and anger. *Legal & Criminological Psychology, 9*, 279–294.

Britt, E., Blampied, N.M., & Hudson, S.M. (2003). Motivational interviewing: A review. *Australian Psychologist, 38*, 193–201.

Brookoff, D., O'Brien, K.K., Cook, C.S., Thompson, T.D., & Williams, C., (1997). Characteristics of participants in domestic violence. Assessment at the scene of domestic assault. *Journal of the American Medical Association, 277*, 1369–1373.

Burke, B.L., Arkowitz, H., & Menchola, M. (2003). The efficacy of motivational interviewing: A meta-analysis of controlled clinical trials. *Journal of Consulting and Clinical Psychology, 71*, 843–861.

Burke, B.L. , Dunn, C.W., Atkins, D.C., & Phelps, J.S. (2004). The emerging evidence base for motivational interviewing: A meta-analytic and qualitative inquiry. *Journal of Cognitive Psychotherapy: An International Quarterly, 18*(4), 309–322.

Cadsky, O., Hanson, R.K., Crawford, M., & Lalonde, C. (1996). Attrition from a male batterer treatment program: Client-treatment congruence and lifestyle instability. *Violence and Victims, 11*, 51–64.

Chanut, F., Brown, G.T., & Dongier, M. (2005). Motivational interviewing and clinical psychiatry. *Canadian Journal of Psychiatry, 50*, 715–721.

Chen, H., Bersani, C., Myers, S.C., & Denton, R. (1989). Evaluating the effectiveness of a court-sponsored abuser treatment program. *Journal of Family Violence, 4*, 309–322.

Dailey, D.C., & Zuckoff, A. (1999). *Improving treatment compliance: Counseling and systems strategies for substance abuse and dual disorders.* Center City, MN: Hazelden.

Daley, D.C., & Zuckoff, A. (1998). Improving compliance with the initial outpatient session among discharged inpatient dual diagnosis clients. *Social Work, 43*, 470–473.

Davis, R.C., & Taylor, B.G. (1999). Does batterer treatment reduce violence? A synthesis of the literature. *Women and Criminal Justice, 10*, 69–93.

DiClemente, C.C. & Velasquez, S.K. (2002). Motivational interviewing and the stages of change. In. S.R. Miller & S. Rollnick (Eds). *Motivational interviewing: Preparing people for change* (2nd ed.). New York: The Guildford Press.

Dench, S., & Bennett, G. (2000). The impact of brief motivational intervention at the start of an outpatient day programme for alcohol dependence. *Behavioural and Cognitive Psychotherapy, 28*, 121–130.

Donovan, D.M., Rosengren, D.B., Downey, L., Cox, G.B., & Sloan, K.L. (2001). Attrition prevention with individuals awaiting publicly funded drug treatment. *Addiction, 96*, 1149–1160.

Dutton, D.G., Bodnarchuk, M., Kropp, R., Hart, S.D., & Ogloff, J.R.P. (1997). Wife assault treatment and criminal recidivism: An 11-year follow-up. *International Journal of Offender Therapy and Comparative Criminology, 41*, 9–23.

Easton, C., Swan, S., & Sinha, R. (2000). Motivation to change substance use among offenders of domestic violence. *Journal of Substance Abuse Treatment, 19*, 1–5.

Eckhardt, C.I., Babcock, J., & Homack, S. (2004). Partner assaultive men and the stages of process of change. *Journal of Family Violence, 19*, 81–93.

Edleson, J.G., & Syers, M. (1991). The effects of group treatment for men who batter: An 18-month follow-up study. *Research on Social Work Practice, 1*, 227–243.

Hamberger, L.K., & Hastings, J.E. (1989). Counseling male spouse abusers: Characteristics of treatment completers and dropouts. *Violence and Victims*, 4, 275–286.

Hettema, J., Steele, J., & Miller, W.R. (2005). Motivational interviewing. *Annual Review of Clinical Psychology*, 1, 91–111.

Holzworth-Munrow A., & Stuart, G.L., 1994. Typologies of male batterers: Three subtypes and the differences among them. *Psychological Bulletin*, 116, 476–497.

Ingersoll, K.S., Wagner, C.C., & Gharib, S. (2000). *Motivational groups for community substance abuse programs*. Richmond, VA: Mid-Atlantic Addiction Technology Transfer Center, Center for Substance Abuse Treatment (Mid-ATTC/CSAT)

Jackson, S., Feder, L., Forde, D.R., Davis, R.C., Maxwell, C.D., & Taylor, B.G. (June 2003). Batterer intervention programs: Where do we go from here? *Special NIJ Report*, Washington DC: National Institute of Justice, U.S. Department of Justice.

Knight, K.M., McGowan, L., Diskens, C., & Bundy, C. (2006). A systematic review of motivational interviewing in physical health care settings. *British Journal of Health Psychology*, 11, 319–332.

Kistenmacher, B.R., & Weiss, R.L. (2008). Motivational interviewing as a mechanism for change in men who batter: A randomized control trial. *Violence and Victims*, 5, 558–570.

Levesque, D.A., Gelles, R.J., & Velicer, W.F., (2000). Development and validation of a stages of change measure for men in batterer treatment. *Cognitive Therapy and Research*, 24, 175–199.

Mattson, M., DelBoca, F., Cooney, N., DiClemente, C.C., Donovan, D.M., Rice, C.L., & Zweben, A. (1998). Patient compliance in Project MATCH: Session attendance predictors and relationship to outcome. *Alcoholism Clinical and Experimental Research*, 11, 1328–1339.

Miller, W.R. (1983). Motivational interviewing with problem drinkers. *Behavioural Psychotherapy*, 11, 147–172.

Miller, W.R. (1985). Motivation for treatment: A review with special emphasis on alcoholism. *Psychological Bulletin*, 98, 84–107.

Miller, W.R. (1994). Motivational interviewing: III. On the ethics of motivational intervention. *Behavioural and Cognitive Psychotherapy*, 22, 111–123.

Miller, W.R. (1999a). Pros and cons: Reflections on motivational interviewing in correctional settings. *The Motivational Interviewing Newsletter: Updates, Education and Training*, 6, 2–3.

Miller, W.R. (1999b). Toward a theory of Motivational Interviewing. *The Motivational Interviewing Newsletter: Updates, Education and Training*, 6, 2–4.

Miller, W.R., Benefield, R.G., & Tonigan, J.S. (1993). Enhancing motivation for change in problem drinking: A controlled comparison of two therapist styles. *Journal of Consulting and Clinical Psychology*, 61, 455–461.

Miller, W.R., & Rollnick, S. (2002). *Motivational interviewing: Preparing people for change* (2nd ed.). New York: The Guildford Press.

Miller, W.R., & Rollnick, S. (1991). *Motivational interviewing: Preparing people to change addictive behavior*. New York: Guilford.

Miller, W.R., & Sovereign, R.G. (1989). The check-up: A model for early intervention in addictive behaviors. In T. Løberg, W.R. Miller, P.E. Nathan, & G.A. Marlatt (Eds.), *Addictive behaviors: Prevention and early intervention* (pp. 219–231). Amsterdam: Swets & Zeitlinger.

Miller, W.R., Zweben, A., DiClemente, C.C., & Rychtarik, R.G. (1992). *Motivational enhancement therapy manual: A clinical research guide for therapists treating individuals with alcohol abuse and dependence.* Rockville, MD: National Institute on Alcohol Abuse and Alcoholism.

Minnesota Program Development, Inc. (2007). The Duluth model web site downloaded from http://www.duluth-model.org/ on August 30, 2007.

Musser, P.H., Semiantin, J.N., Taft, C.T., & Murphy, C.M. (2008). Motivational interviewing as a pregroup intervention for partner violent men. *Violence and Victims,* 23, 539–557.

Murphy, C.M., & Baxter, V.A. (1997). Motivating batterers to change in the treatment context. *Journal of Interpersonal Violence,* 12, 607–619.

Nielson, B., Nielson, A.S., & Wraae, O. (1998). Patient-treatment matching improves compliance of alcoholics in outpatient treatment. *The Journal of Nervous and Mental Diseases,* 186, 752–760.

Paymar, M. (2002). *Violence no more: Helping men end domestic abuse.* Alameda, CA: Hunter House.

Pence, E., & Paymar, M. (1985). *Power and control: Tactics of men who batter.* Duluth, MN: Domestic Abuse Intervention Project.

Pence, E., & Paymar, M. (1993). *Education groups for men who batter: The Duluth model.* New York: Springer.

Pirog-Good, M., & Stets, J. (1986). Programs for abusers: Who drops out and what can be done. *Response,* 9, 17–19.

Prochaska, J.O., & DiClemete, C.C. (1983) Stages and processes of self-change of smoking: Toward an integrative model of change. *Journal of Consulting and Clinical Psychology,* 51, 390–395.

Prochaska, J.O., & DiClemete, C.C. (1984). *The transtheoretical approach: Crossing the traditional boundaries of therapy.* Malabar, FL: Krieger.

Reid, S.C., Teesson, M., Sannibale, C., Matsuda, M., & Haber, P.S. (2006). The efficacy of compliance therapy in pharmacotherapy for alcohol dependence: a randomized controlled trial. *Journal of the Studies of Alcohol,* 66, 833–41.

Rivera, F.P., Mueller, B.A., Somes, G., Mendoza, C.T., Rushforth, N.B., & Kellermann, A.L. (1997). Alcohol and illicit drug abuse and the risk of violent death in the home. *Journal of the American Medical Association,* 278, 569–575.

Rollnick, S., Heather, N., & Bell, A. (1992). Negotiating behaviour change in medical settings: The development of brief motivational interviewing. *Journal of Mental Health.* 1, 25–37.

Rollnick, S., & Miller, W.R. (1995). What is motivational interviewing? *Behavioral and Cognitive Psychotherapy,* 23, 325–334.

Rollnick, S., Miller, W.R., & Butler, C.C. (2007). *Motivational interviewing in health care: Helping patients change behavior, applications of motivational interviewing,* The New York: Guilford Press.

Rosengren, D. & Wagner, C.C. (2001). Motivational interviewing: Shall we dance? In Coombs R. (Ed.), *Addiction recovery tools: A practitioner's handbook.* Thousand Oaks, CA: Sage.

Rubak, S, Sandboek, A., Lauritzen, T., & Christensen, B. (2005). Motivational interviewing: a systematic review and meta-analysis. *British Journal of General Practice,* 55, 305–312.

Saunders, B., Wilkinson, C., & Phillips, M. (1995). The impact of a brief motivational intervention with opiate users attending a methadone program. *Addiction*, 90, 415–424.

Schippers, G.M., Brokken L.C.M.H. and Otten, J. (1994). *Doorlichting, voorlichting alcoholgebruik. Handleiding [Manual, Dutch motivational drinker's check-up]*. Bureau Beta, Nijmegen.

Simmons, C.A., Lehmann, P., & Cobb, N. (2008) A comparison of women versus men charged with intimate partner violence: General risk factors, attitudes regarding using violence and readiness to change, *Violence and Victims*, 23, 571–585.

Shepard, M.F., & Pence, E.L. (Eds.). (1999). *Coordinating community responses to domestic violence: Lessons from Duluth and beyond*. Thousand Oaks, CA: Sage.

Stott, N.C. II., Rollnick, S., Rees., M.R., & Pill, R.M. (1995). Innovation in clinical method: Diabetes care and negotiating skills. *Family Practice*, 12, 413–418.

Stuart, G.L., Temple, J.R., & Moore, T.M. (2007). Improving batterer intervention programs through theory-based research. *Journal of the American Medical Association*, 298, 560–562.

Taft, C.T., Murphy, C.M., Elliott, J.D., & Morrel T.M. (2001). Attendance enhancing procedures in group counseling for domestic abusers. *Journal of Counseling Psychology*, 48, 51–60.

Taft, C.T., Murphy, C.M., King, D.W., Musser, P.H. & DeDeyn, J.M. (2003). Process and treatment adherence factors in group cognitive-behavioral therapy for partner violent men. *Journal of Consulting and Clinical Psychology*, 71, 812–820.

Taft, C.T., Murphy, C.M., Musser, P.H., & Remington, N.A. (2004). Personality, interpersonal and motivational predictors of the working alliance in group cognitive-behavioral therapy for partner violent men. *Journal of Consulting and Clinical Psychology*, 72, 349–354.

Vansteenkiste, M., & Sheldon, K.M. (2006). There's nothing more practical than a good theory: Integrating motivational interviewing and self determination theory. *British Journal of Clinical Psychology*, 45, 63–82.

Vasilaki E.I., Hosier S.G., & Cox W.M. (2006). The efficacy of motivational interviewing as a brief intervention for excessive drinking: a meta-analytic review. *Alcohol and Alcoholism*, 41, 328–35.

Winarski, Silver, & Kraybill, (2003). Motivational Interviewing: Applications for path service providers, an edited transcript of the PATH national Teleconference. Downloaded from http://www.pathprogram.samhsa.gov/text_only/tech_assist/Transcripts/MotivationalInterviewing_2_2003.asp on October 9, 2008.

5

Narrative Therapy: Addressing Masculinity in Conversations with Men who Perpetrate Violence

TOD AUGUSTA-SCOTT

After 27 years I never got to know who Rosemary was. I knew she was my wife but I never got to know her.
> **—George, reflecting during his final session of group therapy**

To end men's violence against their female partners, addressing the social-political context of men's violence is important.[1] This social-political context influences men who decide to control and abuse their partners (Adams, 2007; Bancroft, 2003; Jenkins, 1990; Pence and Paymar, 1993; Paymar, 2000; Stark, 2007; White, 1994). I was initially trained in the education approach that used blunt oppositional confrontation to address issues such as sexism (Adams, 2007; Bancroft, 2003; Pence and Paymar, 1993; Paymar, 2000; Stark, 2007). After years of using this approach, I was introduced to the ideas and practices of narrative therapy (Jenkins, 1990; White, 1994, 2007). Through this approach, I learned respectful, collaborative, and effective ways of addressing sexism in conversations with men. Specifically, I learned about externalizing problems and inviting men to take a position on them (White, 2007). Externalizing involves separating people's identities from problems.

In this chapter, I will draw on my work primarily with men who have been mandated to attend counseling in a rural community organization.

---

[1] To be congruent with the Narrative Therapy style, this chapter is written in the first person.

Most of the men are white, straight, and live on low-incomes. I will focus on externalizing dominant or hegemonic masculinity (Connell, 1995) and inviting men to take a position on it. Men are invited to notice the ways in which dominant masculinity leads them to avoid both taking responsibility for mistakes and the shame that comes with making them. As a result, many men act accordingly by minimizing the seriousness of the abuse, denying it, or blaming it on external factors. Externalizing dominant masculinity makes it more possible for men to take responsibility for their violence. An important part of taking responsibility involves listening to and acknowledging their partners' experiences of the violence. As men become better able to deal with mistakes and pain, they are better able to listen to their partners' pain and suffering as a result of the violence.

Male violence in relationships is often both a mistake and not a mistake. The violence is intentional. In as much as the violence results in power and control, it is "working" and not a mistake. Often, there are unintentional effects of the abuse as well. Men often do not intend to devastate their relationships with their partners and children over time. In the context of wanting long term, caring and respectful relationships, choosing to use violence in a relationship for many men can also be constructed as a "mistake" (Augusta-Scott, 2003, 2008).

Inviting men to take a position on the problem of masculinity is one of the ways I work collaboratively with them. The process of inviting the men to take a position on dominant masculinity involves: 1) negotiating a name for the problem, 2) naming the effects of the problem, 3) evaluating the effects of the problem as acceptable, unacceptable, or both, and 4) justifying why participants evaluate these effects as they do. By externalizing dominant masculinity and inviting men to take a position on it, alternative constructions of masculinity begin to develop.

HISTORY

I was initially trained in and practiced the education approach to working with men who had perpetrated violence against their female partners (Adams, 1988, 1989, 2002; Adams & Cayouette, 2002; Adams & McCormick, 1982; Bathrick, Carlin, Kaufman & Vodde, 1992; Pence and Paymar, 1993; Paymar, 2000, Pence, 2002; Yllo & Bograd, 1988). This approach has made some important contributions to the field. It emphasized the importance of addressing the social context of violence; that is, addressing issues of power and gender (Dobash & Dobash, 1979). The education approach focuses on men's responsibility and accountability, and has assisted in coordinating community and legal efforts to address the issue of domestic violence (Pence & Paymar, 1993).

The education approach also offered an important critique of therapeutic approaches that individualized and pathologized men's violence (Bograd, 1982, 1984; Almeida & Bograd, 1991; Schecter, 1982). Therapy was also critiqued for not clearly focusing on the man's responsibility for choosing to abuse and for stopping further abuse. Further, therapy was criticized for "colluding" with men's excuses and justifications that support perpetrating violence. Feminists specifically critiqued the field of family therapy for similar reasons (Avis, 1989, Bograd, 1986; Hare-Mustin & Maracek, 1986; Goldner, 1985, 1987).

In response, the education approach adopted an anti-therapeutic stance, thus the term "education" to describe workers' conversations with men. The education approach focused on the way that dominant masculinity leads men to feel entitled to power and control over their female partners. This strategy adopted an oppositional engagement with men. To avoid colluding with men, I believed I had to challenge and confront them to take responsibility. Men had to be directly challenged to give up their power and control, and then adopt anti-sexist ideas and practices.

In response, some therapists countered the education approach by simply insisting that gender is unrelated to the issue of violence in intimate relationships (e.g., Dutton, 1994). Out of the field of family therapy, however, narrative therapy developed, which moved away from dichotomous debates arguing for either an education or therapeutic approach (White & Epston, 1990; Jenkins, 1990). Instead, narrative therapy recognizes the importance of both the *collaborative* engagement of the therapeutic approach and the social-political analysis of the education approach.

Narrative therapy began to develop during the 1980s with Michael White (1984, 1986a, 1986b, 1987, 1988, 1994) and David Epston's work (White & Epston, 1990), which was significantly influenced by Gregory Bateson (1972, 1979) and Michel Foucault (1965, 1973). Other developments in the field have come from philosophers such as Derrida (1978) and Vygotsky (1986). Likewise, Alan Jenkins (1990, 1991, 1994, 1996, 1997, 1998a, 1998b, 2007; Jenkins, Joy & Hall, 2002) developed an invitational approach to working with men, which was significantly influenced by White's work. Since then there have been other developments in the field (Augusta-Scott, 2001; 2006, 2007a, 2007b, 2007c, 2008; Augusta-Scott & Dankwort, 2002; Brownlee, Ginter & Tranter, 1998; Calder, 2007; Chapman, 2007; Denton, 2007; Fisher, 2005a, 2005b; Gordon, 2005; Gray, 2006; Mills, 2003; Nurnberger & Robichaud-Smith 2004; Newman, 2007; Nylund & Corsiglia, 1998; Paré, Bondy & Malhotra, 2006).

MASCULINITIES

Masculinity is not the same for all men. Differences occur along various social locations such as race, class, sexual orientation, and so forth (Denborough, 1996; McLean, 1996). I work with men who are primarily white, straight, and live on low-incomes. Men in this rural community define dominant masculinity in terms of having power and control over women. This dominant construction of masculinity influences how they construct their identities in a variety of ways. Men perform this identity by both controlling and abusing their partners.[2] Further, men in this community also report that the social expectations of dominant masculinity are that men are to "be perfect," "never make mistakes," "know everything," and avoid pain (Smith, 1996). These social expectations lead men to irresponsibly avoid acknowledging mistakes and shame. As a result, men often silence their partners, preventing them from voicing their painful experiences of male violence. In contradiction to the expectation of "be perfect," dominant masculinity also gives men messages such as "boys will be boys," which also fosters irresponsible behavior.

Many men who are mandated to counseling with me have not studied how they present their individual masculinities. These social expectations about masculinity are taken for granted, assumed, and habitual. As a result, men often initially report, "I don't know why I do it. I just lose it." Some men have a momentary realization of why they have perpetrated abuse after an incident. The realization of their responsibility is accompanied by shame, which men are expected to avoid. As a result, men minimize the seriousness of abuse and deny it rather than seek to understand their abusive behavior.

In response to men reporting that they are unaware of why they use violence, I affirm that perpetrating abuse is often habitual and can happen quickly. I report to the participants that I believe he does not know why he perpetrates abuse. I then suggest that to stop the abuse, some men have previously reported that it is helpful to study past incidents slowly to find out what ideas led to this behavior (i.e., find out *why* they chose to perpetrate abuse).[3] Studying past incidents renders visible the ideas that are influencing men's choices to perpetrate abuse in those moments. When studying past incidents of abuse, men often notice how ideas about masculinity they took for granted have lead them to make choices to abuse their female partners (e.g., "needing to win," "needing to be right," etc.). Upon externalizing these ideas and studying their influence, men can begin to confront them, rather than letting the ideas lead them toward perpetrating abuse.[4]

Externalizing the Problem

Externalizing problems involves separating men's identities from the problem (White, 2007).[5] The problem is defined in terms of the ideas people are influenced by and participate in, such as dominant masculinity. Rather than defining the man as the problem, the externalizing conversations focus on the relationship a man has with the problem. Further, externalizing conversations center on the type of relationship the man might prefer to have with the problem. While dominant masculinity defines men as the problem, the process of externalizing defines men's participation in the difficulty of dominant masculinity. By externalizing the problem and defining it in social terms, men are better able to take responsibility for their participation in the problem.

The process of externalizing the problem contrasts with traditional practices of internalizing problems. Internalizing the problem means defining the problem as something internal to the person, that is, the problem is inherent, biological, and "natural." Making people the problem relies on an internal understanding of the self. In the case of violence, the problem is often defined as essential to the aggressors' identities as men. Patriarchal cultures purport that being a man is innate and biological—something essential to their being and not socially constructed (e.g., "that is just the way men are"). These types of internal understandings of the self lead men to believe they do not have a choice about how they are; they are simply being men – the self is static and unchangeable. In traditional therapy, the process of internalizing the problem is done through individualizing and pathologizing the problem. Within this framework, men's problems are understood as biologically determined.

Unlike therapeutic intervention, the education approach inherent to traditional batterers defines the problem in social terms (Pence and Paymar, 1993; Adams, 2007; Bancroft, 2003; Pence and Paymar, 1993;

Paymar, 2000; Stark, 2007). In my earlier practice, however, rather than focusing on the *influence* of social expectations on men, I *defined* men according to the social expectations. I totalized them as only wanting power and control in their relationships. With this approach, identity was still defined primarily in fixed, static terms. This education approach retains a social determinism: dominant masculinity is monolithic and all men are influenced by it in the same manner. The problem is still defined as something internal or *essential* about men. Implicit in the men's identities being static and fixed was the idea that men would not change. Male static identity was reflected in totalizing labels such as "batterers," "abusers," and so forth.[6] As long as I was defining men as the problem and solely seeing them in terms of their participation in the problem, I was unable to notice alternative stories of masculinity, and how men might prefer to be. However, within a narrative context, I observed many men with stories of both participating in and resisting the social expectations of dominant masculinity.

With respect to patriarchy, men I talk with often believe initially that dominant masculinity is fixed, static, and therefore unchangeable: "that's just the way men are." Many of the men have made attempts to change themselves by making promises that they will never abuse again, yet they continue to do so. Often implicitly and sometimes explicitly, men conclude the abuse continues despite their efforts to the contrary simply because this is the way they are. The men often feel they have no choice over who they are or how they act. They simply are the way they are. These notions of the self support men in continuing to perpetrate violence.

Recognizing how men develop identity allows these men to notice how they adopt very different positions and behaviors in different contexts. Masculine identities are never fixed, always in formation, and are far from universal or consistent. The realization that men actively build on their identities opens up possibilities for inviting and taking responsibility for the gendered ways in which they act. (Denborough, 1996).

Collaborative Practice

By externalizing the problem of dominant masculinity and noticing men's multiple relationships to the problem, I have been able to develop a collaborative approach to my conversations with men. Acknowledging male resistance to dominant masculinity allowed me the opportunity to join with men to address violence. In this collaborative relationship, I acknowledge that my values and politics are shaping the conversation. I negotiate the purpose of therapeutic conversations with men, as well as the manner in which these conversations will happen and the definitions that are given to problems, solutions, identities and politics. By acknowledging how I am *centered* in the conversation, I increase my sense of accountability and responsibility for the power I have in the conversations.

My collaborative posture lead to acknowledging and taking responsibility for my helpful use around the ideas of power because it clarifies the influences that have shaped my curiosity and questions. My curiosity is influenced by the many previous conversations I have had with others about what is helpful and unhelpful in relationships. Furthermore, my interest is influenced by my own ideas about social justice. Of course, one such idea is that men are responsible for their choice to abuse. I think it is undesirable and even impossible to suggest that I can have a conversation about men's violence that seeks to suspend these influences. In fact, part of my working position is that the values, knowledge, and skills of the men consulting with me must also be at the center of the conversation for it to be helpful. I want to acknowledge that we are both "centered" and "experts" in the conversation.

When I believed men only wanted power and control, I was unable to engage them collaboratively. I adopted an oppositional posture with them that often replicated the dominant masculinity I wanted to change (Augusta-Scott, 2003). The result of this oppositional engagement with men was that they either retreated from the conversation by simply agreeing with me, or they would become angry with me for unilaterally defining their experience. This therapeutic posture lead the conversations to remain superficial and ineffective in moving men toward disclosing incidents of violence and taking responsibility for this violence.

In sum, I had adopted a posture in which I alone was the expert. This "expert" posture has a long tradition in paternalistic medical and therapeutic practice. The conversations were primarily about what I thought. In retrospect, I realize I adopted an attitude of not listening to men. Before a man walked into my office, I assumed that I already knew why he was violent, how he was violent, and what he wanted to get out of it: he wanted power and control, used power and control (tactics), and attained it by perpetrating abuse (Pence and Paymar, 1993; Adams, 2007; Bancroft, 2003; Pence and Paymar, 1993; Paymar, 2000; Stark, 2007). I imposed this analysis on the men by confronting them any time they veered from my singular version of their experience and the experience of their partners; if the men veered from the power and control story. Thus, alternative stories about men's relationships with dominant masculinity were rendered invisible.

STATEMENT OF POSITION MAP

One of the ways narrative practice works collaboratively with men is by inviting them to develop their own positions on problems. These conversations are facilitated through the "statement of position map" (White, 2007). In the early stages of counseling, I often invite men to take a position on the problem of dominant masculinity. I do this early because often the influence of dominant masculinity prevents men from participating in counseling conversations, taking responsibility, and listening to their female partners.

The process of inviting men to establish their position on a problem such as dominant masculinity involves a four-part process: 1) The first is negotiating a definition of the problem; 2) the next stage involves the men identifying the effects of the problem on themselves and others; 3) in the third stage, men are encouraged to evaluate these effects as acceptable, not acceptable, or both; 4) finally men are encouraged to justify why they evaluate the problem the way they do. Men are encouraged to explore the values they have that lead them to evaluate the effects as acceptable, unacceptable, or both.

Negotiating a Definition of the Problem

The first category of inquiry of the "statement of position map" is negotiating a definition of the problem. This process involves making visible the taken for granted, assumed, habitual ideas of dominant masculinity that influence men's identities and choices to abuse. Further, men are invited to consider where they learned these ideas.

For example, I might ask, "What are the social messages that men generally learn about sharing problems and mistakes with others?" When asking this question, I often have to clarify that I am not asking men about their ideas on how men are supposed to be, but simply asking them what the social expectations are.

In response, men report that they are expected not to ask for help, not to talk about problems, not admit mistakes, and so forth. I then invite a man to consider questions such as, "If a man was influenced by these ideas, how might these ideas lead him to act?"[7] Men often report these ideas would prevent men from sharing their mistakes, instead pretending to "be perfect" or to "know everything." I also ask men to consider where men generally learn these ideas.

Consideration of these hypothetical questions (e.g., "if a man was influenced . . .") about a theoretical third-person can provide men with the opportunity to name the social expectations and effects they might have on a man. These hypothetical questions help men think about what is often a new idea – the social expectations of dominant masculinity, and the possibility that gender is also socially constructed rather than biologically determined. A helpful distance is provided between the therapeutic conversation and the men's particular situation. It reduces the possible defensiveness men may experience in this conversation, because at this point I am only asking him to consider the merit of theory and ideas rather than to talk about his experience (Denton, 2007).

Giving men the opportunity to talk about some of these ideas generally provides a platform for them to consider the influence of these ideas in their lives. These questions also give men the opportunity to reflect quietly on their connections with other men. A man is able to identify privately any struggles he is having with dominant masculinity as a struggle he may share with other men. He begins to understand dominant masculinity as *social* rather than simply an individualized experience that he alone is having. Eventually, as a man privately makes these connections to other men, he commonly will begin to relay his own experience of learning about dominant masculinity. Some men report being beaten for making mistakes, for crying, and so forth. Men also begin to speak about the influence of dominant masculinity on men's choices to perpetrate abuse. Men decide themselves when they want to share their own stories rather than the therapist deciding for them. It is significant, with respect to men's agency, that they propose the connections between hypothetical states of affairs and their own experience, rather than me trying to convince or persuade them to make these connections (Denton, 2007).

Previously, when I only relied on the power and control story, I believed the only ideas men had were social expectations. By not making distinctions between men and the problem of dominant masculinity, I had conflated men's ideas with the social expectations. As a result, I simply asked men, "How do you think women and men are supposed to be?" and "How have these ideas influenced you?" If men's responses did not accord with the social expectations, I concluded they were being dishonest. In retrospect, I can see that I did not give men the opportunity to identify the social expectations. They simply became defensive because of the accusatory tone of the questions. Alternatively, at the same time men may have wanted power and control, but I did not consider that men might also hold views contrary to the social expectations of dominant masculinity. Now when men say they hold views contrary to dominant masculinity, I want to honor their recognition rather than dismiss it.

The following excerpt illustrates the first stage of the "statement of position map." The problem being externalized from the man's identity is part of the social expectations of dominant masculinity. The man's name is Jacob, and this is his second individual conversation. Jacob is a laborer who lives on a low income. He has been abusive to his partner for a number of years. He also has two children. I, Tod, the therapist, invite Jacob to first name the problem: the social expectations about the emotions men are supposed to avoid. This leads to a conversation about avoiding mistakes, pain, and disappointment by becoming angry.

Tod: What are the messages guys get about expressing emotions other than anger?

Jacob: Guys are supposed to be rough and tough.

Tod: What feelings are guys supposed to avoid sharing? What are guys expected to keep to themselves?

Jacob: Disappointment, fear, being sad. They're allowed to show anger and being cranky. Those ideas – that's, that's society.

Tod: Avoid feelings like being . . . sad?

Jacob: No, no, no don't show sadness.

Tod: So you avoid those feelings.

Jacob: Well if you're really drunk, people don't really care then.

Tod: Then they've got an excuse.

Jacob: Yeah, "I'm drunk, I'm drunk."

Tod: And not show fear?

Jacob: No, you ain't allowed to show fear.

Tod: Or disappointment?

Jacob: No, no. Disappointment – fuck it.

Tod: Fuck it.

Jacob: Fuck it. A short version of disappointment is – "fuck it."

Tod: Where do guys learn to avoid problems and pain by simply becoming angry?

Jacob: There are lots of ways that, you know, movies, magazines, everything, television, support that – real men don't cry and that whole thing. . . .

Tod: What are the messages that guys get about expressing their feelings other than anger? If a guy shows his feelings, what are the messages he gets?

Jacob: "Pussy," "wimp," whatever, you know, "chicken shit"—whatever they call you.

Jacob is naming the problem of gender expectations and the practices that they lead toward, like avoiding painful feelings by becoming angry instead. As this conversation develops, I make distinctions that "the problem" is not simply that men cannot show emotions other than anger. Many men recognize that they can express other emotions in ways that are still controlling and manipulative (McLean, 1996). The problem gets more clearly defined as avoiding experiences of pain—hers and his—as it relates to him being responsible for perpetrating abuse (Augusta-Scott, 2008). The conversation also includes a discussion on how he learned these ideas, which undermines the idea that men's behaviors are innate and therefore unchangeable.

As we continue to define the problem, I invite Jacob to consider other social messages men get about "making mistakes." Jacob informs me that men are not supposed to make mistakes. Men are supposed to be perfect and know everything. Jacob states that men are expected not to have problems, or, if they do, they are supposed to handle them on their own. I then inquire, "If a man was influenced by these ideas, would they lead him to take more responsibility for his mistakes over time or less?" I then invite him to explore the various ways that men avoid taking responsibility, by denying they made a mistake or minimizing the seriousness of how their behavior may have negatively affected others.

Effects of the Problem

I continue the conversation by inviting Jacob to consider the potential effects of the problem. The problem has been named as the social expectations of men needing to "be perfect" and "not express emotions" other than anger. The inquiry begins with hypothesizing about how a man would be affected by these social expectations if he were under their influence. Again, I begin this process by asking hypothetical questions such as, "If a man was influenced by the idea that he should not share his problems, what kind of effect might this idea have on him over time? How would it affect his relationship to his partner? How would it affect his partner?"

By externalizing these ideas, men are able to study them safely rather than be concerned that I am making assumptions about their relationship to the problem. I am not assuming that I know how the man is influenced by social expectations or how he participates in or resists them. I do not make assumptions about how much these social expectations have influenced men's identities. This process provides the opportunity for Jacob to consider in a non-defensive manner what a man might do if he was influenced by these social expectations. As they respond to these hypothetical questions, men are then able to privately consider how these social expectations may have affected both them and others over time. Often as I am inquiring about the experiences of "other men," a man will begin to talk about his own connection to this experience. Men also talk about how they try to avoid this pain through drinking, becoming angry, and so forth. Men often talk about how denying mistakes and avoiding shame leads toward ignoring their partner's expressions of pain over the violence. Men also talk about the isolation and pain this creates for their partners and children.

In the conversation with Jacob, once he identifies these social expectations, he begins to privately consider his relationship to them and how he may be influenced by them. I adopt a respectful and curious posture rather than being judgmental when talking about the relationships of "other men" to these social expectations. As Jacob witnesses my approach and, in turn, feels safe and respected enough, he begins to trust that I will adopt a similar posture with him.

Tod: If a guy thinks that, you know, the only thing he can show is his anger and all that kind of stuff and he needs to keep all this sad, hurt feelings to himself, what kind of effect would that have on him over time?

Jacob: You're probably looking for a hospital bed somewhere, probably the N.S. [local mental health hospital], I imagine. . . . They are probably going to be sitting in this chair or on that couch. [Pointing to the couch beside him.]

Tod: So if you are not sharing that stuff with anybody, just keeping it to yourself . . .

Jacob: You're going to bottle it up.

Tod: And if a guy were influenced by these ideas, would he feel more able to handle his feelings of disappointment over time or less able?

Jacob: Probably less. It's going to get harder on you . . . I know . . .

By stating, "I know," Jacob gives another indication that he is privately making connections to the conversation about "other men." He is beginning to think about the social expectations and how the problem affects him. I continue this conversation by investigating how the social expectation of men needing to be right or perfect affects a man over time. Jacob articulates how the social expectations "wear a man down over time." Jacob considers how these ideas decrease a man's willingness to take responsibility for making mistakes and deal with the pain that comes in making those mistakes. Jacob talks about how a man might begin drinking or use sex to avoid the painful feelings that result from making mistakes.

I then invite him to also consider how these social expectations would affect a man's partner over time.

Tod: What are some of the other costs of these old ideas about what it means to be a man? What are the costs to the relationship with a partner? How would they affect a man's relationship with his partner?

Jacob: There would be a lot of disrespect there.

Tod: Ah yeah. So she'd be feeling disrespected?

Jacob: Sure. Why the hell wouldn't she? You out all night drinking. All you want to come home for is sex. You don't even know you've got two kids.

Jacob has two children. He is beginning to reveal his own relationship to the social expectations.

Tod: I hear what you're saying. And if a guy wanted to be close to his wife and these ideas were affecting him . . . what would go on then? Would these ideas lead him to be closer to her over time or further apart?

Jacob: Oh, you're just going to be in for a disappointment.

Tod: Would these ideas make it easier for him to be close to somebody or harder?

Jacob: You get close to nobody but yourself. I wasn't, anyway.

As Jacob begins to identify the negative effects these social expectations have on men and their partners, he begins to gain distance from these ideas. By externalizing these ideas he is in more of a position to evaluate them and take a stand on them, rather than simply continuing to habitually live by them. By stating, "I wasn't, anyway," Jacob continues to move the conversation from talking about "other men" to talking about himself. Jacob continues to talk about how expressing only anger can result in a partner never talking about his abuse, his mistakes, and the pain his violence has caused her. Further in this conversation, Jacob identifies that partners would become "resentful" over time and feel disrespected if the man always had to be right and she had to be wrong. He reported it would be "hard on a relationship" if the man could never admit to making mistakes.

Evaluate the Effects of the Problem

The next component of the "statement of position map" involves inviting men to evaluate the effects of the problem of sexism and abuse on their lives. Men evaluate the effects as acceptable, unacceptable, or both. As men begin to evaluate the negative effects of dominant masculinity, they begin to distance themselves from the problem and alterative ways of being begin to develop.

As the conversation develops, I begin to invite Jacob to evaluate the impact of the social expectation that a man needs to "not make mistakes" and "not share painful feelings." By talking about "other men" a scaffold has been created for him to understand and reflect on the expectations of dominant masculinity. As a result, I begin to ask him questions directly about himself.

Tod: And how do you feel about the effects these ideas are having on you?

Jacob: Well it didn't work the way I was running her . . .

Tod: So these ideas were leading you astray?

Jacob: Ah yeah.

Tod: It makes sense. Sounds like they didn't lead you or relationships where you wanted to go.

Jacob: Well they didn't.

Tod: Cause I think often people say these ideas are going to work . . .

Jacob: Last four or five years of my life Tod I have been living in fear, fear and anger.

Throughout the conversation, I continue to ask him specifically to evaluate the effects of not taking responsibility for mistakes and not facing his feelings over these mistakes. He reports that "it is wrong" that his partner is left feeling unheard, disrespected and isolated as a result of him participating in the practices of dominant masculinity. In turn, he identifies that these practices are devastating to his relationship over time. While men articulate the costs of the social expectations, in accordance with the power and control story, men also report there are "benefits." For example, many men report that perpetrating abuse gives them "relief" from painful feelings and a sense of "power." They also identify, however, that these experiences are often fleeting. Many men are faced with weighing these benefits against the short and long-term costs of perpetrating violence against their families.

Justify the Evaluation of the Effects

The final category of the "statement of position map" is to invite men to justify their evaluation of the effects of the problem on their partners, themselves and their relationships. This process involves inviting men to think *why* they consider the effects to be acceptable, unacceptable, or both. Many men identify that they find the impact of not facing problems, for example, unacceptable because of the pain it causes to themselves or others. Men identify the values they have that lead them to conclude these effects are unacceptable. For example, men often state that they value and prefer to be caring and respectful fathers and partners. These values are underscored when men report that they feel ashamed for abusing their partners and children. Further, men often report that they respect themselves more for taking responsibility rather than avoiding their mistakes or blaming them on others. Toward this end, men identify that the abuse will only stop once they face up to mistakes and shame by listening to their partner's experiences. As long as men continue to deny and minimize the seriousness of what they have done, the abuse continues.

In the conversation with Jacob, I ask him to justify *why* the effects of social expectations on men in general as well as himself are unacceptable for his partner and children. Jacob reported that avoiding problems simply made them worse. He also reported that he thinks a man should face up to problems rather than avoid them through getting angry, drinking, or so forth. By admitting mistakes and acknowledging his partner's experience, he could do something about the problem. As the session ended, I summarized Jacob's stated position on these social expectations and on what values he based this position. One week later, Jacob returned for another counseling session. He was no longer talking about "other men," but clearly talking about his own relationship with the problem. He related various stories that reflected his preference for acknowledging mistakes rather than pretending he is perfect. He also shared his preference for being able to acknowledge feeling pain over his mistakes rather than only becoming angry. For example, Jacob immediately began to speak of a conversation he had with his Alcoholics Anonymous (AA) sponsor in which he shared his position on some of the social expectations of dominant masculinity.

Jacob: Well, I was talking about that [the social expectations] the other night with my [AA] sponsor.

Tod: Did you? What were you saying?

Jacob: I said, "This program" I said, "I am taking in Truro" I said, "I've noticed that I've got more than one feeling in my body." I said, "I don't have to be mad at everybody. Everybody don't have to be right and I don't always have to be right."

Tod: Or wrong?

Jacob: Well, if I'm right, I'm right, and if I'm wrong, big deal. Big deal.

Tod: Why is it okay to make mistakes?

Jacob: I shouldn't hate myself if I'm wrong and I shouldn't gloat about it if I'm right.

Tod: What difference does it make to take that stand?

Jacob: It makes my mind think totally different.

Tod: And there's kind of unhelpful shame that happens because you don't live up to the social expectations about how to be a man, that you're not perfect. . . .

Jacob: Well, I am a long ways from it . . . and that's okay. Today I notice that.

Jacob gives an example of his position on the value of acknowledging mistakes and not always needing to be right. Articulating these commitments increases his willingness to take responsibility for his "mistake" of using violence in his relationships. I also inquire about how he feels about the pain he might experience from taking responsibility and acknowledging his mistakes. Jacob then relates a story from the previous week in which he was okay with acknowledging a mistake and feeling "blue" over it rather than becoming angry.

Jacob: It's okay for me to feel whatever I want to feel today. I was feeling a little blue this morning. I didn't do things the way I was supposed to, but I didn't get mad over it. No.

Tod: So you were just able to be blue.

Jacob: Blue. Here I am. Welcome to earth.

Tod: And that's okay.

Jacob: It's not that bad of a feeling.

Tod: You can handle it.

Jacob: Well, I'm human.

Tod: And you don't need to avoid it by becoming angry.

Jacob: Acknowledging it and being able just to accept it is a big thing for me. I used to fight it and wind up mad. Everything I'd done, I'd wind up mad. Pissed right off and I'm telling you . . . when I got mad, fuck, I'd upset a building or something. Where my strength came from I couldn't tell ya. I've torn doors right off houses.

Tod: How does it feel to take this position against the social expectations?

Jacob: Well, if I can go through a day without getting in a rage, I'm so happy at bedtime. I am so happy to lay my bones down. . . . It's probably not as wear down to just acknowledge you have them. Right instead of saying, "no I'm not blue, I'm not fucking blue . . ."

Tod: Avoid it and then you are not blue . . . you're angry.

Jacob: You're right, you're not blue—that's the way I worked. But everybody's got feelings—I don't care who you are . . . Now I'm just getting into this. Me sharing feelings and talking about problems is just like a child learning how to walk It's just that for the last years upon years Tod, everything's stacked up in my head, this is the way life has to be . . .

Jacob has taken a position on the problem, on the social expectations of dominant masculinity. He recognizes and has begun to address these taken for granted ideas. Jacob goes on to identify how being able to acknowledge mistakes and pain will better prepare him to listen to his partner's experience of the violence. Listening honestly to his partner will help him slow down and interrupt his violence in the future, leading him to closer to respectful, caring relationships.

CONCLUSION

Narrative therapy can offer helpful ways of addressing the political-social context of men's violence against their female partners. In part, this approach works by collaboratively engaging men in externalizing conversations and inviting them to take a position on the effects dominant masculinity has on themselves, their partners, and their children. The process of inviting men to take a position on dominant masculinity involves 1) negotiating the definition of the problem, 2) defining the effects of the problem, 3) evaluating the effects of the problem and 4) identifying men's values that are implicit in these evaluations. These conversations can begin the process of developing alternative stories of masculinity. These stories develop by inquiring about the men's history of resisting dominant masculinity, responding to injustice, inviting men to consider the types of relationships they prefer, and inviting them to explore the values implicit in the shame they may experience for perpetrating abuse. To change the definition of masculinity is to change what men understand themselves to be and what they can become (McLean, 1996). In turn, narrative practice can help create a foundation for men to listen to women's experiences of men's violence.

ENDNOTES

1. I would like to acknowledge Stephen Madigan and David Denborough, who provided valuable feedback on this chapter.
2. These and other social expectations are what Foucault (1965, 1973) calls "normalizing judgments."
3. The effect of using the word "ideas" rather than "beliefs" makes the process of both externalizing and challenging them easier. I seldom refer to "men's beliefs" because this reference infers a commitment to the ideas, which often increases the difficulty of changing men's relationship to them. Instead, I prefer to use the term "ideas" that men are influenced by, resist, and participate in.
4. The process of deconstructing men's negative identity conclusions often happens in the process of men studying past abusive incidents. Often the negative identity conclusions men have about themselves become apparent after they have perpetrated abuse. At this point, many men (momentarily) acknowledge that they hate themselves for being "losers," for example. To deconstruct these negative identity conclusions, these conclusions can be externalized and the history of how and from whom men learned these negative identity conclusions about themselves can be traced. Often when men realize that they learned these negative ideas about themselves, they begin to challenge the idea that they are innately, and therefore destined always to be, "losers". Through externalizing these negative identity conclusions in this manner, men can gain distance from them and begin to see other possibilities about who they have been and who they may want to be. I have written about this process in men who have perpetrated abuse elsewhere (Augusta-Scott, 2007a).
5. Variations on the ideas and practices of externalizing are quite common. Both therapeutic and religious traditions have relied on the helpfulness of separating people's identities from their problematic behavior (e.g., "hating the sin and not the sinner"). These traditions believe that people are more and can be more than their destructive

behavior suggests. Indeed, in the domestic violence movement, the problems of women who are abused were externalized. The problems were defined as sexism and men. The externalizing of narrative therapy focuses on defining the problem in terms of discourse rather than simply projecting the problem onto someone else (Tomm, 1989).

6. Rather than using labels, I now refer to the men as men. When describing my work, I explain that I have conversations with men about perpetrating abuse. This language makes the process of men taking responsibility for their abusive behavior easier. As part of this process, men no longer need accept that violence defines the totality of their identity. Further, these labels often shame the women and children who are in relationships with these men. The language of simply "talking with men about perpetrating abuse" honors the multiple experiences these women and children have of these men apart from violence. Often these other positive experiences are the basis on which many women decide to stay.

7. This process of asking hypothetical questions is used in a variety of therapeutic inquiries (Denton, 2007; Perakyla, 1995; Tomm, 1987, 1989).

REFERENCES

Adams, D. (1988). Treatment models of men who batter: A profeminist analysis. In K. Yllo & M. Bograd (Eds.), *Feminist perspectives on wife abuse* (pp. 176–199), Newbury Park, CA: Sage

Adams, D. (1989). Feminist-based Interventions for battering men. In L. Caesar & K. L. Hamberger. (Eds.). *Treating men who batter: Theory, practice and programs* (pp. 3–23). New York: Springer.

Adams, D. (2002). The Emerge program. In J. Hammer & C. Itzin (Eds.). *Hometruths about domestic violence: Feminist influence on policy and practice* (pp. 310–322). London, UK: Routledge.

Adams, D. (2007). *Why do they kill? Men who murder their intimate partners.* Nashville, TN: Vanderbilt University Press.

Adams, D., & Cayouette, S. (2002). Emerge—a group education model for abusers. In E. Aldarondo & F. Mederos, (Eds.), *Programs for men who batter: Intervention and prevention strategies in a diverse society* (pp. 4-1–4-32). New York: Civic Research Institute.

Adams, D., & McCormick, A. (1982). Men unlearning violence: A group approach based on the collective model. In M. Roy (Ed.), *The abusive partner* (170–197). New York: Van Nostrand Reinhold.

Almeida, R., & Bograd, M. (1991). Sponsorship: Men holding men accountable for domestic violence. *Journal of Feminist Family Therapy.* 2, 243–59.

Augusta-Scott, T. (2001). Dichotomies in the power and control story: Exploring multiple stories about men who choose abuse in intimate relationships. *Gecko: A Journal of Deconstruction and Narrative Ideas in Therapeutic Practice, 2,* 31–68.

Augusta-Scott, T. (2003). Dichotomies in the power and control story: Exploring multiple stories about men who choose abuse In *Responding to Violence: A collection of papers relating to child sexual abuse and violence in intimate relationships.* (pp. 203–224). Adelaide, South Australia: Dulwich Centre Publications.

Augusta-Scott, T. (2006). Talking with men who have used violence in intimate relationships: An Interview with Tod Augusta-Scott. *International Journal of Narrative Therapy and Community Work.* 4. 23–30. Australia: Dulwich Centre Publications.

Augusta-Scott, T. (2007a). Letters from prison: Re-authoring identity with men who have perpetrated sexual abuse. In C. Brown, & T. Augusta-Scott (Eds.) *Narrative therapy: Making meaning, making lives* (pp. 251–268). Thousand Oaks, CA: Sage.

Augusta-Scott, T. (2007b). Challenging anti-oppressive discourse: Uniting against racism and sexism. In Brown, C. & Augusta-Scott, T. (Eds.) *Narrative therapy: making meaning, making lives* (pp. 211–228). Thousand Oaks, CA: Sage.

Augusta-Scott, T. (2007c). Conversations with men about women's violence: Ending men's violence by challenging gender essentialism. In Brown, C. & Augusta-Scott, T. (Eds.) *Narrative therapy: making meaning, making lives* (pp. 197–210). Thousand Oaks, CA: Sage.

Augusta-Scott, T. (2008). *Narrative therapy: Abuse intervention program. A program to foster respectful relationships. A group facilitator's manual.* Truro: Nova Scotia: Bridges.

Augusta-Scott, T., & Dankwort, J. (2002). Group work with partner abuse: Lessons from constructivist and educational approaches. *Journal of Interpersonal Violence.* 17, 783–805.

Avis, J. (1989). Integrating gender into the family therapy curriculum. *Journal of Feminist Family Therapy*, 1, 3–26.

Bancroft, D. (2003). *Why does he do that?: Inside the minds of angry and controlling men.* San Francisco, CA: Berkley Trade.

Bateson, G. (1972). *Steps to an ecology of mind.* New York: Ballantine Books.

Bateson, G. (1979). *Mind and nature: A necessary unity.* New York: Bantam Books.

Bathrick, D., Kathleen, C. Kaufman, G., & Vodde, R. (1992). *Men stopping violence: a program for change.* Atlanta, GA: Men Stopping Violence, Inc.

Bograd, M. (1982). Battered women, cultural myths and clinical interventions: A feminist analysis. *Women and Therapy*, 1, 69–77.

Bograd, M. (1984). Family systems approaches to wife battering: A feminist critique. *American Journal of Orthopsychiatry*, 54, 558–568.

Bograd, M. (1986). Family therapy and violence agsint women. In M. Riche (Ed.) *Women and family therapy* (pp. 34–50). Rockville, MD: Aspen Systems.

Bograd, M. (1988). Feminist perspectives on wife abuse: An introduction. In K. Yllo & M. Bograd (Eds.), *Feminist perspectives on wife abuse* (pp. 176–199). Newbury Park, CA: Sage.

Brown, C., & Augusta-Scott, T. (2007a). (Eds.) *Narrative therapy: making meaning, making lives.* Newbury Park, CA: Sage Publications.

Brownlee, K., Ginter, C., and Tranter, D. (1998). Narrative intervention with men who batter: An appraisal and extension of the jenkins model. *Family Therapy*, 25, 85–98.

Bruner, J. (2003). *Making stories: law, literature, life.* Cambridge, MA: Harvard University Press.

Calder, J. (2007). A place to stand: A strengths-based therapeutic engagement with violence and anger. *Narrative Network News.* 39, 8–22.

Chapman, C. (2007). "Dilemmas about 'taking responsibility' and cultural accountability in working with men who have abuse their female partners." *International Journal of NarrativeTherapy and Community Work*, 4. 57–62.

Connell, R. (1995). *Masculinities*. Cambridge: MA: Polity Press.

Denborough, D. (1996). "Step by step: Developing respectful and effective ways of working with young men to reduce violence." In C. McLean, M. Carey, & C. White (Eds.). *Men's ways of being: New directions in theory and psychology*. (pp. 91–116). Boulder, CO: Westview Press.

Denton, E. (2007). *Negotiating anger and agency, responsibility, and change: Discourse analysis of narrative therapy for male intimate partner violence*. Unpublished Thesis. Guelph, Ontario: The University of Guelph.

Derrida. J. (1978). *Writing and difference*. London, UK: Routledge.

Dobash & Dobash. (1979). *Violence against wives. A case against the patriarchy*. New York: Harper & Row.

Dutton, D. (1994). Patriarchy and wife assault: The ecological fallacy. *Violence and Victims*. 9, 167–182.

Fisher, A. (2005a). Romance and violence: Practices of visual map making and documentation in conversation about men's abuse to women. In S. Cooper & J. Duvall (Eds). *Catching the winds of change: A conference to inspire healing conversations and hopeful stories with individuals, families, and communities* (pp. 115–123). Toronto, ON1: The Brief Therapy Networker.

Fisher, A. (2005b). Power and the promise of innocent places. *Narrative Network News*. 34, 12–14.

Foucault, M. (1965). *Madness and civilization: A history of insanity in the age of reason*. New York: Random House.

Foucault, M. (1973). *The Birth of the clinic: An archeology of medical perception*. London, UK: Tavistock.

Goldner, V. (1985). Feminism and family therapy. *Family Process*. 24, 31–47.

Goldner, V. (1987). Instrumentalism, feminism and the limits of family therapy. *Journal of Family Psychology*, 1, 109–116.

Gordon, M. (2005). Unexpected conversations: Some reflections on talking with men. *The International Journal of Narrative Therapy and Community Work*, 1, 31–37.

Gray, N. (2006). Responding to men's violence: An interview with Nancy Gray. *The International Journal of Narrative Therapy and Community Work*, 43, 9–14.

Hare-Mustin, R. & Maracek, J. (1986). Autonomy and gender: Some questions for therapists. *Psychotherapy*, 23, 203–212.

Jenkins, A., (2007). A conversation with alan jenkins: The ethics of working with perpetrators of violence. *Narrative Network News*, 38, 34–41.

Jenkins, A. (1998a) Facing shame without shaming: Engaging men who have enacted violence. *Therapeutic Conversations 4*. Toronto, Canada: Yaletown Family Therapy. May 12.

Jenkins, A. (1998b). Invitations to responsibility: Therapeutic engagement with Men who have abused their partners. Guelph, Ontario: Couple and Family Therapy Centre, University of Guelph. October, 15

Jenkins, A. (1997). Alcohol and men's violence: An interview with alan jenkins. *Dulwich Centre Newsletter*, 2&3, 43-47.

Jenkins, A. (1996). Moving towards respect: A quest for balance. In C. McLean, M. Carey & C. White (Eds), *Men's ways of being* (pp. 117–133). Boulder, CO: Westview Press.

Jenkins, A. (1994). Therapy for abuse or therapy as abuse. *Dulwich Centre Newsletter*, 1, 11–19.

Jenkins, A. (1991). Intervention with violence and abuse in families: The inadvertent perpetuation of irresponsible behaviour. *Australia and New Zealand Journal of Family Therapy, 2,* 186–195.

Jenkins, A. (1990). *Invitations to responsibility: The therapeutic engagement of men who are violent and abuse.* Adelaide, South Australia: Dulwich Centre Publications.

Jenkins, A., Joy, M., & Hall, R. (2002). Forgiveness and child sexual abuse: A matrix of meanings. *The International Journal of Narrative Therapy and Community Work, 1,* 35–51.

McLean, C. (1996). The Politics of men's pain: Men's ways of being. In C. McLean, M. Carey & C. White (Eds.), *The politics of men's pain: Men's way of being* (pp. 11–28). Boulder, CO: Westview Press.

Mills, L. (2003). *Insult to Injury: Rethinking our responses to intimate abuse.* Princeton, NJ: Princeton University Press.

Newman, D. (2007) Audience as accountability? Dilemmas in the issue of outsider witness practices in supporting men's anti-violence projects. *International Journal of Narrative Therapy and Community work. 4,* 63–69.

Nurnberger, R., & Robichaud-Smith, D. (2004). A Post-positive enquiry into men's relational motivations: Therapeutic construction and giving credence to men's stories about their use of abuse. *Canadian Social Work Review. 21,* 169–188.

Nylund, D. & Corsiglia, V. (1998). Internalized other questioning with men who are violent: With commentary by Alan Jenkins. In M. Hoyt (Ed.). *The Handbook of constructive therapies: Innovative approaches from leading practitioners* (pp. 401–413). San Francisco, CA: Jossey-Bass.

Paré, D.A., Bondy, J., & Malhotra, C. (2006). Performing respect: Using enactments in group work with men who have abused. *Journal of Systemic Therapies. 25,* 64–79.

Paymar, M. (2000). *Violent no more: Helping men end domestic abuse* (2nd ed.). Alameda, CA: Hunter House Inc.

Pence, E. (2002). The Duluth domestic abuse intervention project. In E. Aldarondo & F. Mederos, *Programs for men who batter: Intervention and prevention strategies in a diverse society* (pp. 6-1–6-46). New York: Civic Research Institute.

Pence, E. & Paymar, M. (1993). *Education groups for men who batter: The Duluth model.* New York: Springer.

Perakyla, A. (1995). *Aids Counseling: Institutional interaction and clinical practice.* Cambridge, MA: Cambridge University Press.

Schecter, S. (1982). *Women and male violence.* Boston: South End Press.

Smith, G. (1996). Dichotomies in the making of men. In C. McLean, M. Carey & C. White (Eds), *The politics of men's pain: Men's way of being* (pp. 29–50). Boulder, CO: Westview Press.

Stark, E. (2007). *Coercive control: How men entrap women in personal life.* New York: Oxford University Press.

Tomm, K. (1989). Externalizing the problem and internalizing personal agency. *Journal of Strategic and Systemic Therapies. 8,* 54–59.

Tomm, K. (1987). Interventive Interviewing: Part II, reflexive questioning as a means to enable self healing. *Family Process. 26,* 167–183.

Vygotsky, L. (1986). *Thought and language.* Cambridge, MA: MIT Press.

White, M. (1984). Pseudoencopresis: From avalanche to victory, from vicious to virtuous cycles. *Journal of Family Systems Medicine. 2,* 150–160.

White, M. (1986b). Negative explanation, restraint, and double description: A template for family therapy. *Family Process.* 25, 169–184.

White, M. (1986b). Practice Notes: The conjoint therapy of men who are violent and the women with whom they live. *Dulwich Centre Newletter,* Spring, pp. 12–16. Republished in White, M. (1989). *Selected Papers.* Adelaide: Dulwich Centre Publications. 101–105.

White M. (1987). Family Therapy and schizophrenia: Addressing the 'in-the-corner' lifestyle. *Dulwich Centre Newsletter,* Spring, 14–21. Republished in White, M. *Selected Papers,* Adelaide: Dulwich Centre Publications, 47–45.

White, M. (1988). The process of questioning: A therapy of literary merit?" *Dulwich Centre Newsletter.* Republished in Epston & White (1992). *Experience, Contradiction, Narrative & Imagination.* Adelaide: Dulwich Center Publications.

White, M. (1991). Deconstruction and therapy. *Dulwich Center Newsletter,* 3. Reprinted in Epston, D. & White, M. (1992), *Experience, Contradiction, Narrative & Imagination.* Adelaide: Dulwich Center Publications.

White, M. (1994). 'A conversation about accountability with Michael White by Chris McLean.' *Dulwich Centre Newsletter,* 2&3, 68–79.

White, M. (1995). *Re-authoring lives: Interviews & essays.* Adelaide: Dulwich Center Publications

White, M. (1997). *Narratives of therapists' lives.* Adelaide: Dulwich Centre Publications

White, M. (2001). Narrative practice and the unpacking of identity conclusions. In *Gecko: a Journal of Deconstruction and Narrative Ideas in Therapeutic Practice.* Dulwich Centre Publications, 1, 28–55.

White, M. (2007). *Maps of narrative practice.* New York: Norton.

White, M. & Epston, D. (1990). *Narrative means to therapeutic ends.* New York: Norton.

Wirtz, H. & Schweitzer, R. (2003) Group work for men who engage in violent and abusive actions. In *Responding to violence: A collection of papers relating to child sexual abuse and violence in intimate relationships.* Adelaide, South Australia: Dulwich Centre Publications pp. 187–201.

Yllo, K. and Bograd, M. (1988). *Feminist perspectives on wife abuse.* Newbury Park, CA: Sage.

6

Cognitive Behavioral Interventions for Partner-Abusive Men

CHRISTOPHER I. ECKHARDT
JACQUELINE SCHRAM

The way you think about your situation largely determines whether you will do anything about it, and what you will do. —*Arthur Freedman*

Despite the multitude of rifts and divisions so seemingly entrenched across areas of intimate partner violence (IPV) research, treatment, and prevention, there are at least two statements of agreement that IPV counselors, advocates, criminal justice staff, and researchers would share: (1) IPV perpetrators' attitudes and cognitive processing style are important correlates, if not determinants, of IPV (e.g., hostile attitudes toward women, positive beliefs about the acceptability of violence to obtain power and coerce others, and a biased style of interpreting the social world); and (2) an important goal of criminal justice efforts to rehabilitate IPV offenders is to produce changes in these attitudes and cognitions as a potent means of preventing future victimization of women. While these topics of general agreement among diverse groups of professionals working in the IPV field often give way to more specific areas of disagreement and "turf" battles, these cognitive themes are important constructs in their own right that form the basis of the cognitive-behavioral therapy (CBT) paradigm.

The CBT approach has had enormous influence in terms of our understanding of IPV etiology and represents a sizable step forward in our efforts to intervene and prevent future IPV victimization. In the present chapter, we will first provide an overview of what it means to be a program that offers CBT, especially in the context of the strengths perspective. Second, we will review the assumption that there is indeed sufficient evidence for a cognitive-behavioral model of IPV *etiology* that suitably justifies the CBT intervention model. Third, we will review whether there is evidence that addressing CBT themes and applying CBT techniques relate to (or actually predict) violence cessation; i.e., is there any evidence that this model works? Finally, we will review recent developments in CBT interventions and apply these techniques in the context of an IPV case.

WHAT IS COGNITIVE BEHAVIORAL THERAPY?

While a detailed review of the developmental history of CBT is beyond the scope of this chapter, the interested reader is referred to several excellent overviews of its history and general components (Beck, 1976; Beck, 1995). Briefly, CBT is a system of psychotherapy in which the therapist and client set the goals of the therapeutic relationship and collaboratively examine, dispute, and restructure cognitive processes so that the client may better regulate negative emotions and demonstrate goal-congruent behavior. The label "CBT" is applied to a wide variety of treatment approaches, with some that have a primary focus on cognitive etiologic and intervention-related foci (Beck, 1995), and others that incorporate a variety of affective and behavioral techniques as well (Dobson, 2001). Despite this heterogeneity, the common factor that defines a CBT-oriented intervention is largely a matter of process (rather than content), such that general CBT is defined by a positive, change-oriented collaboration between client and therapist to affect goal-congruent behavior using empirically supported techniques to modify dysfunctional cognitions and problematic emotions. A variety of meta-analytic reviews support the efficacy and effectiveness of CBT interventions for a wide array of psychological disturbances (Nathan & Gorman, 2007).

Central to the CBT approach is the basic "A-B-C" model, originally outlined by Ellis (1955) and expanded upon by Beck (1963), whereby "A" refers to *Activating Events*, "B" refers to *Belief System*, and "C" signifies the emotional and behavioral *Consequences* that are typically the foci of the intervention. This model, of course, emphasizes that most clients will begin treatment with a strong bias that favors an "A-C" connection, i.e., that feeling badly and behaving ineffectually are caused by environmental events (e.g., annoying people, bad drivers, unreasonable bosses). The task of the CBT therapist is to dissuade the client of the A-C connection and instead illustrate the importance of the mediating effects of one's belief system in understanding how we react to the world around us (the "B-C" connection). Confrontational approaches are typically avoided; therapists do not humiliate (overtly or covertly) clients for the content of their belief system, and they do not issue ultimatums along the lines of "change or else," given the tendency of such approaches to encourage resistance and defensiveness on the part of the client. Having the client working collaboratively with the therapist (whether individually or in a group setting) to understand and modify the content of the belief system is seen as a core aspect of improving the safety of women living with an abusive partner (Murphy & Eckhardt, 2005). In addition to cognitive restructuring, CBT interventions also incorporate emotion regulation techniques and relationship skills training in order to allow clients to understand and control abusive behavior in emotion-arousing situations.

CBT became recognized as a viable treatment for abusive men in the 1980s, with a concentration on cognitive restructuring and problem-solving interventions (Dutton, 1986; Feazell, Mayers & Deschner, 1984; Saunders, 1984). CBT for IPV perpetrators was implemented with several goals, one of which was using techniques to encourage men to accept responsibility for abusiveness and develop an appropriate level of control of their lives and behavior. "The issue here is not blame; it is responsibility for one's own actions, and ultimately, responsibility for acting in a way which can build trust, intimacy, and a sense of personal power that is not achieved at the expense of someone else's powerlessness" (Sonkin, Martin & Walker, 1985; p. 145). Self-described CBT programs for IPV perpetrators have continued to develop over the last 20 years and have been widely applied (e.g., Hamberger, 1997; Hamberger & Lohr, 1989; Jennings, 1987; Roberts, 1984; Saunders, 1984; Sonkin et al., 1985; Sonkin & Durphy, 1997; Stosny, 1995; Wexler, 2006). While several programs adhere to what can be considered a "prototypical" CBT approach (e.g., Wexler, 2000; 2006), others are more accurately described as largely didactic psychoeducational programs that have a focus on cognitive content, but spend little time on cognitive process, emotion regulation, and/or relationship skills training. For example, the Duluth model psychoeducational curriculum (Pence & Paymar, 1993) focuses on altering abusers' misogynistic beliefs in order to promote nonviolence and, as a result, is often described by advocates as being an exemplar of the CBT model (Gondolf, 2002).

The net result of this apparently wide adoption of the CBT designa-tion has been a diffusion of meaning about just what is and what is not CBT. Is a program CBT just because it focuses on thoughts and behav-iors, or is there something more essential that underlies this term? In their meta-analysis of the effectiveness of abuser intervention programs, Babcock, Green, and Robie (2004) noted the difficulties they experi-enced in differentiating between studies investigating CBT and Duluth model treatments, given that both models focus on thoughts in order to impact abusive behavior: "To the extent that CBT groups address patriarchal attitudes, and Duluth model groups address the learned and reinforced aspects of violence, any distinction between CBT and Duluth model groups becomes increasingly unclear" (Babcock et al., 2004; p. 1026). Indeed this lack of clarity may underlie why recent meta-analytic reviews report little difference in effectiveness (e.g., partner reports of IPV recidivism) between CBT and Duluth model interven-tions, with these interventions being associated with small to negligible effects on partner and police-reported IPV relative to comparison inter-ventions (Babcock et al., 2004; Feder & Wilson, 2005). However, it is also clear that there is substantial individual variation in these results. A critical task at this point in the evolution of CBT interventions for part-ner-abusive men is to more carefully examine the core components of the CBT model as they relate to IPV, and to confirm that these compo-nents are indeed being addressed by self-described CBT programs.

CBT and the Strengths Perspective

Is CBT congruent with the basic tenets of the strengths approach to intervening with partner-abusive individuals? The answer is a definitive "it depends!" As will be discussed in more detail in subsequent sections of this chapter, CBT interventions appear to fit squarely with the two essential elements of the strengths perspective as defined by Saleebey (1996): "the power of the self to heal and right itself with the help of the environment, and the need for an alliance with the hope that life might really be otherwise" (p. 303). More specifically, CBT programs for IPV perpetrators generally challenge men about the commonly held belief that abusive behavior is beyond their control (Ganley, 1981). This goal is accomplished through basic CBT techniques of self-monitoring (of thoughts, behaviors, and bodily reactions), emotion control, communi-cation education, and role-playing (Russell, 1994). As control is given back to clients for their emotions and behaviors, they can take more responsibility for how they feel and act despite the demands of others and the difficulties of any particular situation (Ellis, 1973). As the abusive client internalizes this renewed sense of self-control, he (or she) is better able to construct and follow a set of personal goals. These goals, when addressed in the context of a respectful therapeutic relationship, and with the enlistment of other social and community supports, can benefit the client as well as the client's close relationships.

However, the CBT approach has the potential to work against the strengths approach, especially when attempted by therapists who may lack the depth of training to understand its more humanistic and client-centered origins (Ellis, 1973). Many therapists new to the CBT approach may naively believe that because the abusive client shows little insight or awareness into his own biased and distorted attitudes, then it is the job of the clinician to forcefully "educate" the client into the cognitive errors of his ways. When this process occurs before the client is ready to question the validity of his own thinking or even to accept the accuracy of the therapist's message, the client is likely to infer that he and the therapist are working on different goals—the client wants to vent about his insurmountable problems with other unreasonable people, yet the therapist wants to change his thinking. When cognitive challenges occur prematurely, clients may resist this information and maintain a defensive stance against the therapist's change attempts. It is just this sort of client-therapist goal incongruence that has been shown to predict attrition from IPV interventions (Brown et al., 2000), which in turn has been shown to predict IPV recidivism (Gondolf, 2004). Thus, the therapist must "switch on" or enable the strengths-based aspects of CBT interventions, a process that relies upon the therapist's capacity to listen to the client's story, to have empathy for the client's point of view, and to implement the right components of the CBT model at the right time (e.g., Lee, Uken & Sebold, 2007). These elements are reviewed in more detail below.

CLINICAL ASSUMPTIONS AND INTERVENTION IMPLICATIONS

In this section, we will review what is known concerning the four basic and defining targets of CBT interventions for IPV perpetrators: cognitive factors, emotion regulation, relationship skills, and the importance of a strong therapeutic alliance. Within each of these CBT targets, we will first provide an overview of the empirical basis for each construct as "deserving" of its role in the CBT model, briefly outline several intervention techniques that illustrate how CBT addresses each target, and then conclude if there is indeed evidence to indicate whether change in the target variable predicts behavior change.

Cognitive Factors: Theory and Evidence

Diverse models of IPV etiology have consistently suggested that certain attitudes, beliefs, and cognitive distortions are implicated at some level in the onset and maintenance of abusive behavior. As a result, a variety of theoretical models and intervention programs that focus on IPV-related cognitive factors claim CBT as their orientation (Gondolf, 2004). As noted above, initial research on the role of cognitive factors in IPV grew out of profeminist theories of domestic violence (e.g., Dobash & Dobash, 1979), which posit that Western society is built upon patriarchy, defined as "a system of social organization that creates and maintains male domination over women" (Sugarman & Frankel, 1996; p. 14). Males are therefore socialized to hold attitudes that justify or support the patriarchal system. These attitudes and resulting behaviors, when combined with patriarchal practices in the legal system, religious institutions, and other social systems, result in the collective maintenance of male domination over women across social domains, including close relationships, marriage, and domestic life. Therefore, this perspective sees abuse-related attitudes as being the result of long-term exposure to a patriarchal society or community, rather than as psychological processes per se. This exposure has instilled a deeply held belief in male privilege and superiority that covertly and overtly sanctions any means necessary to maintain this unequal power arrangement, including the use of coercion and aggressive force: "Men who batter not as abnormal members of society, but as men carrying out a role defined for them by our own culture" (Pence, 1983; p. 252). Mental healthcare providers and proponents of psychological or interactional models of IPV, in turn, have been criticized by feminist scholars for ways in which their theories and interventions disempower women and blame victims for their experiences of abuse (Adams, 1988; Bograd, 1984; Gondolf, 2007).

While the feminist model and the intervention systems that it is has spawned (e.g., the Duluth model; Pence & Paymar, 1993; Kivel, 1998) represent important starting points in the CBT movement, the model's conceptualization of gender-focused cognitive/attitudinal disturbances as they relate to IPV is incomplete for a number of reasons. First, there is little evidence to support the notion that patriarchal attitudes and power-related beliefs represent *specific proximal contributors* to the enactment of IPV (Malik & Lindahl, 1998; Sugarman & Frankel, 1996). Second, partner abuse is quite prevalent in lesbian and gay male relationships, a fact that is difficult to explain if abuse is a purely gender-based system of oppression (Burke & Follingstad, 1999). Third, recent literature reviews indicate that men in treatment for domestic abuse are not more likely than nonabusive men to endorse sexist beliefs in male privilege or regarding women's roles and rights, as indicated by over a dozen case control studies (Dutton & Corvo, 2006; Eckhardt & Dye, 2000; Sugarman & Frankel, 1996). Unfortunately, such beliefs are characteristic of a great many men across many societies; however, they do not appear to be unique or specific risk factors for IPV perpetration. Finally, and perhaps most importantly from the standpoint of CBT-related cognitive risk factors for IPV, the feminist model says nothing about the cognitive processes that lead to violence. While much attention is focused on specific types of attitudinal content that are indeed correlated with IPV (e.g., positive attitudes toward violence, needs for power), the model does not adequately specify the operations presumed to underlie a purely gendered analysis of IPV. In other words, while the model tells us *what* abusers are likely to think and provides a post hoc rationale for *why* they may think this way, it says little about *how* these thoughts come into consciousness and *how* this immediate cognitive activity may serve as a predictor of acute episodes of IPV.

A clearer theoretical starting point for the CBT model as applied to IPV emerged from the application of social learning theory to interpersonal violence, which focuses on process-level interactions of the individual with the broader social and interpersonal context (Bandura, 1973). The social learning approach predicts that aggressive behaviors are acquired through basic principles of learning (i.e., classical conditioning, operant conditioning, observational learning), and as a result of these direct and vicarious learning experiences, violent individuals' processing of social information is systematically biased toward negative assumptions of others' behavior and positive associations regarding the acceptability and value of aggressive behaviors (Dodge, 1991). Long-standing cognitive distortions further degrade the individual's ability to self-regulate their emotional responses to interpersonal conflict and impair the development of secure attachments with romantic partners (Dutton, Saunders, Starzomski & Bartholomew, 1994). Together, these deficits result in a deficient set of basic relationship skills that favor the use of controlling and abusive behaviors, including belligerent and coercive communication patterns (Jacobson et al., 1994). Thus, a central difference between the social learning and feminist accounts of how cognitive variables relate to IPV is that the social learning model addresses both cognitive content and cognitive processes presumed to be related to IPV, whereas the feminist account focuses almost entirely on biased cognitive content.

Over the last 20 years, researchers have refined the social learning approach in terms of understanding and assessing cognitive mechanisms that may be involved in IPV, again with an eye toward a broader understanding of both cognitive content and process that may translate into CBT intervention advancements. Holtzworth-Munroe (1992) outlined a model of social skill deficits that outlines a sequence of social information-processing stages that can result in marital aggression. During the first stage, *Decoding*, social stimuli are attended to, encoded, and interpreted. However, "various cognitive deficits including unrealistic expectations, faulty attributions, and irrational beliefs could result in the misconstrual of social stimuli," (Holtzworth-Munroe, 1992; p. 607). Thus, specific information-processing distortions, such as Ellis' (1994) irrational beliefs, may distort the significance of incoming stimuli or result in other cognitive products, such as faulty attributions, that may otherwise disrupt accurate, goal-congruent processing of social stimuli. During the second *Decision Making* stage, the individual is confronted with the task of strategically constructing a number of potential responses to manage the demands of the specific situation. After the most appropriate response is selected, the individual decides if there is sufficient skill to enact that response, as well as the response's likely positive and negative consequences. Finally, the third stage describes response *Enactment*, during which the selected response is put into action and its impact is monitored.

Ample evidence supports this model. Briefly, relative to nonviolent males, IPV perpetrators exhibit (a) decoding, interpretation, and hostile attribution biases on questionnaire measures (Fincham et al., 1997) and during imagined conflict scenarios (Eckhardt, Barbour & Davison, 1998; Eckhardt & Jamison, 2002; Holtzworth-Munroe & Hutchinson, 1993); (b) less competent decision making (i.e., greater generation of aggressive response options) on questionnaires (Field, Caetano & Nelson, 2004; Sugarman & Frankel, 1996) and during conflict simulations (Anglin & Holtzworth-Munroe, 1997; Barbour, Eckhardt, Davison &

Kassinove, 1998; Jacobson et al., 1994); and (c) positive evaluations of violence in close relationships (Kaufman-Kantor & Straus, 1990). A number of more detailed review papers that catalog the attitudes and cognitions that differentiate abusive from nonabusive individuals are available (Eckhardt & Dye, 2000; Holtzworth-Munroe, 2000; Murphy & Eckhardt, 2005; Stith et al., 2004).

The social information processing model is a useful mechanism for understanding both the cognitive content and processes associated with IPV. A broad set of common themes apparent in abuser thinking can be deductively derived from this model, which can be seen in Exhibit 6.1.

These themes are drawn from clinical experience and the published literature on abuser attributions, attitudes, and beliefs (Murphy & Eckhardt, 2005). The list is comprised of what can be called *implicit theories* (in bold), as well as their component cognitive distortions commonly held by IPV perpetrators. According to the implicit theory model, which emerged from research on cognitive risk factors for sexual assault (e.g., Polaschek & Ward, 2002), cognitive distortions emerge from individuals' underlying causal theories about the nature of their world, themselves, and their victims. Implicit theories function like scientific theories—they are used to explain events and others' behavior, to make predictions, and to establish empirical regularities about important aspects of the individual's world. Information that supports the implicit theory is retained (e.g., "Women like to be abused"), and disconfirming evidence (e.g., arrest, loss of family and freedom) is ignored or reinterpreted in order to fit the underlying theory (e.g., the system is biased against me). Individual cognitive distortions tend to cluster together in related thematic networks, which provide something akin to a *script* that helps the individual understand and enact an action plan to manage a particular event. As noted by Polaschek and Ward (2000), the implicit theory perspective cuts across theoretical divisions in the violence field. By explicitly addressing the interrelations among diverse types of cognitive content exhibited by violent offenders, better theoretical integration of differing theoretical perspectives is possible, such as feminist proposals about the role of traditional gender-role stereotypes, the role of trauma exposure as it relates to maladaptive attachment themes, and social learning models of the cognitive and emotional consequences of witnessing interparental abuse.

The implicit theory approach may explain why IPV offenders' cognitive activity often seems like little more than shallow minimization and denial. Indeed, the degree to which abusers will practically bend

Exhibit 6.1

SPOUSE-SPECIFIC:

SHE'S IRRATIONAL

- She's inadequate
- She's crazy
- She just wants to bust my balls
- She disrespects me
- She wants to control me

VIOLENCE IS APPROPRIATE

- Sometimes you gotta stick up for yourself. Some people just need a good ass-kicking
- What men do to keep their women in line is a private matter
- It's OK for a man to be violent
- As long as no one gets really hurt, hitting a partner can actually do them some good

SHE GOT WHAT WAS COMING

- She made me do it
- If she starts it then I'm going to finish it
- She just needed to shut up
- She knows how I am/She should know better
- She gave me a good reason
- She got what she deserved
- She could have prevented it

NEED FOR CONTROL

- Never show weakness
- What I say goes
- It's my way or the highway
- If you cross me, you'll pay for it
- I'm no pussy
- Nobody walks all over me
- If you don't like it, then get out

GENERAL:

WOMEN CAN'T BE TRUSTED

- Women are deceitful
- Women like to laugh at men
- If you let them, women like to take advantage of men
- Women think they're so superior
- A woman should know her place

LOW FRUSTRATION TOLERANCE

- She made me mad and I just lost it
- I can't take any more of her crap
- I tried everything but she wouldn't leave me alone/ shut up
- I just got so pissed
- I can't control myself when I'm really pissed
- I just hit my breaking point
- It was more than I could handle
- I couldn't take it any more

over backwards to deny the incident, minimize any injury-related consequences, and blame the event on the actions of the partner is often remarkable. There is typically a fundamental assumption that the perpetrator's denial is motivated and purposeful, designed to manipulate others, and, if unchallenged, is predictive of future violence risk: "He has constructed elaborate walls to avoid an honest self-examination" (Pence & Paymar, 1993, p. 118). But perhaps there are other interpretations of this tendency toward denial. For every abuser who consciously minimizes his abusive actions, there are just as many whose minimization and denial represent either lack of access to alternate cognitive-behavioral *scripts*, or a particularly entrenched set of interconnected beliefs that support a basic aggressogenic implicit theory. The offender who was exposed to abusive trauma in childhood, who was raised in a "might makes right" household, and who may have spent a lifetime learning the behavioral contingencies of a male status-conscious community will predictably exhibit little evidence of remorse or insight into the impact the abusive behaviors he directed toward a female partner. Rather than conceptualizing this as little more than deliberate denial and minimization (deserving of direct confrontation), it may also be the case that this information processing style reflects this particular individual's lifetime of self and social understanding; it is the only *script* this offender has available for use in his daily life (Huesmann. 1988). As such, the counselor must understand that there is unlikely to be a different, more appropriate script that the offender is simply choosing to ignore; this alternative *script* needs to be created as a function of the intervention. It is this latter insight that forms the basis of the CBT intervention approach with violent individuals.

Thus, the social learning and social information processing approaches make the prediction that IPV perpetrators will exhibit distortions in cognitive processing, as well as biased cognitive content relative to nonabusive males. For the most part, the data support this assumption. The final issue concerns whether there is any clear theoretical reason to assume that cognitive distortions are *functionally* related to the onset of IPV. In a recent CBT-oriented analysis of interpersonal violence, Beck (1999) outlined a cognitive vulnerability approach that focuses on the construct of "primal thinking." According to this perspective, adverse childhood experiences produce a tendency to experience situations egocentrically. Individuals with this frame may overinterpret situations in terms of their own self-interest, especially in regard to a preoccupation with perceived present and past injustices, and perceived threats to the self. This tendency of the aggressive individual to overperceive others' behaviors as unjust and deliberate attempts to block his/her goals in a personally threatening manner sets the stage for the individual to take corrective actions, such as punishing acts of aggressive behavior. This process is reinforced by the cognitive distortions identified above, which make the aggressive individual prone to notice negative events as indicative of loss and a threat to the self, leading to the experience of distress and the conclusion that the event is an unjustified violation of a strongly held personal rule. This awareness of a rule violation activates memories of prior violations in similar contexts, which may further intensify affective arousal. When the sense of threat is exaggerated and important details of these encounters are omitted from further processing, the meanings derived tend to be overly personalized and the conclusions excessively broad (e.g., "she's always trying to control me;" "her disrespect will be severely punished"). These immediate categorizations typically lead to interpersonal imperatives (e.g., demandingness), which signify the rules that others should follow, or how the individual expects to be treated in interpersonal contexts ("she needs to leave me alone"). The quality and degree of anger eventually experienced is generated by the final meaning placed on the event by the perceiver, which then sets the stage for the relative acceptability of a violent response.

Cognitive Factors: Clinical Implications

With partner-violent individuals, the cognitive focus is on challenging attitudes and beliefs that promote and maintain abusive behavior, such as negatively biased attributions of blame regarding partner behaviors and positive endorsement of aggression as a means of coping with relationship conflict. The CBT model emphasizes a social learning-based and, from a strengths perspective, optimistic hypothesis that even deeply ingrained attitudes and assumptions about the self and relationship partners can be altered in ways that are goal-promoting and therapeutic. As discussed later in this chapter, it is crucial that before any cognitive restructuring work begin, the therapist clearly articulates that the perpetrator is a client who is a fully active partner in the therapeutic process, rather than a "criminal" mandated to attend a "class." As such, the client is involved in shaping the overall goals of treatment and in setting the priorities for each treatment session. The CBT counselor works with the client in reviewing self-monitoring situations, assessing thoughts and behaviors that occurred in conflict situations, and disputing and modifying dysfunctional patterns of cognition and action.

Importantly, partner-abusive clients often respond quite positively to the empowering message inherent in the CBT model. The CBT approach sends a strong message to the client that is closely aligned with the basic tenets of the strengths approach, and suggests that thought and action are NOT set in stone because of early experiences, are not shameful examples of patriarchal socialization that must be reprogrammed, and are not outside the client's control. Instead, clients learn that they can control the content of their thinking, they can dispute attitudes that are automatically generated but unwanted or unhelpful, and they can positively influence their emotional states by examining and altering maladaptive thought patterns. Clients also learn that personal and relationship goals can be better fulfilled by improving their cognitive and emotional regulation skills.

Following the initial work of Beck and colleagues, the primary cognitive techniques that comprise CBT stem from the principles of guided discovery and collaborative empiricism (Beck et al., 1979). Guided discovery refers to the ways in which the therapist helps the client to unravel experiences, events, and personal history in order to discover themes running through the client's beliefs and misperceptions. This process follows the "downward arrow" technique of uncovering ever deeper layers of problematic thinking, beginning with immediate cognitive content that flashes through consciousness (e.g., "I need to teach her a lesson"), and moving toward more pervasive cognitive biases at the boundary of conscious awareness (e.g., "she's always taking advantage of me"). The process then moves toward underlying generalized assumptions (e.g., "women cannot be trusted"), and finally to basic schemas regarding the self, world, and others (e.g., "I am alone in the world and people will screw me over if I let them") (Beck, 1999). As noted in the previous section, collaborative empiricism refers to the process of the client and counselor working together to gather evidence and test hypotheses derived from the client's social information processing style.

It is also critical for the therapist to communicate the basic A-B-C philosophy that underlies CBT prior to the use of any specific CBT techniques, namely that that as much as the abuser would like to blame his problems on external activating events (A), some of which may be quite aversive, these events by themselves do not cause negative emotional and behavioral consequences (C); it is his beliefs (B) about these events that determines the outcome. This equation typically runs counter to clients' perspectives that unreasonable people are making them get angry and forcing them to act abusively. Self-monitoring greatly facilitates this awareness for many clients. Once the clinician has successfully used clinical interviewing skills and self-monitoring logs to identify and uncover relevant cognitive distortions (for a more detailed discussion of these techniques, see Murphy & Eckhardt, 2005), the process of disputation and cognitive restructuring can begin. It is worth noting that although the terms "disputation" and "restructuring" imply a change process whereby an actively verbal clinician enacts changes in a passive client, the actual process of CBT is very different from this inference. Instead, clients must persuade themselves to change a specific belief or assumption, with the therapist available for consultation and deductive interpretation. The cognitive change process is of necessity *client-directed*, as it requires generalization to their specific life situations.

The CBT clinician, having explained the rationale of the CBT approach and established a strong working bond with the client, is now ready to collaborate with the client on testing and disputing cognitive errors. There are four general types of cognitive challenge: logical, empirical, heuristic, and subversive (DiGiuseppe, 1991), and these are described in order below. The first type of cognitive disputing tactic occurs when the client realizes that a specific thought or belief is not logical, or that it involves some assumption or leap in logic that should not be made (*"How does it follow that because you don't like it when she asks you to do things around the house, that when she does so she is being unreasonable?"*). The second type of cognitive challenge, the empirical challenge, involves the realization that a belief or assumption is simply not in line with the events of one's life, and that therefore there is a more accurate way to conceptualize events (*"Is there any evidence that simply because you don't like something that it will therefore never happen?"*). The third type, the heuristic cognitive challenge, involves the realization that a belief is not useful or functional (regardless of its accuracy), and that an alternative view would be more helpful in achieving personal goals (*"How did it help you to make this law stating that she can never talk about things you don't like—how did that work out for you?"*). The fourth type of cognitive challenge, the subversive challenge, occurs when the client realizes that a specific thought, assumption, or belief is simply not necessary in the first place. Regardless of whether the thought is logical, realistic, or accurate, it is simply not worth the time or effort to worry about it—it just doesn't matter (*"In the whole scheme of things, how critical was it for you to win this battle?"*). Experience suggests that early in the intervention process, heuristic challenges are more effective than the other types, as this approach does not involve disputing the "facts of the case," only whether this particular belief was helpful in achieving a goal. As the client begins to see that not all of his attitudes and beliefs are particularly helpful, he is likely to be more conducive to the other cognitive challenges that involve logical, empirical, and subversive challenges (Murphy & Eckhardt, 2005). As the client and clinician become more comfortable with the disputation process, it is important for this process to extend to deeper-level implicit theories. Such cognitive activity is likely to reveal more strongly biased generalizations centered around gender themes (how women "always" or "never" are), the value of violence (people get what they deserve), relationship assumptions (who is "in charge"), and remnants of earlier attachment processes (themes of loss, vulnerability, and suspicion of others' motives) (Dutton, 2007; Murphy & Eckhardt, 2005).

As alternate attributions are discussed, evaluated, and disputed (if necessary), the therapist must initiate the processes needed for these more adaptive and realistic attributions to generalize to the client's life outside the therapy room. If self-monitoring logs are being used, the therapist can insert a column specifically labeled as "alternate beliefs" in order to encourage the client to practice thinking of alternate reasons for others' behavior. Log entries can be evaluated and/or disputed in the following group or individual session. It is also important for the client and therapist to develop coping dialogues that can be used during role-play exercises, which simulate common situations of difficulty for the client. It simply is not enough to identify and dispute irrational ideas, and it is not always the case that a discussion of more rational alternative beliefs leads to these cognitions being automatically inserted into the client's cognitive frame. Instead, it is important to construct a positive, strengths-based coping dialogue that the client can rehearse and activate when needed. After the client contemplates things that he could be thinking in order to cope with a difficult situation, the therapist can then role model an internal coping dialogue, verbalizing the statements for the client. Next, the client is asked to do the same in session, and then finally outside of the session in *in vivo* practice with increasingly difficult situations.

These coping dialogues need to be extensively rehearsed and modified if they are to become the client's preferred and automatic manner of responding to conflict. One way to do this is to construct various behavioral experiments wherein clients can test the potential effectiveness of newly constructed beliefs in their daily lives. This process is especially helpful when clients don't readily accept that an alternate attitude will be particularly useful. Thus, the client who has long believed that coercion and threats are the only way to get what he wants from difficult people may not completely buy into the notion that compromise and negotiation may also be effective. As the new coping script is developed, the client is asked to approach the next difficult situation with this alternate belief model in place and to bring back "evidence" concerning the effectiveness of this belief system. Typically, the client will report that the new way of thinking wasn't that useful because the situation was still difficult. Here, the therapist has an excellent opportunity to return to the A-B-C model and illustrate that it will always be the case that people will be difficult and situations problematic, but that by maintaining self-control and restraint, he has vastly improved his outcomes.

These are but a few commonly used techniques that specifically target cognitive processes related to IPV. Overall, CBT may help men "take responsibility for what happens in their lives and see how they may set themselves up for negative, as well as positive, events" (Sonkin et al., 1985, p. 91). The interested reader is encouraged to compile the excellent clinical suggestions offered by contributors to the current volume, as well as other cognitive therapy techniques, to bolster the ability to impart meaningful change not only to the client's IPV-related beliefs, but to his general philosophy of life as well (Beck, 1999; Dutton, 2007; Dutton & Sonkin, 2003; Ellis, 1992; Hamberger, 1997; Murphy & Eckhardt, 2005; Stosny, 1995; Wexler, 2000).

Is there Evidence that Changing Cognitions in Partner Violence Interventions Specifically Predicts Nonviolent Outcomes? Surprisingly, the answer is no. To date, there is no published research that clearly demonstrates that cognitive change among IPV perpetrators during the course of an intervention independently predicts either nonviolent change or some other clinically meaningful outcome. That is a disappointing state of affairs. Given that practically all commonly implemented IPV intervention programs consider themselves CBT in orientation, it is alarming that we have no direct evidence that having clients make cognitive changes directly impacts abusive behavior *separate* from the influence of other components of the intervention, or other factors associated with the sample. The available research on this topic involves single-sample pre-post designs, wherein a sample of men are given a paper-and-pencil measure of cognitive distortions early in the program and then at the end of the program. Many studies simply report whether men who successfully complete the program reported improvements in their attitudes and beliefs concerning women, relationships, and related factors (they do!) (e.g., Craig et al., 2006; Schmidt et al., 2007). In other reports, recidivists are compared to nonrecidivists (or completers compared to dropouts) and the findings typically indicate that men who complete the program and remain nonviolent show fewer cognitive distortions than those who drop out of the program and/or reoffend against a partner (Gondolf, 2000; Tutty, Bidgood, Rothery & Bidgood, 2001). Of course there are many problems with these studies, in that the single-sample/no control group design makes it impossible to rule out other extra-treatment reasons for cognitive change over the course of the intervention. Further, the lack of demonstration that cognitive change, rather than a myriad of other variables, actually mediated the relationship between the intervention and the outcome is another problem. Such a finding is best obtained when using suitable comparison groups (to address sample or selection effects), more careful assessment of cognition as it relates to program components, and specific mediation analyses which directly test the effects of a given intervention component relative to other factors on the outcomes of interest. Thus, while it would seem logical to target faulty attitudes and beliefs in interventions for abuse perpetrators, the jury is still out as to whether such changes indeed influence IPV-related outcomes.

REGULATION OF NEGATIVE EMOTIONS: THEORY AND EVIDENCE

One of the core assumptions of the CBT model is that cognitive disturbances intensify the experience of negative emotions and disrupt how these emotions are expressed interpersonally. Decades of theoretical (Ellis, 1962) and empirical (Haaga, 1991) work supports this general proposition, and we think it is fair to say that the cognitively focused interventions spawned from these writings (e.g., Beck et al., 1979) have resulted in some of the most important and beneficial clinical advancements in the history of psychotherapeutic treatments for emotional problems (e.g., Nathan & Gorman, 2007). Nevertheless, much controversy exists within elements of the IPV field concerning the relevance of emotional variables in explaining and treating IPV. Indeed, while one of the authors (C.E.) was giving a recent talk to a group of battered women's advocates and intervention program workers about risk factors for male-to-female IPV, he was met with a chorus of boo's and rather nasty comments from the audience the moment he concluded that the data supported emotional problems and psychopathology as important risk factors for IPV. Why the negative reaction? Generally, there appears to be a general concern among many battered women's advocates and program staff that invoking internal constructs such as psychopathology or emotional problems will lead to a "medical model" approach to IPV that may lead to a focus away from what traditionally have been viewed as the root causes of violence (e.g., community supports which overtly or covertly condone abusive behavior and men's lack of accountability and responsibility). While it would indeed be counterproductive to see the causes of IPV as resting solely with the psychological disturbances of the male perpetrator, it seems similarly unproductive to simply dismiss such factors when ample empirical evidence exists to substantiate these variables as legitimate risk factors.

In the context of IPV, the negative emotion that has garnered the most attention (favorable and not) is *anger*. The role of anger arousal in intimate partner violence (IPV) seems obvious, for it is often assumed that anger and aggression are "inextricably, biologically linked," (Tavris, 1989, p. 24), and one can easily imagine a scenario wherein an abusive male becomes intensely angry and assaults his female partner. From an empirical standpoint, recent quantitative reviews (Norlander & Eckhardt, 2005; Schumacher, Feldbau-Kohn, Slep & Heyman, 2001) have indicated that disturbances in how anger is experienced and expressed distinguish between partner-violent and nonviolent men (effect size: d = +.50). Despite this support, there are few areas more controversial within areas of domestic violence research and advocacy than the issue of anger and IPV. For example, Gondolf (2002; Gondolf & Russell, 1986) has steadfastly maintained that focusing on anger as a cause of IPV or as a legitimate target for batterer intervention programs at best misses the "actual" causes of IPV, and at worst puts women at risk for future acts of aggression. Echoing these concerns, a number of state domestic violence coalitions have issues standards that explicitly outlaw anger-control treatments or else strongly discourage their use (e.g., Austin & Dankwort, 1999). The net result of this stance has not only been a resistance toward anger-based interventions, but a steadfast dismissal of anger as a potential risk factor for IPV. Ultimately, however, all of these concerns must be answered empirically rather than ideologically. So, is there a relationship between anger arousal and IPV?

The answer is yes, although the relationship is moderate in strength. Diverse models of interpersonal violence have suggested that aggressive behavior during provocation can, in part, be predicted by the perpetrator's level of dispositional anger (Anderson & Bushman, 2002; Beck, 1999; Berkowitz, 1993; 2008). Studies using self-report questionnaires consistently indicate that partner-violent males show elevated trait anger, hostility, increased tendency to express anger outwardly, and decreased anger control (Eckhardt, Barbour & Stuart, 1997; Norlander & Eckhardt, 2005). In addition, anger problems are directly related to more severe and frequent perpetration of IPV (Holtzworth et al., 2000). In observational research examining sequential patterns of couple interaction, violent couples demonstrate increased usage of "destructive" forms of anger, involving expressions of contempt, disgust, and belligerence (e.g., Jacobson et al., 1994). Prior research on anger in subtypes of partner-violent men suggests that some, although not all, partner-abusive men exhibit symptoms of excessive and dysregulated anger (e.g., Chase, O'Leary & Heyman, 2001; Dutton, 1988; Hershorn & Rosenbaum, 1991; Saunders, 1992; Holtzworth-Munroe & Stuart, 1994; Waltz, Babcock, Jacobson & Gottman, 2000). Most notably, Holtzworth-Munroe and colleagues (2000) found that the two most severe subtypes of partner-violent men (labeled Generally Violent/Antisocial and Borderline/Emotionally Dysregulated) had significantly higher anger levels than less severe subtypes. Other research suggests that anger interacts with alcohol intoxication to increase the likelihood of IPV during relationship conflicts (Eckhardt, 2007). Finally, recent findings using forensic samples of IPV perpetrators suggest that approximately 20–25% of partner-abusive men judicially mandated to attend batterer intervention programs have clinically significant problems with anger experience and expression (Eckhardt, Samper & Murphy, 2008); and that abusers with problematic anger are less likely to complete such programs and more likely to reassault female partners (Murphy, Taft & Eckhardt, 2007).

But there are inconsistencies as well. Several studies using self-report questionnaires of anger and hostility have not found differences between partner-violent and nonviolent males (see Norlander & Eckhardt, 2005). In addition, researchers using observational methods have typically found that direct statements of anger (e.g., "I'm really mad at you") do not reliably differentiate violent from nonviolent couples (Barbour et al., 1998; Gottman et al., 1995). Thus, while the accumulated data indicate that IPV perpetrators show dysfunctional levels of trait anger and anger-control relative to nonviolent males, even after controlling for relationship distress, and that anger problems portend risk for treatment attrition and criminal recidivism, it is unlikely that partner-violent males can be differentiated from their nonviolent counterparts *solely* on the basis of anger problems; indeed, batterers constitute a heterogeneous group of individuals (e.g., Holtzworth-Munroe & Stuart, 1994) who act abusively as a function of a diverse array of causes and situations (e.g., Babcock et al., 2004). Thus, rather than assuming that anger is *always* or *never* involved in IPV, it is more important to consider *whether* and *for whom* specific patterns of anger problems may be factors deserving of clinical attention (Murphy, Taft & Eckhardt, 2007). From this perspective, the conclusions are straightforward: (1) anger problems differentiate abusive from nonabusive males and are linearly related to IPV severity; (2) a sizeable proportion of IPV perpetrators in the criminal justice system (between 1/4 and 1/3 present with severe anger problems, and (3) perpetrators with anger problems present with a variety of clinical disturbances that will complicate the intervention process (Eckhardt et al., 2008; Murphy et al., 2007; Norlander & Eckhardt, 2005). These conclusions point to the relevance of a CBT approach in intervention programming for partner-abusive males.

NEGATIVE EMOTIONS: CLINICAL IMPLICATIONS

While there is a general acceptance of emotion-related interventions for violent offenders in the general clinical (Del Vecchio & O'Leary, 2004) and offender rehabilitation literatures (e.g., Howells & Day, 2006; McMurran & Gilchrist, 2008), there is very little enthusiasm within the IPV field for applying emotional regulation techniques with IPV perpetrators. Part of this resistance reflects concerns about the extension of a *medical model* approach into intervention programs and what this may imply about etiology. That is, if anger-control interventions work for IPV perpetrators, then this might suggest that anger-related factors may indeed be involved in the etiology of IPV; as noted above, such a conclusion is not exactly a popular one among a large sector of the grassroots advocacy community. Echoing these suspicions, Gondolf (Gondolf, 2002; Gondolf & Russell, 1986) suggested that *anger management* interventions: 1) imply that the victim is to blame; 2) do not account for abuse meant to exert power and control; 3) perpetuate the batterer's denial; 4) may put the female partner at further risk for violence; 5) give communities a reason to shun collective responsibility for IPV; and

6) give perpetrators new tools to coerce and control women. These sentiments are reflected by many advocates for battered women and state domestic violence coalitions (see Healey, Smith & O'Sullivan, 1998), who have lobbied effectively against the use of anger-control treatments for men mandated to attend batterer intervention programs (BIPs). However, as noted by Maiuro, Hager, Lin, and Olson (2002), state standards governing BIP content typically lack *any* empirical justification, calling into question the basis for the ban on anger-control interventions. Indeed, there is little cause for confidence at this point concerning what interventions should and should not be attempted with partner-violent males, given the results of recent literature reviews showing high rates of attrition (Daly & Pelowski, 2000) and small preventive effects on future IPV (Babcock et al., 2004) among traditional batterer intervention programs.

Some forms of anger-focused intervention, such as anger management, use relaxation and self-monitoring techniques to lessen anger arousal, and are based on the notion that offenders are at higher risk for engaging in impulsive and dangerous behaviors during states of intense anger and rage than when they are not in such states. Other interventions are more centrally focused on anger as a clinically distinct phenomenon, and require the establishment of a therapeutic relationship in order to provide a context for change. As such, anger treatment (rather than anger management) focuses on personality processes that underlie dysfunctional anger, cognitive correlates and action tendencies influenced by anger, and general self-regulation deficits common among angry clients (Howells & Day, 2006; Novaco, Ramm & Black, 2000). Thus, learning to identify, dispute, and replace faulty cognitions goes a long way toward producing more adaptive and prosocial emotions and behaviors. The use of role-play methods gives the client a chance to practice newly developed cognitive coping skills, which can then be practiced further in the context of guided anger exposure sessions and *in vivo* behavioral experiments (see Kassinove & Tafrate, 2002, for more discussion of these techniques with angry clients).

Additional techniques are also integral to the emotion regulation components of CBT. Relaxation techniques are commonly used to help clients gain mastery over anger arousal (Wexler, 2000). An extensive body of literature with dysfunctionally angry adults indicates that relative to comparison conditions, individuals receiving relaxation-based interventions report significantly less intense state and trait anger, and fewer negative outcomes associated with anger arousal, such as violence and substance use (Beck & Fernandez, 1998; Deffenbacher, Oetting, Huff & Thwaites, 1995; Deffenbacher & Stark, 1992; DiGiuseppe & Tafrate, 2003; Tafrate, 1995). These techniques range from using progressive muscle relaxation (Bernstein & Borkovec, 1973) to combined cognitive-relaxation methods (Deffenbacher, Thwaites, Wallace & Oetting, 1994). Regardless, the key element to the use of relaxation techniques is rooted in the strengths approach: the client has the ability to master his emotions and can remain focused and goal-directed even in the face of situational adversity and interpersonal conflict. Relaxation is not a cure-all, and it cannot be expected to address the myriad other cognitive and relational problems that the IPV perpetrator will bring to treatment, but when combined with other cognitive techniques (for an example, see Kassinove & Tafrate, 2002) it is exceptionally useful for those clients whose level of anger arousal is extreme, or whose level of emotional arousal consistently leads to antisocial or abusive behavior. As indicated in our prior research (Eckhardt et al., 2008; Murphy et al., 2007), roughly between 1/4 and 1/3 of clients commencing for an abuser intervention program would be expected to show problems deserving of this target of CBT treatment.

A more recent development that has garnered much clinical and research attention is the relevance of acceptance and commitment therapies (ACT) for clients with anger-related problems (Eifert, McKay & Forsyth, 2006). Briefly, the ACT approach teaches clients to accept and learn to live with emotional pain, such as anger and rage, and to develop a commitment to stick to one's core values and personal goals even if they are prone to feel such pain. During episodes of intense anger, the client is encouraged to say "I'm having the thought that I'm angry," and to avoid reifying the experience into something that must be overcome before anything else of worth or value can be attained. By learning to accept the experience, the client becomes more focused on goal achievement and living a value-conscious life. In the context of IPV, this might involve instructing abusive clients to learn to live with anger and frustration, to label it with language and identify it as a mere thought, and to stay committed to remaining nonviolent even with this pain. Importantly, the ACT model de-emphasizes the identification, evaluation, and disputation of cognitive distortions (Hayes, Strosahl & Wilson, 1999), because this singular focus on the cognitive underpinnings of anger (e.g., What am I telling myself about this event? Do I have evidence that she is acting this way for that reason?) may actually make the client more focused on his anger, rather than focused on behaving effectively. While this proposition has yet to be confirmed, the ACT approach may have potential from a strengths perspective, in that its message is solely focused on allowing the client to commit to his values and goals, no matter what internal processes are occurring from moment to moment. More research and clinical experimentation is needed to evaluate the potential relevance of ACT-based techniques for interventions with partner-abusive clientele.

Is there Evidence that Changing Negative Emotions Such as Anger in Partner Violence Interventions Specifically Predicts Nonviolent Outcomes? No. Overall, there have been relatively few controlled studies of CBT interventions for partner-abuse perpetrators (for a review and commentary, see Wathen & MacMillan, 2004), and no published research exists concerning whether anger or emotion-focused techniques *specifically* reduce IPV risk. Again, this state of affairs is surprising and disappointing, especially in the context of the often vehement pronouncements against the usage of anger-focused interventions for IPV perpetrators (Adams, 1988; Gondolf, 2002), for one would assume that such negative evaluations would be based on actual evidence that would support such a position. Important research needs to be conducted to investigate whether interventions that have an emotion-regulation component are more effective relative to standard interventions without such a component. In addition, work needs to be done to examine whether there is a client-treatment matching effect with anger-focused interventions; perhaps CBT interventions with an anger focus become the intervention of choice for perpetrators with emotion regulation difficulties (Eckhardt et al., 2008; Murphy et al., 2007).

INTERPERSONAL SKILLS: THEORY AND EVIDENCE

Prior reviews of risk factors for IPV have concluded that the context of IPV is indeed the relationship—violent couples also tend to be very distressed and unhappy couples (Dobash & Dobash, 1979; Schumacher et al., 2001). But does relationship distress lead to IPV, or does violence in the relationship lead to other relationship problems? In a 4-year prospective study, Rogge and Bradbury (1999) reported that communication problems (but not violence) predicted relationship distress over the 4-year period; the presence of violence in the relationship uniquely predicted relationship dissolution. Thus, this and other studies (O'Leary et al., 1989) indicate that problematic couple communication patterns are strong determinants of relationship distress, and that lower levels of relationship satisfaction differentiate violent from nonviolent couples. IPV tends to accompany relational distress and verbal arguments (O'Leary, 1999), and is itself a strong predictor of relationship termination. It follows, then, that the many existing strategies for the treatment of relationship dysfunction can be usefully applied to this population. In addition, the available evidence indicates that abusive behavior can play an important role in relationship stability, a fact that may prove crucial in motivating abusive clients to seek treatment, remain in treatment, and change their behavior.

One of the hallmark assumptions of feminist-informed models of CBT is that relationship disturbances of relevance to IPV are largely related to the male's malevolent use of relationship power and control tactics. As noted in a previous section, the central theme of these models is that the patriarchal society in which we live provides an enormously influential and reinforcing context for men to use power and control tactics to subjugate their female partners and promote male privilege. Aggressive manifestations of abuse are but one example of power and control tactics, as men may also utilize psychological or emotional abuse, economic coercion, and restriction of social contacts to intimidate, isolate, and control the partner. Research has not been consistently supportive of the specific links between relationship power and IPV (Malik & Lindahl, 1998). For example, Babcock, Waltz, Jacobson & Gottman (1993) found no relationships between power bases (i.e., education, income, SES) and IPV, and only a modest relation among power-related outcomes (i.e., control over decision making) and IPV. However, violent husbands reported greater pursuit-and-demand tactics during conflict discussions, while wives reported withdrawing or shutting down. This husband-demand/wife-withdraw communication pattern was also reported by Holtzworth-Munroe, Smutzler, and Stuart (1998). Thus, it may be the case that while the power-and-control model provides an important distal context from which to explore violence toward women, the motivations underlying partner-violent acts are usually complex and multidetermined, rather than simple or straightforward expressions of dominance and control.

For example, many abusive clients will automatically reject the notion that they are coercive and power-driven, not typically because of denial or minimization efforts, but because (cognitively) they often view themselves as subject to others' (e.g., their partners') unreasonable demands, against which they are powerless to defend themselves. As program counselors have heard many times, what else was he supposed to do when, after all, she was the one who started it? Was the abuser's narrative objectively accurate? Probably not, but this perception of personal victimization on the part of the abuser is critical, regardless of its veracity, and is in keeping with the implicit assumption that anger and violence are caused by external factors rather than personal responsibility. Functionally, it is often the case that the violence and abuse sometimes leads to partner compliance or other desired outcomes in the short term, resulting in an increased likelihood of an abusive action the next time the partner exhibits the unwanted behavior. However, this strategy typically has long-term negative consequences, as abusive behaviors impair relationship satisfaction, create trauma, confusion, and mistrust on the part of the abused partner, and often presage the eventual dissolution of the relationship. Thus, the cognitive and emotional elements of the perpetrator's experience of victimization and the resulting sense of powerlessness are important targets of intervention in many partner-abuse cases, and also imply the importance of the poor interactional skills that often give rise to conflicts and power struggles.

Discussing the relationship context in which abuse occurs does not mean that victims of IPV are somehow to blame for their own victimization. However, it seems reasonable to suggest that a complete understanding of IPV requires knowledge of the context in which it occurs, and that this context also includes the behavior of both partners (Jacobson, 1994; Murphy & Eckhardt, 2005). Research on the mutual nature of IPV further illustrates the importance of contextual factors in abusive behavior. When one partner has been physically aggressive in a relationship, it is highly likely that the other partner has been physically aggressive as well (Archer, 2000). Therefore, it becomes critical to understand the usual ways that couples with a violent male interact about matters both mundane and serious, and to integrate this information into effective clinical interventions. An important area of research in this regard is based on the analysis of the sequential behavioral patterns associated with IPV. After discussing a typical topic of conflict for 15 minutes in the lab, researchers have found that relative to nonviolent couples, violent couples exhibit more offensive negative behaviors during conflict discussions as well as more reciprocal patterns of negative communication (Berns et al., 1999; Burman et al., 1993; Cordova et al., 1993; Jacobson et al., 1994; Margolin et al., 1988). In particular, violent couples seem to be locked in a pattern of reciprocated belligerence, contempt, disgust, and overt hostility, with both partners responding to the other's negative behavior with similarly negative reactions (Gottman, 1994). This back-and-forth, "negative reciprocity" sequence is longer-lasting and involves more negative behaviors in violent couples than among nonviolent couples. While few differences have been observed on these variables between husbands and wives *within* violent couples, violent males tend not to stop this negative communication pattern even after their wives exhibit fear or try to terminate the conflict. In addition, alcohol appears to worsen this pattern of hostile communication and negative reciprocity (Leonard & Roberts, 1998). These data suggest what has long been observed in clinical settings: Among couples experiencing male-to-female IPV, both partners are likely to be negative, reactive, and locked in a competitive battle to defeat the other. This contextual reality neither absolves the male from his decision to act abusively, nor blames the victim for her victimization.

One of the central conclusions at this point of the narrative is fairly straightforward: IPV perpetrators tend to be unskilled communicators in close relationships. Beyond those data already presented, ample research supports this inference. For example, abusive men tend to exhibit deficits not only in emotional experience (as reviewed above) but also in *emotional expression*. On the research side, we (Barbour et al., 1998; Eckhardt, Jamison & Watts, 2002) have found that during laboratory anger induction, violent males expressed fewer statements reflective of anger and annoyance relative to nonviolent males, even though self-report measures revealed that they indeed felt angrier than nonviolent controls. Instead, partner-violent men appear to "skip over" the affective communication step, and go directly to verbal insults, threats, and other forms of belligerent communication styles, perhaps in an attempt to "win" the interactional battle. Others have found that during imaginary marital conflicts, the coping responses of partner-violent men were significantly less competent than nonviolent men (Holtzworth-Munroe & Anglin, 1991; Holtzworth-Munroe & Smutzler, 1996). These skill deficits appear to reflect generalized problems with social skills, although the deficits are particularly pronounced in the relationship domain, as well as during states of emotional arousal (Anglin & Holtzworth-Munroe, 1997).

Related to these findings is another key relationship skill, assertiveness, or "the ability to express one's feelings or wants, particularly as it relates to refusing requests from others, making requests of others, or initiating contact with others" (Schumacher et al., 2001, p. 328). The research examining general assertiveness among IPV perpetrators is inconsistent, with some data suggesting that IPV men are less assertive, and other data suggesting no differences in general assertiveness between violent and nonviolent males. However, spouse-specific assertiveness problems are more consistently associated with IPV, with two studies showing that IPV perpetrators exhibit lower spouse-specific assertiveness than nonviolent men in discordant relationships (Dutton & Strachan, 1987; Rosenbaum & O'Leary, 1981), and one study showing a difference between partner-violent and martially satisfied nonviolent groups (O'Leary & Curley, 1986). Clinical experience suggests that many abusive individuals are likely to have immense difficulty making assertive requests of their partners, and easily fall back upon well-learned behavioral patterns that tend toward abuse and coercion.

Interpersonal Skills: Clinical Implications. As noted elsewhere (Murphy & Eckhardt, 2005), it would seem obvious that partner-abusive clients would be motivated to fix what's not working, to alter those thought, emotion, and action patterns that have gotten them to this point: in trouble with the law, on the outs with their relationship partners, and in danger of losing their freedom as well as their families. But it is only after clients are ready to accept some responsibility for their abusive actions, to make a commitment to monitor and challenge abuse-promoting thoughts, and make concerted efforts to stay in emotional control that they are ready to change their actual relationship behaviors. And for many clients, this step is the most difficult. They often have not given thought to their actions in relationship situations as being comprised of "skills," a term which implies behaviors that need to be learned, shaped, and practiced. Instead, clients often have the belief that "this is just the way I am," or that they had no choice in acting the way they did. Many clients report having very poor role models in the context of basic relationship behaviors, and there is often a sense of helplessness about what one's options are in difficult relationship situations, i.e., "What else was I supposed to do when she laughed at me?" Though some in the field see this perspective as yet another example of perpetrators' tendency to minimize and deny their abusiveness, it is at least as plausible to assume something more simple and straightforward that follows from the social learning model: Numerous, if not most, abusive individuals have a deficient repertoire of relationship-specific behavioral skills.

In the context of CBT interventions for abusive clients, treatment typically focuses on active listening, emotional expression, and negotiation/compromise. For each of these skills, the counselor or therapist must first establish a context for change to occur; most men, regardless of their abuse history, are not ready to make wholesale changes to the way they interact with their female partners simply because a therapist tells them to do so. Rather, the therapist needs to develop a basic set of strategies for imparting relationship skills to abusive clients using a basic set of steps common to general CBT for problem behaviors: provide information about the skill ("consider this . . ."), establish a positive mindset about the skill ("Here's how things improve if you could do this. . . ."), common situations that involve the skill ("Here's when you do this . . ."), role-playing exercises ("Let's practice this together . . ."), and generalization ("Let's see how we can use this in other situations . . ."). In essence, training is designed to help the client understand what the skill is, when to use it, and how it is done (Murphy & Eckhardt, 2005).

Partner-abusive clients have massive difficulty listening to what their partners are trying to communicate, as their intense negative emotions, conflict-escalating self-talk, and tendency to see communication as conflict impedes accurate understanding of what the partner is saying. Simply put, a great deal of partner abuse can be prevented if abusive clients learn to listen effectively while modulating emotional reactivity. This supposition is supported by recent research indicating that listening skills, as rated by group facilitators, were the most powerful protective factor in predicting partner aggression outcomes in a teen dating violence prevention program (Wolfe et al., 2003). While communication in close relationships consists of a speaker and a listener, with each role defined by a distinct set of skills, marital therapists have long noted that the most efficient way to improve communication is to primarily work on listening skills (Jacobson & Margolin, 1979). This is not the typical focus of abuse perpetrators, who are more likely to describe communication problems in terms of the need for more self-expression so that the partner will better understand the problem, rather than the need to better understand the partner.

Thus, the major step in encouraging better listening is to point out the nonverbal cues that convey disdain for the partner, including dismissive responses to what is being said, or signs of an impulsive need to respond (e.g., eye rolling, head shaking, smiling, averting gaze to another stimulus, interrupting, etc.). Conversely, nonverbal behaviors that convey active listening include turning to face the speaker, making eye contact, and displaying facial expressions consistent with interest and concern. Fairly basic instructions are often needed, as many abusive clients need explicit instruction to mute the television, turn away from the computer, or to otherwise stop engaging in distracting activities when the partner is attempting to communicate. In addition, therapists will often need to help clients rethink long-held notions about such nonverbal cues ("She asks me about the bills during the game on purpose"), and to positively frame new skills as indicating that the client has concern and caring for the partner. As noted elsewhere (Murphy & Eckhardt, 2005), improvement in basic nonverbal listening behaviors, along with exploration and change in the attitudes and beliefs that prevent effective listening, typically provide the most significant clinical improvements in this area. Once nonverbal cues have been addressed, the therapist, using a combination of didactic and experiential/role-play methods, can instruct the client to modify verbal responses used to convey understanding, such as paraphrasing and validation techniques.

A second major area of emphasis in relationship skills training is emotional expression. This may sound surprising; hasn't the client gotten into trouble for "over-expressing" certain emotions and behaviors in the context of abusive behavior? Indeed, some abusive men fit into the pattern of "undercontrolled" aggression; as such, they describe themselves as having a hot temper, with little psychological control over the next time they yell and scream. They may also seem emotionally sensitive and easily provoked to express extreme anger and jealousy. However, other abusers may correspond to a more "overcontrolled" pattern of aggression (Hershorn & Rosenbaum, 1991). This group reports infrequent anger and aggression outbursts, and a general tendency toward emotional suppression. However, when aggression does occur, it tends to be more severe and frequent than in undercontrolled males. Interestingly, this tendency to suppress and avoid emotional awareness (alexithymia) is elevated among abusive clients (Yelsma, 1996).

Thus, very different behavioral skill targets may be needed for effective expression of negative emotions, and they will vary depending upon the specific style and features of each individual abusive client. In brief, the skill requires (1) awareness, tracking, and labeling of one's emotional experiences (including not only classic emotions such as fear and sadness, but also thoughts and wishes or desires); (2) expression of feelings and wishes in a clear and nonthreatening fashion. Self-expression of feelings and desires is most successful in the context of active listening, which tends to facilitate receptivity in the other person to communication. For undercontrolled individuals, the therapeutic task involves encouraging the recognition that they are more threatening and less effective when they use angry, dominant display tactics during conflicts, and that a more controlled response will result in positive outcomes without instilling fear, sadness, and disappointment in others. Overcontrolled males will need explicit assistance with verbal labels for emotional states, especially as it relates to emotions of varying intensity, using structured self-monitoring and guidance in expression. For example, many abusive men need to learn the difference between annoyance and anger as it relates to affective expression, and to be convinced that it is acceptable to state assertively that they feel annoyed about something a family member has done. This kind of basic training in affective communication not only leads to fewer major conflicts between relationships partners, but also teaches the client that words matter, i.e., that different words can be used to specifically convey the intensity of the emotion they are experiencing.

Negotiation and compromise represent the process whereby partners formulate solutions to conflicts and other problems, and provide the maximum of positive outcomes for all involved. Effective negotiation and compromise is greatly facilitated by making the commitment to accept the influence of the partner, to steadfastly resist the urge to win all battles, and to understand the priorities of both oneself and one's partner. This process draws upon a mature understanding of relationships as involving give and take, reciprocity, mutual respect, and the recognition that one cannot always get one's way (Murphy & Eckhardt, 2005). The individual must use all the skills outlined above; the client must be attuned to toxic cognitive distortions that may derail the negotiation process. The client must also work at regulating internal emotional states and the assertive expression of these emotions, and use active listening, paraphrasing, and validation techniques. The ability to compromise is a critical skill that involves deliberate problem solving to consider a range of options that will promote both partners,' and not just the client's, interests. It is this technique of generating alternative responses and carefully examining the likely outcomes of each that becomes the primary technique at this largely problem-solving phase of the intervention. As the client rehearses the steps involved in brainstorming and imagining the outcomes of each solution, the process, which will be painfully slow at the outset, will gradually become more automated as the client's repertoire of potential responses is bolstered.

Is there Evidence that Modifying Interpersonal and Communication Skills in Partner Violence Interventions is Associated with Nonviolent Change? Yes. Recent research indicates that interventions based upon improving couple communication and relationship skills are at least as effective at preventing new IPV episodes as standard intervention programs or other comparison interventions (for a more detailed review see Murphy & Eckhardt, 2005). For example, Dunford (2000) randomly divided up 861 men in the U.S. Navy stationed in San Diego into a 26-week cognitive-behavioral group BIP, a 26-week couples therapy group, a rigorous monitoring group, or a no-treatment control group. Follow-up reports from female partners of male participants gathered 6 and 12 months post-treatment indicated that although individuals assigned to all treatments exhibited reductions in IPV, no differences in recidivism were found in male-to-female physical aggression across the four groups. In addition, using couples volunteering for treatment at a university marital distress clinic, O'Leary, Heyman and Neidig (1999) found no difference between men assigned to either couples treatment versus a group using Duluth model intervention. Similar results using a court-referred sample were reported by Brannen and Rubin (1996). Thus, one can either conclude that treatment focused on improving relationship skills is unwarranted because it does no better than more traditional group treatments, or one can perhaps see couples treatment as a useful alternative for some violent couples (especially those who are clearly planning on staying together), because it appears to work just as well as traditional interventions. However, the clinician interested in implementing couples' treatment must take extreme care to make sure the couple is indeed appropriate for the intervention, and that the intervention does not exacerbate existing problems in ways that increase risk of future IPV victimization (for more, see LaTaillade, Epstein & Werlinich, 2006; Murphy & Eckhardt, 2005).

The Collaborative Therapeutic Alliance: Evidence and Clinical Implications

As mentioned in each of the preceding sections, the specific techniques suggested for use in modifying cognitive, affective, and relationship factors assume a strong working relationship between therapist and client. This relationship is ideally one based upon the basic CBT tenets of guided discovery and collaborative empiricism, which when applied appropriately results in an empathic clinician and a motivated client. However, one of the more problematic aspects of the application of CBT techniques with abuse perpetrators is the issue of motivation to change. CBT assumes a client who is ready to change; most psychotherapy clients are motivated to seek treatment for their presenting problem, and are invested in the task of working with the clinician toward the successful completion of specific therapeutic goals. This working alliance is essentially a collaborative relationship between therapist and client (Bordin, 1979), making the strengths perspective a core element of the CBT system. The alliance is typically thought to have three components, a warm bond between therapist and client, agreement on the goals of treatment, and agreement on the tasks or strategies needed to attain those goals.

Working with abuse perpetrators mandated to attend an intervention program is a much different picture. The collaborative alliance is a controversial concept in partner violence intervention, as supportive and empathic therapist behaviors thought to promote a strong alliance have been seen by some in the field as promoting collusion with the abuser's negative outlook. It is also important to note that the alliance, as currently conceived, is not a therapist-delivered entity, but rather a relationship-level, two-person construct. Thus, it is expected that both the client and therapist contribute to the establishment of the working alliance, and that client personal characteristics may impede alliance formation. In particular, many angry, resistant, and interpersonally difficult clients pose a particular challenge as it relates to the establishment of a therapeutic alliance. As discussed elsewhere (DiGiuseppe, Tafrate & Eckhardt, 1994; Kassinove & Tafrate, 2002), the therapist must work especially hard in these cases to let the client know that he or she is on the client's side and is willing to "walk a mile in the client's shoes" during the early stages of the treatment process.

Indeed, one of the challenges inherent in CBT interventions from a strengths perspective is how to convey the basic philosophy of the intervention without it seeming as though the therapist is on a mission to blame the client for all of his misfortunes. CBT therapists (especially those new to the model) are likely to devote much time early in the intervention to identifying and challenging cognitive distortions, irrational ideas, biased attitudes, extreme emotions, and incompetent relationship behaviors. There is much potential for the client to believe that not only has he been labeled a criminal by the justice system and thought of in intensely negative terms by family and friends, but that *even the therapist* blames everything on the terrible qualities of the client as well! This can be a potentially humiliating appraisal that can reduce motivation to change (why bother?) and increase the potential of treatment attrition. In addition, the unskilled CBT therapist who is on the immediate search for cognitive distortions and dysfunctional emotions may not properly hear the client's story and engage in the first steps of the collaborative process. Typically, the angry client's narrative involves a common theme of "it's all her/their fault!"—if only the client had done better at managing all the crazy and unreasonable people in his life, this whole thing could have been avoided (Deffenbacher, 1995; DiGiuseppe et al., 1994; Kassinove & Tafrate, 2002). If the CBT therapist fails to respond with an empathic understanding of this narrative and instead launches into a lecture on how the client's cognitive distortions are the true culprit, then the client is likely to perceive the therapist as yet another person in authority who doesn't want to hear what he has to say. In order for the therapist to have any chance of modifying these faulty attributions of blame, the client and therapist must work together to establish a bond, agree on a set of treatment goals, and agree on the tasks needed to accomplish these goals. This is a step that is often omitted, given the coercive nature of the referral source among men in court-mandated treatment programs.

Is there Evidence that a Strong Working Alliance in Partner Violence Interventions Predicts More Favorable Outcomes? Yes. In general, motivation to change is a strong predictor of the working alliance (Taft, Murphy, Musser & Remington, 2004), program attrition, and criminal recidivism (Eckhardt et al., 2008). Among investigations of abusive couples and self-referred males (Brown et al., 2000), as well as a study of cognitive-behavioral group treatment for court-referred abusive men (Taft, Murphy, King, Musser & DeDeyn, 2003), ratings of the working alliance predicted lower levels of self-reported and partner-reported abusive behavior post-treatment. Interestingly, therapist ratings of the alliance late in group treatment (at sessions 11 and 13 of a 16-session program) were the most strongly associated with outcome, as compared to client ratings and early session ratings of both client and therapist (Taft et al., 2003). With this often interpersonally-challenged and treatment-resistant population, it may take some time for the alliance to develop and/or for the therapist to have a clear picture of the quality of the alliance. Additional factors that have been found to predict successful change in other areas of psychosocial treatment research have also enjoyed some predictive success in partner violence treatment. Compliance with homework assignments in CBT (i.e., participation in active change strategies) was associated with lower levels of psychological abuse after treatment. In addition, client ratings of positive group cohesion were associated with lower levels of both physical and psychological abuse at follow-up (Taft et al., 2003).

In brief, the available research to date, although limited, indicates that partner-violent clients are quite similar to other psychosocial treatment populations in responding to therapist support and reflective empathy. Factors that predict successful outcomes in other areas of psychotherapy and behavior change likewise appear to predict cessation of physical assault and reduction of emotionally abusive behavior in this treatment population. Although we do not as yet have sound empirical support for this speculation, careful reading of many existing treatment manuals in this area indicate that high levels of therapist confrontation, and critical or punitive attitudes toward abusive clients by service providers may impede the development of the working collaborative alliance and other active elements of the helping relationship.

CBT INTERVENTIONS FOR PARTNER ABUSE: GROUP OR INDIVIDUAL?

A variety of excellent CBT intervention programs have been developed over the last two decades (for other reviews, see Dutton, 2007; Dutton & Sonkin, 2003). These programs, by and large, are the product of the developers' openness to the use of empirically supported treatments in the context of IPV. As a consequence, most CBT programs are open and flexible to modifications as long as there are clear and objectively based reasons for changing elements of the intervention. One such question concerns modality—is there an optimal approach to delivering CBT interventions that can maximize client strengths in the treatment process? State standards are quite clear about this. In their review of state standards for batterer programs, Austin and Dankwort (1999) reported that 86% of states identified group intervention as the preferred format, and that more than two-thirds (68%) of states indicated that "one-on-one" interventions were inappropriate as a primary format, with some indicating that exceptions may be necessary in special circumstances (e.g., active psychosis, language problems, adolescent status, or significant cultural differences). Approximately 1/3 of states mandate a group intervention format. But is this the best strategy? While there may be sound reasons (e.g., economic reasons) to treat abuse perpetrators in a group format, there are also compelling reasons to consider the potential benefits of an individual approach for some abusive individuals. The high degree of substance problems (Leonard, 2001), comorbid psychopathology (Ehrensaft, Moffitt & Caspi, 2006), minimal readiness to change (Eckhardt et al., 2008), and literature suggesting that group programs for aggressive adolescents may actually have iatrogenic effects on aggressive outcomes (e.g., Dishion, McCord & Poulin, 1999) are compelling reasons to at least consider the potential benefit of individualized interventions for some perpetrators.

One such effort to develop an individual treatment approach was reported by Murphy and Eckhardt (2005) in an extensive treatment manual. The individualized CBT intervention is centered around the clinical construct of case formulation. CBT case formulation for partner-abusive individuals uses a detailed assessment of problem behaviors, associated cognitions, and personal strengths and resources to develop hypotheses involving key intervention targets and change strategies. A detailed assessment of problem behaviors that focuses on their specific forms and patterns, the life contexts and situations in which they occur, associated emotions and cognitions, and behavioral consequences is used to develop hypotheses about the associations among various presenting problems, the functions of abusive behavior, and relevant implicit cognitive themes. These hypotheses, in concert with an evaluation of the individual's strengths and resources, guide the formulation of intervention targets and the selection of intervention strategies to promote nonviolent change through a series of four phases.

We will illustrate those phases in the context of a clinical case. "Nick" was referred by an urban probation department for IPV-related treatment. Nick was arrested for misdemeanor spousal assault following an altercation with his wife. He had initially been referred to a standard group treatment for IPV but dropped out after one session "because the people in charge made up their mind about me before I even opened my mouth—it was like they knew enough about me to hate me, and I didn't get that." Nick was subsequently referred to an academic outpatient clinic to work with clinical staff trained in the individualized treatment approach outlined by Murphy and Eckhardt (2005). Briefly, Nick was a 34-year-old Caucasian male who was employed as a carpenter, living in an urban southwestern community. Lisa, his wife, worked part-time in the mornings at a local medical office. They had been married for 7 years with a 3-year-old daughter. Nick reported a "basic" upbringing, growing up in a small farming community, playing football and baseball, and attending, but not really excelling, at school. Nick's only sibling (a sister) died in a farming accident when he was in grade school. Nick stated that after this point, his mother (a stay-at-home mom) was very overprotective and emotionally volatile, e.g., she would be violently enraged and crying when he came home after curfew as a teenager. Nick reported that his father was distant and cold, and that he did not have a close relationship with his father at any point. His father was described as a "typical" farmer: "He woke up, grabbed some coffee, working by 7 and home ready for dinner by 7 at night, asleep by 10:00." His father, with whom Nick was not close, died when Nick was in his 20s.

Regarding the altercation that led to Nick's arrest, he had come home after a later-than-usual day at work, and upon walking through the door, he reported that Lisa pointed to their crying 3-year-old daughter and said, "I'm done, she's all yours." Nick reported feeling very upset at this point, because "all I wanted to do was grab dinner and have a beer and relax a little." During the ensuing argument, Nick reported that Lisa accused of him of being too rough with their daughter (Nick does not appear to have ever abused his daughter but has on occasion spanked the child following misbehavior). Following this, Nick reported feeling enraged and "ready to explode;" Nick pushed Lisa and the subsequent yelling and screaming, which could be heard through their open windows, caught the attention of a neighbor, who called the police. Nick contemplated pleading not guilty and fighting the assault charge ("It wasn't fair that I took the fall for stuff we both said and did"), but decided to not pursue this course. After a 2-month separation, Nick and Lisa reconciled and appear committed to their marriage.

The first phase of the individualized CBT intervention involves enhancement of motivation to change (Miller & Rollnick, 2002). This aspect of treatment is essential for those individuals who arrive at treatment not yet ready to commit to an active plan for behavior change, which, as noted above, represents a large percentage of court-mandated IPV perpetrators (e.g., Eckhardt et al., 2008). The motivational phase of treatment may be relatively brief for those who recognize that they have a problem and want to resolve it, but can take up many sessions for those who are in early stages of change. Although periodic attention to motivational issues is helpful throughout treatment, the motivational phase can be thought to end when the individual has clearly articulated goals for change and, in collaboration with the therapist, has committed to a plan for working on change-related goals. MI relies largely on reflective listening strategies, with judicious use of change-relevant advice, exploration of factors that encourage or limit change, and use of structured change-planning strategies. In addition, MI provides an atmosphere that promotes client strengths, in which more directive treatment techniques can be delivered.

Nick reported that he felt relieved to be out of the group that he was originally assigned to attend following his adjudication, but that he was still uncertain about whether he really needed "'therapy.'" As is common among early stage abusive clients, the therapist's initial response and handling of this ambivalence in the initial sessions is critically important, as it sets the stage for the development of a trusting alliance and creates a norm that values a collaborative effort at goal achievement.

Therapist (T): So tell me why you're here.

Nick (N): I don't know.

T: So you're not quite sure about the reasons why you're coming here?

N: Well, I mean . . . of course there's a reason, but . . . well, you know what it is.

T: Tell me about it in your own words.

N: Look, no offense or anything, but—you know—I just don't think I need to be here.

T (noting the ambivalence): So it sounds like there is a reason to be here but at the same time you personally don't think you need what I might be offering? Is that right?

N: Look, the probation guy said I have to come, but what happened between my wife and me . . . it wasn't that bad and—you know—the whole thing has been blown way up by everyone.

T: Right, that sounds frustrating. Can you explain it to me?

N: Oh . . . you mean what happened with my wife or how the whole thing played out, you know, in court and all that?

T: Whichever you want to talk about.

Nick proceeds to discuss the details of the incident that led to his arrest. The therapist asks open-ended questions to elicit more detail, but does not ever question the validity of what or how Nick is describing the incident.

T: So your point is that you both were saying nasty things and you were both pushing each other.

N: Exactly, but then she accused me of abusing my daughter and I . . . I mean . . . you can't just say stuff like that and get away with it.

T: You were angry.

N: I was pissed! And at that moment I just thought about all the things I've tried to—you know—do better than my own parents with my kid and that comment—you know—it was such a low blow.

T: So it sounds like you feel that your response to Lisa was justified, given what she said to you?

N: Yeah . . . well no. I didn't think it would lead to all this, but at the time . . . how can you just let that stuff go?

T: You sound conflicted, like you needed to punish her for what she said but you're frustrated at what's happened since?

N: Yeah . . .

T: Tell me more about that.

N: OK, it's like one day you're doing your thing and not really worried about crap, you know, and then you do something dumb and you almost lose everything just like that. I—I dunno . . . I just want this to all go away now.

At this point, the therapist has elicited an important, if rather half-hearted, statement from Nick, i.e., that he was at least somewhat culpable in the incident and that there might actually be a good reason to come to treatment. The therapist notes several of Nick's cognitive distortions that can be discussed in subsequent sessions (anger can't be controlled, people need to be punished, I deserve more respect, others don't understand me). The next step in the initial MI stage is to examine Nick's goals in the context of the intervention.

T: If you could make it all go away, how would things be different for you?

N: Well, you know, I wouldn't have had the whole thing with the cops and the judge and all that . . . they threatened to take my daughter away, my neighbors think I'm a convict or whatever, Lisa's family hates me, all that.

T: So it sounds like you'd like to say out of trouble—how are you going to do that?

N: Well, I guess—you know—I can work on it here, right?

This initial elicitation of a personal goal was the initial step in helping Nick articulate some important personal and interpersonal goals, and to connect these outcomes to the intervention. The therapist has allowed the client to take control of this early stage in treatment, rather than the therapist dictating what the goals should be. Thus, after 45 minutes, the therapist has learned important details about the arresting incident, and Nick has had the chance to tell "'his side'" of the story without the listener rejecting his version of the incident. With this approach, the therapist and Nick have established the framework of a working relationship, agreed on a set of goals, and can now construct a series of therapeutic tasks that allow for the potential completion of these goals.

In the second phase, the therapist works to promote safety and stabilization for the client, partner, and family in terms of life or relationship instabilities. Careful examination of the referring incident for criminally charged cases, exploration of difficult or abusive relationship scenarios, and/or analysis of other violent situations outside the family are undertaken to develop hypotheses about the eliciting conditions and functions of abusive and violent behavior. Nonviolent alternatives are addressed and worked on, particularly for crisis or emergency situations with the potential to escalate to physical violence. Attitudes and beliefs that support the use of violence may be identified and addressed. These efforts typically meld into more general relationship skills training and relationship enhancement characterized as the next phase of treatment.

For Nick, this phase of treatment primarily related to concerns about the long-term viability of his marriage to Lisa. Early in treatment, Nick was uncertain about whether Lisa would want to remain married to him, and as arguments intensified, he too was uncertain about his commitment to remain with Lisa. The theme of emotional stability and personal accountability was an important theme throughout these discussions, as it focused Nick on broader issues as a partner and parent that were important to him. As his positive commitment to his marriage became clearer to him, this helped Nick and the therapist to further refine his treatment goals and increase his willingness to continue with the intervention. In addition to issues surrounding his marriage, the therapist used these early stages of treatment to address other instability-engendering circumstances in Nick's life, including problems with family finances, child care arrangements that limited Lisa's work opportunities, and the extent of Nick's alcohol use. The effective therapist is able to encourage personal stability through support and focused problem solving as an indirect means to achieve the primary goals of relationship competence and the cessation of abuse.

Once Nick saw the benefits of a goal of personal stabilization, this allowed the therapist to "unpack" two additional elements of CBT: emotion regulation skills and cognitive restructuring. Regarding emotion regulation, Nick's typical anger regulation strategy involved experiencing a high frequency and intensity of anger experience in response to certain situations (e.g., statements from his wife that he perceived as humiliating or nasty) and suppressing this negative affect until it had dissipated. In collaboration with Nick, the therapist first trained Nick in the use of anger-coping statements that would allow him to actively control his anger and calm himself during conflict situations ("I don't like this, but I can take it"). Then, the therapist used different imaginary and in-session exposure techniques wherein Nick would be asked to imagine anger-inducing statements that (for example) his wife might say to him ("You're selfish and you only think about yourself!"). Exposure sessions would last up to one hour and involved a variety of self- and therapist-initiated anger-eliciting statements or situations over 6 sessions; through basic habituation processes as well as usage of anger-coping statements, Nick learned to take a more active role in controlling and reducing his angry feelings. The goal here was not to "turn off" his anger response, but to instead show him that he had the strength and personal resources to control what he used to regard as an uncontrollable reaction to long-term anger suppression.

The next cognitive restructuring step involved self-monitoring of cognitive activity, discussion of the self-monitoring logs, and a review of the basic A-B-C model. Nick's primary implicit theories concerned the distortion that Lisa deserved to be punished for saying something he regarded as unacceptable ("she got what was coming"), cognitive distortions about others having no right to tell him what to do ("need for control"), and a strong belief that if he felt angry for a particular duration, he was entitled to lose control and express himself in any way he saw fit ("low frustration tolerance"). The therapist was careful to not begin the disputation process too early, as Nick would argue persistently in defense of these cognitive distortions ("If I don't let it all out I'll go crazy"). Given this, the therapist focused on heuristic disputes during the beginning sessions during this phase ("So how did it work out for you when you lost control of your emotions?"). As Nick became more comfortable with the idea that he did not always have it quite right, the therapist switched to more rational and logical disputes to elicit alternate cognitions that could be beneficial during his problem solving efforts. During the last stages of the intervention, Nick became more interested in trying to connect some of his cognitive distortions to his memories of childhood, specifically to the lack of emotional connection to his father, which he was determined to not repeat with his daughter. These sessions were also useful in the context of the next phase of the intervention, which focused on basic relationship skills described below.

The third phase involves relationship skills training and relationship enhancement efforts (i.e., "Relationships 101"). Especially for couples who clearly plan on staying together, it is ideal for the bulk of treatment to be devoted to the enhancement of close relationship skills. These treatment targets represent the predominant strategies to prevent escalation of otherwise normal relationship conflicts to abusive behaviors. Case formulation helps to identify the specific problematic relationship beliefs possessed by each individual client, along with limitations in interpersonal/relationship skills, as well as personal strengths that can be deployed during difficult situations. As discussed above, the main areas of relationship skills training involve basic issues in listening skills, assertive self-expression, negotiation and compromise, and noncoercive emotional expression.

Nick, like many males in abuser intervention programs, was a poor listener, especially when he was experiencing negative affect, such as during a conflict with Lisa. Thus, Nick would often overgeneralize and awfulize certain aspects of Lisa's behavior ("Why does she always have to get on my case the second I come home from work?"); as a result, he only heard what he regarded as nagging, and ignored other salient information that was being presented to him during these conflicts, such as the specific nature of the complaint, Lisa's concern about the topic, and her wish that he might take on more household and parenting responsibilities. The therapist worked on eliminating his aversive nonverbal tendencies during these conflicts, which for Nick involved smiling, shaking his head, and looking away from Lisa. After working on his implicit assumption that he can't control his anger, role-plays were used to give Nick a chance to work on listening, paraphrasing, and validating Lisa's concerns, and assertively verbalizing when these requests made him feel annoyed or taken by surprise. The therapist frequently returned to the arresting incident via imagination, as a means to transfer these new techniques to a situation Nick tended to regard as the worst situation he could imagine from his married life. As he progressed with these techniques in the sessions, Lisa was brought in for several sessions so that the therapist could provide some education and modification of their arguing style (this was only done after the therapist, in consultation with both Lisa and Nick, determined that doing so would not put Lisa at risk for IPV). Both Nick and Lisa seemed intent on winning whatever argument they were in, which provided further cognitive data for the therapist to work on in subsequent sessions ("Let's assume Lisa wins every argument you ever have, from here on out; really imagine that. What would this mean for you?"). During this phase of CBT, Nick was becoming more adept at using the A-B-C-D (disputation) model on his own without therapist guidance, and was able to see the connections between self-talk, emotion regulation, and the ability to behave effectively during relationship conflicts.

In the fourth and final phase, trauma recovery and relapse prevention, clients with histories of witnessed or experienced abuse in childhood are given clinical attention to aspects of their social development that continue to put them at risk for relationship conflict. Such interventions can include cognitive interventions that aim to provide insight and modification of how adverse events during childhood have shaped expectations and emotions (Resick & Schnicke, 1993), as well as interventions that utilize trauma exposure techniques (Rothbaum, Meadows, Resick & Foy, 2000). Relapse prevention is relevant to all who undergo a change process, given the relatively high probability of vulnerable individuals returning to earlier patterns of problematic behavior. Some partner-violent individuals slide back into old patterns of controlling and abusive behavior rather quickly after making initial changes, and may benefit greatly from ongoing support and encouragement. In addition, a variety of therapeutic techniques can be used toward the latter stages of the intervention that emphasize the role of lifestyle imbalance and stress in stimulating a return to problematic behavior. These techniques denote the distinction between a temporary lapse (such as an insulting comment during an argument) and a more complete relapse to problematic behavior (consistent use of controlling and violent behaviors), and provide training regarding the cognitive and emotional factors that predict relapse in high-risk situations (Marlatt & Gordon, 1985).

For Nick, this last phase of treatment represented an opportunity to make connections between childhood memories and his worries about his own family's future. As is often the case among abusive men with children of their own, a very powerful source of insight can be found when men realize that they are making many of the same mistakes that their own parents made, and they now have an opportunity to prevent these misfortunes from happening to their own children. Thus, the therapist had Nick engage in several therapeutic writing sessions designed to facilitate his expression of trauma-related memories regarding emotionally abusive actions from his mother and his lack of emotional connection to his father. These writing sessions allowed Nick to disclose information that he had trouble articulating with the therapist. His involvement with a motivational-enhancement alcohol treatment program provided another important resource to promote stability and nonviolence in his life. Nick completed the 26- week program with one absence and participated in monthly follow-up telephone sessions for six months thereafter. At the six-month follow-up, Lisa reported that while they continue to argue more than she would like, there had been no incidents of abuse since the end of the intervention.

CONCLUSION

Substantial progress has been made in the development of interventions for individuals who assault their relationship partners. Over time, there has been a notable shift away from early ideologies that were solely focused on gender themes as being the dominant model to understand the etiology and treatment of IPV (e.g., Adams, 1988). Modern ideologies have moved toward an approach that attempts to broaden this point of view with less ideologically-based and more empirically-based findings concerning risk factors for IPV and how this understanding of risk relationships may translate into more focused interventions for perpetrators (Dutton & Corvo, 2006). An outcome of this approach is the emergence of CBT-themed interventions for IPV perpetrators as the empirically-based standard for sound practice with this population. The CBT approach as applied to perpetrators of IPV is based on clear theoretical underpinnings and a solid body of confirming findings. Relative to non-perpetrators, partner-violent individuals exhibit a variety of social information processing disturbances and show more favorable attitudes toward violence as an acceptable conflict resolution strategy. In terms of emotion regulation, the limited research available indicates that IPV perpetrators show more disturbances in anger experience and expression, relative to nonviolent comparison samples, and that problems relating to anger control are linearly related to the severity and frequency of IPV perpetration. Laboratory studies indicate that relative to nonviolent males, IPV perpetrators induced to feel angry are more likely to respond to relationship conflict situations with expressions of verbal aggression, belligerence, and hostile conflict strategies. Data also clearly indicate the relational nature of violent conflict tactics: abusive behavior, while always the responsibility of the individual perpetrator, emerges in particular relationship contexts and follows a sometimes-predictable pattern of reciprocated and escalating interpersonal processes. In addition, the CBT approach emphasizes a collaborative approach to fostering therapeutic change, one that values the client's point of view and creates a respectful, strengths-based, change-focused therapeutic relationship.

Together, these findings make for a compelling framework around which to structure intervention programs for nonviolent change.

But, as noted by Stuart (2005), there is still quite a distance left to travel if we as a field are to make the paradigm shift toward an approach to addressing IPV that takes advantage of the most that social and behavioral sciences have to offer. Unfortunately, it is still the case that large sectors of the abuser intervention community are devoted to an exclusive gender-themed ideology that leaves little room for dissenting voices or incompatible data (Dutton & Nichols, 2005; Stuart, 2005). Many have wondered if this approach extends into the therapeutic process; perhaps this "ideologically narrowed view of domestic violence distorts and limits other approaches to behavioral and psychological change, and generates an atmosphere in the client group that cannot be conducive to honest exchange, vulnerability, trust, or disclosure" (Dutton & Corvo, 2006, p. 461). The CBT approach represents an important stage in this paradigm shift, especially in light of recent, largely unenthusiastic outcome studies regarding more traditional abuser intervention programs that have the potential to signal to those in the criminal justice community that such programs are simply not worth the effort. Why mandate an intervention that men have little motivation to attend, that at best has a small impact on criminal recidivism, and that doesn't really fit the bill as a punishment, an educational experience, or a therapeutic intervention? Given the strong empirical base with which to justify the CBT approach and the encouraging, if emerging, outcome literature of its impact on important outcomes concerning victim safety, there is much to be hopeful about in the context of improving interventions for IPV perpetrators.

REFERENCES

Adams, D. (1988). Treatment models of men who batter: A profeminist analysis. In K. Yllö, & M. Bograd (Eds.), *National conference for family violence researchers* (pp. 176–199). Thousand Oaks, CA: Sage.

Anderson, C.A., & Bushman, B.J. (2002). Human aggression. *Annual Review of Psychology, 53*, 27–51.

Anglin, K., & Holtzworth-Munroe, A. (1997). Comparing the responses of maritally violent and nonviolent spouses to problematic marital and nonmarital situations: Are the skill deficits of physically aggressive husbands and wives global? *Journal of Family Psychology, 11*, 301–313.

Archer, J. (2000). Sex differences in aggression between heterosexual partners: A meta-analytic review. *Psychological Bulletin, 126*, 651–680.

Austin, J.B., & Dankwort, J. (1999). Standards for batterer programs: A review and analysis. *Journal of Interpersonal Violence, 14*, 152–168.

Babcock, J.C., Green, C.E., & Robie, C. (2004). Does batterers' treatment work? A meta-analytic review of domestic violence treatment. *Clinical Psychology Review, 23, 1023–1053.*

Babcock, J.C., Waltz, J., Jacobson, N.S., & Gottman, J.M. (1993). Power and violence: The relation between communication patterns, power discrepancies, and domestic violence. *Journal of Consulting and Clinical Psychology, 61*, 40–50.

Bandura, A. (1973). *Aggression: A social learning analysis.* Oxford, England: Prentice-Hall.

Barbour, K.A., Eckhardt, C.I., Davison, G.C., & Kassinove, H. (1998). The experience and expression of anger in maritally violent and maritally discordant-nonviolent men. *Behavior Therapy, 29*, 173–191.

Beck, A.T. (1963). Thinking and Depression: 1. Idiosyncratic content and cognitive distortions. *Archives of General Psychiatry, 9*, 324–333.

Beck, A.T. (1976). *Cognitive therapy and the emotional disorders.* NY: International Universities Press.

Beck, A.T. (1999). *Prisoners of hate: The cognitive basis of anger, hostility, and violence.* New York, NY: HarperCollins.

Beck, J. (1995). *Cognitive therapy: Basics and beyond.* NY: Guilford.

Beck, R., & Fernandez, E. (1998). Cognitive-behavioral therapy in the treatment of anger: A meta-analysis. *Cognitive Therapy and Research, 22*, 63–74.

Beck, A.T., Rush, A.J., Shaw, B.F., & Emery, G. (1979). *Cognitive therapy of depression.* New York: Guilford.

Berkowitz, L. (1993). *Aggression: Its causes, consequences, and control.* New York, NY: Mcgraw-Hill.

Berkowitz, L. (2008). On the consideration of automatic as well as controlled psychological processes in aggression. *Aggressive Behavior, 34*, 117–129.

Berns, S.B., Jacobson, N.S., & Gottman, J.M. (1999). Demand-withdraw interaction in couples with a violent husband. *Journal of Consulting and Clinical Psychology, 67*, 666–674.

Bernstein, D.A., & Borkovec, T.D. (1973). *Progressive relaxation training: A manual for the helping professions.* Champaign, IL: Research Press.

Bograd, M. (1984). Family systems approaches to wife battering: A feminist critique. *American Journal of Orthopsychiatry, 54*, 558–568.

Bordin, E.S. (1979). The generalizability of the psychoanalytic concept of the working alliance. *Psychotherapy: Theory, Research & Practice, 16*, 252–260.

Brannen, S.J., & Rubin, A. (1996). Comparing the effectiveness of gender specific and couples groups in court-mandated spouse abuse treatment programs. *Research on Social Work Practice, 16*, 252–260.

Brown, P.D., & O'Leary, K.D. (2000). Therapeutic alliance: Predicting continuance and success in group treatment for spouse abuse. *Journal of Consulting and Clinical Psychology, 68*, 340–345.

Burke, L.K., & Follingstad, D.R. (1999). Violence in lesbian and gay relationships: Theory, prevalence, and correlational factors. *Clinical Psychology Review, 19*, 487–512.

Burman, B., Margolin, G., & John, R.S. (1993). America's angriest home videos: Behavioral contingencies observed in home reenactments of marital conflict. *Journal of Consulting and Clinical Psychology, 61*, 28–39.

Chase, K.A., O'Leary, K.D., & Heyman, R.E. (2001). Categorizing partner-violent men within the reactive-proactive typology model. *Journal of Consulting and Clinical Psychology, 69,* 567–572.

Cordova, J.V., Jacobson, N.S., Gottman, J.M., Rushe, R., & Cox, G. (1993). Negative reciprocity and communication in couples with a violent husband. *Journal of Abnormal Psychology, 102,* 559–564.

Craig, M.E., Robyak, J., Torosian, E.J., & Hummer, J. (2006). A study of male veterans' beliefs toward domestic violence in a batterer intervention program. *Journal of Interpersonal Violence, 21,* 1111–1128.

Daly, J.E., & Pelowski, S. (2000). Predictors of dropout among men who batter: A review of studies with implications for research and practice. *Violence and Victims, 15,* 137–160.

Deffenbacher, J.L. (1995). Ideal treatment package for adults with anger disorders. In H. Kassinove (Ed.), *Anger disorders: Definition, diagnosis, and treatment.* (pp. 151–172). Philadelphia, PA: Taylor & Francis.

Deffenbacher, J.L., Oetting, E.R., Huff, M.E., & Thwaites, G.A. (1995). Fifteen month follow-up of social skills and cognitive-relaxation approaches to general anger reduction. *Journal of Counseling Psychology, 42,* 400–405.

Deffenbacher, J.L., & Stark, R.S. (1992). Relaxation and cognitive-relaxation treatments of general anger. *Cognitive Therapy and Research, 12,* 167–184.

Deffenbacher, J.L., Thwaites, G.A., Wallace, T.L., & Oetting, E.R., (1994). Social skills and cognitive-relaxation treatments for general anger. *Journal of Counseling Psychology, 41,* 386–396.

Del Vecchio, T., & O'Leary, K.D. (2004). *Effectiveness of anger treatments for specific anger problems: A meta-analytic review.* Clinical Psychology Review, 24, 15–34.

DiGiuseppe, R. (1991). Comprehensive cognitive disputing in RET. In M.E. Bernard (Ed.), *Using rational-emotive therapy effectively: A practitioner's guide* (pp. 173–195). New York, NY Plenum Press.

DiGiuseppe, R., & Tafrate, R.C. (2003). Anger treatment for adults: A meta-analytic review. *Clinical Psychology: Science and Practice, 10,* 70–84.

DiGiuseppe, R., Tafrate, R., & Eckhardt, C.I. (1994). The treatment of dysfunctional anger: Review of the literature and clinical hypotheses. *Cognitive and Behavioral Practice, 1,* 111–132.

Dishion, T., McCord, J., & Poulin, F. (1999). When interventions harm: Peer groups and problem behavior. *American Psychologist, 54,* 755–764.

Dobash, R.E., & Dobash, R. (1979). *Violence against wives: A case against the patriarchy.* New York: Free Press.

Dobson, K. (Ed.) (2001). *Handbook of cognitive- and behavioral therapies* (2nd ed.). NY: Guilford Press.

Dodge, K.A. (1991). The structure and function of reactive and proactive aggression. In D.J. Pepler, & K.H. Rubin (Eds.), *Earlscourt symposium on childhood aggression* (pp. 201–218). Hillsdale, NJ: Erlbaum.

Dunford, F.W. (2000). The San Diego Navy experiment: An assessment of interventions for men who assault their wives. *Journal of Consulting and Clinical Psychology, 68,* 486–476.

Dutton, D.G. (1986). Wife assaulter's explanations for assault: The neutralization of self-punishment. *Canadian Journal of Behavioral Science, 18,* 381–390.

Dutton, D.G. (1988). Profiling of wife assaulters: Preliminary evidence for a trimodal analysis. *Violence and Victims, 3*, 5–29.

Dutton, D.G. (2007). *The abusive personality: Violence and control in intimate relationships* (2nd ed.). New York, NY: Guilford Press.

Dutton, D.G. & Corvo, K. (2006). Transforming a flawed policy: A call to revive psychology and science in domestic violence research and practice. *Aggression and Violent Behavior, 11*, 457–483.

Dutton, D.G., & Nicholls, T.L. (2005). The gender paradigm in domestic violence research and theory: Part 1- The conflict of theory and data. *Aggression and Violent Behavior, 10*, 680–714.

Dutton, D.G., Saunders, K., Starzomski, A., & Bartholomew, K. (1994). Intimacy-anger and insecure attachment as precursors of abuse in intimate relationships. *Journal of Applied Social Psychology, 24*, 1367—1386.

Dutton, D., & Sonkin, D.J. (2003). Introduction: Perspectives on the treatment of intimate violence. *Journal of Aggression, Maltreatment & Trauma, 7*, 1–6.

Dutton, D.G., & Strachan, C.E. (1987). Motivational needs for power and spouse-specific assertiveness in assaultive and nonassaultive men. *Violence and Victims, 2*, 145–156.

Eckhardt, C.I. (2007). Effects of alcohol intoxication on anger experience and expression among partner assaultive men during anger arousal. *Journal of Consulting and Clinical Psychology, 75*, 61–71.

Eckhardt, C.I., Babcock, J., & Homack, S. (2004). Partner assaultive men and the stages and processes of change. *Journal of Family Violence, 19*, 81–93.

Eckhardt, C.I., Barbour, K.A., & Davison, G.C. (1998). Articulated irrational thoughts in maritally violent and nonviolent men during anger arousal. *Journal of Consulting and Clinical Psychology, 66*, 259–269.

Eckhardt, C.I., Barbour, K.A., & Stuart, G.L. (1997). Anger and hostility in maritally violent men: Conceptual distinctions, measurement issues, and literature review. *Clinical Psychology Review, 17*, 333–358.

Eckhardt, C.I., & Dye, M.L. (2000). The cognitive characteristics of maritally violent men: Theory and evidence. *Cognitive Therapy and Research, 24*, 139–158.

Eckhardt, C.I., & Jamison, T.R. (2002). Articulated thoughts of male perpetrators of dating violence during anger arousal. *Cognitive Therapy and Research, 26*, 289–308.

Eckhardt, C.I., Jamison, T.R., & Watts, K. (2002). Experience and expression of anger among male perpetrators of dating violence. *Journal of Interpersonal Violence, 17*, 1102–1114.

Eckhardt, C., Murphy, C., Black, D., & Suhr, L. (2006). Intervention programs for perpetrators of intimate partner violence: Conclusions from a clinical research perspective. *Public Health Reports, 121*, 369–381.

Eckhardt, C.I., Holtzworth-Munroe, A., Norlander, B., Sibley, A., & Cahill, M. (2008). Readiness to change, partner violence subtypes, and treatment outcomes among men in treatment for partner assault. *Violence and Victims, 23*, 446–475.

Eckhardt, C.I., Samper, R., & Murphy, C. (2008). Anger disturbances among perpetrators of intimate partner violence: Clinical characteristics and outcomes of court-mandated treatment. *Journal of Interpersonal Violence, 23*, 1600–1617.

Ehrensaft, M.K., Moffitt, T.E., & Caspi, A. (2006). Is domestic violence followed by an increased risk of psychiatric disorders among women but not among men? A longitudinal cohort study. *American Journal of Psychiatry, 163*, 885–892.

Eifert, G.H., McKay, M., & Forsyth, J.P. (2006). *Act on life not on anger: The new acceptance & commitment therapy guide to problem anger.* Oakland, CA: New Harbinger Publications.

Ellis, A. (1955). Psychotherapy techniques for use with psychotics. *American Journal of Psychotherapy, 9,* 452–476.

Ellis, A. (1962). *Reason and emotion in psychotherapy.* New York: Citadel Press.

Ellis, A. (1973). *Humanistic psychotherapy.* NY: McGraw-Hill.

Ellis, A. (1994). *Reason and emotion in psychotherapy (2nd Ed.).* New York: Citadel Press.

Feazell, C.S., Mayers, R.S., & Deschner, J. (1984). Services for men who batter: Implications for programs and policies. *Family Relations, 33,* 217–223.

Feder, L., & Wilson, D. (2005). A meta-analytic review of court-mandated batterer intervention programs: Can courts affect abusers' behavior? *Journal of Experimental Criminology, 1,* 239–262.

Field, C.A., Caetano, R., & Nelson, S. (2004). Alcohol and violence related cognitive risk factors associated with the perpetration of intimate partner violence. *Journal of Family Violence, 19,* 249–253.

Fincham, F.D., Bradbury, T.N., Arias, I., Byrne, C.A., & Karney, B.R. (1997). Marital violence, marital distress, and attributions. *Journal of Family Psychology, 11,* 367–372.

Ganley, A.L. (1981). *Court-mandated counseling for men who batter: A three-day workshop for mental health professionals. Participant's Manual.* Washington D. C.: Center for Women Policy Studies.

Gondolf, E.W. (2002). *Batterer intervention systems.* Thousand Oaks, CA: Sage Publications

Gondolf, E.W. (2004). Evaluating batterer counseling programs: A difficult task showing some effects and implications. *Aggression and Violent Behavior, 9,* 605–631.

Gondolf, E.W. (2007). Theoretical and research support for the Duluth model: A reply to Dutton and Corvo. *Aggression and Violent Behavior, 12,* 644–657.

Gondolf, E.W., & Russell, D. (1986). The case against anger control treatment programs for batterers. *Response to the Victimization of Women & Children, 9,* 2–5.

Gottman, J.M. (1994). *What predicts divorce? The relationship between marital processes and marital outcomes.* Hillsdale, NJ: Erlbaum.

Gottman, J.M., Jacobson, N.S., Rushe, R.H., Shortt, J.W., Babcock, J.C., LaTaillade, J.J., & Waltz, J. (1995). The relationship between heart rate reactivity, emotionally aggressive behavior, and general violence in batterers. *Journal of Family Psychology, 9,* 227–248.

Haaga, D.A., Dyck, M.J., & Ernst, D. (1991). Empirical status of cognitive theory of depression. *Psychological Bulletin, 110,* 215–236.

Hamberger, L.K. (1997). Cognitive behavioral treatment of men who batter their partners. *Cognitive and Behavioral Practice, 4,* 147–169.

Hamberger, L.K., & Lohr, J.M. (1989). Proximal causes of spouse abuse: A theoretical analysis for cognitive-behavioral interventions. In P.L. Caesar and L.K. Hamberger (Eds.), *Treating men who batter: Theory, practice, and programs* (pp. 53–76). New York: Springer.

Hayes, S.C., Strosahl, K.D., & Wilson, K.G. (1999). *Acceptance and commitment therapy: An experiential approach to behavior change.* New York: Guilford Press.

Healey, K., Smith, C. & O'Sullivan, C. (1998). *Batterer intervention: Program approaches and criminal justice strategies*. Washington DC: National Institute of Justice.

Hershorn, M., & Rosenbaum, A. (1991). Over- vs. undercontrolled hostility: Application of the construct to the classification of maritally violent men. *Violence and Victims, 6*, 151–58.

Holtzworth-Munroe, A. (1992). Social skill deficits in maritally violent men: Interpreting the data using a social information processing model. *Clinical Psychology Review, 12*, 605–617.

Holtzworth-Munroe, A. (2000). Social information processing skills deficits in maritally violent men: Summary of a research program. In Vincent, J.P., & Jouriles, E.N. (Eds.), *Domestic violence: Guidelines for research-informed practice* (pp. 13–36). London: Jessica Kingsley Publishers.

Holtzworth-Munroe, A., & Anglin, K. (1991). The competency of responses given by maritally violent versus nonviolent men to problematic marital situations. *Violence and Victims, 6*, 257–269.

Holtzworth-Munroe, A., & Hutchinson, G. (1993). Attributing negative intent to wife behavior: The attributions of maritally violent versus nonviolent men. *Journal of Abnormal Psychology, 102*, 206–211.

Holtzworth-Munroe, A., & Smutzler, N. (1996). Comparing the emotional reactions and behavioral intentions of violent and nonviolent husbands to aggressive, distressed, and other wife behaviors. *Violence and Victims, 11*, 319–339.

Holtzworth-Munroe, A., Smutzler, N., & Stuart, G.L. (1998). Demand and withdraw communication among couples experiencing husband violence. *Journal of Consulting and Clinical Psychology, 66*, 731–743.

Holtzworth-Munroe, A., & Stuart, G.L. (1994a). Typologies of male batterers: Three subtypes and the differences among them. *Psychological Bulletin, 116*, 476–497.

Howells, K., & Day, A. (2006). Affective determinants of treatment engagement in violent offenders. *International Journal of Offender Therapy and Comparative Criminology, 50*, 174–186.

Huesmann, L.R. (1988). An information processing model for the development of aggression. *Aggressive Behavior, 14*, 13–24.

Jacobson, N. (1992). Rewards and dangers in researching domestic violence. *Family Process, 33*, 81–85.

Jacobson, N.S., & Margolin, G. (1979). *Marital therapy: Strategies based on social learning and behavior exchange principles*. NY: Brunner/Mazel.

Jacobson, N.S., Gottman, J.M., Waltz, J., Rushe, R., Babcock, J., & Holtzworth-Monroe, A. (1994). Affect, verbal content, and psychophysiology in the arguments of couples with a violent husband. *Journal of Consulting and Clinical Psychology, 62*, 982–988.

Jennings, J.L. (1987). History and issues in the treatment of battering men: A case for unstructured group therapy. *Journal of Family Violence, 2*, 193–214.

Kassinove, H., & Tafrate, R.C. (2002). *Anger management: The complete treatment guidebook for practitioners*. Atascadero, CA: Impact Publishers.

Kaufman-Kantor, G. & Straus, M.A. (1990). The "drunken bum" theory of wife beating. In M. Straus & R. Gelles (Eds.), *Physical violence in American families* (pp. 203–224). New Brunswick, NJ: Transaction.

Kivel, P. (1998). *Men's work: How to stop the violence that tears our lives apart*. San Francisco, CA: Hazelden.

LaTaillade, J.J., Epstein, N.B., Werlinich, C.A. (2006). Conjoint treatment of intimate partner violence: A cognitive behavioral approach. *Journal of Cognitive Psychotherapy, 20*, 393–410.

Lee, M.Y., Uken, A., & Sebold, J. (2007). The role of self-determined goals in predicting recidivism in domestic violence offenders. *Research on Social Work Practice, 17*, 30–41.

Leonard, K. (2001). Alcohol and substance abuse in marital violence and child maltreatment. In C. Wekerle & A. Wall (Eds.), *The violence and addiction equation* (pp. 194–219). NY: Brunner-Routledge.

Leonard, K.E. & Roberts, L.J. (1998). The effects of alcohol on the marital interactions of aggressive and nonaggressive husbands and their wives. *Journal of Abnormal Psychology, 107*, 602–615.

Maiuro, R.D., Hagar, T.S., Lin, H., & Olson, N. (2002). Are current state standards for domestic violence perpetrator treatment adequately informed by research? A question of questions. *Journal of Aggression, Maltreatment & Trauma, 5*, 21–44.

Malik, N.M., & Lindahl, K.M. (1998). Aggression and dominance: The roles of power and culture in domestic violence. *Clinical Psychology: Science and Practice, 5*, 409–423.

Margolin , G., John, R.S., & Gleberman, L. (1988). Affective responses to conflictual discussions in violent and nonviolent couples. *Journal of Consulting and Clinical Psychology, 56*, 24–33.

Marlatt, G.A. & Gordon, J.R. (Eds.) (1985). *Relapse prevention: Maintenance strategies in the treatment of addictive behaviors.* New York: Guilford.

McMurran, M., & Gilchrist, E. (2008). Anger control and alcohol use: Appropriate interventions for perpetrators of domestic violence? *Psychology, Crime, & Law, 14*, 107–116.

Miller, W.R., & Rollnick, S. (2002). *Motivational interviewing: Preparing people to change addictive behavior (2nd ed.).* New York: Guilford.

Murphy, C.M., & Eckhardt, C.I. (2005). *Treating the abusive partner: An individualized cognitive-behavioral approach.* NY: Guilford.

Murphy, C.M., Taft, C.T., & Eckhardt, C.I. (2007). Anger problem profiles among partner violent men: Differences in clinical presentation and treatment outcome. *Journal of Counseling Psychology, 54*, 189–200.

Nathan, P.E., & Gorman, J.M. (2007). *A guide to treatments that work (3rd ed.).* New York, NY: Oxford University Press.

Norlander, B., & Eckhardt, C. (2005). Anger, hostility, and male perpetrators of intimate partner violence: A meta-analytic review. *Clinical Psychology Review, 25*, 119–152.

Novaco, R.W., Ramm, M., & Black, L.(2000) Anger treatment with offenders. In C. Hollin (Ed.), *Handbook of offender assessment and treatment* (pp. 281–296). London: John Wiley and Sons.

O'Leary, K.D. (1999). Psychological abuse: A variable deserving critical attention in domestic violence. *Violence and Victims, 14*, 3–23.

O'Leary, K.D., Barling, J., Arias, I., Rosenbaum, A., Malone, J., & Tyree, A. (1989). Prevalence and stability of physical aggression between spouses: A longitudinal analysis. *Journal of Consulting and Clinical Psychology, 57*, 263–268.

O'Leary, K.D., & Curley, A.D. (1986). Assertion and family violence: Correlates of spouse abuse. *Journal of Marital and Family Therapy, 12*, 281–289.

O'Leary, K.D., Heyman, R.E., & Neidig, P.H. (1999). Treatment of wife abuse: A comparison of gender-specific and conjoint approaches. *Behavior Therapy, 30,* 475–506.

Pence, E. (1983). The Duluth domestic abuse intervention project. *Hamline Law Review, 6,* 247–275.

Pence, E., & Paymar, M. (1993). *Education groups for men who batter: The Duluth model.* New York: Springer.

Polaschek, D.L., & Ward, T. (2002). The implicit theories of potential rapists: What our questionnaires tell us. *Aggression and Violent Behavior, 7,* 385–406.

Resick, P.A., & Schnicke, M.K. (1993). *Cognitive processing therapy for rape victims: A treatment manual.* Newbury Park, CA: Sage.

Roberts, A. (1984). Intervention with the abusive partner. In Roberts, A. (Ed). *Battered women and their families* (pp. 65–83). New York: Springer.

Rogge, R.D., & Bradbury, T.N. (1999). Till violence does us part: The differing roles of communication and aggression in predicting adverse marital outcomes. *Journal of Consulting and Clinical Psychology, 67,* 340–351.

Rosenbaum, A., & O'Leary, K.D. (1981). Marital violence: Characteristics of abusive couples. *Journal of Consulting and Clinical Psychology, 49,* 63–71.

Rothbaum, B.O., Meadows, E.A., Resick, P., & Foy, D.W. (2000). Cognitive behavioral therapy. In E. Foa, T. Keane, & M. Friedman (Eds.), *Effective treatments for PTSD* (pp. 60–83). NY: Guilford.

Russell, M.A. (1994). *Confronting abusive beliefs: A group treatment program for men who abuse their partners.* Thousand Oaks, CA: Sage.

Saleebey, D. (1996). The strengths perspective in social work practice: Extensions and cautions. *Social Work, 41,* 296–305.

Saunders, D. (1984). Helping husbands who batter. *Social Casework, 65,* 347–353.

Saunders, D.G. (1992). A typology of men who batter: Three types derived from cluster analysis. *American Journal of Orthopsychiatry, 62,* 264–275.

Schmidt, M.C., Kolodinsky, J.M., Carsten, G., Schmidt, F.E., Larson, M., & MacLachlan, C. (2007). Short-term change in attitude and motivating factors to change abusive behavior of male batterers after participating in a group intervention based on the pro-feminist cognitive-behavioral approach. *Journal of Family Violence, 22,* 91–100.

Schumacher, J.A., Feldbau-Kohn, S., Slep, A.M.S., & Heyman, R.E. (2001). Risk factors for male-to-female partner physical abuse. *Aggression and Violent Behavior, 6,* 281–352.

Sonkin, D.J., & Durphy, M. (1997). *Learning to live without violence: A handbook for men.* Volcano, CA: Volcano Press.

Sonkin, D.J., Martin, D., & Walker, L.E.A. (1985). *The male batterer: A treatment approach.* New York: Springer.

Stith, S.M., Smith, D.B., Penn, C.E., Ward, D.B., & Tritt, D. (2004). Intimate partner physical abuse perpetration and victimization risk factors: A meta-analytic review. *Aggression and Violent Behavior, 10,* 65–98.

Stosny, S. (1995). *Treating attachment abuse: A compassionate approach.* New York: Springer.

Stuart, R.B. (2005). Treatment for partner abuse: Time for a paradigm shift. *Professional Psychology: Research and Practice, 36,* 254–263.

Sugarman, D.B., & Frankel, S.L. (1996). Patriarchal ideology and wife-assault: A meta-analytic review. *Journal of Family Violence, 11,* 13–40.

Tafrate, R.C. (1995). Evaluation of treatment strategies for adult anger disorders. In Kassinove, H. (Ed). *Anger disorders: Definition, diagnosis, and treatment* (pp. 109–129). Philadelphia, PA: Taylor & Francis.

Taft, C.T., Murphy, C.M., King, D.W., Musser, P.H., & DeDeyn, J.M. (2003). Process and treatment adherence factors in group cognitive-behavioral therapy for partner violent men. *Journal of Consulting and Clinical Psychology, 71*, 812–820.

Taft, C.T., Murphy, C.M., Musser, P.H., & Remington, N.A. (2004). Personality, interpersonal, and motivational predictors of the working alliance in group cognitive-behavioral therapy for partner violent men. *Journal of Consulting and Clinical Psychology, 72*, 349–354.

Tavris, C. (1989). *Anger: The misunderstood emotion (rev. ed.).* NY: Touchstone.

Tutty, L.M., Bidgood, B.A., Rothery, M.A., & Bidgood, P. (2001). An evaluation of men's batterer treatment groups. *Research on Social Work Practice, 11*, 645–670.

Waltz, J., Babcock, J.C., Jacobson, N.S., & Gottman, J.M. (2000). Testing a typology of batterers. *Journal of Consulting and Clinical Psychology, 68*, 658–669.

Wathen, C.N., & MacMillan, H.L. (2004). Interventions for violence against women: A scientific review. *Journal of the American Medical Association, 289*, 589–600.

Wexler, D.B. (2000). *Domestic violence 2000: An integrated skills program for men. Group leaders manual.* New York: Norton.

Wexler, D.B. (2006). *Stop domestic violence: Innovative skills, techniques, options, and plans for better relationships. Group leader's manual.* New York: Norton.

Wolfe, D.A., Wekerle, C., Scott, K., Straatman, A.L., Grasley, C., Reitzel-Jaffe, D. (2003). Dating violence prevention with at-risk youth: A controlled outcome evaluation. *Journal of Consulting and Clinical Psychology, 71*, 279–291.

Yelsma, P. (1996). Affective orientations of perpetrators, victims, and functional spouses. *Journal of Interpersonal Violence, 11*, 141–161.

7

Application of the Broaden-and-Build Theory of Positive Emotions to Intimate Partner Violence

ERIC L. GARLAND
BARBARA L. FREDRICKSON

> But penance need not be paid in suffering . . . it can be paid in forward motion. Correcting a mistake is a positive move, a nurturing move.
> **—*Barbara Hall*, A Summons to New Orleans**

While intimate partner violence (IPV) has a multifaceted etiology, it is often triggered by stressful events. When factors such as financial strain, legal troubles, disagreement over child rearing, and martial conflict are perceived to be overwhelmingly taxing, this appraisal triggers negative emotions. Stress-induced emotions are complex, multi-component processes that involve a psychophysiological cascade, including neural, cardiovascular, endocrine, and muscular changes, cognitive-emotional alterations, and the activation of behavioral routines patterned from primitive "fight or flight" instincts (Garland, 2007a). In the context of a society that historically condoned the oppression of women,[1] these behavioral routines, when learned through the modeling of aggression from one's family of origin, may eventuate in physical violence committed by one partner against the other. The fear, anger,

---

[1] We are aware that not only men commit intimate partner violence. Females also batter their partners. The ideas within this chapter should apply in those cases as well. Even so, our pronouns throughout the chapter reflect the modal case, given that most batterers are males acting within the context of a society that has historically condoned violence against women.

sadness, and shame that co-occur with such destructive interactions perpetuate stress reactivity and maintain aggressive behavior, undermining the safety of relationship partners and well-being of the relationship. Conversely, positive affective states such as joy, humor, affection, love, hope, and wonder serve as a bulwark against the stress of life; if engendered and harnessed in an intentional manner, positive emotions might help to break the cycle of violence. The purpose of the following chapter is to outline Barbara Fredrickson's broaden-and-build theory of positive emotions and discuss its potential contribution to strengths-based batterer interventions.

HISTORY OF THE RESEARCH ON POSITIVE EMOTIONS

While the scientific study of the human mind has classically focused on pathology and deficit, today's groundswell of positive psychology has brought positive emotions under the purview of basic science and clinical research. Until recently, the evolutionarily value of positive affective states had been largely ignored by researchers for several reasons. First, unlike negative emotions, positive emotions lack clearly differentiated physiological profiles, making them more difficult to measure; the response of the autonomic nervous system remains the same across the variety of positive affective states (Fredrickson, 2003; Fredrickson & Branigan, 2005). Correspondingly, although there are characteristic facial muscle signatures for different negative emotions, positive emotions all evoke a similar Duchenne smile, involving the curl of the lips and the contraction of muscles around the eyes to produce characteristic "crow's feet" wrinkles (Fredrickson, 1998). Also, there are no specific action tendencies associated with the embodiment of particular positive emotions, as opposed to negative emotions, which do seem to show specificity regarding associated actions (Fredrickson, 2003). For instance, anger drives the impulse to attack, while fear drives the impulse to flee. Positive emotions like contentment and joy, however, are not linked to specific, evolutionarily adaptive behaviors, and thus their value was marginalized by behaviorally-oriented social scientists who dominated the field of emotion research for decades.

Another important reason for the neglect of positive emotions in the social sciences is the fact that fields such as psychology and social work tend to focus on psychopathology and social problems, rather than the salutary elements of the human condition. Negative emotions have been implicated in the etiologies of a number of physical, emotional, and behavioral disorders (Fredrickson, 1998). As such, they have become the target of both scientific research and clinical interventions. In contrast, positive affective states rarely lead to social problems, and thus have received little attention in the literature. This historical omission is ironic, in that positive emotion may be the key that unlocks salutogenic processes and provides the solution to many societal ills.

Theoretical Overview

Despite their lack of specificity and differentiation, positive emotions do have beneficial effects. According to Fredrickson's broaden-and-build theory (1998), pleasant affective states have two intertwined consequences: 1. They enhance cognitive processes by widening attentional focus from local details to a more encompassing, global view; and 2. They drive engagement in an enlarged scope of resource-building behaviors. For instance, emotions such as contentment and love tend to evoke broadened cognitive states of oneness or self-other overlap, leading to affiliation, attachment, and social support (Fredrickson, 1998; Waugh & Fredrickson, 2006). With positive emotions, myopic egocentricity expands to altruistic concern for others. Similarly, when one experiences joy and interest, he or she may be more likely to engage in novel activities outside the range of typical or automatic behavior patterns. Indeed, such positive emotions often eventuate in play and exploration, behaviors which are theorized to promote skill acquisition (Fredrickson, 1998) and deepen social bonds (Gervais & Wilson, 2005). Whereas negative emotions narrow attention and restrict behavior to stereotypic, scripted patterns of cognition and activity, transient positive emotions broaden repertoires of thought-action tendencies, which when implemented build durable physical, intellectual, and social resources (Fredrickson, 1998; Fredrickson & Branigan, 2005).

Research Associated with the Theory

There is a substantial body of empirical evidence to support this theory. First, positive emotions have been shown to broaden cognition. The work of Isen has demonstrated that positive emotions enhance creative thinking, enlarge semantic categories to include more disparate concepts, and increase one's ability to make meaningful associations (1987). Fredrickson and Branigan (2005) found that pleasant feelings expand visual attention from a focus on fine visual details to viewing objects as wholes. Recent experimental research by Anderson complements and extends this work, showing that positive affective states result in enhancements in semantic associations between remotely related terms that are correlated with increased breadth of visual attention (Rowe, Hirsh & Anderson, 2007).

Second, positive emotions increase behavioral variation, stimulating the individual to generate unusual or novel patterns of action. People induced to feel positively are able to generate a larger variety of possible activities than those exposed to neutral or negative emotion inductions, and they feel a greater number of urges to engage in activity (Fredrickson & Branigan, 2005). Persons experiencing positive affect perform better on experimental tasks that require innovative solutions (Isen, 1987), and children engage in a larger range of play when experiencing interest in the play object (Renninger, 1992).

Third, positive emotions bolster social resources. This benefit is most apparent in the case of early infant smiles, which build infant-caregiver attachment by providing affectively reinforcing interactions (Jones & Raag, 1989; Messinger, Fogel & Dickson, 2001). Even between adults, emotional episodes of gratitude form in part the basis of reciprocal social ties; for instance, gratitude increases helping behaviors, even when the provision of assistance is costly to the individual (Bartlett & DeSteno, 2006). Persons induced to feel gratitude are also more likely to help others (Emmons & McCullough, 2003). In addition, positive emotions are correlated with feelings of merging or communion between self and others, and persons experiencing positive emotions tend to have a more sophisticated understanding of other's motives and behaviors (Waugh & Fredrickson, 2006). Similarly, experimentally eliciting joy has been shown to reduce the own-race bias, the tendency of individuals to be less able to identify and distinguish persons of another race (Johnson & Fredrickson, 2005).

Fourth, positive emotions facilitate coping processes (Folkman & Moskowitz, 2000), and are used intuitively by psychologically resilient people to down-regulate the emotional and psychophysiological consequences of stressful experiences (Tugade & Fredrickson, 2004). For instance, when faced with the threat of a time-pressured public speaking task, persons identified as having more resilient personality styles reported experiencing more positive emotions and recovered more quickly from the heightened cardiovascular reactivity triggered by the stressor (Tugade & Fredrickson, 2004). This finding offers additional evidence for the empirical observation that positive emotions undo the residual cardiovascular effects of negative affective states (Fredrickson & Levenson, 1998).

The instances of cognitive, behavioral, and social broadening evidenced above may be mediated by neuroplastic changes to brain structure. Indeed, groundbreaking discoveries in neuroscience have demonstrated that the affective centers of the brain are "plastic" and malleable by life experience (for reviews, see Davidson, Jackson, & Kalin, 2000; Goleman, 2003). In the same way that novel sensory experiences and learning new behaviors triggers neuronal growth in the brain (Draganski et al., 2004; Elbert, Pantev, Wienbruch, Rockstroh & Taub, 1995; Jenkins, Merzenich, Ochs, Allard & Guic-Robles, 1990; Nudo, Milliken, Jenkins & Merzenich, 1996; Pascual-Leone, Amedi, Fregni & Merabet, 2005), new or augmented neural circuitry may result from the neurochemical cascades triggered by positive emotions. The modern science of functional genomics, the study of how genes interact with the environment to be expressed as characteristics, is consistent with the suggestion that positive affective states trigger adaptive changes in the brain and body that are regulated through the activation of the genome (Rossi, 2002a). Novel or enriching experiences that produce positive feelings of fascination and wonder have been shown to increase activity-dependent gene expression, the driving force behind the genesis and increased connectivity of neurons (Rossi, 2002b). Such positive emotion-induced neuroplasticity may mediate the long-range increases in durable cognitive and behavioral repertoires predicted by Fredrickson's broaden-and-build theory.

IMPLICATIONS FOR USE WITH THE INTIMATE PARTNER VIOLENCE OFFENDER POPULATION

The Client

While there are numerous theoretical lenses for conceptualizing the etiology of intimate partner violence, systems and social learning theory perspectives are best supported by the empirical literature. Partner violence appears to be transmitted across generations; a prospective study of 543 children over 20 years found that child abuse and exposure to violence between parents were significant predictors of later patterns of adult partner violence (Ehrensaft et al., 2003). Children who were diagnosed with conduct disorder in adolescence were more likely to commit violence against their partners as adults, as were those adolescents who experienced more severe levels of power-assertive punishment. Doubtlessly, there are positive feedback loops between these variables that create complex systems. To illustrate, children reared in violent environments may be at greater risk to develop behavior problems, which then in turn tend to evoke more punitive forms of discipline from parents. This pattern eventuates in the increased likelihood of acting out by conduct-disordered adolescents, which subsequently results in these at-risk teens being subject to even more aggressive forms of punishment. With such a childhood history of aggression, it is no wonder that many of these persons commit acts of intrafamilial violence as adults.

Other studies have found converging evidence in support of a social learning framework of intimate partner violence. For instance, an analysis of data from a nationally representative sample indicated that experience of corporal punishment in adolescence, when mediated by marital conflict, normative approval of violence, and depression, is predictive of later martial violence (Straus & Yodanis, 1996). It is clear that families exposed to economic, social, and environmental stressors are at risk for raising children with behavioral, cognitive, or affective liabilities, who in turn tend to place greater parenting demands upon their caregivers, compounding stress within the household. In this context of heightened stress, parents are more likely to use corporal punishment, especially with children who present them with disciplinary challenges. Among societies with a cultural precedent of legitimized spousal assault, families with a history of domestic violence tend to pass this aggressive behavior on to their offspring through implicit and explicit forms of social learning, such as observation, modeling, and external attributions (i.e. "Your mother deserved it.") (Straus & Yodanis, 1996). By observing repeated physical assaults against their mothers, children learn that such behavior is socially normative and an appropriate means of dealing with marital conflict. Exposed to a familial environment characterized by repeated spousal assault and corporal punishment, children have less opportunity to learn nonviolent forms of conflict resolution and problem solving, and therefore develop into adults more likely to replicate such aggressive behaviors.

The developmental psychopathology of intrafamilial violence occurs through neurobiological as well as social pathways. Indeed, individuals at greater risk for impulsive aggression tend to evince marked affective dysregulation, which has been observed via functional magnetic resonance imaging studies of prefrontal cortical activity during emotion regulation tasks (Davidson, Putnam & Larson, 2000). Similarly, disruption of the serotonin systems of the brain has been observed in populations with histories of aggression. These observations support the hypothesis that persons with deficits in neural circuits responsible for suppressing, inhibiting, and coping with negative emotions are more susceptible to impulsive acts of aggression (Davidson, Putnam, & Larson, 2000). While genetic factors contribute to the diathesis for neurobiological vulnerability, stressors such as exposure to trauma and violence shape the plastic, developing brain, providing the stimulus for the expression of aggressive phenotypes (Davidson, Jackson, & Kalin, 2000). Thus, the interplay between experience and heritable predisposition translates into the intergenerational transmission of violence within families.

Whatever its etiology and biobehavioral correlates, when viewed through the lens of the broaden-and-build theory, intimate partner violence may be seen to arise out of negative affective balances within relationships. Research has shown that there is a tipping point in the emotional balance between partners that is predictive of the health and stability of their relationships. Gottman (1994), a preeminent researcher of intimate relationships, determined that stable marriages are characterized by a ratio of five positive reactions to every one negative reaction during conflict discussions, whereas unstable marriages are characterized by less than one positive reaction for every one negative reaction. Critically, Gottman (1998) observed that such unsound marriages tend to become entrenched in negative affect reciprocity; cyclic, interactional patterns in which both partners become absorbed in self-perpetuating and escalating hostile or distressed emotional states.

Building upon this work, Fredrickson and Losada (2005) found that when there are three or fewer positive emotions to every negative emotion experienced by partners, the relationship may be defined as languishing, characterized by emotional distress and social impairment; conversely, a relationship of more than three positive emotions to every one negative emotion may be described as flourishing, characterized by coherence, acceptance, and resilience. In light of these findings, the batterer may be viewed as acting within the context of a relationship that has been destabilized by a pathological affective balance and negative affect reciprocity. From a biopsychosocial framework, given a familial history of domestic violence and a neurobiological vulnerability to affective dysregulation, the batterer has few ways to cope with emotional distress arising from relational conflict, which is often compounded by economic or legal stressors. As a complement to other interpretations, the act of battering may be more than an immoral assertion of coercive power; it can be conceptualized as an impulsive, desperate act committed by an individual whose ability to manage destructive emotions has been compromised.

From the perspective of the broaden-and-build theory, psychosocial interventions designed to augment well-being by leveraging positive emotions hold the promise of salutogenesis even for those members of society who have been cast as pathological. According to the new sciences of neuroplasticity and psychosocial genomics, persons diagnosed with psychiatric disorders related to intimate partner violence, such as mood disorders, antisocial personality disorder, intermittent explosive disorder, and substance use disorders are not condemned to repeat their past behaviors. If psychiatric illnesses are in part a result of genetic abnormalities and their concomitant disruptions in biochemical and hormonal equilibrium, these neurobiological disorders should be subject to remediation through psychosocial intervention. Similarly, if the cognitive, affective, and behavioral dysfunctions common to batterers result from a history of trauma or vicariously modeled aggression, clinical treatments may redress and retrain these maladaptive patterns. Through novel, positive experiences, mental training, and engaging in new behaviors, clients can alter their brains and compensate for constitutional or learned vulnerabilities (Begley, 2006; Davidson, Jackson, & Kalin, 2000; Garland, unpublished manuscript; Goleman, 2003).

Assessment

Assessment of intimate partner violence from the lens of the broaden-and-build theory would involve a careful exploration of emotional dynamics within relationships. Specifically, triggers of negative emotions would be assessed as a means of identifying critical links in the relational behavior chain leading to violence. Similarly, patterns of control would be explored for their emotional concomitants; batterers would be interviewed about the emotional insecurities that motivate them to attempt to exert control over their partners (Johnson & Ferraro, 2000). Johnson and Ferraro highlight the need to distinguish "intimate terrorism" from "common couple violence" by the quality of power and control dynamics in the conflict. While common couple violence is often mutual and results from poor emotion regulation in the face of relational strife, intimate terrorism occurs when one partner attempts to use violent tactics to exert control over the other (Johnson & Ferraro, 2000). Assessment should involve identifying which form of intimate partner violence is more prevalent in the relationship, while maintaining an awareness that both types of violence may be subsumed under a more general, compensatory model in which individuals attempt to control their partner as a means of maintaining a sense of mastery when their level of control is threatened (Stets, 1995). In fact, "from the phenomenological standpoint of the batterer, we may discover that the controlling and destructive behaviors are used to defend against an underlying fear of being out of control, powerless, unmanly, or feminine" (Mankowski, Haaken & Silvergleid, 2002, p. 176).

Along with this investigation of the emotional antecedents of partner violence, batterers could be assessed for their physiological response to conflict. Specifically, observation of autonomic response under duress could potentially identify persons with the dysfunctional neural circuits outlined by Davidson et al. (2000). While access to psychophysiological measures is beyond the means of most clinicians, careful scrutiny of observable signs of distress, such as increased heart rate, muscle tension, sweat, facial flushing, etc., in the midst of verbal conflict between partners could help identify whether the perpetrator is sociopathic or emotionally labile. Research by Jacobson, Gottman, and colleagues has successfully discriminated between these two subtypes of batterers – the former exhibiting internal calm, emotional detachment, and lack of physiological reactivity during verbal attacks, and the latter exhibiting marked physiological activation in tune with their emotional displays (1995; 1994). Clinicians might interview couples and use these psychophysiological indices to determine the most appropriate form of treatment for the subtype of emotional response observed, with sociopaths receiving more empathy training and affectively unstable persons receiving more instruction in emotion regulation.

Given the broaden-and-build theory's focus on positive emotions, clinical assessment of intimate partner violence would involve careful attention to pleasant affective content. Batterers and partners would be interviewed for recall of positively-valenced memories of the relationship, as well as recollections of their own individual experiences of accomplishment, flow, or joy. The consequences of such positive emotional experiences would be explored, with a focus on how the thought-action repertoires of the batterer may have been broadened during emotionally flourishing times in the relationship. Note would be made about which durable personal and relational resources have maintained over time, despite the incidents of violence.

The assessment would also explore the supportive, affectionate, and loving actions that each partner desires from the other. A critical and pragmatic series of questions could focus on which behaviors elicit genuine positive emotions from each partner. This form of evaluation could parallel solution-focused couples therapy assessment (Weiner-Davis, 1993). Attention would be paid to the interactional sequences of the couple, specifically to situations where there is either a "turning toward" or "turning away" from one's partner during ordinary exchanges, such as when a spouse approaches a partner to discuss a childcare concern and he or she is met with disinterest because the partner is preoccupied with a hobby. A higher proportion of turning away compared with turning toward leads to feeling spurned, and often initiates criticism that typically reciprocates into a negative affective cycle; conversely, more frequent turning toward by showing interest in a partner's concerns can lead to the development of a positive tone in the relationship (Gottman, 1998).

Overall, assessment of battering from a broaden-and-build perspective is centered on the exploration of affective dynamics between partners for the purpose of identifying potential linchpins for creating an upward, positive spiral of emotional flourishing. The ultimate aim of such assessment is to ascertain how the therapist might best help batterers to generate feelings of contentment, affection, and empathy toward their partners and themselves, because in the end, each individual is responsible for his or her own sense of well-being.

Treatment

Given the core idea of the broaden-and-build theory that positive emotions enlarge the scope of attention from a narrow focus to a more global, holistic view (Fredrickson & Branigan, 2005), batterer interventions could capitalize on this phenomenon to affect change. Specifically, the induction of positively-valenced affective states could help batterers transcend their egocentric need to maintain control and adopt a more compassionate, empathetic stance toward their partners and women in general. Before such empathy can be developed in the treatment process, self-centered concerns must be laid to rest. Feelings of self-loathing associated with memories of one's own violent actions or being out of control can lead to perseverative cognition, which amplifies stress and anxiety (Brosschot, Gerin & Thayer, 2006). These feelings can also lead to general defensiveness that can inhibit treatment and the learning of new skills. Preoccupation with one's own emotional distress inhibits concern for others. Conversely, having self-compassion, a caring and kind acceptance of one's own shortcomings and mistakes (Neff, 2003), allows one to take responsibility for his or her part in disastrous life events without being overwhelmed by negative affect (Leary, Tate, Adams, Allen & Hancock, 2007). Hence, treatment should address self-directed, destructive feelings first, through the induction of the positive affective state of self-compassion.

Once the batterer is able to experience a sense of calm, peace, interest, curiosity, and/or well-being, treatment should utilize these positive affective states to broaden attentional focus and build thought-action repertoires. Exercises involving the development of empathy and compassion for one's partner will be more successful when the batterer's attention has been broadened from a "local," egocentric focus to a more global orientation. Similarly, the communication skill training, conflict resolution, tension-reduction exercises, problem solving, and anger management techniques common to batterer interventions (Feder & Wilson, 2005) will be more successful when batterers are infused with positive emotions. According to the broaden-and-build theory, positive emotions impel persons to think more creatively and engage in novel behaviors (Fredrickson & Branigan, 2005). Hence, while feeling positively about self and others, batterers may show more interest in learning new skills and have more motivation to put them into practice. Indeed, empirical observation indicates that positive emotional experiences during therapy sessions may facilitate cognitive-behavioral skill learning (Rudd, Joiner & Rajab, 2001). Ultimately, the evocation of pleasant emotion through treatment may lead to positive rather than negative affect reciprocity between partners, leading to a general positive sentiment that can override transient negative emotions and buffer against future escalating cycles of hostility (Gottman, 1998).

The treatment approach suggested by the broaden-and-build theory is counter to other prominent batterer interventions, which often adopt a pejorative, moralizing, blaming stance toward the batterer. The commonly used Duluth model, rooted in feminist theory, involves confrontational tactics designed to stamp out sexist and controlling attitudes by taking a punitive, authoritarian approach toward batterers. This approach has been criticized as recapitulating the very power and control dynamics with which offending men are charged (Mankowski et al., 2002). In the wake of this model, cognitive-behavioral, psychoeducational interventions often adopt a similar politicized stance toward batterers (Feder & Wilson, 2005). However, "in a confrontational environment clients may be more likely to change their self-presentation . . . than to internalize any change in attitudes, beliefs, or behavior" (Mankowski et al., 2002, p. 175). The unstructured, psychodynamic model of batterer treatment is also counter to the broaden-and-build theory, in that its focus on feelings of vulnerability and experience of victimization (Mankowski et al., 2002) does not actualize the therapeutic benefit of positive affective states. Contrary to these forms of conventional treatment, the tenets of the broaden-and-build theory suggest that behavior change is most fruitfully evoked through the induction of positive emotions rather than negative feelings of shame, guilt, or powerlessness.

In the context of therapy, positive affective states may be induced by a variety of means. A brief outline of eight potentially useful techniques for batterer treatment is offered below. This list is not meant to be exhaustive, but instead is intended to be heuristic for the development and implementation of similar therapeutic strategies designed to elicit positive emotions.

Positive Affirmations. Positive affirmations are statements self-generated with the guidance of the clinician, designed to inculcate the client with optimistic internal attributions in an attempt to induce a positive interpretational bias. The client is directed to verbalize these phrases out loud, and also to his or herself, in order to "reprogram" deeply ingrained negative beliefs about oneself. For example, a batterer could be encouraged to repeat the phrase: "At heart, I am a good person who can learn to control his temper." While initially such statements may come across as saccharine or altogether ersatz to the client, with repetition comes habituation and a gradual entrenchment of the affirmation. Ultimately, the client needs to find the affirmations plausible and genuine; hence, this process can be reinforced through cognitive-behavioral therapy homework exercises, such as having clients keep a log of their own actions and experiences, which provide evidence for the veracity of the new positive belief. Positive self-affirmations have been empirically demonstrated to stop ruminative, negativistic thinking (Koole, Smeets, van Knippenberg & Dijksterhuis, 1999).

Positive Reappraisal/Reframing. Positive reappraisal, first articulated by Lazarus and Folkman (1984) in their transactional theory of stress and coping, is the adaptive process by which stressful events are re-construed as benign, valuable, or beneficial. When this process is leveraged within the context of therapy, it is known as reframing. During psychotherapy, the clinician may assist in reframing the offending incident so that it takes on new significance (de Shazer, 1988). In treating a batterer, therapy via reframing may help the client to envision his offense as an act done not by an evil or pathological person, but instead as a misguided attempt to cope with stressful life events. Empirical research has shown reframing or reappraisal to be a central constituent of successful bio-psychosocial outcomes (Carver et al., 1993; Folkman, 1997; Himelein & McElrath, 1996; Major, Richards, Cooper, Cozzarelli & Zubek, 1998; Penley, Tomaka & Wiebe, 2002). Positive reappraisal is an active coping strategy (Folkman, 1997), not a defense mechanism used to repress or deny. Unlike suppressing the expression of emotions, positive reappraisal does not lead to physiological or psychosocial complications (Gross, 2002; Ochsner et al., 2002). In addition, unlike suppression and denial, positive reappraisal is often the first step toward a reengagement with the stressor event.

By inducing positive affect via a solution-focus on the batterer's successes in life, attentional broadening may be evoked. Such a broadening of the attentional field may enable batterers to re-construe the painful memories of their offenses within a novel context wherein the experiences might gain new meaning. Hence, the violent offense, with its corresponding emotional memories of fear, anger, disgust, pleasure, shame, etcetera, might be reframed within the enlarged scope of attention that results from positive emotions generated in psychotherapy. The therapeutic process of reframing may be mediated through neuroplasticity, where the act of cognitive-emotional reconstruction of life events drives the development of new, or augmented neural connections (Garland, unpublished manuscript). This process may parallel the

> activity-dependent process of reactivating a fear memory in order to extinguish and reconstruct it on the level of gene expression, protein synthesis, and brain plasticity, (including synaptogenesis, neurogenesis) [which] is the psychobiological essence of creative replay in the practice of therapeutic hypnosis and psychotherapy (Rossi, 2005).

In addition to modifying their own internal attributions, clients can be taught to positively reappraise or reframe the events in their lives. This positive interpretational bias training is especially salient for batterers, who may tend to interpret the ambiguous behaviors of their partners as threats to their relationship. For example, a batterer might interpret his wife's going out to lunch with a male coworker as evidence of her intent to commit adultery. Such threat interpretations may lead to the batterer's sense of a loss of control over his relationship and consequently trigger acts of violence. Experimental induction of benign interpretational bias has been shown to result in significant reductions in trait-level anxiety (Mathews, Ridgeway, Cook & Yiend, 2007).

Recall of Positive Memories. Another means of inducing positive affect is the intentional recall of positive memories. Clinicians can ask clients to recall when they've been at their personal best, or when they experienced their relationship as most warm and loving. Memory recall is biased in humans, whose autobiographical selves consist of constantly reconstructed narratives shaped by social, cultural, and historical context. Batterers, who may suffer from affective dysregulation (Davidson, Putnam, & Larson, 2000), often have histories of abuse and depression (Ehrensaft et al., 2003; Straus & Yodanis, 1996) that provide a negativistic context for their future relationships. A large corpus of research details negative memory bias in depression, in which depressed individuals, relative to nondepressed persons, have a greater tendency to remember and recall negatively-valenced events (e.g. Mathews & MacLeod, 1994, 2005; Watkins, Vache, Verney, Muller & Mathews, 1996). However, positive memory bias is an integral component to healthy relationships; intimate partners who report greater marital satisfaction tend to remember more positive events about their relationships, and view them in an idealized manner (Gagne & Lydon, 2004). By training batterers to recall the positive features and circumstances of their partners and relationships, negative, depressogenic memory bias may be offset, which has been shown to enhance personal happiness (Bryant, Smart & King, 2005). Similarly, batterers could be encouraged to recall instances when they observed the healthy resolution of conflict, or positive, loving interactions between other couples. Such memories could be used for modeling adaptive behavior.

Mental Imagery. Mental imagery has a potent influence on emotion (Holmes & Mathews, 2005). Emotions can be represented by mental images, and mental images co-occur with intense affective states, such as in posttraumatic stress disorder, where intrusive imagery associated with the traumatic event elicits powerful feelings of fear, anger, and disgust (Holmes, Grey & Young, 2005). Given the tight interconnection between internal imagery and mood, clinicians can guide clients to intentionally generate imagery of a positive nature to induce positive emotional states. Training in positive imagery induction improves mood and can lead to positive interpretation bias of ambiguous events (Holmes, Mathews, Dalgleish & Mackintosh, 2006). For example, batterers could be instructed to imagine themselves in loving, enjoyable, or relaxing scenarios with their partners, or alternately invoke metaphorical images of peace and well-being, such as being suffused with a calming, healing radiance. Meta-analysis has demonstrated that clinical hypnosis, a technique that heavily involves the use of mental imagery, can significantly potentiate cognitive-behavioral therapy efforts (Kirsch, Montgomery & Sapirstein, 1995).

Focus on Solutions. Following a solution-focused therapy approach (de Shazer, 1988), clinicians can intentionally focus therapeutic conversations on solutions. By focusing on strengths and past successes rather than pathology and behavioral dysfunction, typically-resistant, involuntary clients often become more amenable to the therapy process, as has been observed during positive emotion-focused clinical interventions with suicidal, involuntarily hospitalized clients (Rudd et al., 2001). In addition, this approach can produce rapid behavioral changes that are often associated with feelings of accomplishment, surprise, and joy. Such positive emotions facilitate solution-focused therapy work. If positive emotions broaden people's mindsets, then they can facilitate the generation of solution-oriented, cognitive-behavioral strategies. Within the realm of batterer treatment, a focus on solutions might entail a series of questions designed to tap into times when the batterer successfully controlled urges to strike his partner and used alternative means of resolving relational conflict. Additionally, batterers could be asked to discuss instances when they were satisfied with their relationship, in an effort to discover actions that supported the positive emotional tone of those occasions. By gathering this information, the clinician can then prescribe the client to carry out these solution-oriented behaviors in an effort to recreate similar successful interactions.

Compliments. Solution-focused therapy also involves the strategic use of compliments (de Shazer, 1988), which, as a rule, are delivered to clients prior to any change-oriented directives. These compliments should highlight how the client has successfully managed difficult situations, persevered despite challenges, or otherwise prevented his situation from becoming worse. Clinicians can augment clients' motivation to change as well as their sense of self-efficacy by administering genuine compliments in a deliberate fashion throughout the therapy process. Fascination, amazement, and enthusiasm on the part of the therapist in response to the client's description of solutions can evoke positive emotions. One can only speculate if such enthusiastic demonstrations from the therapist generate positive affect in the client via activation of the mirror neuron system, which is involved in the recognition of other's intentions through the entrainment of brain activity during the act of behavioral observation (E. L. Rossi & Rossi, 2006). In support of this conjecture, a conceptual synthesis of the neuroscience litera-ture by Gervais and Wilson suggests that the contagiousness of laughter and positive affect involves the reciprocal activation of mirror neuron circuits in the brains of individuals who are coupled together in social exchange (Gervais & Wilson, 2005).

The "Miracle Question." Another potent solution-focused technique is the use of the "miracle question," first formulated by Steve de Shazer and Insoo Kim Berg to assist clients who were experiencing difficulty recog-nizing exceptions to the problems in their lives (de Shazer, 1988). The "miracle question" asks clients to imagine how they would live their lives differently if a miracle had occurred and the problem that had brought them into therapy was gone. A positive affective tone can be elicited by asking the batterer to envision a miracle in which he and his relation-ship partner feel joy, interest, contentment, and love. Oftentimes, just the asking of this question evokes positive emotions of surprise, curios-ity, and a sense of wonder. However, the miracle question may be chal-lenging to answer, particularly for clients who are especially entrenched in feelings of hopelessness about their situation. Hence, engagement in this therapeutic process can initiate heightened states of arousal and positive stress (eustress) that are theorized to drive neuroplasticity, lead-ing to new learning (E. L. Rossi, 2002, 2004). The broaden-and-build theory suggests a hypothesis about the mechanism that may undergird this technique: the miracle question may help clients generate creative solutions to their difficulties by evoking positive emotions, leading to attentional broadening and the expansion of thought-action repertoires.

Meditative Techniques: Loving-Kindness and Mindfulness. Although social work, psychology, and psychiatry have addressed psychopathology in the West for nearly a century, the millennia-old traditions of Buddhism offer a sophisticated system with which to understand and ameliorate the destructive emotions implicated in psychosocial problems such as intimate partner violence. According to Buddhist psychology, affective states such anger, desire, craving, or jealousy are considered mental afflictions (*kleshas* in Sanskrit) that cause suffering and distort one's view of reality (Goleman, 2003). These afflictions are thought to arise out of a deeply rooted grasping or attachment to the concept of an immutable self, which is subjectively experienced as vulnerable and in constant need of external fulfillment. As the Buddha observed thousands of years ago, this attachment is the root of all human suffering because it leads to the fundamental ignorance of the true nature of existence: the impermanent, ever-changing quality of phenomenal experience (Kalupahana, 1987). By resisting or denying the ephemeral character of existence, one suffers and experiences negative emotions. Clinging to a sense of an unchanging self inevitably leads to emotional distress, as life events alter aspects of self that had been previously held as one's identity (Garland, 2007a). Out of this fundamental attachment are derived the most rudimentary of emotions: attraction to what is deemed pleasant, and the aversion to what is deemed unpleasant. When one is thwarted from obtaining what one is attracted to or forced to deal with what one has an aversion toward, a whole host of negative emotions arise that bias accurate sensory perception of reality.

The notion that conceptual processes can influence perception via emotional states is wholly congruent with the findings of affective neuroscience, which has delineated functional pathways between prefrontal cortical, limbic, and sensory brain structures (Davidson, Jackson, & Kalin, 2000; Davidson et al., 2002; Davidson, Putnam, & Larson, 2000; Goleman, 2003). Thus, the brain itself is wired such that cognition and expectation can influence both emotion and sensation.

Given the astonishingly precise and detailed theory of mental life offered by Buddhist psychology, it is perhaps unsurprising that this spiritual tradition offers a number of "antidotes" to the negative affective states associated with battering. For instance, feelings of anger or fear that might otherwise trigger a relapse of violent behavior can be short-circuited by the practice of mindfulness meditation; the intentional regulation of attention in a nonjudgmental, receptive manner (Kabat-Zinn, 1982). Mindfulness, which involves the cultivation of a metacognitive state of awareness (Garland, 2007a), attenuates emotional distortions of stimuli perception by facilitating nonevaluative contact with phenomenological experience (Brown, Ryan & Creswell, in press). Hence, mindfulness training can enable batterers to gain a more accurate view of their partners, and help them to discern when they are experiencing irrational or unjustified anxieties. Through the practice of mindfulness, a batterer may experience the urge to lash out at his partner without reacting to the impulse by stepping back, or "decentering" (Segal, Williams & Teasdale, 2002), from the mental experience of anger. Mindfulness may also facilitate positive reappraisal of stressful circumstances, allowing for psychological adjustment in the face of adversity (Garland, 2007b). In addition to diffusing negative emotions, mindfulness training can induce states of well-being, leading to significant changes in brain function, such as asymmetrical left anterior prefrontal cortex activation, a known neural correlate of positive emotions (Davidson et al., 2003). A recent study of a mindfulness-based relationship enhancement program found that the intervention improved emotional intimacy and reduced conflict within participating couples (Carson, Carson, Gil & Baucom, 2004), suggesting that this form of training could be especially useful for batterer treatment.

However, the "antidote" most congruent with the broaden-and-build theory is loving-kindness meditation, called *metta* in Sanskrit, a form of mental training in which the practitioner intentionally cultivates a sense of compassion by wishing joy, love, and peace, and freedom from suffering upon self and others (Kristeller & Johnson, 2003). By invoking the memory of a person who elicits unconditional feelings of tenderness and love (e.g., a trusted caregiver), the loving-kindness practitioner generates affective states of warmth and empathy, and then successively applies these emotions to internal images of a benefactor or teacher, a friend, themselves, a neutral person, someone with whom one is experiencing interpersonal conflict, an enemy, and finally to all living beings. This practice of generating a state of unconditional compassion and benevolence can lead to marked alterations in the synchronization of neurons in the brain (Lutz, Greischar, Rawlings, Ricard & Davidson, 2004) indicative of coherent and integrated psychological functioning (Williams et al., 2005). Increased neural synchrony as a result of loving-kindness meditation has been found not only during the meditative state, but also when long-term practitioners are not meditating (Lutz et al., 2004), suggesting that long-term mental practice can induce lasting, trait-level changes mediated by structural modifications to the brain (Begley, 2006). Given these findings, it seems likely that through loving-kindness training, batterers can learn to develop empathy and compassion toward themselves, their partners, and people in general, in spite of possible family histories of domestic violence and neurobiological propensities to affective dysregulation. For, as Gottman so eloquently stated, "Admiration is the antidote for contempt." (1998, p. 192).

All the aforementioned techniques generate positive emotions and therefore may facilitate both the broadening of mindsets and the building of durable personal resources, thus enhancing batterer treatment. Some of these techniques, such as loving-kindness or mindfulness practice, could be used as stand-alone therapies like the meditation-based relationship program of Carson and colleagues (2004) or in combination with psychoeducational skills-training, while others could be used to augment extant intimate partner violence interventions.

Positive emotions such as loving feelings toward one's partner or oneself are both physically and mentally salubrious (Esch & Stefano, 2005a). It is known that the experience of love involves secretion of endogenous chemicals such as oxytocin, dopamine, and serotonin (Esch & Stefano, 2005b), critical neurotransmitters and neuromodulators involved in autoregulation and adaptation to stress (Stefano & Esch, 2005). For example, self-reported feelings of being supported by one's partner are correlated with decreases in blood pressure and greater oxytocin levels (Grewen, Girdler, Amico & Light, 2005), and physical affection via hugs exert similar salutary physiological effects (Light, Grewen & Amico, 2005). It therefore stands to reason that self-regulatory processes can be enhanced through the induction of positive affect. Indeed, this has been substantiated through empirical research (Fredrickson, 2003; Fredrickson & Levenson, 1998; Tugade & Fredrickson, 2004). Given this finding, a broaden-and-build approach to batterer treatment could prevent future acts of violence by enhancing emotion regulation and altruistic concern for others, while decreasing stress reactivity. The act of battering may be seen to arise within the context of a historically patriarchal, misogynistic culture and out of conditions of affective dysregulation and deep insecurity manifested as the desire to control one's partner. From this perspective, what could be a better antidote to such a social ill than the evocation of positive feelings of love, empathy, and compassion?

Case Study Illustration

The following case study is a composite of several clients who have received therapy for relational aggression from a broaden-and-build perspective:

Mike, a 35-year-old Caucasian auto mechanic, was court-referred for treatment after being arrested on domestic violence charges against his wife Patty, who reported him to police after an occasion when he had given her a black eye after slapping her repeatedly. After the arrest and for the bulk of the subsequent therapy process, Mike and Patty were separated; Mike remained in their home while Patty moved in with her mother, who lived in the same town as the couple.

In his initial biopsychosocial assessment, Mike reported slapping Patty when he was "stressed about money" and when he saw her "talking with other guys." Using emotional probing techniques, Mike disclosed a deep-rooted insecurity that Patty, like the other women in his life (including his own mother), would abandon him when he was "down and out." This insecurity seemed to intensify when Mike received criticism from his boss at work and when his paycheck was insufficient to cover the monthly bills. After exploring these negative affective triggers, the assessment attended to positive emotional dynamics in the relationship. At first, it was difficult for Mike to recall positive experiences in his marriage, but eventually he began to smile broadly as he discussed how good he felt when Patty called him "her hero" after he fixed her car in their second week of dating. He also recalled times when Patty would hug him after a hard day of work and tell him that "everything would be alright" despite getting yelled at by his boss. When soothed in this manner, Mike reported being more willing to talk with Patty, being better able to listen to her concerns, and keeping a more even temper at work.

Mike's treatment began with several sessions of cognitive restructuring and solution-focused therapy aimed at disrupting the self-denigrating belief "I must be an evil man if I hit my wife" by asking him to recall times when he had in fact exhibited kindness and compassion toward others. In the context of therapy, Mike developed a positive affirmation, "I am a good person who can learn from his mistakes," which he was encouraged to potentiate with a visualization of himself five years in the future "after a miracle has occurred and your problem with violence is now gone." As a daily practice, Mike was directed to identify three pieces of evidence to support this new belief (e.g. helping an elderly woman who slipped on the sidewalk outside of the auto shop). Next, therapy targeted Mike's interpretations of Patty's behaviors. Instead of seeing Patty's concern about the monthly budget as a sign that she wanted to have an affair with a wealthier man, Mike was taught to reinterpret her behavior as a sign of how much she cared about his welfare and the wellbeing of their relationship.

To foster positive affective states and develop a compassionate stance toward others, Mike was given meditation instruction during later therapy sessions. First, Mike was taught how to become mindful of his breath. By focusing his awareness on his breathing patterns, Mike learned how to decenter from worries or frustrations and develop a sense of equanimity. Next, Mike was instructed in loving-kindness meditation, where he initially visualized experiencing unconditional love for his maternal grandmother, who had cared for him during childhood when his mother had been hospitalized. Using this visualization as a reference point for feelings of love and compassion, Mike was taught to apply this affective state to images of his coworkers, Patty, and ultimately, even his boss. After several sessions of loving-kindness meditation, Mike expressed feeling happy and relieved knowing that he could be a "caring person."

When Mike's self-loathing had significantly abated, treatment focused on taking a hard look at his abusive behaviors. Because Mike was not as guilt-ridden and defensive as he had been at the inception of therapy, he was able to take accountability for his violent, out-of-control behavior and recognize how he had taken his own insecurities and stresses out on Patty. At this point, the therapist contacted Patty to ascertain her willingness to attend couples' therapy. Patty expressed her desire to move back in with Mike if "he really has his stuff together this time." The therapist urged Patty to remain cautious and suspend any decision to move back in together until she and Mike had worked together in couples' therapy. Couples' therapy was oriented toward increasing the positive-to-negative affective balance in the relationship and learning conflict resolution skills. Mike and Patty were able to identify behaviors in the other partner that evoked joy, contentment, and security, and they were encouraged to practice these behaviors in and out of therapy. After a seven-month course of therapy and incrementally increased time spent together on dates, Patty moved back in with Mike. They continued couples' counseling every other week to maintain their therapeutic gains.

Hopeful Outcomes

The ideal outcome of batterer interventions based on the broaden-and-build theory is to reduce the likelihood of future violence through the batterer's development of affective competence, the ability to regulate one's emotions even in the face of significant economic, social, or relational stressors. Through pursuit of this aim, treatment would help the batterer to build durable personal resources (physical, intellectual, psychological, and social), including the capacity to access positive emotional states and experience empathy for others. The latter achievement is of evident value; in qualitative interviews of reformed batterers, empathy is one of the most frequently endorsed variables as critical to changing abusive behavior (Scott & Wolfe, 2000). However, the former quality, the ability to internally generate positive emotions rather than rely on external wish-fulfillment to establish a sense of well-being, has been undervalued both in batterer treatment and in psychotherapy at large. This oversight is unfortunate, because reduced dependency on partners is another factor deemed essential by reformed batterers in the change process (Scott & Wolfe, 2000). Through a positive emotion-focused intervention, the batterer may realize that he alone is responsible for his own happiness, not his partner – thus he has no right to attempt to control the behavior of others in order to obtain a sense of security or satisfaction. In this respect, the broaden-and-build theory converges with the accountability-based philosophies of extant models of batterer treatment.

In the end, the long-term goal of any such treatment is to rectify the root of the problem of aggression. More than simply learning new, adaptive behaviors and taking accountability for one's past actions, for change to be enduring, the violent offender must undergo a radical transformation that touches the very substrates of his being. There is hope for the possibility of such change, for through intensive training, even the structure of the adult brain may be transformed, as neuroscientific investigations of long-term meditation practitioners have shown (Goleman, 2003; Lazar et al., 2005). However, the onus for such conversion does not lie upon the shoulders of the batterer alone, because ultimately it is society that must embrace and support the batterer in his redemption from disgrace. Perhaps as a culture we can find no better exemplar than the Baemba tribe of South Africa, wherein

> when a person acts irresponsibly or unjustly, he is placed in the center of the village, alone and unfettered. All work ceases, and every man, woman, and child in the village gathers in a large circle around the accused individual. Then each person in the tribe speaks to the accused, one at a time, about all the good things the person . . . has done in his lifetime. All his positive attributes, good deeds, strengths, and kindnesses are recited carefully and at length. The tribal ceremony often lasts several days. At the end, the tribal circle is broken, a joyous celebration takes place, and the person is symbolically and literally welcomed back into the tribe. (Walker, 2007).

REFERENCES

Bartlett, M.Y., & DeSteno, D. (2006). Gratitude and prosocial behavior: helping when it costs you. *Psychological Science, 17*, 319–325.

Begley, S. (2006). *Train your mind, change your brain: How a new science reveals our extraordinary potential to transform ourselves.* New York: Ballantine.

Brosschot, J.F., Gerin, W., & Thayer, J.F. (2006). The perseverative cognition hypothesis: a review of worry, prolonged stress-related physiological activation, and health. *Journal of Psychosomatic Research, 60*, 113–124.

Brown, K.W., Ryan, R.M., & Creswell, J.D. (in press). Mindfulness: Theoretical foundations and evidence for its salutary effects. *Psychological Inquiry.*

Bryant, F., Smart, C., & King, S. (2005). Using the past to enhance the present: Boosting happiness through positive reminiscence. *Journal of Happiness Studies, 6*, 227–260.

Carson, J.W., Carson, K.M., Gil, K.M., & Baucom, D.H. (2004). Mindfulness-based relationship enhancement. *Behavior Therapy, 35*, 471–494.

Carver, C.S., Pozo, C., Harris, S.D., Noriea, V., Scheier, M.F., Robinson, D.S., et al. (1993). How coping mediates the effect of optimism on distress: A study of women with early stage breast cancer. *Journal of Personality and Social Psychology, 65*, 375–390.

Davidson, R.J., Jackson, D.C., & Kalin, N.H. (2000). Emotion, plasticity, context, and regulation: perspectives from affective neuroscience. *Psychological Bulletin, 126*, 890–909.

Davidson, R.J., Kabat-Zinn, J., Schumacher, J., Rosenkranz, M., Muller, D., Santorelli, S.F., et al. (2003). Alterations in brain and immune function produced by mindfulness meditation. *Psychomatic Medicine, 65*, 564–570.

Davidson, R.J., Lewis, D.A., Alloy, L.B., Amaral, D.G., Bush, G., Cohen, J.D., et al. (2002). Neural and behavioral substrates of mood and mood regulation. *Biological Psychiatry, 52*, 478–502.

Davidson, R.J., Putnam, K.M., & Larson, C.L. (2000). Dysfunction in the neural circuitry of emotion regulation—a possible prelude to violence. *Science, 289*(5479), 591–594.

de Shazer, S. (1988). *Clues: Investigating solutions in brief therapy.* New York: W.W. Norton & Company.

Draganski, B., Gaser, C., Busch, V., Schuierer, G., Bogdahn, U., & May, A. (2004). Neuroplasticity: changes in grey matter induced by training. *Nature, 427*(6972), 311–312.

Ehrensaft, M.K., Cohen, P., Brown, J., Smailes, E., Chen, H., & Johnson, J.G. (2003). Intergenerational transmission of partner violence: a 20-year prospective study. *Journal of Consulting and Clinical Psychology, 71*, 741–753.

Elbert, T., Pantev, C., Wienbruch, C., Rockstroh, B., & Taub, E. (1995). Increased cortical representation of the fingers of the left hand in string players. *Science, 270*(5234), 305–307.

Emmons, R.A., & McCullough, M.E. (2003). Counting blessings versus burdens: an experimental investigation of gratitude and subjective well-being in daily life. *Journal of Personality & Social Psychology, 84*, 377–389.

Esch, T., & Stefano, G.B. (2005a). Love promotes health. *Neuroendocrinology Letters, 26*(3), 264–267.

Esch, T., & Stefano, G.B. (2005b). The Neurobiology of Love. *Neuroendocrinology Letters, 26*, 175–192.

Feder, L., & Wilson, D.B. (2005). A meta-analytic review of court-mandated batterer intervention programs: Can courts affect abusers' behavior? *Journal of Experimental Criminology, 1,* 239–262.

Folkman, S. (1997). Positive psychological states and coping with severe stress. *Social Science and Medicine, 45,* 1207–1221.

Folkman, S., & Moskowitz, J.T. (2000). Positive affect and the other side of coping. *American Psychologist, 55,* 647–654.

Fredrickson, B.L. (1998). What good are positive emotions? *Review of General Psychology, 2,* 300–319.

Fredrickson, B.L. (2003). The value of positive emotions: The emerging science of positive psychology is coming to understand why it's good to feel good. *American Scientist, 91,* 330–335.

Fredrickson, B.L., & Branigan, C. (2005). Positive emotions broaden the scope of attention and thought-action repertoires. *Cognition and Emotion, 19,* 313–332.

Fredrickson, B.L., & Levenson, R.W. (1998). Positive emotions speed recovert from the cardiovascular sequelae of negative emotions. *Cognition and Emotion, 12,* 191–220.

Fredrickson, B.L., & Losada, M.F. (2005). Positive affect and the complex dynamics of human flourishing. *American Psychologist, 60,* 678–686.

Gagne, F.M., & Lydon, J.E. (2004). Bias and accuracy in close relationships: An integrative review. *Personality and Social Psychology Review, 8,* 322–338.

Garland, E.L. (2007a). The meaning of mindfulness: A second-order cybernetics of stress, metacognition, and coping. *Complementary Health Practice Review, 12,* 15–30.

Garland, E.L. (2007b). *Mindfulness in positive reappraisal: A metacognitive focal point for psychotherapeutic interventions.* Paper presented at the National Council on Family Relations: Theory Construction and Methodology Workshop.

Garland, E.L. (unpublished manuscript). The biopsychosocial paradigm in the 21st century: Neuroplasticity, psychosocial genomics, and the science of empowerment.

Gervais, M., & Wilson, D.S. (2005). The evolution and functions of laughter and humor: a synthetic approach. *The Quarterly Review of Biology, 80,* 395–430.

Goleman, D. (2003). *Destructive emotions: How can we overcome them?* New York: Bantam Dell.

Gottman, J.M. (1994). *What predicts divorce?* Hillsdale, NJ: Erlbaum.

Gottman, J.M. (1998). Psychology and the study of marital processes. *Annual Review of Psychology, 49,* 169–197.

Grewen, K.M., Girdler, S.S., Amico, J., & Light, K.C. (2005). Effects of Partner Support on Resting Oxytocin, Cortisol, Norepinephrine, and Blood Pressure Before and After Warm Partner Contact. *Psychosomatic Medicine,* (Vol. 67, pp. 531–538).

Himelein, M.J., & McElrath, J.V. (1996). Resilient child sexual abuse survivors: Cognitive coping and illusion. *Child Abuse & Neglect, 20,* 747–758.

Holmes, E.A., Grey, N., & Young, K.A. (2005). Intrusive images and "hotspots" of trauma memories in Posttraumatic Stress Disorder: an exploratory investigation of emotions and cognitive themes. *Journal of Behavior Therapy and Experimental Psychiatry, 36,* 3–17.

Holmes, E.A., & Mathews, A. (2005). Mental imagery and emotion: a special relationship? *Emotion, 5,* 489–497.

Holmes, E.A., Mathews, A., Dalgleish, T., & Mackintosh, B. (2006). Positive interpretation training: effects of mental imagery versus verbal training on positive mood. *Behavior Therapy, 37,* 237–247.

Isen, A.M. (1987). Positive affect, cognitive processes, and social behavior. *Advances in Experimental Social Psychology, 20,* 203–253.

Jacobson, N.S., Gottman, J.M., & Shortt, J.W. (1995). The distinction between Type 1 and Type 2 batterers—Further considerations: Reply to Ornduff et al. (1995), Margolin et al. (1995), and Walker (1995). *Journal of Family Psychology, 9,* 272–279.

Jacobson, N.S., Gottman, J.M., Waltz, J., Rushe, R., Babcock, J., & Holtzworth-Munroe, A. (1994). Affect, verbal content, and psychophysiology in the arguments of couples with a violent husband. *Journal of Consulting and Clinical Psychology, 62,* 982–988.

Jenkins, W.M., Merzenich, M.M., Ochs, M.T., Allard, T., & Guic-Robles, E. (1990). Functional reorganization of primary somatosensory cortex in adult owl monkeys after behaviorally controlled tactile stimulation. *Journal of Neurophysiology, 63,* 82–104.

Johnson, K.J., & Fredrickson, B.L. (2005). We all look the same to me: Positive emotions eliminate the own-race bias in face recognition. *Psychological Science, 16,* 875–881.

Johnson, M.J., & Ferraro, K.J. (2000). Research on domestic violence in the 1990s: Making distinctions. *Journal of Marriage and the Family, 62,* 948–963.

Jones, S.S., & Raag, T. (1989). Smile production in older infants: the importance of a social recipient for the facial signal. *Child Development, 60,* 811–818.

Kabat-Zinn, J. (1982). An outpatient program in behavioral medicine for chronic pain patients based on the practice of mindfulness meditation: Theoretical consideratoins and preliminary results. *General Hospital Psychiatry, 4,* 33–47.

Kalupahana, D.J. (1987). *The principles of Buddhist psychology.* Albany: State University of New York Press.

Kirsch, I., Montgomery, G., & Sapirstein, G. (1995). Hypnosis as an adjunct to cognitive-behavioral psychotherapy: a meta-analysis. *Journal of Consulting and Clinical Psychology, 63,* 214–220.

Koole, S.L., Smeets, K., van Knippenberg, A., & Dijksterhuis, A. (1999). The cessation of rumination through self-affirmation. *Journal of Personality and Social Psychology, 77*(1), 111–125.

Kristeller, J.L., & Johnson, T. (2003). *Cultivating loving-kindness: A two-stage model for the effects of meditation on compassion, altruism, and spirituality.* Paper presented at the Works of Love: Scientific and Religious Perspectives on Altruism.

Lazar, S.W., Kerr, C.E., Wasserman, R.H., Gray, J.R., Greve, D.N., Treadway, M.T., et al. (2005). Meditation experience is associated with increased cortical thickness. *Neuroreport, 16,* 1893–1897.

Lazarus, R.S., & Folkman, S. (1984). *Stress, Appraisal, and Coping.* New York: Springer.

Leary, M.R., Tate, E.B., Adams, C.E., Allen, A.B., & Hancock, J. (2007). Self-compassion and reactions to unpleasant self-relevant events: the implications of treating oneself kindly. *Journal of Personality and Social Psychology, 92,* 887–904.

Light, K.C., Grewen, K.M., & Amico, J.A. (2005). More frequent partner hugs and higher oxytocin levels are linked to lower blood pressure and heart rate in premenopausal women. *Biological Psychology, 69,* 5–21.

Lutz, A., Greischar, L.L., Rawlings, N.B., Ricard, M., & Davidson, R.J. (2004). Long-term meditators self-induce high-amplitude gamma synchrony during mental practice. *The Proceedings of the National Academy of Sciences USA, 101,* 16369–16373.

Major, B., Richards, C., Cooper, M.L., Cozzarelli, C., & Zubek, J. (1998). Personal resilience, cognitive appraisals, and coping: an integrative model of adjustment to abortion. *Journal of Personality and Social Psychology, 74,* 735–752.

Mankowski, E.S., Haaken, J., & Silvergleid, C.S. (2002). Collateral damage: An analysis of the achievements and unintended consequences of batterer intervention programs and discourse. *Journal of Family Violence, 17*, 167–184.

Mathews, A., & MacLeod, C. (1994). Cognitive approaches to emotion and emotional disorders. *Annual Review of Psychology, 45*, 25–50.

Mathews, A., & MacLeod, C. (2005). Cognitive vulnerability to emotional disorders. *Annual Review of Psychology, 1*, 167–195.

Mathews, A., Ridgeway, V., Cook, E., & Yiend, J. (2007). Inducing a benign interpretational bias reduces trait anxiety. *Journal of Behavior Therapy and Experimental Psychiatry, 38*, 225–236.

Messinger, D.S., Fogel, A., & Dickson, K.L. (2001). All smiles are positive, but some smiles are more positive than others. *Developmental Psychology, 37*, 642–653.

Neff, K. (2003). Self-compassion: An alternative conceptualization of a healthy attitude toward oneself. *Self and Identity, 2*, 85–102.

Nudo, R.J., Milliken, G.W., Jenkins, W.M., & Merzenich, M.M. (1996). Use-dependent alterations of movement representations in primary motor cortex of adult squirrel monkeys. *Journal of Neuroscience, 16*, 785–807.

Pascual-Leone, A., Amedi, A., Fregni, F., & Merabet, L.B. (2005). The plastic human brain cortex. *Annual Review of Neuroscience, 28*, 377–401.

Penley, J.A., Tomaka, J., & Wiebe, J.S. (2002). The association of coping to physical and psychological health outcomes: a meta-analytic review. *J Behav Med, 25*(6), 551–603.

Renninger, K.A. (1992). *Individual interest and development: Implications for theory and practice.* Hillsdale, NJ: Erlbaum.

Rossi, E.L. (2002). A conceptual review of the psychosocial genomics of expectancy and surprise: neuroscience perspectives about the deep psychobiology of therapeutic hypnosis. *American Journal of Clinical Hypnosis, 45*, 103–118.

Rossi, E.L. (2002a). *The psychobiology of gene expression.* New York: Norton.

Rossi, E.L. (2002b). Psychosocial genomics: gene expression, neurogenesis, and human experience in mind-body medicine. *Advances in Mind Body Medicine, 18*, 22–30.

Rossi, E.L. (2004). Stress-induced alternative gene splicing in mind-body medicine. *Advances in Mind and Body Medicine, 20*, 12–19.

Rossi, E.L. (2005). The ideodynamic action hypothesis of therapeutic suggestion: Creative replay in the psychosocial genomics of therapeutic hypnosis. *European Journal of Clinical Hypnosis, 6*, 2–12.

Rossi, E.L., & Rossi, K. (2006). The neuroscience of observing consciousness & mirror neurons in therapeutic hypnosis. *American Journal of Clinical Hypnosis, 48*, 263–278.

Rowe, G., Hirsh, J.B., & Anderson, A.K. (2007). Positive affect increases the breadth of attentional selection. *The Proceedings of the National Academy of Sciences USA, 104*, 383–388.

Rudd, M.D., Joiner, T., & Rajab, M.H. (2001). *Treating suicidal behavior: An effective time-limited approach.* New York: Guilford.

Scott, K.L., & Wolfe, D.A. (2000). Change among batterers: Examining men's success stories. *Journal of Interpersonal Violence, 15*, 827–842.

Segal, Z., Williams, J.M., & Teasdale, J.D. (2002). *Mindfulness-based cognitive therapy for depression.* New York: The Guilford Press.

Stefano, G.B., & Esch, T. (2005). Love and stress. *Neuroendocrinol Letters, 26*, 173–174.

Stets, J.E. (1995). Role identities and person identities: Gender identity, mastery identity, and controlling one's partner. *Sociological Perspectives, 38,* 129–150.

Straus, M.A., & Yodanis, C.L. (1996). Corporal punishment in adolescence and physical assaults on spouses in later life: What accounts for the link? *Journal of Marriage and the Family, 58,* 825–841.

Tugade, M.M., & Fredrickson, B.L. (2004). Resilient individuals use positive emotions to bounce back from negative emotional experiences. *Journal of Personality and Social Psychology, 86,* 320–333.

Walker, A. (2007). Sunbeams. *The Sun, July* 2007(379).

Watkins, P.C., Vache, K., Verney, S.P., Muller, S., & Mathews, A. (1996). Unconscious mood-congruent memory bias in depression. *Journal of Abnormal Psychology, 105,* 34–41.

Waugh, C.E., & Fredrickson, B.L. (2006). Nice to know you: Positive emotions, self-other overlap, and complex understanding in the formation of a new relationship. *The Journal of Positive Psychology, 1,* 93–106.

Weiner-Davis, M. (1993). *Divorce busting: A step-by-step approach to making your marriage loving again.* New York: Simon & Schuster.

Williams, L.M., Grieve, S.M., Whitford, T.J., Clark, C.R., Gur, R.C., Goldberg, E., et al. (2005). Neural synchrony and gray matter variation in human males and females: integration of 40 Hz gamma synchrony and MRI measures. *Journal of Integrative Neuroscience, 4,* 77–93.

8

Applying the Good Lives Model to Male Perpetrators of Domestic Violence

ROBYN L. LANGLANDS
TONY WARD
ELIZABETH GILCHRIST

The quality of life is determined by its activities.   *—Aristotle*

Domestic violence is a pervasive social problem that has devastating emotional, physical, psychological, and financial costs for individuals, families, and communities (Chrisler & Ferguson, 2006; Healey, Smith & O'Sullivan, 1998). Between 1998 and 2002, 3.5 million Americans were victimized by a family member, while close to 14 million were the victims of violent crimes perpetrated by a boyfriend, girlfriend, friend, or acquaintance (Bureau of Justice Statistics, 2005).

Feminist activists worked tirelessly in the 1970s to bring the problem of "wife battering" to the attention of the public and lawmakers, and as a result, domestic violence was typically conceptualized within a gendered framework (McHugh & Frieze, 2006). This perspective drew attention to how the patriarchal structure of society both caused and maintained male violence against women by endorsing general beliefs of male entitlement and differential power between males and females. However, this approach has been criticized for failing to attend to individual differences, because across all societies the risk of abuse differs greatly from one individual to another. Furthermore, the gendered approach to domestic violence does not include other patterns of violence and abuse, such as those that may occur within same-sex relationships.

217

Since then, considerable research has been conducted in the field of what is now interchangeably referred to as domestic violence, family violence, interpersonal violence, spouse abuse, and intimate partner violence. Contemporary interventions for domestic violence tend to utilize a combined theoretical approach grounded in the feminist-driven Duluth model (Pence & Paymar, 1993a), and cognitive behavioural therapy (CBT; Babcock, Green & Robie, 2004; Bowen, Brown & Gilchrist, 2002; Davis & Taylor, 1999). Unfortunately, despite the widespread use of such intervention programs, recent reviews have demonstrated that they only have a small impact on the reduction of recidivism (Babcock, Green & Robie, 2004; Sartin, Hansen & Huss, 2006; Smedslund, Dalsbø, Steiro, Winsvold & Clench-Aas, 2007).

Many researchers have acknowledged that the limited evidence for efficacy of treatment programs may be due, in part, to methodological difficulties (Babcock, Green & Robie; Sartin, Hansen & Huss, 2006; Wathen & MacMillan, 2003). These include a lack of consensus on the operational definitions of key terminology (Johnson, 2006; Sartin, Hansen & Huss, 2006), difficulties in accurately measuring true rates of recidivism (Babcock, Green & Robie, 2004; Guterman, 2004; Dobash & Dobash, 2000; Sartin, Hansen & Huss, 2006), an absence of randomized, controlled trials and longitudinal studies (Guterman, 2004; Sartin, Hansen & Huss, 2006), high attrition rates (Sartin, Hansen & Huss, 2006), and a narrow focus on physical violence to the exclusion of psychological and sexual abuse (Bennett Cattaneo & Goodman, 2005; McHugh & Frieze, 2006).

It is clear that we have not as yet arrived at a reliable and effective evidence-based intervention for individuals who inflict harm on their partners. In addition to the methodological limitations discussed above, one reason for this may be that interventions are primarily focused on offenders' deficits or risk factors, and therefore fail to engage them in the complex and difficult process of turning their lives around. In our view, it is important to consider alternative approaches alongside the continued use and refinement of traditional models. The purpose of this chapter is to investigate how the Good Lives Model (GLM; Ward & Gannon, 2006; Ward & Stewart, 2003) can be used to frame domestic violence interventions, and the potential impact of this model on the high attrition rates exhibited by domestic violence offenders.

The GLM is a strengths-based approach to offender rehabilitation that seeks to equip individuals with the capabilities to achieve personal goals in ways that also reduce their risk of reoffending (Ward & Maruna,

2007; Ward, Polaschek & Beech, 2006). While the GLM has been applied to sexual and violent offending (e.g., Ward & Stewart, 2003; Whitehead, Ward & Collie, 2007), it has not been utilized with perpetrators of domestic violence. However, we believe that the individualized approach to offender rehabilitation advocated by the GLM may be productive in overcoming some of the difficulties that practitioners have when trying to engage domestically violent offenders in treatment.

To begin, we will outline the empirical basis for the GLM and the core assumptions of the model. We will then describe the good lives approach to the assessment and treatment of domestically violent men. Finally, we will consider future directions for the use of the GLM in domestic violence interventions. For the purposes of this chapter, we will use the term domestic violence to encompass a range of violent actions as included in the broad definitions adopted by both professionals in the USA (e.g., the power and control wheel of the Duluth model of intervention, Pence & Paymar, 1993b) and in the UK (as identified in the "constellation of abuses" Dobash & Dobash, 1980). We have also chosen to limit our discussion to male perpetrators of domestic violence against females. While we acknowledge that domestic violence can be carried out by women, and that it does occur within some same-sex relationships, these groups are beyond the scope of this paper.

THE GOOD LIVES MODEL (GLM)

The GLM (Ward & Gannon, 2006; Ward & Maruna, 2007; Ward & Stewart, 2003) is a capabilities or strengths-based approach to offender rehabilitation (Rapp, 1998), in which the aim of treatment is to equip individuals with the necessary psychological and social conditions and resources to achieve well-being in socially acceptable and personally satisfying ways. The goal of strengths-based approaches is to enhance individuals' capacities to live meaningful, constructive, and ultimately satisfying lives so they can desist from further offending (Ward & Maruna, 2007; Ward, Polaschek & Beech, 2006). The GLM is a comprehensive theory of offender *rehabilitation* that focuses on promoting individuals' important personal goals, while at the same time reducing and managing their risk for future offending (for greater detail on the GLM see Ward, 2002; Ward & Brown, 2004; Ward & Gannon, 2006; Ward & Marshall, 2004; Ward & Stewart, 2003). It is a *strength-based* approach in two respects: (a) it takes seriously offenders' personal preferences and values (that is, the things that matter most to them in the world) and draws upon these primary goods to motivate individuals to live better lives; and (b) clinicians using the model seek to provide offenders with the competencies (internal conditions) and opportunities (external conditions) to implement treatment plans based on these primary goods.

Fundamental to the GLM is the notion of a *Good Lives Plan* or *Conception*—a plan for living that incorporates important and valued goods that individuals, as active psychological agents, seek to achieve. This plan for living leads to meaningful, satisfactory, and worthwhile lives that are not conducive to offending (Ward & Gannon, 2006; Ward & Stewart, 2003; Ward et al., 2006). The good lives plan represents a type of "blueprint" that includes those goals and activities that are important in achieving the type of life the individual would like to attain and reflect the kind of person he wishes to become.

The GLM is underpinned by three related, core ideas, all of which are integral to the construction of each individual's good lives conception:

1. Humans are active, goal-seeking beings who consistently attempt to construct a sense of meaning and purpose in their lives;
2. The majority of human actions reflect attempts to meet inherent human needs or *primary human goods* (Emmons, 1999; Ward, 2002); and
3. *Instrumental* or *secondary goods* provide the concrete means or strategies to pursue and achieve primary human goods.

Primary human goods are actions, states of affairs, or experiences that are inherently beneficial to human beings. These goods are naturally sought for their own intrinsic properties, rather than as means to some other end (Arnhart, 1998; Deci & Ryan, 2000; Emmons, 1999; Schmuck & Sheldon, 2001). Secondary goods represent the means to achieve primary goods and, as such, have instrumental value.

The pursuit and achievement of primary human goods are integral to individuals' sense of meaning and purpose in their lives, and, in turn, their well-being. In other words, when individuals are able to secure the full range of primary human goods (i.e., to meet their inherent human needs), their well-being flourishes. For such individuals, their good lives conception is working well. However, when individuals are unable to secure a number of primary human goods, constructing meaningful and purposeful lives is frustrated and well-being is compromised; in this case, their good lives conception is dysfunctional. It is proposed that men who abuse their partners have, at least in part, a flawed good lives conception, and that enhancing their well-being, in tandem with risk management, can function to reduce risk for reoffending.

The psychological, social, biological, and anthropological research evidence provides support for the existence of at least ten groups of primary human goods (Arnhart, 1998; Aspinwall & Staudinger, 2003; Cummins, 1996; Deci & Ryan, 2000; Emmons, 1999; Linley & Joseph, 2004; Murphy, 2001; Nussbaum, 2000; Rescher, 1993). The ten primary goods are: life, knowledge, excellence in work and play, agency, inner peace, relatedness, community, spirituality, happiness, and creativity. No individual good is more important to attain than others; rather, all goods in some form or another are necessary to achieve a fulfilling life. These primary human goods are multifaceted, and the names of each good are general labels for thematically related clusters of goods. For example, the primary good of relatedness may be further divided into sub-goods of intimacy, friendship, support, caring, and so on.

In addition to these primary goods, *instrumental* or secondary goods represent the particular ways (i.e., means) of achieving primary goods. Using the example of relatedness, it is possible to secure this primary good via romantic, parental, or other personal relationships, and the specific means will be highly individualized. The notion of instrumental goods or means is particularly important when applying the GLM to offending behavior, as within this model it is assumed that individuals commit offenses in the pursuit of obtaining more abstract primary goods, albeit in destructive and ultimately unsatisfying ways.

From the perspective of the GLM, all primary goods serve as instrumental goods, as well as constituting ends in themselves—that is, outcomes that are worth seeking for their own sake. For example, the primary good of knowledge can be a desired end in and of itself as well as a means to achieve another good, such as relatedness. That is, in order to establish a relationship with another person, an individual must understand what another person is experiencing in addition to his or her needs and wants, as well as what kinds of actions would ease establishment of a relationship with the person in question. Furthermore, primary goods are abstract and people are not usually aware of them as ultimate ends, but more typically speak of secondary goods as their values and everyday goals. As such, in assessment, primary human goods are most likely to be inferred indirectly from more concrete goals and life objectives.

It is important to note that these primary goods are not considered hierarchical—that is, the occurrence of one good is not dependent upon the preexistence of another. In addition, individuals are unique in the priorities or weightings they give to different goods due to personal preferences, strengths, opportunities, developmental history, and cultural context. For example, an individual from a culture that places greater social value on *relatedness* than on *agency* may internalize the value of relatedness and prioritize the pursuit of group mastery over individual mastery. In this example, the individual will achieve greater well-being when the group does well than when the individual does well. Thus, all individuals have their own unique *good lives conceptions* that reflect the priority given to the various primary human goods, as well as the secondary goods or strategies chosen to achieve the primary goods. Within the GLM, a good life is attainable when an individual possesses the internal skills and capabilities, and the external opportunities and supports, to achieve primary human goods in a socially acceptable manner. For a fulfilling and balanced life, it is important that the full range of primary goods is attained within an individual's lifestyle (Ward & Maruna, 2007; Ward & Stewart, 2003).

Flaws in the Good Lives Plan

According to the GLM, criminogenic needs (dynamic risk factors) are internal or external *obstacles* that frustrate and block the acquisition of primary human goods. The responses to these obstacles are learned and conditioned throughout the individual's life. What this means is that the individual lacks the ability to obtain important outcomes (i.e., goods) in his life, and in addition, is frequently unable to think about his life in a reflective manner. It is assumed that failure to acquire certain goods results from problems inherent in the good lives conception or its implementation, and in the manner that individuals go about seeking human goods. The GLM proposes *four specific flaws* that reflect problems in the manner that individuals pursue primary goods and seek to meet inherent human needs; essentially what have been called criminogenic needs (i.e., the flaws) in the forensic psychological literature (Andrews & Bonta, 2003). These flaws negatively affect individuals' abilities to acquire primary human goods and to attain valued goals and objectives. The flaws also lead individuals to attempt to attain goods in harmful and socially unacceptable ways.

First, individuals may demonstrate problems with the *means* used to secure goods. As described above, individuals seek primary human goods via more concrete secondary or instrumental goods. Behaviors that individuals engage in to attain these goods can be problematic (e.g., seeking control or emotional relief through intimidating or assaulting one's partner), thus presenting a problem with the means or the manner by which the individual seeks to attain the good.

Second, a lack of *scope* or *variety* among goods being sought may result in chronic dissatisfaction or lack of a sense of fulfillment. Individuals demonstrating problems in scope insufficiently value a particular good, resulting in an incomplete good lives conception. In short, in this type of situation, individuals live unbalanced lives with crucial goods not evident in their lifestyle. This absence of critical goods is traced back to problems in the good lives conception or plan (e.g., the individual may not consider equal relationships to be important), or in implementation (e.g., they may believe that the best way to assure their partner's fidelity is through intimidation and threats).

Third, a lack of *coherence* in the good lives plan may result in conflict amongst goods sought. This occurs when individuals simultaneously attempt to attain a good in ways or circumstances that are incompatible, resulting in behavior that actually functions to inhibit achievement of one or more goods. A lack of coherence also results in psychological distress. An example of conflict in a good lives plan is when a person seeks a sense of empowerment within an intimate relationship by inappropriately dominating his partner and as a result reduces the quality of the relationship. In this instance, there is conflict between the way the person concerned pursues the goods of agency and relatedness.

Fourth, a *lack of skills or capacity* may inhibit or prevent the individual from forming a good lives conception. Within the GLM, a lack of capacity or skills refers to an inability to achieve the good sought because of the absence of psychological, social, or other resources. The lack of capacity can be *internal*, associated with skill deficits or problematic attitudes, or *external*, including such factors as poor social support, a lack of educational and work resources, and cultural constraints. In some situations, a change in external circumstances may result in a specific strategy that was previously effective becoming ineffective in securing the good in question (e.g., when a change of job requires a different profile of employment skills).

Utilizing the GLM with Domestically Violent Men

The GLM was initially developed as a model for use with sexual offenders (Ward & Stewart, 2003), and later was extended to work with violent offenders (see Whitehead, Ward & Collie, 2007). While it has not yet been used with domestic violence offenders, the GLM is a broad intervention framework that can incorporate both the evaluative tenets of the Duluth model and the capacity-building focus of CBT in two ways.

First, the important focus of the Duluth model on gender socialization issues is addressed by the GLM's insistence that human beings are interdependent and rely on a range of social resources and relationships to achieve their goals. Furthermore, the ability to effectively implement a GLM plan is critically reliant upon internal and external conditions. For example, the achievement of a healthy intimate relationship requires certain external conditions such as the provision of social resources (e.g., dating partners, supportive networks, etc.) and internal conditions, such as appropriate gender and relationship norms and intimacy skills. In certain social circumstances, individuals may not possess the requisite set of internal and external conditions, and may establish unequal and ultimately destructive relationships.

Second, with respect to CBT approaches, the GLM offender treatment is an evaluative and capacity (skill) building process, and therefore specific CBT techniques can be useful in this process. However, the emphasis on equipping offenders with the ability to adequately assess and choose warranted norms means that techniques are always in the service of appropriate goals and values.

What the GLM adds over and above existing programs is an individualized approach that focuses on each offender's strengths and goals, rather than primarily on his deficits. Utilizing a deficit-driven approach is a mistake because offenders become defensive, unmotivated, and more difficult to engage. As noted earlier, one of the major problems with programs for domestic violence offenders is the high attrition rate. Sartin, Hansen, and Huss (2006) hypothesize that the failure of domestic violence interventions to cater to needs of each individual offender may be one of the reasons that many offenders drop out of treatment. Additionally, the lack of treatment readiness exhibited by many domestic violence offenders is hardly surprising, considering that the majority are court-mandated to attend programs. It is likely that the GLM will increase the chance of motivating individuals to invest in the intervention process by attending to offenders' primary values and interests, offering them alternative means of achieving their goals and, at the same time, reducing their level of risk.

The Good Lives Approach to Assessment

Given the dual focus of goods promotion and risk management advocated by the GLM framework, assessment protocols ought to be designed for use in conjunction with systematic evaluation of an offender's individual, social, and psychological risk factors, self-regulation capacity, and personal circumstances, yielding a comprehensive case formulation that guides assessment, treatment, and supervision (Ward & Maruna, 2007). The aim of this case formulation is to provide a comprehensive understanding and conceptual model of individual offenders' good lives plans, goals with respect to this plan, pathways to offending, goals with respect to offending, risk factors, internal and external capabilities and constraints, and the interrelationships between these factors that will direct intervention and function as a guide for treatment implementation.

The basic steps in this process are described below. It is noted that this case formulation, though constructed by the clinician based on assessment, is developed in a collaborative manner with the offender in the form of mutual goal-setting, particularly with respect to treatment targets and the development of a good lives plan. It is suggested that such collaboration will increase engagement with treatment, and can be revisited with individuals periodically throughout treatment to evaluate progress and to ensure the relevance of the plan.

The *first step* in this case conceptualization process concerns detection of the clinical phenomena implicated in individuals' abusive behaviors. In other words, what kind of problems do they present with, and what criminogenic needs and dynamic risk factors are evident? To accomplish this assessment, clinicians need to use empirically validated risk assessment instruments, which will assist in both determining the appropriate intensity level of treatment, as well as criminogenic needs to be addressed in treatment. Dynamic risk factors (criminogenic needs) empirically related to risk and recidivism include such factors as negative social influences, antisocial lifestyles, intimacy deficits, problems with general self-regulation (e.g., problem solving, impulsivity, emotion regulation), cognitive distortions, sexual self-regulation deficits (e.g., sexual deviance), and lack of cooperation with supervision (Hanson, Harris, Scott & Helmus, 2007; Hanson & Morton-Bourgon, 2005; Ward & Beech, 2004). Criminogenic and non-criminogenic need factors are also addressed. These factors influence engagement with treatment and are associated with responsivity issues such as attachment problems and problems with self-esteem, motivation, learning styles, cognitive abilities, language, personality, and culture (Andrews & Bonta, 2003; Marshall, Anderson & Fernandez, 1999; Marshall, Marshall, Serran & Fernandez, 2006; Serin & Kennedy, 1997). The degree to which these factors are present will vary from case to case, and each requires comprehensive assessment and inclusion in case formulation and treatment planning. Finally, any additional clinical phenomena, such as mental disorders, personality disorders, and psychological functioning are also assessed and included in the case formulation.

In the *second step* of the case formulation approach, the function of offending (i.e., what the individual expected to achieve via offending) is established through the identification of primary goods that are directly or indirectly linked to the abusive actions. In addition, the identification of the *overarching good* or value around which the other goods are oriented should also be ascertained. The overarching good informs clinicians about what is most important in a person's life and hints at his fundamental commitments. By this stage in the assessment process, the clinician will have a good sense of why the person is domestically abusive, his level of risk, the flaws in his good lives plan, and whether the link between his pursuit of primary goods is directly or indirectly connected to his offending. The clinician will also have insight into the person's offense pathway, offense-related goals and strategies, self-regulation styles and capacities, dynamic risk factors, and any other clinical phenomena requiring intervention.

In the *third step,* the selection of the overarching good(s) or value(s) around which the other goods are oriented should be identified and made a focus of the treatment plan. For example, an offender might be particularly committed to doing well in his job and have a strong work ethic. In this situation, it would make sense to use work-related mastery as a key motivator and a pivot for any GLM reintegration plan while also ensuring that the other primary goods are present to a sufficient degree and support rather than conflict with the offender's major goals. Of course, from a therapeutic and ethical perspective it is necessary to ensure that there are no inherent conflicts between the offender's overarching goals and the other aspects of his life. Balance is an important consideration, as is the need to not import the strategies used in one domain into another. For example, while possibly necessary in the context of work, striving for mastery and dominance could prove disastrous and ultimately related to violence in an intimate relationship.

In the *fourth step*, the selection of secondary goods or values that specify how the primary goods will be translated into ways of living and functioning is undertaken. These will be linked to dynamic risk factors, and the treatment plan will include specific interventions for targeting criminogenic needs and skill development. For example, an intervention could include identifying ways that an individual can achieve a sense of autonomy or agency within a relationship without resorting to abusive actions, and then developing strategies to assist him in achieving this. Unlike work settings that may be hierarchical, acceptance of the norms of equality within relationships means that it is never appropriate to seek to control or dominate one's partner. In such a context, respecting the autonomy of a partner means respecting the partner's right to make his or her own decisions and learning to negotiate over disputed matters, rather than simply issuing directives. In this example, the offender's strong valuing of work-related achievement and need for respect and some degree of control is carefully distinguished from the other domains of his life. Furthermore, his pursuit of respect and status in the work setting is tailored in way that also guarantees respect for the other employees while maintaining the integrity of his particular role.

In the *fifth step*, the contexts or environments in which the person is likely to be living during or following treatment are identified. This is the ecological aspect of the GLM, and is strongly supported by its etiological assumptions concerning the relationship between human beings and the contexts in which they live their lives. This also ensures that the treatment plan and expected outcomes are personally relevant to the individual and the contexts in which he or she lives, including the opportunities and limitations that will be present, thus assuring that the plan is relevant, realistic, and achievable. Addressing the context or environment in which offenders live their lives is critical for domestic violence offenders, considering that their offending behaviors are carried out within the context of interpersonal relationships.

In the *sixth step*, the clinician constructs a treatment plan for the offender based on the above considerations and information. Taking into account the kind of life that would be fulfilling and meaningful to the individual (i.e., primary goods, secondary goods, and his relationship to ways of living and possible environments), the clinician notes the relevant environments and internal (e.g., competencies, beliefs) and external (e.g., opportunities, social environment) conditions required to achieve primary goods and manage risk. The plan also explicitly includes ways to target dynamic risk factors, offense pathways and attendant treatment needs, and follow-up treatment and supervision needs with respect to both risk management and the acquisition and maintenance of good lives (Yates, 2003; Ward & Maruna, 2007). This good lives plan therefore fully integrates treatment targets and risk management plans in a comprehensive manner.

The Good Lives Approach to Therapy

An exploration of an offender's good lives plan can assist the clinician in formulating a reintegration plan that provides the opportunity for the individual to achieve greater satisfaction and well-being, alongside planning for risk management. If the offender is able to see how the treatment plan will directly benefit him in terms of goods that he values, he will be more likely to engage and invest in treatment, and an effective therapeutic alliance can be formed. Increased engagement with treatment can lead to reduced dropout rates, which is particularly important given the high attrition rates among domestic violence offenders (Sartin, Hansen & Huss, 2006), and evidence that demonstrates that offenders who do not complete treatment reoffend at higher rates than those who complete treatment (Hanson & Bussière, 1998; Hanson et al., 2002).

As stated above, the GLM has a twin focus with respect to therapy for offenders: (a) to promote goods and (b) to manage/reduce risk. What this means is that a major aim of therapy is to equip the offender with the skills, values, attitudes, and resources necessary to lead a different kind of life, one that is personally meaningful and satisfying, and does not involve inflicting harm. In other words, a life that has the basic primary goods and ways of effectively securing them built into it. These aims reflect the etiological assumptions of the GLM that offenders are either directly seeking basic goods through the act of offending, or else commit an offense because of the indirect effects of a pursuit of basic goods. Furthermore, according to the GLM, risk factors represent omissions or distortions in the internal and external conditions required to implement a good lives plan in a specific set of environments. Instilling the necessary internal (i.e., skills, values, beliefs) and external (i.e., resources, social supports, opportunities) conditions is likely to reduce or eliminate each individual's set of criminogenic needs.

One of the virtues of the GLM is its ability as a theory to integrate practices and factors already accepted as important in the rehabilitation arena. Because treatment is focused on obtaining outcomes (in socially acceptable ways) that offenders value, they are more likely to see therapy as relevant to their lives rather than as something imposed by clinicians and correctional agencies (see Ward & Maruna, 2007). The advantage of treating offenders within the GLM framework is that it reminds therapists to actively consider several critical elements of treatment that tend to be *underemphasized* in the traditional risk management approach. For one thing, the combined approach to treatment outlined in this chapter ensures that clinicians deal explicitly with offender goals and values (motivation), and helps them to appreciate the importance of process variables and the therapeutic alliance. The combined approach also incorporates psychological, social, cultural, environmental, and biological factors in the treatment plan, bridges the gap between etiological and treatment considerations, and understands that offenders are best viewed as psychological agents seeking meaning rather than mechanisms that need to be "restructured" (Maruna, 2001). It is a deeply humanistic and empirically guided approach to treatment that takes seriously the fact that therapy is an art as well as a science. These features reveal the integrative and unifying power of the GLM rehabilitation framework.

CASE STUDY

In order to make the rather abstract nature of the GLM more concrete we have constructed a case study of a violent offender from our experience of working with a number of domestically violent individuals.

Mr. X is a 35-year-old New Zealand Maori (i.e., indigenous) man who was a prisoner and subsequent parolee under the mandate of the New Zealand Department of Corrections. At the time of Mr. X's initial contact he was an active patched member of a criminal gang with a notorious reputation. He was heavily tattooed on his face and body, with many tattoos vividly denoting his gang allegiance. He had past convictions for sexual and nonsexual violence against strangers and his female partners. Mr. X disclosed a number of notable features about his family background and early development during clinical interview that are all too frequently the precursors of persistent aggression. He was the middle child of two siblings (brother and sister) and was raised in a family where he was exposed to interpersonal violence and sexual abuse. He alternated between living with his parents and his grandfather, who were of Maori descent. Mr. X had reported that he often chose to live with his grandfather in order to avoid severe physical punishment from his parents. Mr. X was assessed as a high-risk violent offender on the basis of an actuarial measure, psychopathy assessment, and the additional information disclosed by him during clinical interview.

Mr. X's earlier treatment engagement seemed largely motivated by the prospect of parole. Accordingly, the potential beneficial effects of his treatment were limited by his lack of internal treatment readiness over multiple criminogenic domains. As described above, the GLM of offender rehabilitation proposes a twin focus on goods promotion (approach goals) and risk management (avoidance related goals), with each complimenting the other. Examination of the theoretical concepts of the GLM indicated it provided three potential benefits in Mr. X's case. First, the GLM provided an overall framework for treatment integration by acknowledging Mr. X's long-term future well-being at the macro level but embracing the risk-needs framework at the micro level. Second, the GLM could potentially facilitate Mr. X's treatment readiness by triggering or motivating him to apply his prior acquired knowledge. Third, by focusing on approach goals Mr. X could potentially access positive affective states and begin to visualize a new sense of identity. At the same time, GLM provides him the impetus to implement the skills necessary to manage his future risk and prevent reoffending.

An initial step from a GLM perspective is to assess a client's own goals, life priorities, and aims for the intervention in order to establish relevant treatment goals. This step can be defined as finding the dream factor: what did clients see themselves doing when they were children, what goals do they have for their lives, and what have they always wanted to achieve? Using such questions is a means to explore the concept of a good life where the therapist attends to the client and takes into account the kind of life that would be fulfilling and meaningful to the individual (i.e., his primary goods, secondary goods, and his relationship to ways of living and possible environments). This also facilitated a therapeutic change whereby Mr. X shifted from a predominantly present-focused orientation to a predominantly future-focused orientation. In this regard, life had previously been represented by the highs of drugs, alcohol, multiple partners, quick money, violence, and collegial brotherhood through the gang. Now, life was beginning to be represented by the values associated with education (i.e., he wanted to go to a university to study Maori history and language), equality and respect, intimacy (i.e., he wanted a happy and loving relationship with a woman), collegial support through pro-social endeavors, and self-fulfillment. He began to forge a new identity based on these values and success at having achieved mastery at working toward his goals. Essentially, the GLM was invaluable in enabling Mr. X to visualize and begin working toward a life for himself that he would never have previously considered.

Mr. X's approach goals included: attending university in order to further his interest in Maori studies, concepts, and spirituality; obtaining a drivers license; having improved relationships with members of the opposite sex; and making his family "proud." The resultant criminogenic effects included reducing his drug usage, forming pro-social peers and accordingly disassociating with antisocial peers, interacting with society, and adopting new pro-social attitudes, particularly around violence, power and control, and his pledge of life-long allegiance to the gang. When examining the criminogenic factors frustrating access to human goods, a plan was formulated that revolved around drug reduction, relationship skills, and antisocial thinking in order to achieve the client's desired outcomes. The important part of this phase is to listen carefully to the client, have him desire a better (i.e., good) life, and in turn address his identified criminogenic needs so he can achieve his valued goals. As Mr. X examined his approach goals he began to realize through self-reflection that implementation of his risk management plan was essential to the attainment of his primary human goods. Thus, Mr. X began to recognize that in order to attend university, acquire a driver's license, and develop cultural expertise he would have to dissociate from his gang, form a new peer group, and reduce his drug and alcohol intake.

Mr. X made a number of profound life changes and achievements that were not foreseeable prior to embarking on a GLM approach. His sexual predatory and violent behaviour is no longer reinforced by antisocial peers, he has reduced his drug intake, he remains in a committed relationship (with no violent episodes), he has had success in establishing a new peer group through his university studies, he is developing prosocial leisure pursuits (e.g., diving), and he has utilised his support network appropriately. As a result, his sense of identity is being formed around prosocial achievements and aspirations rather than gang affiliation and criminal activities. Therapeutic techniques were effectively "wrapped around" Mr. X's core goals and were used in part to help him obtain capabilities to pursue and achieve his GLM plan. In order to achieve his goal of attending university (good of knowledge) and a loving and sound intimate relationship, Mr. X needed to reduce his drug and alcohol intake, deal with his anger and frustrations more adaptively, and engage in some degree of problem solving when faced with obstacles. In other words, equipping Mr. X with the internal and external resources to achieve his GLM plan enabled him to also reduce his risk of reoffending (e.g., violence against his partner and others, drug-taking, property offences, etc).

CONCLUSION

The GLM has the capacity to integrate both the feminist-based tenets of the Duluth model and the skills management techniques promoted by CBT, while increasing the motivation of individual offenders to participate in treatment. One of the differences between current interventions for domestic violence offenders and the GLM is the highly individualized focus of the latter. Interventions for domestic violence offenders tend to focus on group work and while the GLM as a rehabilitation framework can incorporate this form of treatment, it is essential that clinicians also work with individual offenders to develop relevant and realistic good lives plans.

Future research will need to examine the extent to which the GLM functions as an effective rehabilitation model for domestic violence offenders. As discussed earlier, the GLM has been successfully applied to sexual and violent offenders (Ward & Stewart, 2003; Whitehead, Ward & Collie, 2007), and at present there are a number of treatment programs underway throughout the world for violent, psychopathic, juvenile, and substance dependent offenders. Reports from therapists working with these offenders are encouraging and point to greater therapy participation and motivation (Ward & Maruna, 2007). In addition, recent research evidence has emerged that is extremely supportive of the GLM's contention that offenders want to focus on a broad range of personal concerns that are related to well-being and living better lives, and also that the presence of GLM goods can help individuals to desist from further offending (e.g., McMurran, Theodosi, Sweeney & Sellen, 2008; Willis & Grace, 2008). Given that domestic violence encompasses both sexual and physical abuse, parallels can be drawn between the offense types that have been addressed within the GLM framework and domestic violence. By constructing in-depth case formulations and subsequent good lives plans for each individual offender, the GLM also has the potential to target psychological abuse more effectively than current interventions, which adopt a more general approach.

REFERENCES

Andrews, D.A., & Bonta, J. (2003). *The psychology of criminal conduct* (3rd ed.). Cincinnati, OH: Anderson.

Arnhart, L. (1998). *Darwinian natural right: The biological ethics of human nature.* Albany, NY: State University of New York Press.

Aspinwall, L.G., & Staudinger, U.M. (Eds.). (2003). *A psychology of human strengths: Fundamental questions and future directions for a positive psychology.* Washington, DC: American Psychological Association.

Babcock, J.C., Green, C.E., & Robie, C. (2004). Does batterers' treatment work? A meta-analytic review of domestic violence treatment. *Clinical Psychology Review, 23*, 1023–1053.

Bennett Cattaneo, L., & Goodman, L.A. (2005). Risk factors for reabuse in intimate partner violence: A cross-disciplinary critical review. *Trauma, Violence, and Abuse, 6*, 141–175.

Bowen, E., Brown, L., & Gilchrist, E. (2002). Evaluating probation based offender programmes for domestic violence perpetrators: A pro-feminist approach. *The Howard Journal of Criminal Justice, 41*, 221–236.

Bureau of Justice Statistics. (2005). *Family violence statistics: Including statistics on strangers and acquaintances.* Washington, DC: US Department of Justice.

Chrisler, J.C., & Ferguson, S. (2006). Violence against women as a public health issue. *Annals of the New York Academy of Science, 1087*, 235–249.

Cummins, R.A. (1996). The domains of life satisfaction: An attempt to order chaos. *Social Indicators Research, 38*, 303–328.

Davis, R.C., & Taylor, B.G. (1999). Does batterer treatment reduce violence? A synthesis of the literature. *Women & Criminal Justice, 10*, 69–93.

Deci, E.L., & Ryan, R.M. (2000). The "what" and "why" of goal pursuits: Human needs and the self-determination of behavior. *Psychological Inquiry, 11*, 227–268.

Dobash, R.E., & Dobash, R.P. (2000). Evaluating criminal justice interventions for domestic violence. *Crime & Delinquency, 46*, 252–270.

Dobash, R.E., & Dobash, R.P. (1980). *Violence against wives: A case against the patriarchy.* London: Open Books.

Emmons, R.A. (1999). *The psychology of ultimate concerns.* New York: Guilford.

Gilchrist, E., Johnson, R., Takriti, R., Beech, A., Kebbell, M., & Weston, S. (2003). Domestic violence offenders: Characteristics and offending related needs. *Findings No. 217.* London: Home Office.

Gilchrist, E., & Kebbell, M. (2004). Domestic violence: Current issues in definitions and intervention. In J. Adler (Ed.), *Forensic Psychology: Debates, concepts, practice.* Devon, UK: Willan.

Guterman, N.B. (2004). Advancing prevention research on child abuse, youth violence, and domestic violence: Emerging strategies and issues. *Journal of Interpersonal Violence, 19*, 299–321.

Hanson, R.K., & Bussière, M.T. (1998). Predicting relapse: A meta-analysis of sexual offender recidivism studies. *Journal of Consulting and Clinical Psychology, 66*, 348–362.

Hanson, R.K., Gordon, A., Harris, A.J.R., Marques, J.K., Murphy, W., Quinsey, V.L., et al. (2002). First report of the collaborative outcome data project on the effectiveness of psychological treatment for sex offenders. *Sexual Abuse: A Journal of Research and Treatment, 14*, 169–194.

Hanson, R.K., Harris, A.J.R., Scott, T., & Helmus, L. (2007). *Assessing the risk of sexual offenders on community supervision: The dynamic supervision project.* User Report No. 2007-05. Ottawa: Public Safety Canada.

Hanson, R.K., & Morton-Bourgon, K. (2005). The characteristics of persistent sexual offenders: A meta-analysis of recidivism studies. *Journal of Consulting and Clinical Psychology, 73*, 1154–1163.

Healey, K., Smith, C., & O'Sullivan, C. (1998). *Batterer intervention: Program approaches and criminal justice strategies.* Washington, D.C.: Report to the National Institute of Justice.

Johnson, M.P. (2006). Conflict and control: Gender symmetry and asymmetry in domestic violence. *Violence Against Women, 12*, 1003–1018.

Johnson R., Gilchrist E., Beech, A.R., Weston, S., Takriti, R., & Freeman, R. (2006). A psychometric typology of U.K. domestic violence offenders. *Journal of Interpersonal Violence, 21*, 1270–85.

Linley, P.A., & Joseph, S. (2004). Applied positive psychology: A new perspective for professional practice. In P.A. Linley & S. Joseph (Eds.), *Positive psychology in practice* (pp. 3–12). New Jersey, NY: John Wiley & Sons.

Marshall, W.L., Anderson, D., & Fernandez, Y.M. (1999). *Cognitive behavioral treatment of sexual offenders.* Chichester, UK: Wiley.

Marshall, W.L., Marshall, L.E., Serran, G., & Fernandez, Y.M. (2006). *Treating sexual offenders: An integrated approach.* New York, NY: Routledge.

Maruna, S. (2001). *Making good: How ex-convicts reform and rebuild their lives.* Washington, DC: American Psychological Association.

McHugh, M.C., & Frieze, I.H. (2006). Intimate partner violence: New Directions. *Ann. N.Y. Acad. Sci., 1087*, 121–141.

McMurran, M., Theodosi, E., Sweeney, A., & Sellen, J. (2008). What do prisoners want?: Current concerns of adult male prisoners. *Psychology, Crime, & Law, 14*, 267–274.

Murphy, M.C. (2001). *Natural law and practical rationality.* New York: Cambridge University Press.

Nussbaum, M.C. (2000). *Women and human development: The capabilities approach.* New York: Cambridge University Press.

Pence, E., & Paymar, M. (1993a). *Education groups for men who batter: The Duluth mModel.* New York: Springer Publishing Company.

Pence, E., & Paymar, M. (1993b). *Domestic violence information manual: The Duluth domestic abuse intervention project.* Springer Publishing Company, Inc., http://www.duluth-model.org/, accessed October 2007.

Rapp, C.A. (1998). *The strengths model: Case management with people suffering from severe and persistent mental illness.* New York: Oxford University Press.

Rescher, N. (1993). *A system of pragmatic idealism. Vol. II: The validity of values.* Princeton, NJ: Princeton University Press.

Sartin, R.M., Hansen, D.J., & Huss, M.T. (2006). Domestic violence treatment response and recidivism: A review and implications for the study of family violence. *Aggression and Violent Behavior, 11*, 452–440.

Schmuck, P., & Sheldon, K.M. (Eds.). (2001). *Life goals and well-being.* Toronto, ON: Hogrefe & Huber Publishers.

Serin, R., & Kennedy, S. (1997). *Treatment readiness and responsivity: Contributing to effective correctional programming.* Canada: Correctional Services Research Report.

Smedslund, G., Dalsbø, T.K., Steiro, A.K., Winsvold, A., & Clench-Aas, J. (2007). Cognitive behavioural therapy for men who physically abuse their female partner. *Cochrane Database of Systematic Reviews, Issue 3.* Art. No.: CD006048. DOI: 10.1002/14651858.CD006048.pub2.

Ward, T. (2002). Good lives and the rehabilitation of offenders: Promises and problems. *Aggression and Violent Behavior, 7,* 513–528.

Ward, T., & Beech, A. (2004). The etiology of risk: A preliminary model for sexual offenders. *Sexual Abuse: A Journal of Research and Treatment, 16,* 271–284.

Ward, T. & Brown, M. (2004). The good lives model and conceptual issues in offender rehabilitation. *Psychology, Crime, & Law, 10,* 243–257.

Ward, T., & Gannon, T. (2006). Rehabilitation, etiology, and self-regulation: The good lives model of sexual offender treatment. *Aggression and Violent Behavior, 11,* 77–94.

Ward, T. & Marshall, W.L. (2004). Good lives, etiology and the rehabilitation of sex offenders: A bridging theory. *Journal of Sexual Aggression, 10,* 153–169.

Ward, T., & Maruna, S. (2007). *Rehabilitation: Beyond the risk paradigm.* London, UK: Routledge.

Ward, T., Polaschek, D.L.L., & Beech, A.R. (2006). *Theories of sexual offending.* Chichester, UK: John Wiley & Sons.

Ward, T., & Stewart, C.A. (2003). The treatment of sex offenders: Risk management and good lives. *Professional Psychology: Research and Practice, 34,* 353–360.

Wathen, C.N., & MacMillan, H.L. (2003). Interventions for violence against women: Scientific review. *JAMA, 289,* 589–600.

Whitehead, P.R., Ward, T., & Collies, R.M. (2007). Time for a change: Applying the good lives model of rehabilitation to a high-risk violent offender. *International Journal of Offender Therapy and Comparative Criminology, 51,* 578–598.

Willis, G., & Grace, R. (2008). The quality of community reintegration planning for child molesters: Effects on sexual recidivism. *Sexual Abuse: A Journal of Research and Treatment, 20,* 218–240.

Yates, P.M. (2003). Treatment of adult sexual offenders: A therapeutic cognitive-behavioral model of intervention. *Journal of Child Sexual Abuse, 12,* 195–232.

Practical Tools and a Look Forward

PART III

Application of Strengths-Based Approaches

9

CATHERINE A. SIMMONS
JOY D. PATTON
JULIE A. SUTTER
PETER LEHMANN

Basically we are all the same human beings with the same potential to be a good human being or a bad human being . . . the important thing is to realize the positive side and try to increase that: realize the negative side and try to reduce. That's the way. **—*The Dalai Lama***

Application of strengths-based intervention with intimate partner violence (IPV) offending clients* is grounded in the idea that reducing abusive behaviors is dependent on building the positive side of the person's potential. Clearly, violence, manipulation, anger, and intentionally harming others are abusive behaviors that must not continue. However, to end these behaviors, traditional IPV intervention approaches (a.k.a. traditional batterer intervention programs) tend to focus on shame, confrontation, and deficits in a manner that has proven to be ineffective (for meta analyses please see Babcock, Green & Robie, 2004: Feder & Wilson, 2005; Levesque & Gelles, 1998). In contrast, the strengths-based approaches included in this book attempt to elicit lasting client change by turning the center of attention away from deficits, instead focusing on the client's strengths and

---

* For consistency and to remain strengths based, the population is referred to as *IPV offending clients* in this chapter. However, in the literature they are also referred to under a variety of other terms, including (but not limited to) batterers, domestic assaulters, abusers, and IPV offenders.

resources—thus building a cycle of competencies (McCashen, 2005) that does not include abusive behavior.

In his general discussion about strength-based approaches with all client populations, McCashen (2005) wrote *"a focus on strengths sets the tone for practice that enables people to see themselves and their experiences differently . . . it creates positive expectations that open the way for the development of competencies"* (p. 11). Translating these ideas into intervention with IPV offending clients is a paradigm shift with exciting potential to move the field forward. The six theoretical approaches included in this text provide some (but not all) of the strengths-based initiatives applicable to this population. From these theories, ideas, and concepts, the following chapter is designed to help move practice with IPV offending clients toward a strengths-based paradigm by presenting a few practical ways family violence professionals can integrate strengths into intervention.

STRENGTHS-BASED PERSPECTIVE

Before providing specific strengths-based intervention tools, one must first understand that the strengths-based perspective is not a single theory or model that attempts to explain, describe, or logically represent a particular aspect, situation, or occurrence of family violence. Instead, the strengths-based perspective should be thought of as an overarching way to view the intervention process. Saleebey (2006) eloquently stated that a strengths-based perspective *"provides us with a slant on the world, built of words and principles . . . it is a lens through which we choose to perceive and appreciate"* (p. 16).

As discussed throughout this text, strengths-based approaches encompass a different set of assumptions. First, the IPV offending client is not the problem. Rather, his or her abusive behavior is the problem. Framing the client's abusive behavior as something that is wrong yet does not define the client changes the focus of intervention. In this process, the family violence professional can view the client as a person with the ability to change. Likewise, IPV offending clients can take responsibility for their actions while reducing disempowering beliefs. Second, strengths-based approaches view IPV offending clients as the experts on their own lives and behavior. IPV offending clients have the ability to make sense of why they behave in an abusive manner. They know themselves better than anyone else, thus, they should be treated as knowledgeable about what will help generate change within them. Third, strengths-based approaches focus on the sharing of power between the family violence professional and the client. In this way, the relationship is balanced, collaborative, and respectful. By understanding these three core assumptions, the family violence professional can move the focus of intervention away from deficits, helping clients change by building their unique competencies.

When applying strengths-based approaches, the abilities and resources clients bring to the treatment process are always considered. They have the power and capacity to produce the desired effect within themselves and should be supported in this quest to deal with life more advantageously (Koenig & Spano, 2007; Saleebey, 2006). Often referred to as self-efficacy, Bandura (1993) purports *"it is partly on the basis of judgments of personal efficacy that people choose what to do, how much effort to invest in activities, and how long to persevere in the face of obstacles and failure experiences"* (p. 122). With this in mind, family violence professionals should be respectful, considering IPV offending clients' values when assessing their needs and creating a treatment plan. This consideration acquiesces an understanding about the connection between the client and his environment while keeping in mind the traits and capacities that have allowed the client to become resilient, resourceful, and motivated (Koenig & Spano, 2007; Saleebey, 2006).

It is also important to develop and maintain an affirming therapeutic partnership, as evidence indicates this relationship predicts more positive outcomes (i.e., less abusive behavior reported by both the partner and the perpetrator) (Eckhardt, Murphy, Black & Suhr, 2006). Family violence professionals have the ability to inspire positive expectations by focusing on the present and future, thus creating a sense of change that is built on developing resources that already exist within the client (Laursen, 2003).

Approaches to Assessment and Treatment

As previously discussed, strengths-based assessment and treatment with IPV offending clients is a relatively new area of research and practice. Although a growing number of practitioners and researchers are moving the pertinent body of knowledge forward, the empirical foundation of this approach within the family violence community is in its infancy. However, general strengths-based knowledge can be adapted to this population in a straightforward manner. To this end, the following section provides practical recommendations for family violence professionals who are starting to incorporate strengths-based concepts into practice with IPV offending clients.

Suggestions for Strengths-Based Assessment

As should be the case with all client assessment, strengths-based assessment with IPV offenders is both a process and a product. The intent of a strengths-based assessment is to (a) aid clients in reflecting on the context of their situation (Rankin, 2007), (b) join forces with them to understand, define, and clarify the problem, and (c) evaluate and give meaning to factors that impact clients (Saleebey, 2001). The assessment process includes a brief summary of the situation and challenges the client must cope with, as well as evaluation and analysis of the factors that have an impact on the client's presenting circumstances (Cowger, 1994; Cowger, Anderson & Snively, 2006; Saleebey, 2001).

It is from this evaluation and analysis that family violence professionals are able to identify internal and external strengths the client can use to make change happen. Internal strengths include such things as the client's cognitive abilities, emotional strengths, interpersonal skills, hopes, desires, dreams, successes, and motivations (Rankin, 2007). The fact that the IPV offending client is there in the treatment environment is in itself a strength that can be utilized in this process. External strengths can include the client's family, friends, community, volunteer organizations, public institutions, and work environment (Rankin, 2007). It is important to remember that regardless of their current situation, all individuals have a wealth of resources available to them. In the assessment process, the family violence professional has the important job of helping the client identify these preexisting strengths in a manner that is helpful to elicit change.

Although not specific to family violence, a number of authors have addressed strengths-based assessment with the general population (e.g. Cowger, 1994; Cowger, Anderson & Snively, 2006; Rankin, 2007; Saleebey, 2001). From this general knowledge, Exhibit 9.1 outlines seven general guidelines that are helpful in changing the assessment from deficit-focused to competency-focused. At first, incorporating these ideas with IPV offending clients may appear a bit therapeutically incongruent. For example, Cowger (1994) emphasizes giving preeminence to the client's understanding of the facts, and believing these facts.

Exhibit 9.1

GENERAL GUIDELINES FOR ASSESSMENT

1. Nonconfrontational acknowledgement
2. Discover what the client wants
3. Seek multidimensional strengths
4. Discover the client's uniqueness
5. Use language the client can understand
6. Approach assessment as a joint activity
7. Remember, it's a process not a product

General Guidelines for Assessment were adapted from the work of Cowger (1994), Cowger, Anderson & Snively (2006), Rankin (2007), and Saleeby (2001).

Referred to in this text as *nonconfrontational acknowledgement*, this concept is sometimes difficult when working with involuntary IPV offending clients because much empirical evidence indicates this population tends to minimize its abusive behavior, (e.g., Henning, Jones & Holdford, 2005; Henning & Feder, 2004) being untruthful and/or unreliable. Therefore, as strengths-based family violence professionals it is important to acknowledge the client's view of events, without agreeing with them. Even though events may have occurred differently than presented, to clients, their point of view is correct. In strengths-based assessment, confronting these misperceptions head-on is not as important as understanding how the client views the problem and what, within the confines of treatment; they believe they need to work on. In this process the IPV offending client and the family violence professional work together to *discover what the client wants*, both from the intervention process and in relation to his current situation. It is important to clarify that this does not mean abusive behavior is condoned or accepted; it's just not directly confronted in the early stages of intervention.

Nonconfrontational acknowledgement and purposefully *discovering what the client wants* is often a disarming experience. Most people who present to batterer intervention programs (BIPs) have interfaced with the criminal justice system (e.g., Healey, Smith & O'Sullivan, 1998), and thus are at some level aware, whether they admit to it or not, that they have done something wrong. Generally, they expect to be confronted in the treatment setting and are prepared to defend themselves in manners such as passive aggression, direct denial, confabulation, or simply telling the therapist what they want to hear. For those unfamiliar (or uncomfortable) with strengths-based assessments, it may make the process a bit easier to understand by framing intervention as separate from punishment. The criminal justice system is responsible for punishment, and needs clients to be accountable and take responsibility for their actions. The family violence professional, on the other hand, is there to help IPV offending clients change their behaviors, not to punish them. Within this context, insisting the client take responsibility for past acts becomes less important than changing current and future behavior. Nonconfrontational acknowledgement and purposefully seeking the IPV offending client's desires facilitates the therapeutic alliance, changing the focus and tone of the relationship. It is a different way of approaching assessment and intervention than traditional confrontational approaches.

In addition to the two previously addressed general guidelines, (*discovering what the client wants* and *nonconfrontational acknowledgement*), remembering to *seek multidimensional strengths* is also important when conducting strengths-based assessments (e.g. Cowger, 1994; Cowger, Anderson & Snively, 2006; Rankin, 2007; Saleebey, 2001). The family violence professional needs to include personal and environmental assets that will help the client progress toward a resolution. *Discovering the client's uniqueness* includes finding internal and external strengths that provide the framework for evaluating various solutions (e.g. Cowger, 1994; Cowger, Anderson & Snively, 2006; Rankin, 2007; Saleebey, 2001). It should not be assumed that all clients with similar situations will behave in the same manner, nor will they all have the same strengths or combinations of strengths. Because all clients are unique, strengths-based assessment is never considered a one-size-fits-all approach. It is the family violence professional's charge to discover this uniqueness and work with it to develop solutions.

The general guideline *use language the client can understand* emphasizes the idea that it is important to speak to clients in a way they are comfortable and identify with (e.g. Cowger, 1994; Cowger, Anderson & Snively, 2006; Rankin, 2007; Saleebey, 2001). At the center of all work with IPV offending clients is the use of verbal and nonverbal communication. Through this communicative interchange, the meaning of events, of self, of behavior, of change, of good, and of bad are interpreted. Professional language serves to separate the family violence professional from the client in a way that could (a) alter the meaning of the communication and (b) damage any collaborative efforts to elicit participation. Therefore, speaking with the client in everyday terms they understand, not at or about the client, is essential to strengths-based assessments.

Similar to using language clients understand, the general guideline *approach assessment as a joint activity* (e.g. Cowger, 1994; Cowger, Anderson & Snively, 2006; Rankin, 2007; Saleebey, 2001) encompasses the idea that, by design, strengths-based assessment is a collaboration between the family violence professional and the IPV offending client. The family violence professional's role is to assist clients in discovering, clearly expressing, and taking ownership of their experiences. Although initial assessment often develops a product (such as an assessment report), assessment is considered an ongoing dialogue and relationship, rather than a product. Questions that can be utilized in this process include: What are some of your recent successes? What is one thing you did that was a lot of hard work? What have you done that you are proud of? What kinds of things do people compliment you on? Have you or anyone in your family been able to stop a habit that was hard to stop? From these questions, the family violence professional can develop a clearer understanding of the client in a mutually beneficial way.

The final general guideline reiterates the statement at the beginning of this section that assessment is a *process, not a product* (Cowger, Anderson & Snively, 2006). Although the courts and other funding sources generally require a written assessment to guide criminal justice, treatment, and funding decisions, this product is not the assessment itself. Assessment is a continual process that starts before the first client interview and continues throughout the intervention. Family violence professionals are charged with the responsibility of working with IPV offending clients to continually assess and evaluate their needs, strengths, environment, and movement toward change. To aid in this process, a number of instruments family violence professionals can use are included at the end of this section. As discussed later in this chapter, some of these have greater empirical validation than others and none are a one-size-fits-all solution. Therefore, it is important to remember that these instruments can be used as guides, but are not appropriate for all situations, nor are they guaranteed.

SUGGESTIONS FOR STRENGTHS-BASED TREATMENT/INTERVENTION

Each of the six strengths-based models included in this book recognize that intervention and treatment are predicated on tapping into individual strengths in a way that will help the client develop useful goals toward positive change. All IPV offending clients have strengths that they utilize in times that they are not aggressive or violent, and they often use other (nonviolent) means to resolve conflicts. It is from these competencies that strengths-based batterer interventions and treatment are focused. Although each of the six theories included in this book use slightly different methods for intervention, some common themes are inherent. For example, all view the progression of change as a continuous rather than a linear process. Likewise, all the approaches work with the IPV offending client to develop useful individually focused goals, provide feedback regarding the change process, and work to consolidate ongoing change. Indeed, all of the approaches included in this text are grounded in the belief that helping IPV offending clients to build their competencies will produce longer-lasting change than focusing on deficits. As stated by Garland and Fredrickson (2009) in chapter 7 of this text, *"for change to be enduring, the violent offender must undergo a radical transformation that touches the very substrates of his being* (p. 210)." It is the belief of the editors and authors included in this book that utilizing strengths will elicit greater transformation than approaches that focus on deficits, shame, and confrontation.

Signs of Safety Approach

Making a radical, life-changing transformation is often difficult for IPV offending clients, and safety is always a concern. To aid this transformation while simultaneously addressing safety, Milner and Singleton (2008) adapted the Signs of Safety approach (Turnell & Edwards, 1997; 1999; Turnell & Essex, 2007; Turnell, Elliott & Hogg, 2007) to work with men and women who are violent in their intimate partner relationships. The Signs of Safety approach was originally designed to be a compassionate, safe, and rigorous way to deal with difficult child protection cases (Turnell & Edwards, 1997; 1999; Turnell & Essex, 2007; Turnell, Elliott & Hogg, 2007). Adapting these principles to IPV offending clients is straightforward, as (a) concerns related to child abuse and IPV are often similar, and (b) the two forms of family violence commonly co-occur. The main goal of the Signs of Safety approach is to help offenders identify existing strengths (signs of safety) and expand on them so that a safe treatment plan can be implemented (Milner & Singleton, 2008; Lehmann & Simmons, 2009). In this process, clinicians help offenders make the radical changes needed in their lives while being held accountable for current and future behavior (Milner & Singleton; Lehmann & Simmons).

To study the effectiveness of a unique solution-focused domestic violence program in the United Kingdom (UK), Milner and Singleton

(2008) incorporated the six Signs of Safety practice principles into their program design. The outcomes of a three-and-a-half-year study of men (N = 52) and women (N = 16) participating in their individualized treatment regime show promising results, with none of the program completers reoffending (per self-report, partner-report, and police-report). Although it is important to note the dropout rate from their program was 26.5%, this is comparable to the estimated 30%–60% dropout rate of other UK domestic violence programs (Milner & Singleton, 2008). Because of the initial success of this study and the importance the Signs of Safety approach is having in the child welfare community (Turnell & Edwards, 1997, 1999; Turnell & Essex, 2007; Turnell, Elliott & Hogg, 2007), incorporating these ideas into practice with IPV offending clients is promising.

At the heart of the Signs of Safety approach are the fundamental notions of good practice and intervention, i.e., aspiring to partnership and creating conversations of solution-building. To help conceptualize how the Signs of Safety approach can be helpful in work with IPV offending clients, Exhibit 9.2 outlines the six practice principles with sample questions that can serve as a guide for family violence professionals wanting to incorporate this approach into their practices. The principles can overlap one another, and with the exception of principle 1 do not necessarily need to be followed in sequential order.

Principle 1: Understand the Position of Each Family Member.[*] The key to understanding the position of each family member is for the domestic violence professional to not only listen for and notice clinical issues, but also to give all available family members a chance to talk about their experiences. Respect for all family members is demonstrated by respectfully listening to them (IPV offending client included) while also being aware of the plight of the victim who has suffered the abuse. Respectfulness avoids direct confrontation by not reframing the IPV offender's concerns as denial, resistance, poor motivation, or victim blaming. Instead, the Signs of Safety approach encourages seeking IPV offending clients' cooperation by listening respectfully to their accounts of their life situations while encouraging them to explore the meaning of

---

[*] The six principles, discussion, and questions are based on the six Signs of Safety practice principles developed by Turner and Edwards (1997, 1999) for child welfare, adapted by Milner and Singleton (2008) for work with men and women in a domestic violence offenders program, and by Lehmann and Simmons (2009) for work with families of children exposed to domestic violence.

Exhibit 9.2

PRINCIPLES AND QUESTIONS BASED ON THE SIX SIGNS OF SAFETY PRACTICE PRINCIPLES

Principle 1: *Understand the Position of Each Family Member* can be elicited by asking the following:

1.   Would you be interested in telling me your side of things?
2.   What did you think would happen as a result of our meeting today?
3.   What are you hoping will happen today?
4.   Are there some things about yourself you'd like to mention?
5.   If things are near to getting out of hand again, is there anything you will do differently this time?

Principle 2: *Find Exceptions to the Violence* can be elicited by asking the following:

1.   Has there been a time when you could have been violent but stopped yourself?
2.   What steps do you remember taking? What do you think you might have said to yourself that helped?
3.   Has there been a time when you and your partner solved your differences without any violence?
4.   Tell me a time when you were at your best as a husband? What was that like?
5.   Have there been moments when you felt you had the right to say mean things, but instead you pulled back because you thought doing that would make everything worse?

Principle 3: *Discover Strengths and Resources* can be elicited by asking the following:

1.   What do you do best at work?
2.   If you are in a jam, who can you turn to?
3.   How would you describe yourself as a husband/father?
4.   When you are at your best as a husband, what does that look like?
5.   What's one of your personal strengths you think I need to know?

Exhibit 9.2

Principle 4: *Focus on Safety* can be elicited by asking the following:

1. What do you want to get out of being here?
2. What do you imagine your life will be like in 6 months if things continue as they are? What do you want to be different?
3. If you were to pick one small goal you could accomplish what do you think it would be?
4. If this is your goal, how do you think accomplishing it will help you?
5. How many steps are you away from reaching that goal today?

Principle 5: *Scale Safety and Progress* can be elicited by asking the following:

1. What specifically is different about you now compared to 4 weeks ago?
2. On a scale of 0 to 10, where 10 is you "lost it" and 0 is you were fully in charge of yourself, how would you rate the conflict you had with your partner this week?
3. Tell us about the steps you took to prevent yourself from getting even angrier.
4. Give us the details of how you took the steps you did to walk away.
5. If 10 is you are totally certain you'll never use violence again, where are you today? How do you know that? What are you doing now at home that makes you certain?

Principle 6: *Assess Willingness, Confidence, and Capacity to Change* can be elicited by asking the following:

1. You could refuse to come to group or even drop out. What keeps you coming?
2. So, you'll never hit her again...What gives you this much confidence? What are you doing that tells you this will never happen? Give us a couple of scenarios you've been through that show us just how confident you are.
3. Tell us why you are capable of handling money conflicts differently now.
4. Are you willing to give group a try? Why, besides the PO checking in on you?
5. You sound confident about problem solving without resorting to using your fists. Tell us about that.

their behavior and the underpinning beliefs in a non-colluding way. It is much easier for IPV offending clients to accept responsibility for changing their behavior when they have been listened to and permitted to explore their own beliefs and meanings. In addition, when appropriate, it is also important to work with the other family members to develop an understanding of the entire family system, including them in the safety planning, goal setting, and other aspects of the change process.

Principle 2: Find Exceptions to the Violence. Perpetrators of intimate partner violence are not violent all the time. Finding examples of occasions in which IPV offending clients were not violent helps them to realize that they have control over their violent behavior. These nonviolent experiences are considered *signs of safety* that can be tapped into and transferred across situations. In applying this principle, the family violence professional can work with the IPV offending client to find occasions when the client was frustrated, annoyed, or angry but chose behavior that was not violent or abusive. The "when, where, and how" of these situations can be examined in great detail to uncover and encourage strengths that can be used in similar situations that arise in the future. Indeed, these occasions do not have to be directly related to the referring incident, or even to the intimate partner relationship. For example, a client who is violent with his spouse but not with his co-workers can be encouraged to discuss the "when, where, and how" of these workplace situations. Identifying the reasons and the things clients do to be nonviolent in other situations can then be applied to their family situation, often with much success (please see Milner & Singleton, 2008). Where the client is not able to identify possible exceptions, the dangerousness of the client situation is increased and should be treated accordingly by the family violence professional.

Principle 3: Discover Strengths and Resources. Discovering the IPV offending client's strengths, capacities, and resources is an essential component of all strengths-based interventions. Just as very few people are completely good all the time, so too are very few people completely evil all the time. A truism of human nature is that people become discouraged when the focus is solely on their deficits and shortcomings. By looking first at strengths, IPV offending clients' abilities are validated, thus preparing them to accept the things about themselves they need to change. Discovering these assets, abilities and competencies helps provide a framework for the change process, making the interaction between the IPV offending client and family violence professional less threatening while also uncovering the tools they need to make radical life changes. Indeed, the ongoing discovery of the IPV offending client's strengths and exceptions can be a way of building on mastery that may already exist.

Principle 4: Goals that Focus on Safety. Essential to the intervention process, goal setting defines, clarifies, focuses, and guides behavior change. When working with IPV offending clients it is important to focus on the goals that ensure the safety of all members of the family. Inquiring about what the client wants out of therapy, what his objectives are, and what is the smallest thing he wishes to "start on" may be useful in this process. Setting goals helps the IPV offending client to better understand the nature of his problem, as well as what can be done to solve it.

The goals set by the IPV offending client should be measurable, attainable, ethical, and negotiated by all parties involved. Goals also need to be detailed, concrete, and specific, as these goals ultimately become the central focus of therapeutic work. At the same time, the family violence professional should have a clinical understanding of whether goals are doable, within reach, and small enough so that they can be accomplished. In addition, an important therapeutic goal when working with this population is to develop an action plan that addresses freedom from violence. One way to look at goal setting is to break up the steps needed to stop violence into the things that need to happen differently to assure the safety of all family members.

Principle 5: Scale Safety and Progress. It is not unusual for IPV offending clients to have difficulty with goal setting early in the therapeutic relationship. When this happens, scaling can be a useful tool. Stemming from principle 4, scaling safety and progress on a scale of 1 to 10 (1 = not at all safe; 10 = completely safe) can be useful in safety assessment, priority setting, and measuring change. Although subjective, scaling responses provide an evaluation of where one stands in relation to taking some action and reaching goals (de Shazar et al., 2007). Macdonald (2007) has also characterized scaling as a means to help clients move from an all-or-nothing position to something more manageable. Whenever possible, scaling should be done from the point of view of the IPV offending client, as well that of as his partner and other family members. Eliciting input from others in the IPV offending client's life allows them to acknowledge when progress is lagging without creating awkwardness.

It also provides both the ability to track progress and the impetus for creating expanding goals.

Principle 6: Assess Willingness, Confidence and Capacity to Change. Throughout the change process it is important to assess and encourage the willingness, confidence, and capacity to change. As stated previously, for change to be enduring, the IPV offending client must make a radical transformation. Following through on safety plans, setting new rules for nonviolence, saying no to drugs and alcohol, agreeing to show respect, speaking softly, walking away, and the myriad of other tasks needed to create a safe family environment may be hard to accomplish. The IPV offending client's willingness, confidence, and desire to take these steps will wax and wane, becoming weaker and stronger at different stages of the change process. It is the charge of family violence professionals to encourage, support, and work with IPV offending clients as they make these changes. The final principle, assess willingness, confidence and capacity to change, is intended to motivate, continually building belief and hope for the client in small sustainable ways.

Additional Instruments and Tools

In addition to the chapters included in this book and the six Signs of Safety practice principles outlined above, an array of tools and techniques are available to move intervention with IPV offending clients toward a strengths focus. To help facilitate this move forward, 20 practical instruments that family violence professionals can use in the treatment setting are included at the end of this chapter. In addition, an annotated bibliography including additional resources with empirically based citations is also included. It is important to note that the authors do not make guarantees about validity, reliability, or effectiveness of any of the instruments (included or cited), as evidentiary support is at varying stages. Although each brings unique elements to the assessment and treatment process and can be used as guides, further empirical investigation to support effectiveness is clearly needed. Despite the obvious limitations, family violence practitioners are encouraged to incorporate strengths-based ideas proven effective with other populations into the assessment and treatment process with IPV offending clients. In so doing, they are also encouraged to develop the evidentiary foundation of these approaches through empirical research and clinical evaluation.

When reviewing the instruments included at the end of this chapter, it is important to remember that strengths-based approaches to intervention with IPV offending clients are not one-size-fits-all approaches, nor are they manualized type endeavors. Different measures will be appropriate for different programs and different clients at different stages of the change process. Likewise, the 20 instruments and annotated bibliography included at the end of this chapter are just a few of the many relevant tools available to the family violence professional. Therefore, the measures included represent a range of available tools that may or may not be helpful to the reader. The first eleven of the instruments are scales and questionnaires that can be used in both assessment and ongoing treatment processes. For example, instrument 2, the *Strengths Interview Questions for Domestic Violence* (Lehmann, 2007) is a qualitative questionnaire that can be given to clients as part of the initial assessment to determine what they see as their strengths, or it can be utilized later in the relationship as a homework assignment. Likewise, instrument 5, the *Satisfaction with Life Scale* (Diener, Emmons, Larsen & Griffin, 1985) is a 5-question scale that can be included with the intake assessment instruments and also used as an ongoing clinical evaluation measure. More information about usage, validity, and reliability of these scales may be ascertained by contacting the instrument's author, cited below each.

In addition to the scales and questionnaires, instruments 12–16 include examples of activities that can be used for either goal setting in the initial stages of treatment or homework assignments later in the process. Each of these instruments is currently in use with the IPV offending population during various stages of the change process. Finally, instruments 17–20 are examples from the *Goals to Solutions* program at the Fort Worth Brief Therapy Center, Fort Worth, Texas. These four instruments progress through the intervention process, starting at the treatment plan agreement, and followed by an outcome measure, a treatment plan review, and a client satisfaction survey. Family violence professionals are encouraged to review these instruments with an open yet critical mind. The goal of selecting instruments to assist with the treatment process is to help the client elicit lasting change by incorporating his unique strengths, skills, and resources. The intent is to build a cycle of competencies (McCashen, 2005) that does not include abusive behavior. In so doing, these resources can be used as guides and helpful instruments. However, as previously stated, none are applicable to all clients and all situations.

HOPEFUL OUTCOMES

The shift toward a paradigm of strength-building in assessment and treatment of IPV offending clients takes into account heterogeneity, individualization of approaches, and a focus on the outcome. The domestic violence professional assists clients in discovering, clarifying, and articulating the internal and external strengths already in existence within themselves: discovering possibilities they may not have realized existed. This process includes the need to find balance between the very real risks IPV offending clients pose with the idea that they do in fact have strengths as well. To help the client undergo the radical transformation needed for lasting change, these competencies, skills, and resources need to be discovered, accessed, and developed. The ultimate goal and the hopeful outcome of the strengths-based approach, therefore, is to help the IPV offending client to discover and understand not only his abusive and violent behavior, but the abilities and competencies that will help him to change his behavior. This shifting paradigm offers hopeful outcomes that allow an expansion of ideas and new forms of practice that will be helpful in protecting victims, changing IPV offenders, and stopping intimate partner violence.

REFERENCES

Babcock, J.C., Green, C.E., & Robie, C. (2004). Does batterers' treatment work? A meta-analytic review of domestic violence treatment. *Clinical Psychology Review*, 23, 1023–1053.

Bandura, A. (1993). Perceived self-efficacy in cognitive development and functioning. *Educational Psychology, 28,* 117–148.

Cowger, C.D. (1994). Assessing client strengths: Clinical assessment for client empowerment. *Social Work, 39,* 262–268.

Cowger, C.D., Anderson, K.M., & Snively, C.A. (2006). Assessing strengths: The political, context of individual, family, and community empowerment. In D. Saleebey, *The strengths perspective in social work practice* (4th ed.) pp 93–115. Boston, MA: Pearson.

Diener, E., Emmons, R.A., Larsen, R.J., & Griffin, S. (1985). The Satisfaction with Life Scale. *Journal of Personality Assessment,* 49, 71–75.

Eckhardt, C.I., Murphy, C., Black, D., & Suhr, L. (2006). Intervention programs for perpetrators of intimate partner violence: Conclusions from a clinical research perspective. *Public Health Reports, 121,* 369–381.

Feder, L., & Wilson, D.B. (2005). A meta-analytic review of court-mandated batterer intervention programs: Can courts affect abusers' behaviors. *Journal of Experimental Criminology,* 1, 239–262.

Garland, E., & Fredrickson, B. (2009). Application of the Broaden-and-Build theory of positive emotions to intimate partner violence. In P. Lehmann & C.A. Simmons (Eds.), *Strength's-based batterer intervention: A new paradigm in ending family violence* (pp. 189–215). New York: Springer Publishing.

Healey, K., M. Smith, C., & O'Sullivan, C. (1998). *Batterer intervention: Program approaches and criminal justice strategies.* Washington, DC: Department of Justice. Retrieved October 23, 2008 from http://www.ncjrs.gov/pdffiles/168638.pdf.

Henning, K., & Feder, L. (2004). A comparison between men and women arrested for domestic violence: Who presents the greater threat? *Journal of Family Violence,* 19, 69–81.

Henning, K., Jones, A., & Holdford, R. (2005). 'I didn't do it, but if I did I had a good reason': Minimization, denial and attributions of blame among male and female domestic violence offenders. *Journal of Family Violence,* 20, 131–139.

Koenig, T., & Spano, R. (2007). The cultivation of social workers' hope in personal life and professional practice. *Journal of Religion and Spirituality in Social Work,* 26, 45–61.

Laursen, E.K., (2003). Frontiers in strength-based treatment. *Reclaiming Children and Youth,* 12, 12–17.

Lehmann, P., & Simmons, C.A. (2009). Children Exposed To Domestic Violence: Building Safety. In A.R. Roberts & G.J. Greene (Eds.), *Social Workers' Desk Reference,* 2nd ed. (pp. 1082–1091). New York, NY: Oxford University Press.

Levesque, D.A., & Gelles, R.J. (1998, July). *Does treatment reduce recidivism in men who batter: A meta-analytic evaluation of treatment outcome.* Paper presented at the Program Evaluation and Family Violence Research: An international Conference: Durham, NH.

Macdonald, A. (2007). *Solution-focused therapy: Theory, research, & practice.* Los Angeles, CA: Sage.

McCashen, W. (2005). *The strengths approach: A strengths-based resource for sharing power and creating change.* Victoria, Australia: St. Luke's Innovative Resources.

Milner, J., & Singleton, T. (2008). Domestic violence: solution focused practice with men and women who are violent. *Journal of Family Therapy,* 30, 29–53.

Rankin, P. (2007). Exploring and describing the strengths-empowerment perspective in social work. *Journal of Social Work Theory and Practice,* 14, 1–26.

Saleebey, D. (2001). The diagnostic strengths manual. *Social Work,* 42(2), 183–187.

Saleebey, D. (2006). *The strengths perspective in social work practice* (4th ed.). Boston: Pearson Education, Inc.

de Shazar., S., Dolan, Y., Korman, H., Trepper, T., McCollum, E., & Berg Insoo, K. (2007). More than miracles: The state of the art of solution-focused brief therapy. New York, New York: Haworth.

Turnell, A., & Edwards, S. (1997). Aspiring to partnership: The signs of safety approach to child protection. *Child Abuse Review,* 6, 179–190.

Turnell, A., & Edwards, S. (1999). *Signs of Safety. A solution oriented approach to child protection casework.* New York and London: W. W. Norton.

Turnell, A., & Essex, S. (2007). *Working with denied child abuse. The resolutions approach.* Maidenhead: Open University Press.

Turnell, A., Elliott, S., & Hogg, V. (2007). Compassionate, safe and rigorous child protection practice with biological parents of adopted children. *Child Abuse Review,* 16, 108–119.

CHAPTER 9 APPENDIX

Practical Instruments That Can Be Used During Strengths-Based Intervention

1.	Solution-Focused Recovery for Abuse Survivors©	Yvonne Dolan
2.	Strengths Interview Questions for Domestic Violence	Peter Lehmann
3.	Fordyce Emotions Questionnaire©	Michael Fordyce
4.	Solution Identification Scale©	Yvonne Dolan and Ron Krall; Jeffrey Goldman and Mary Baydarian
5.	Satisfaction with Life Scale©	Ed Diener
6.	Beliefs About Romantic Partner©	Jennifer Frei and Phillip R. Shaver
7.	Meaning of Life Questionnaire©	Michael F. Steger
8.	Respect for Partner Scale©	Susan S. Hendrick and Clyde Hendrick
9.	Relationship Assessment Scale©	Susan S. Hendrick
10.	Subjective Happiness Scale©	Sonja Lyubomirsky and Heidi A. Lepper
11.	Session Rating Scale© (SRS V.3.0) and Outcome Rating Sale© (ORS)	Scott D. Miller
12.	Exercise/Homework Activity: Utilizing Goals to Create a Context for Change: Treating Domestic Violence Offenders	Mo Yee Lee, Adriana Uken, and John Sebold
13.	Exercise/Homework Activity: Accountability Timeline	Ken Bennett
14.	Exercise/Homework Activity: Writing About the Benefits of My Experience Task	Michael McCullough, Lindsey Root, and Adam Cohen
15.	Exercises/Homework Activity: Relationship Values and Distractions	Tod Augusta-Scott
16.	Exercises/Homework Activity: Gratitude Visit, Three Good Things, and You At Your Best	M.E.P. Seligman
17.	Goals to Solutions: Treatment Plan Agreement	Blaine Moore and Elliott Connie
18.	Goals to Solutions: Outcome Measure	Blaine Moore and Elliott Connie
19.	Goals to Solutions: Treatment Plan Review	Blaine Moore and Elliott Connie
20.	Goals to Solutions: Client Satisfaction Survey	Blaine Moore and Elliott Connie

Solution-Focused Recovery for Abuse Survivors[1]

Name_____ Date: _____

Circle the number that applies to you today:	Not at all	Just a little	Occasionally	Some of the time	Frequently or most of the time
A. I am able to think/talk about the past violence with my partner when it is appropriate.	0	1	2	3	4
B. I am able to think/talk about things other than the violence with my partner.	0	1	2	3	4
C. I sleep adequately; I don't feel unusually sleepy in the daytime.	0	1	2	3	4
D. I feel part of a supportive family.	0	1	2	3	4
E. I stand up for my self (I am reasonably assertive).	0	1	2	3	4
F. I maintain physical appearance (weight, hair, nails etc.)	0	1	2	3	4
G. I go to work; I am on time, I am reasonably productive.	0	1	2	3	4
H. I am satisfied with my work.	0	1	2	3	4
I. I engage in social activities outside the home.	0	1	2	3	4
J. I have a healthy appetite.	0	1	2	3	4
K. I care for child, loved ones, pets. (I can take care of others.)	0	1	2	3	4
L. I adapt to new situations.	0	1	2	3	4
M. I initiate contact with friends, loved ones.	0	1	2	3	4
N. I show a sense of humor.	0	1	2	3	4
O. I am interested in future goals.	0	1	2	3	4
P. I pursue leisure activities.	0	1	2	3	4
Q. I exercise regularly.	0	1	2	3	4
R. I take sensible protective measures inside and outside house.	0	1	2	3	4
S. I choose supportive relationships over non-supportive ones.	0	1	2	3	4
T. I am able to relax without drugs or alcohol.	0	1	2	3	4
U. I seem to tolerate constructive criticism well.	0	1	2	3	4
V. I seem to accept praise well. I thank the person giving the praise.	0	1	2	3	4
W. I enjoy a healthy sexual relationship. I can give and accept intimacy.	0	1	2	3	4
X. I have long-term friendships.	0	1	2	3	4
Y. I am satisfied with relationship with spouse or partner.	0	1	2	3	4
Z. My partner or spouse would say that relationship is healthy and satisfying.	0	1	2	3	4
AA. My dreams are usually tolerable and not very upsetting.	0	1	2	3	4
BB. My attention span is fairly good and I can concentrate well.	0	1	2	3	4
CC. I experience a wide range of emotions, both pleasant and unpleasant.	0	1	2	3	4
DD. People would say I am more calm than jumpy	0	1	2	3	4

Instrument 2

Strengths Interview Questions for Domestic Violence[2]

1. What are your 3 best skills or talents?

    1.)

    2.)

    3.)

2. What qualities about yourself are you most proud of? _____

_____

_____

3. What do you enjoy most about your life? _____

_____

_____

4. What achievements in your life are you most proud of? _____

_____

_____

5. You've been through some really challenging times in your life – what has helped you cope?

_____

_____

6. What advice would you have for someone else going through your situation? _____

_____

_____

Fordyce Emotions Questionnaire[3]

PART 1 DIRECTIONS: Use the boxes below to answer the following question: IN GENERAL, HOW HAPPY OR UNHAPPY DO YOU USUALLY FEEL? Check the *one* statement below that best describes *your average happiness*

☐ 10. Extremely happy (feeling ecstatic, joyous, fantastic)

☐ 9. Very happy (feeling really good, elated)

☐ 8. Pretty happy (spirits high, feeling good)

☐ 7. Mildly happy (feeling fairly good and somewhat cheerful)

☐ 6. Slightly happy (just a bit above neutral)

☐ 5. Neutral (not particularly happy or unhappy)

☐ 4. Slightly unhappy (just a bit below neutral)

☐ 3. Mildly unhappy (just a little low)

☐ 2. Pretty unhappy (somewhat "blue," spirits down)

☐ 1. Very unhappy (depressed, spirits very low)

☐ 0. Extremely unhappy (utterly depressed, completely down)

Check just one of those boxes!

PART II DIRECTIONS: Consider your emotions a moment further. *On the average,* what percent of the time do you feel happy? What percent of the time do you feel unhappy? What percent of the time do you feel neutral (neither happy nor unhappy)? Write down your best estimates, as well as you can, in the space below. Make sure the three figures add up to equal 100%

ON THE AVERAGE:

The percent of time I feel happy   _____%

The percent of time I feel unhappy   _____%

The percent of time I feel neutral   _____%

TOTAL: _____%

Instrument 4

Solution Identification Scale[4]

Person filling out scale_____ Date_____

Person being described (e.g., self, wife, husband)_____

Please answer the following.	On a scale of 1 to 10, with 1 being never and 10 being always.									
	Never									Always
1. Is respectful to spouse/partner	1	2	3	4	5	6	7	8	9	10
2. Is comfortable in new situations	1	2	3	4	5	6	7	8	9	10
3. Is able to make/keep new friends	1	2	3	4	5	6	7	8	9	10
4. Cooperates with partner/spouse	1	2	3	4	5	6	7	8	9	10
5. Is trustworthy	1	2	3	4	5	6	7	8	9	10
6. Shows trust in spouse/partner	1	2	3	4	5	6	7	8	9	10
7. Is considerate of others	1	2	3	4	5	6	7	8	9	10
8. Settles disagreements peacefully	1	2	3	4	5	6	7	8	9	10
9. Copes with frustration effectively	1	2	3	4	5	6	7	8	9	10
10. Respects the rights of others	1	2	3	4	5	6	7	8	9	10
11. Usually has a positive outlook	1	2	3	4	5	6	7	8	9	10
12. Speaks up for self	1	2	3	4	5	6	7	8	9	10
13. Accepts constructive criticism	1	2	3	4	5	6	7	8	9	10
14. Thinks before acting	1	2	3	4	5	6	7	8	9	10
15. Understands feelings of spouse/partner	1	2	3	4	5	6	7	8	9	10
16. Understands behavior of children	1	2	3	4	5	6	7	8	9	10
17. Identifies feelings other than anger	1	2	3	4	5	6	7	8	9	10
18. Expresses feelings other than anger	1	2	3	4	5	6	7	8	9	10
19. Is affectionate with spouse/partner	1	2	3	4	5	6	7	8	9	10
20. Nurtures children	1	2	3	4	5	6	7	8	9	10
21 Can express anger by talking	1	2	3	4	5	6	7	8	9	10
22. Values safety in relationship/family	1	2	3	4	5	6	7	8	9	10
23. Admits mistakes	1	2	3	4	5	6	7	8	9	10
24. Able to compromise and negotiate	1	2	3	4	5	6	7	8	9	10
25. Abstains from alcohol/drug abuse	1	2	3	4	5	6	7	8	9	10
26. Follows through with commitments	1	2	3	4	5	6	7	8	9	10
27. Shares decision making	1	2	3	4	5	6	7	8	9	10
28. Is considerate during love making	1	2	3	4	5	6	7	8	9	10
29. Supports spouse's/partner's friendships	1	2	3	4	5	6	7	8	9	10
30. Has outside interests	1	2	3	4	5	6	7	8	9	10

SWLS (Satisfaction with Life Scale)[5]

elow are five statements that you may agree or disagree with. Using the 1-7 scale below, indicate your greement with each item by placing the appropriate number on the line preceding that item. Please be open and onest in your responding.

7 – Strongly agree
6 – Agree
5 – Slightly agree
4 – Neither agree nor disagree
3 – Slightly disagree
2 – Disagree
1 – Strongly disagree

_____   In most ways my life is close to my ideal.

_____   The conditions of my life are excellent.

_____   I am satisfied with my life.

_____   So far I have gotten the important things I want in life.

_____   If I could live my life over, I would change almost nothing.

Instrument 6

Beliefs About Romantic Partner[6]

Instructions: The following statements concern how you think about your romantic partner. If you *are* currently involved in a romantic relationship, please think of your partner in that relationship while responding to these statements. If you *are not* currently involved in a romantic relationship, please think about your partner in your *most important previous* relationship while responding to the statements. Respond to each statement by indicating how much you agree or disagree with it.

	Disagree Strongly			Neutral/Mixed		Agree Strongly	
1. S/he shows interest in me, has a positive attitude, is willing to spend time with me.	1	2	3	4	5	6	7
2. S/he does not respect my views and opinions; insists on his/her own wishes.	1	2	3	4	5	6	7
3. S/he is helpful, supportive, present when needed; tries to fulfill my needs.	1	2	3	4	5	6	7
4. S/he is sensitive to and considerate of my feelings.	1	2	3	4	5	6	7
5. S/he does not have admirable or respect-worthy talents, abilities, accomplishments	1	2	3	4	5	6	7
6. S/he is not loving; s/he does not provide unconditional love.	1	2	3	4	5	6	7
7. S/he is not open and receptive.	1	2	3	4	5	6	7
8. S/he is not nice, kind, considerate.	1	2	3	4	5	6	7
9. S/he fosters good, open, two-way communication.	1	2	3	4	5	6	7
10. S/he is not honest and truthful.	1	2	3	4	5	6	7
11. S/he fosters mutuality and equality.	1	2	3	4	5	6	7
12. S/he is caring, compassionate.	1	2	3	4	5	6	7
13. S/he does not have admirable or respect-worthy moral qualities (such as dignity, humility, self-control, good judgment, dedication).	1	2	3	4	5	6	7
14. S/he calms me, puts me at ease, and makes me feel comfortable.	1	2	3	4	5	6	7
15. S/he follows the Golden Rule (treats others as others wish to be treated, or as the person him/herself would like to be treated).	1	2	3	4	5	6	7
16. S/he is cruel or hurtful.	1	2	3	4	5	6	7
17. S/he is concerned, protecting.	1	2	3	4	5	6	7
18. S/he is not committed to me.	1	2	3	4	5	6	7
19. S/he is someone I look up to, am proud of, believe in.	1	2	3	4	5	6	7
20. S/he is not understanding and empathic.	1	2	3	4	5	6	7

Meaning of Life Questionnaire (MLQ)[7]

MLQ   Please take a moment to think about what makes your life and existence feel important and significant to you. Please respond to the following statements as truthfully and accurately as you can, and also please remember that these are very subjective questions and that there are no right or wrong answers. Please answer according to the scale below:

Absolutely Untrue	Mostly Untrue	Somewhat Untrue	Can't Say True or False	Somewhat True	Mostly True	Absolutely True
1	2	3	4	5	6	7

1. _____ I understand my life's meaning.
2. _____ I am looking for something that makes my life feel meaningful.
3. _____ I am always looking to find my life's purpose.
4. _____ My life has a clear sense of purpose.
5. _____ I have a good sense of what makes my life meaningful.
6. _____ I have discovered a satisfying life purpose.
7. _____ I am always searching for something that makes my life feel significant.
8. _____ I am seeking a purpose or mission for my life.
9. _____ My life has no clear purpose.
10. _____ I am searching for meaning in my life.

Respect for Partner Scale[8]

Feelings of respect are important for many types of social relationships. We are interested in how respect might be related to romantic relationships. Whenever possible, answer the questions below with your current romantic partner in mind. For each statement:

A = Strongly agree with the statement

B = Moderately agree with the statement

C = Neutral – neither agree nor disagree

D = Moderately disagree with the statement

E = Strongly disagree with the statement

1. ____ I respect my partner.
2. ____ I am interested in my partner as a person.
3. ____ I am a source of "healing" for my partner.
4. ____ I honor my partner.
5. ____ I approve of the person my partner is.
6. ____ I communicate well with my partner.

Scoring: Items 1-6 can be summed and averaged.

Relationship Assessment Scale[9]

Please mark on the answer sheet the letter for each item that best answers that item for you.

---

1. How well does your partner meet your needs?

A	B	C	D	E
Poorly		Average		Extremely Well

---

2. In general, how satisfied are you with your relationship?

A	B	C	D	E
Unsatisfied		Average		Extremely Satisfied

---

3. How good is your relationship compared to most?

A	B	C	D	E
Poor		Average		Excellent

---

4. How often do you wish you hadn't gotten in this relationship?

A	B	C	D	E
Never		Average		Very Often

---

5. To what extent has your relationship met your original expectations?

A	B	C	D	E
Hardly at All		Average		Completely

---

6. How much do you love your partner?

A	B	C	D	E
Never		Average		Very Much

---

7. How many problems are there in your relationship?

A	B	C	D	E
Hardly Any at All		Average		Many

(NOTE: Items 4 and 7 are reverse scored)

Instrument 10

Subjective Happiness Scale[10]

Instructions to participants: For each of the following statements and/or questions, please circle the point on the scale that you feel is most appropriate in describing you.

1. In general, I consider myself:

1	2	3	4	5	6	7
not a very happy person					a very happy person	

2. Compared to most of my peers, I consider myself:

1	2	3	4	5	6	7
less happy					more happy	

3. Some people are generally very happy. They enjoy life regardless of what is going on, getting the most out of everything. To what extent does this characterization describe you?

1	2	3	4	5	6	7
not at all					a great deal	

4. Some people are generally not very happy. Although they are not depressed, they never seem as happy as they might be. To what extend does this characterization describe you?

1	2	3	4	5	6	7
not at all					a great deal	

Session Rating Scale (SRS V.3.0)[11]

Please rate today's session by placing a hash mark on the line nearest the desciption that best fits your experience.

Relationship:

I did not feel heard,   [- -]   I felt heard, understood,
understood, and respected   and respected

Goals and Topics:

We did not work on, or talk [- -]   We worked on and talked
about what I wanted to   about what I wanted to
work on and talk about   work on and talk about

Approach or Method:

The therapist's approach is [- -]   The therapist's approach
not a good fit for me   is a good fit for me

Overall:

There was something   [- -]   Overall, today's session
missing in the session today   was right for me

Outcome Rating Scale (ORS)[11]

Looking back over the last week, including today, help us understand how you have been feeling by rating how well you have been doing in the following areas of your life, where marks to the left represent low levels and marks to the right indicate high levels.

Individually:
(Personal well-being)

[- -]

Interpersonally:
(Family, close relationships)

[- -]

Socially:
(Work, School, Friendships)

[- -]

Overall:
(General sense of well-being)

[- -]

Exercise and/or Homework Activity

Utilizing Goals to Create a Context for Change:
Treating Domestic Violence Offenders[12]

1. "We want *you* to create a goal for *yourself* that will be *useful* to *you* in improving your life" (a self-determined goal to enhance commitment).

2. "The goal should be one that is *interpersonal* in nature, which means that when you work on the goal, another person will be able to *notice* the changes you've made and potentially they could be affected by the change in how you behave" (interpersonally related, observable, and specific).

3. "Another way to think about this is that if you brought us a video tape of yourself working on your goal, you would be able to point out the different things you were *doing* and maybe even note how these changes affected the other people on the tape" (goal specificity).

4. "The goal does need to be something *different*, a behavior that you have not generally done before" (different and new).

5. "The goal does not need to be something big. In fact, it is better to keep it small and doable" (self-efficacy to enhance confidence to work the goal).

The goal statement

_____

_____

_____

_____

_____

_____

_____

Exercise and/or Homework Activity

The Accountability Time Line[13]

The accountability timeline is a strengths-based tool that helps men take accountability for their assaultive behavior (termed the explosion) as well as every incident that led to the assault. With the cycle of violence, one often sees an increase in tension building before the explosion, followed by regret and remorse. This tool allows the client, along with the group, to process specific things that could have been done differently during the tension-building phase to head off the explosion.

The star represents any violent behavior/explosion. In the diagram below, we see three dotted lines, each representing different behavioral options that could have been demonstrated. When a group member says "she made me hit her": we draw the time line on the board, and process what led up to the explosion, i.e., the assault. Next we ask, what could have been done differently?

In the first dotted line he might have used better communication skills to express his feelings, in the second dotted line he could have minimized tension through relaxation or positive self-talk. Finally, at the third dotted line he could have taken a time-out. This tool helps clients see they are accountable for the actual incident or explosion, but also helps to chart multiple ways of demonstrating nonviolence.

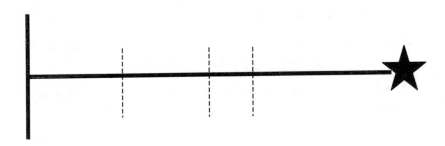

Exercise and/or Homework Activity

Writing About the Benefits of My Experience Task[14]

Directions: Read introduction out loud and follow up with asking men/women to respond to the questions below.

> We at the _____ think that getting arrested, jailed, and charged with a class A misdemeanor domestic violence offense has probably been an unpleasant experience for you. At the same time, when negative things happen they can turn into something positive. For example, have there been any positive consequences as a result of what happened to you? Perhaps you became aware of some of your personal strengths, perhaps your relationship has changed for you, or perhaps you have become a stronger or wiser person.

Please answer some of the questions below to the best of your ability.

1. What personal benefits came out of this experience for you? _____

_____

_____

2. Have you become a better person than before as a result of what happened? If yes, how? _____

_____

_____

3. Are you the same or a different person because of what happened? _____

_____

_____

4. If you could predict yourself into the future, are there other things that might benefit you as a result of what has happened?

_____

_____

Exercise and/or Homework Activity

Relationship Values[15]

Name: _____   Date: _____

, What is important to you in a relationship with a partner?

, What type of relationship would you prefer?

, What do you want your children to learn from you? What kind of role model do you want to be for them?

, Who did you learn these values from? Who else would share these values and support you in living them?

, How do you prefer to respond and to think when you make mistakes and feel ashamed?

, What responses and ideas do you want to avoid or challenge when you make mistakes and feel ashamed?

Exercise and/or Homework Activity

Distractions

Name: _____   Date: _____

. What ideas in the past may have (inadvertently) distracted you from "taking responsibility" for building the relationship you want and instead led you toward abuse?

. What ideas do you remind yourself of now that help you challenge these dangerous ideas?

. While under the influence of these dangerous ideas, what practices/ "quick fixes" did you choose that led you away from "taking responsibility" and building the relationships you really want?

Exercises and/or Homework Activities

Gratitude Visit
Three Good Things
and
You At Your Best[16]

Gratitude visit. Participants take one week to write and then deliver a letter of gratitude in person to someone who had been especially kind to them but had never been properly thanked.

Three good things in life. Participants are asked to write down three things that went well each day and their cause, every night, for one week. In addition, they were asked to provide a causal explanation for each good thing.

You at your best. Participants are asked to write about a time when they were at their best and the to reflect on the personal strengths displayed in the story. They were told to review their story once every day for a week and reflect on the strengths they had identified.

Goals to Solutions

Treatment Plan Agreement[17]

What are your best hopes for this group? What would you like to be different when you complete this group? Please set your own goal for this group. The goal should be something that is achievable, different, measurable (track progress), and observable by others. It is also important that the goal be something that you can routinely practice because you will be asked to report your progress throughout the program.

Your Goal Statement

What difference will achieving each goal have for you, your partner, children, and family? How will you and your family be affected as a result of you reaching these goals?

Are there times when pieces of this goal are already occurring? If so, please describe them.

How close do you suppose you are to reaching this goal? Please rate this on the scale below where ten equals the goal has been reached and zero equals the opposite; circle the number that best fits with where you currently are on the scale.

| 0 | 1 | 2 | 3 | 4 | 5 | 6 | 7 | 8 | 9 | 10 |

Where would the person most close to you place you on this scale? _____

How will you discover that you are moving up the scale?

What do you suppose is the first step you would need to take in order to move half a point up the scale toward your goal?

You will receive a copy of your treatment plan for your records. The treatment plan will be reviewed with you during your exit interview to measure change.

Goals to Solutions

Outcome Measure[18]

The purpose of this is questionnaire is to measure progress. You will be given this questionnaire again when you complete the program. For the following scales below, please circle the number that applies to you as of today.

1. Ten equals you have control of anger and zero equals anger has control of you.

0   1   2   3   4   5   6   7   8   9   10

2. Ten equals you have control of stress and zero equals stress has control of you.

0   1   2   3   4   5   6   7   8   9   10

3. Rate how satisfied you are with your parenting where ten equals you are the parent that you want to be and zero equals you have doubts about how good a parent you currently are. ___check if no children.

0   1   2   3   4   5   6   7   8   9   10

4. How often are you able to relax without the use of drugs or alcohol where ten equals always and zero is the opposite?

0   1   2   3   4   5   6   7   8   9   10

5. How often is there clear communication in your relationship where ten equals there are no misunderstandings and zero equals misunderstandings occur all of the time?

0   1   2   3   4   5   6   7   8   9   10

6. Ten equals you and your partner have control over conflict in your relationship and zero equals conflict in your relationship has control over you and your partner.

0   1   2   3   4   5   6   7   8   9   10

7. How often is there shared trust between you and your partner where ten equals always and zero equals the opposite?

0   1   2   3   4   5   6   7   8   9   10

8. How satisfying is your relationship where ten equals very satisfying and zero equals the opposite?

0   1   2   3   4   5   6   7   8   9   10

9. How often do you have a sense of yourself in your relationship where ten equals always and zero equals the opposite?

0   1   2   3   4   5   6   7   8   9   10

10. How confident are you that you will be able to keep yourself out of the situation that brought you in to group where ten equals absolute confidence and zero equals the opposite?

0   1   2   3   4   5   6   7   8   9   10

Goals to Solutions

Treatment Plan Review[19]

Your Goal Statement

What differences have you noticed since you started working on this goal? What has improved? Have you noticed any differences in your family members?

You have completed the group, where are you today with reaching your goal? Please rate this on the scale below where ten equals the goal has been reached and zero equals the opposite; circle the number that best fits with where you currently are on the scale.

| 0 | 1 | 2 | 3 | 4 | 5 | 6 | 7 | 8 | 9 | 10 |

Are you satisfied where you are on this scale? If not, what is the next step to move up from where you are today?

Where would the person most close to you place you on this scale today? _____

What would the person most close to you say that he or she has noticed that is different about you?

May we contact you in the future to check up on where you are with continuing this goal?

Please circle: yes or no

Goals to Solutions

Client Satisfaction Survey[20]

Please answer the following questions based on your personal experiences in the groups.

	Strongly Disagree	Disagree	Neutral	Agree	Strongly Agree
1. The therapists asked about my previous stories of success in various situations.	1	2	3	4	5
2. Group topics were relevant to my learning about what I can do to improve my family relationships.	1	2	3	4	5
3. I feel heard, understood, and respected by the therapists.	1	2	3	4	5
4. The therapists asked about my strengths and competencies.	1	2	3	4	5
5. The therapists encouraged me to participate in the group discussions.	1	2	3	4	5
6. The therapists were able to effectively answer my questions.	1	2	3	4	5
7. The therapists are very knowledgeable over the topics discussed in the groups.	1	2	3	4	5
8. The therapist encouraged group discussion between group members during group.	1	2	3	4	5
9. The therapist asked the group members for their opinions on topics to be discussed in the group.	1	2	3	4	5
10. I feel like the therapist has confidence that I can make a difference in my life.	1	2	3	4	5

11. What did the therapist do well? _____

_____

_____

12. What did the therapist do that was helpful to me? _____

_____

_____

13. Do you have any other comments on your experiences in the group? _____

_____

_____

Annotated Bibliography

An array of tools and techniques are available to move intervention with IPV offending clients toward a strengths focus. The contents of this book present just some of the many instruments, ideas, scales, questionnaires, assignments, and procedures that may be helpful for work with IPV offending clients. To aid the reader in locating other appropriate instruments the following annotated bibliography lists a few additional resources that family violence professionals may find helpful. A brief description of each instrument is included, followed by a few relevant citations.

Adult Hope Scale (AHS): Written by C.R. Snyder, the AHS is a 12-item, self-report questionnaire grounded on an 8-point Likert scale broken into three categories (pathway thinking, agency thinking, and filler questions), with four questions in each category. Additional information on this scale can be found in the following citations:

- Lopez, S.J. & Snyder, C.R. (2002). *The handbook of positive psychology*. New York: Oxford University Press.
- Snyder, C.R., Harris, C., Anderson, J.R., Holleran, S.A., Irving, L.M., Sigmon, S.T., et al. (1991). The will and the ways: Development and validation of an individual differences measure of hope. *Journal of Personality and Social Psychology, 60*, 570–585.
- Snyder, C.R. (1994). *The psychology of hope: You can get there from here*. New York: Free Press.
- Snyder, C.R. (2002). Hope theory: Rainbows in the mind. *Psychological Inquiry, 13*, 249–275.

Attributional Style Questionnaire (ASQ): Written by Martin E.P. Seligman, Ph.D., the ASQ is a self-report event rating instrument that assesses causal attributions for the good and bad events in a person's life; internal versus external, stable versus unstable, and global versus specific causes. First, 12 hypothetical events, half good and half bad, then the test-taker is asked to write down the one major cause of each event, rating the cause along a 7-point continuum. Additional information on this questionnaire can be found in the following citations:

- Buchanan, G. & Seligman, M.E.P. (Eds.). (1995). *Explanatory Style*. Hillsdale, NJ: Erlbaum.

- Peterson, C., Semmel, A., vonBaeyer, C., Abramson, L.Y., Metalsky, G.I., & Seligman, M.E.P. (1982). The attributional style questionnaire. *Cognitive Therapy and Research, 6,* 287–300.
- Seligman, M.E.P., Nolen-Hoeksema, S., Thornton, N., & Thornton, K.M. (1990). Explanatory style as a mechanism of disappointing athletic performance. *Psychological Science, 1,* 143–146.
- Seligman, M.E.P., & Schulman, P. (1986). Explanatory style as a predictor of productivity and quitting among life insurance agents. *Journal of Personality and Social Psychology, 50,* 832–838.

Curiosity and Exploration Inventory (CEI): Written by Todd B. Kashdan, Ph.D., Paul Rose, B.A., and Frank D. Fincham, Ph.D., the CEI is a 7-item self-report assessment tool that explores dimensions of exploration and adaption (Kashdan, Rose & Fincham, 2004). Grounded in a 7-point Likert scale ranging from strongly disagree to strongly agree, the CEI measures differences in the way novel and challenging experiences are recognized, pursued, and integrated. Additional information on this inventory can be found in the following citations:

- Kashdan, T.B., Rose, P., & Fincham, F.D. (2004). Curiosity and exploration: Facilitating positive subjective experiences and personal growth opportunities. *Journal of Personality Assessment, 82,* 291–305.
- Kashdan, T.B. (2002). Social anxiety dimensions, neuroticism, and the contours of positive psychological functioning. *Cognitive Therapy and Research, 26,* 789–810.
- Kashdan, T.B. (2004). The neglected relationship between social interaction anxiety and hedonic deficits: Differentiation from depressive symptoms. *Journal of Anxiety Disorders, 18,* 719–730.
- Kashdan, T.B., Elhai, J.D., & Breen, W.E., (2008). Social anxiety and disinhibition: An analysis of curiosity and social rank appraisals, approach-avoidance conflicts, and disruptive risk-taking behavior. *Journal of Anxiety Disorders, 22,* 925–939.

Gratitude Questionnaire-6 (CQ-6): Written by Michael E. McCullough, Ph.D., Robert A. Emmons, Ph.D., and Jo-Ann Tsang, Ph.D., the CQ-6 is a 6-item self-report measure of the disposition of a person to experience gratitude. Rated in a 7-point Likert scale, the instrument authors state that "the disposition toward gratitude is associated with tendencies toward positive emotions and well-being, prosocial traits, and spirituality" (McCullough, Emmons & Tsang, 2002, p. 123). Additional information on this questionnaire can be found in the following citation:

■ McCullough, M.E., Emmons, R.A., & Tsang, J. (2002). The grateful disposition: A conceptual and empirical topography. *Journal of Personality and Social Psychology, 82,* 112–127.

Inspiration Scale (IS): Written by Todd M. Thrash and Andrew J. Elliot, the IS consists of four 2-item frequency and intensity subscales measuring the motivational resource inspiration. Grounded on a 7-point Likert scale, the IS measures inspiration as characterized by evocation, motivation, and transcendence. Additional information on this scale can be found in the following citation:

■ Thrash, T.M., & Elliot, A.J. (2003). Inspiration as a psychological construct. *Journal of Personality and Social Psychology, 84,* 871–889.

Mindful Attention Awareness Scale (MAAS): Written by Kirk Warren Brown, Ph.D., and Richard M. Ryan, Ph.D., the MAAS is a 15-item, self-report, 6-point Likert scale questionnaire assessing mindfulness as defined by receptive awareness of and attention to what is taking place in the present (Brown & Ryan, 2003). Additional information on this scale can be found in the following citation:

■ Brown, K.W. & Ryan, R.M. (2003). The benefits of being present: Mindfulness and its role in psychological well-being. *Journal of Personality and Social Psychology, 84,* 822–848.

Personal Growth Initiative Scale (PGIS): Written by Christine Robitschek, Ph.D., the PGIS is a six-item, self-report instrument based on a 6-point Likert scale assessing active and intentional involvement in changing and developing as a person. Additional information on this scale can be found in the following citations:

■ Robitschek, C. (1998). Personal growth initiative: The construct and its measure. *Measurement and Evaluation in Counseling and Development, 30,* 183–198.

■ Robitschek, C. (1999). Further validation of the personal growth initiative scale. *Measurement and Evaluation in Counseling and Development, 31,* 197–210.

■ Robitschek, C., & Cook, S.W. (1999). The influence of personal growth initiative and coping styles on career exploration and vocational identity. *Journal of Vocational Behavior, 54,* 127–141.

■ Robitschek, C., & Kashubeck, S. (1999). A structural model of parental alcoholism, family functioning, and psychological health: The mediating effects of hardiness and personal growth orientation. *Journal of Counseling Psychology, 46,* 159–172.

Quality of Life Inventory (QOLI): Written by Michael Frisch, the QOLI is a two-part measure that assesses the individual's satisfaction within 16 different life domains (Huprich & Frisch, 2004). The first part assesses for the importance the respondent places on each life domain, using a three-point Likert scale to rate the domains (Huprich & Frisch, 2004). The second part assesses for the respondent's satisfaction with each domain, using a seven-point Likert scale (Huprich & Frisch, 2004). Additional information on this inventory can be found in the following citations:

■ Frisch, M.B. (1992). Use of the Quality of Life Inventory in problem assessment and treatment planning for cognitive therapy of depression. In A. Freeman & F.M. Dattilio (Eds). *Comprehensive casebook of cognitive therapy* (pp. 27–52). New York: Plenum.

■ Frisch, M.B., Cornell, J., Villanueva, M., & Retzlaff, P.J. (1992). Clinical validation of the Quality of Life Inventory: A measure of life satisfaction for use in treatment planning and outcome assessment. *Psychological Assessment: A Journal of Consulting and Clinical Psychology, 4,* 92–101.

■ Huprich, S.K. & Frisch, M.B. (2004). The depressive personality disorder inventory and its relationship to the quality of life, hopefulness, and optimism. *Journal of Personality Assessment, 83,* 22–28.

Ryff's Scales of Psychological Well-Being (SPWB): Written by Carolyn Ryff, the SPWB is a 6-dimension scale, with 3 to 12 items per subscale, that measures the 6 dimensions of well-being conceptualized by the author: autonomy, environmental mastery, personal growth, positive relations with others, purpose in life, and self-acceptance. The scale format requires respondents to respond to various statements, indicating on a 6-point Likert scale how representative each statement is of themselves. Additional information on this inventory can be found in the following citations:

- Ryff, C.D. (1989). Happiness is everything or is it? Explorations on the meaning of psychological well-being. *Journal of Personality and Social Psychology, 57,* 1069–1081.
- Ryff, C.D., & Keyes, C.L.M. (1995). The structure of psychological well-being revisited. *Journal of Personality and Social Psychology, 69,* 719–727.
- Ryff, C.D., & Singer, B.H. (1998). The contours of positive human health. *Psychological Inquiry, 9,* 1–28.
- Ryff, C.D., & Singer, B. (2002). From social structure to biology: Integrative science in pursuit of human health and well being. In C.R. Snyder & S.J. Lopez (Eds.). *Handbook of positive psychology* (pp. 541–555). New York: Oxford.

Steen Happiness Index (SHI): Written by Martin E.P. Seligman, Tracy Steen, Nansook Park, and Christopher Peterson, the SHI is a 20-item index measuring the three kinds of pathways to happiness: the pleasant life, the engaged life, and the meaningful life (Seligman, Steen, Park & Peterson, 2005). For each of the 20 items the respondent chooses an appropriate response from a choice of five items, ranging from negative responses to extremely positive responses (Seligman, Steen, Park & Peterson, 2005). Additional information on this index can be found in the following citation:

- Seligman, M.E.P., Steen, T.A., Park, N., & Peterson, C. (2005). Positive psychology progress: Empirical validation of interventions. *American Psychologist, 60,* 410–421.

Transgressional-Related Interpersonal Motivations Inventory (TRIMS): Written by Michael E. McCullough, K. Chris Rachal, Steven J. Sandage, Everett L. Worthington, Jr., Susan Wade Brown, and Terry L. Hight, the TRIMS is a 12-item, self-report instrument that assesses the motivations assumed to underlie forgiving: avoidance and revenge. Additional information on this inventory can be found in the following citations:

- McCullough, M.E., Fincham, F.D., & Tsang, J. (2003). Forgiveness, forbearance, and time: The temporal unfolding of transgression-related interpersonal motivations. *Journal of Personality and Social Psychology, 84,* 540–557.

- McCullough, M.E., Rachal, K.C., Sandage, S.J., Worthington, E.L., Brown, Susan W., & Hight, T.L. (1998). Interpersonal forgiving in close relationships: II. Theoretical elaboration and measurement. *Journal of Personality and Social Psychology, 75,* 1586–1603.
- McCullough, M.E., Hoyt, W.T., & Rachal, K.C. (2000). What we know (and need to know) about assessing forgiveness constructs. In M.E. McCullough, K.I. Pargament, & C.E. Thoresen (Eds.), *Forgiveness: Theory, research, and practice* (pp. 65–88). New York: Guilford Publications.
- McCullough, M.E., Bellah, C.G., Kilpatrick, S.D., & Johnson, J.L. (2001). Vengefulness: Relationships with forgiveness, rumination, well-being, and the big five. *Journal of Personality and Social Psychology Bulletin, 27,* 601–610.

University of Rhode Island Change Assessment—Domestic Violence (URICA—DV): Written by Deborah A. Levesque, Richard Gelles, and Wayne F. Velicer, and based on the Transtheoretical Model of change, the (URICA—DV) is a 20-item four-dimensional stage instrument measuring a profile of scores along a continuum to determine respondent's attitudes about being ready to end their violence (Levesque, Gelles & Velicer, 2000). Respondents indicate the extent to which they agree to each of the items on a 5-point Likert scale (1 = strongly disagree to 5 = strongly agree). The items are then summed into a single score by adding each of the 4 subscales. Additional information on this instrument can be found in the following citations:

- Eckhardt, C.I., Babcock, J., & Homack, S. (2004). Partner assaultive men and the stages and processes of change. *Journal of Family Violence, 19,* 81–93.
- Levesque, D.A., Gelles, R.J., & Velicer, W.F., (2000). Development and Validation of a Stages of Change Measure for Men in Batterer Treatment. *Cognitive Therapy and Research, 24,* 175–199.

Values in Action Inventory of Strengths Survey: Written by Martin Seligman and based on the 6 virtues and 24 character strengths outlined in Positive Psychology, the VIA inventory of Strengths is a 240-item instrument designed to identify a person's signature strengths. Additional information on this instrument can be found in the following citations:

- Linley, P.A., Maltby, J., Wood, A.M., Joseph, S., Harrington, S., Peterson, C., Park, N., & Seligman, M.E.P. (2007). Character strengths in the United Kingdom: The VIA Inventory of Strengths. *Personality and Individual Differences, 43,* 341–351.

■ Peterson, C. (2006). The Values in Action (VIA) Classification of Strengths. In M. Csikszentmihalyi & I.S. Csikszentmihalyi (Eds.), *A life worth living: Contributions to positive psychology,* (pp. 29–48) New York: Oxford.

■ Peterson, C., & Seligman, M.E.P. (2004). *Character strengths and virtues: A classification and handbook.* Washington, DC: American Psychological Association.

■ Seligman, M.E.P., Park, N., & Peterson, C. (2004). The Values In Action (VIA) classification of character strengths. *Ricerche di Psicologia, 27,* 63 s–78.

CHAPTER 9 APPENDIX NOTES

1. The Solution-Focused Recovery for Abuse Survivors © 1988, 1993 is adapted for this text with permission from Yvonne Dolan, M.A. The instrument may not be reprinted without permission of the author.

2. Strengths Interview Questions for Domestic Violence is printed with permission from Peter Lehmann, Ph.D., Domestic Violence Diversion Program, University of Texas at Arlington. The instrument may be reprinted without permission of the author.

3. The Fordyce Emotions Questionnaire © is printed with permission from Michael Fordyce, Ph.D. (gethappy.net). Please contact the author for information about reprinting. Additional information on this questionnaire can be found in the following citations: (1) Fordyce, M. (1988). A review of research on the happiness measures: A sixty-second index of happiness and mental health. *Social Indicators Research, 20,* 355–381; (2) Seligman, M. (2002). *Authentic Happiness: Using the New Positive Psychology to Realize Your Potential for Lasting Fulfillment.* New York: Free Press.

4. The Solution Identification Scale © by Yvonne Dolan & Ron Krall, 1988, as adapted for PATH by Jeffrey Goldman & Mary Baydanan, 1990, reprinted for this text with permission from the authors. The instrument may not be reprinted without permission of the author. Additional information on this questionnaire can be found in the following citations: (1) Doland, Y.M. (1991). *Resolving sexual abuse: Solution focused therapy and Ericksonian hypnosis for adult survivors.* New York: Norton; (2) Goldman, J., & Baydanan, M. (1990). *Solution Identification Scale.* Denver, CO: Peaceful Alternatives in the Home.

5. The Satisfaction With Life Scale (SWLS) is reprinted with permission of Ed Diener, Dept. of Psychology, University of Illinois, Champaign, IL. Scale is not to be reprinted without permission of the author. Additional information on this scale can be found in the following citations: (1) Diener, E., Emmons, R.A., Larsen, R.J., & Griffin, S. (1985). The Satisfaction with Life Scale. *Journal of Personality Assessment, 49,* 71–75; (2) Pavot, W., & Diener, E. (1993). Review of the Satisfaction with Life Scale. *Psychological Assessment, 5,* 164–172; (3) Pavot, W., & Diener, E. (2004). Findings on subjective well-being: Applications to public police, clinical interventions, and education. In P.A. Linley & S.A. Joseph (Eds.), *Positive psychology in practice* (pp. 679-692). Hoboken, NJ: Wiley; (4) Pavot, W., & Diener, E. (2008). The Satisfaction with Life Scale and the emerging construct of life satisfaction. *Journal of Positive Psychology, 3,* 137–152.

6. The Beliefs About Romantic Partner © is reprinted with permission of author Jennifer Frei, Dept. of Psychology, University of California at Davis. Scale is not to be reprinted without permission of the author. Additional information on this scale can be found in the following citation: Frei, J.R., & Shaver, P.R. (2002). Respect in close relationships: Prototype definition, self-report assessment, and initial correlates. *Personal Relationships, 9,* 121–139.

7. The Meaning of Life Questionnaire © (MLQ) is reprinted with permission. The copyright for this questionnaire is owned by the University of Minnesota. This questionnaire is intended for free use in research and clinical applications. Please contact Michael F. Steger prior to any such noncommercial use (http://michael.f.steger.googlepages.com/home). This questionnaire may not be used for commercial purposes. Additional information on this scale can be found in the following citations: (1) Steger, M. F., Frazier, P., Oishi, S., & Kaler, M. (2006). The Meaning in Life Questionnaire: Assessing the presence of and search for meaning in life. *Journal of Counseling Psychology, 53,* 80–93; (2) Steger, M.F., & Fazier, P. (2005). Meaning in life: One link in the chain from religion to well-being. *Journal of Counseling Psychology, 52(4),* 574–582.

8. The Respect for Partner Scale © is reprinted with permission of authors Susan S. Hendrick, Ph.D., and Clyde Hendrick, Ph.D., Dept. of Psychology, Texas Tech University. Scale is not to be reprinted without the consent of the authors. Additional information on this scale can be found in the following citation: Hendrick, S.S., & Hendrick, C. (2006). Measuring respect in close relationships. *Journal of Social and Personal Relationships, 23,* 881–899.

9. The Relationship Assessment Scale © is reprinted with permission of the author Susan S. Hendrick, Ph.D., Dept. of Psychology, Texas Tech University. Scale is not to be reprinted without the consent of the author. Additional information on this scale can be found in the following citation: Hendrick, S.S., Dicke, A., & Hendrick, C. (1998). The relationship assessment scale. *Journal of Social and Personal Relationships, 15,* 137–142.

10. The Subjective Happiness Scale © is reprinted with permission from author Sonja Lyubomirsky, Ph.D. Scale is not to be reprinted without the consent of the author. Additional information on this scale can be found in the following citations: (1) Lyubomirsky, S., & Lepper, H.S. (1999). A measure of subjective happiness: Preliminary reliability and construct validation. *Social Indicators Research, 46,* 137–155; (2) Lyubomirsky, S., & Kennon, S. (2005). Pursuing happiness: The architecture of sustainable change. *Review of General Psychology, 9,* 111–131; (3) Lyubomirsky, S., & Ross, L. (1999). Changes in attractiveness of elected, rejected, and precluded alternatives: A comparison of happy and unhappy individuals. *Journal of Personality and Social Psychology, 76,* 988–1007; (4) Lyubomirsky, S., & Tucker, K. L. (1998). Implications of individual differences in subjective happiness for perceiving, interpreting, and thinking about life events. *Motivation and Emotion, 22,* 155–186.

11. Session Rating Scale (SRS V.3.0) © 2002, Scott D. Miller, Barry L. Duncan, & Lynn Johnson, and Outcome Rating Sale (ORS) © 2000, Scott D. Miller & Barry L. Duncan, exam copy reprinted with permission from Scott D. Miller, Institute for the Study of Therapeutic Change, Chicago, IL. The ORS/SRS V.3.0 are available in 15 languages. Neither scale can be reprinted without the consent of the authors. Requests should be directed to Barry L. Duncan, PsyD, 8611 Banyan Ct., Tamarac, FL 33321. E-mail: barrylduncan@cs.com or www.talkingcure.com. Additional information on this scale can be found in the following citations: (1) Bringhurst, D.L., Watson, C.W., Miller, S.D., & Duncan, B.L. (2006). The reliability and validity of the outcome rating scale: A replication study of a brief clinical measure, *Journal of Brief Therapy, 5,* 23–30; (2) Duncan, B.L., Miller, S.D., Sparks, J.A., Claud, D.A., Reynolds, L.R., Brown, J., & Johnson, L.D. (2003). The session rating scale: Preliminary psychometric properties of a "working" alliance measure. *Journal of Brief Therapy, 3,* 3–12; (3) Miller, S.D., Duncan, B.L., Brown, J., Sparks, J., & Claud, D. (2003). The outcome rating scale: A preliminary study of the reliability, validity, and feasibility of a brief visual analog measure. *Journal of Brief Therapy, 2,* 91–100.

12. Utilizing Goals to Create a Context for Change: Treating Domestic Violence Offenders is reprinted with permission from authors Mo Yee Lee, Ph.D., Adrian Uken, L.C.S.W., & John Sebold, L.C.S.W. Exercise/homework activity is not to be reprinted without the permission of the authors. Additional information on this exercise/homework activity can be found in the following citations: (1) Lee, M.Y., Sebold, J., & Uken, A. (2003). *Solution-focused treatment of domestic violence offenders: Accountability for change.* New York: Oxford University Press; (2) Lee. M.Y., Uken. A., Sebold, J. (2004). Accountability for solutions: Solution-focused treatment with domestic violence offenders. *Families in Society, 85,* 463–476; (3) Lee M.Y., Uken. A., Sebold, J. (2007). Role of self-determined goals in predicting recidivism in domestic violence offenders. *Research on Social Work Practice, 17,* 30–41.

13. The Accountability Time Line is reprinted with the permission of author Ken Bennett, L.M.S.W., Opportunities Counseling, Fort Worth, Texas. Exercise/homework activity is not to be reprinted without permission of the author.

14. Writing About The Benefits Of My Experience Task is adapted, with permission, from a writing questionnaire developed by Michael E. McCullough, Dept. of Psychology, University of Miami, mikem@miami.edu. Exercise/homework activity is not to be reprinted without permission of the authors. Additional information on this exercise/homework activity can be found in the following citation: McCullough, M.E., Root, L.M., & Cohen, A.D. (2006). Writing about the benefits of an interpersonal transgression facilitates forgiveness. *Journal of Consulting and Clinical Psychology, 74,* 887–897.

15. Both Relationship Values and Distractions are reprinted with permission of author Tod Augusta-Scott of Bridges—A domestic violence counseling, research, and training institute, Nova Scotia, Canada, tod@bridgesinstitute.org. Exercise/homework activity is not to be reprinted without permission of the author. Additional information on this exercise/homework activity can be found in the following citation: Augusta-Scott, T. (2008). *Narrative therapy: Abuse intervention program. A program to foster respectful relationships. A group facilitator's manual.* Nova Scotia: Bridges.

16. The Gratitude Visit, Three Good Things, and You At Your Best are reprinted with permission form author M.E.P. Seligman, Ph.D., Positive Psychology Center, University of Pennsylvania. Exercise/homework activity is not to be reprinted without permission of the author. Additional information on these exercises/homework activities can be found in the following citations: (1) Seligman, M. (1990). *Learned Optimism: How to change your mind and your life.* New York: Free Press; (2) Seligman, M. (2002). *Authentic Happiness: Using the New Positive Psychology to Realize Your Potential for Lasting Fulfillment.* New York: Free Press; (3) Seligman, M., & Csikszentmihalyi. M. (2000) Positive psychology: An introduction. *American Psychologist, 55,* 5–14.

17. "Goals to Solutions" Treatment Plan Agreement is reprinted with permission from author Blaine Moore, M.S.S.W., L.M.S.W., and Elliott Connie, M.A., L.P.C., Ph.D. (cand.), Fort Worth Brief Therapy, Fort Worth Texas. Do not reprint without permission of the author.

18. "Goals to Solutions" Outcome Measure is reprinted with permission from author Blaine Moore, M.S.S.W., L.M.S.W., and Elliott Connie, M.A., L.P.C.; Ph.D. (cand.), Fort Worth Brief Therapy, Fort Worth Texas. Do not reprint without permission of the author.

19. "Goals to Solutions" Treatment Plan Review is reprinted with permission from author Blaine Moore, M.S.S.W., L.M.S.W., and Elliott Connie, M.A., L.P.C., Ph.D. (cand.), Fort Worth Brief Therapy, Fort Worth Texas. Do not reprint without permission of the author.

20. "Goals to Solutions" Client Satisfaction Survey is reprinted with permission from author Blaine Moore, M.S.S.W., L.M.S.W., and Elliott Connie, M.A., L.P.C. (cand.), Ph.D. (cand.), Fort Worth Brief Therapy, Fort Worth Texas. Do not reprint without permission of the author.

Looking Forward

10

PETER LEHMANN
CATHERINE A. SIMMONS

The best thing about the future is that it comes only one day at a time.

—*Abraham Lincoln*

Batterer intervention programs (BIPs) are a relatively new response to the problems surrounding intimate partner violence (IPV). From the field's modest beginnings in the 1970s and up to the present, family violence professionals continue to ask the important questions, "what else can be done to improve intervention?" and "are there other ways of responding that are helpful?" In raising these questions, it is clear that the field is ahead of where it started, yet certainly has a long way to go.

The purpose of this text has been to address these questions and others by introducing the idea that a strengths-based paradigm will move intervention with IPV offenders in a new direction; one that advances, contributes, and constructively changes what currently exists. In developing the argument for a changing paradigm, the authors/editors made no attempt to resolve the differing opinions about controversial issues within the field. The argument for a paradigm shift is instead about broadening the view of intervention with IPV offenders in a manner that is different from current thinking. Consequently, a number of considerations arise. Seeded throughout the contributed chapters are ideas for changing the language used in and about batterer intervention. In addition, the need to change the overall approach to work with IPV offenders is apparent.

Thus, this final chapter offers some pragmatic comments about change and working with the IPV offending population. These changes include moving from a first to a dual language, and changing batterer intervention by supporting depth of practice and incorporating a dual language. From these changes the need to incorporate strengths-based outcomes into research and clinical evaluation is emphasized. Arising from this discussion are the hopeful possibilities of new dialogues, novel yet innovative interventions, and expanded outcomes with people who are IPV offenders taking part in batterer programming.

FROM FIRST LANGUAGE TO DUAL LANGUAGE

At the heart of all work with IPV offenders is the use of language as a means to communicate. Language is an activity, an ongoing transfer of words and symbols that allow each person to make sense of, reflect on, and respond within a particular socially constructed context (Gergen, 1985; McNamee, 2004). The act of using language as a tool of communication is the instrument for how the meaning of events, of self, of behavior, of change, and of good or bad are interpreted. Such language occurs with partners, police, probation officers, lawyers, therapists, and in the interchange within the group process. At the heart of every interaction between the family violence professional and the IPV offending client is a language both influencing and influenced by these relationships. For the past three decades a *first language* has developed, shaped, and grown from the field. However, there are aspects of the *first language* that are limiting. Thus, as the family violence field looks toward a paradigm that is strengths-based, the language used in discussions around family violence needs to change to a *dual language*.

First Language

The field of family violence has created what we consider a *first language* of meaning around and about people who use violence in their relationships. These "meanings" are value-laden (see Augusta-Scott, this volume) and shaped by three decades of activities by practitioners, advocates, academia, and researchers; each devoting lifetimes of dedicated labor toward ending relationship violence. In some ways this *first language* has come to represent the best of what we know, understand, and have learned about IPV.

A number of very important concepts have emerged from this *first language*. Although the list is not exhaustive, it does include such examples as: violence against women occurs with great frequency, her risk of danger is very real, and that many women are hurt and even murdered. It also includes the following ideas: that the abuse of power and control in relationships is detrimental to one's well being; men's anger and rage make women and children unsafe; batterer intervention programming is an important element in stopping violence; some men who are violent are vulnerable to mental illness and/or substance abuse; and cultural contexts can define the roles of men who are abusive. The *first language* is an important, valued position of dialogue because it creates an appreciation for the fact that one can *never* ignore the very real consequences of IPV.

Although the *first language* has developed and shaped important strides in theory, research, outreach, and intervention, there are elements of this language that have blocked the field from progressing. Much of the problem revolves around how we view, talk to, and communicate with people who enter family violence programs as IPV offenders. At the heart of much of the work with IPV offenders is the *first language* created from the need to acknowledge the very real problems surrounding IPV, and to encourage safety. This *first language* forms the foundation for how we, as practitioners, construct conversations about change.

It is important to keep in mind that the process of using language in BIP work is a socially constructed activity (Gergen, 1985; McNamee, 2004), part of which stems from what we have come to know. It is also an activity where an ongoing back-and-forth exchange of words and symbols between group leaders and group participants allows each person to make sense of, reflect on, and respond. It is in this process that the meaning of events (such as incidents of IPV), of behavior ("my use of violence is troubling to me"), of change ("can I be forced to change?"), and of good or bad ("am I a good person or bad person?") are interpreted. Although the *first language* has developed and shaped theory, research, outreach, advocacy, and direct practice, there may be elements that discourage IPV offenders from participating in the change process. All too often, clients' failure to accept this *first language* early in intervention leads to confrontation, denial, frustration, and other behaviors generally labeled "resistance" by the family violence profession. In sum, the concepts inherent in the *first language* are important and should not be ignored; however, a broadening of its conceptualization is clearly needed.

Dual Language

As the field matures, the family violence profession needs to recontextualize its work surrounding the *first language* (what we already know) while still preserving its primacy (being committed to ending violence against women) (Eisikovits, Enosh & Edleson, 1996). To that end, the chapters presented in this text are preliminary efforts to provide a vision to the family violence field, specifically BIP work, by introducing a second language to be used in conversations about the future of intervention. The discussions presented in this text represent an inclusion of a second discourse for meeting the professional challenges of working with IPV offenders. What is enclosed is a potential *dual language* of words and ideas that can be part of the dialogue between the family violence professional (e.g., therapist/group facilitator) and IPV offender. It is a conversation that looks to talk (or inquire) both about (a) the IPV offender's strengths, competencies, resources and (b) the very real problem of violence and abuse. Much of the evolution from deficits to strengths-based language in the human service professions (e.g., Duckworth, Steen & Seligman, 2005; Saleebey, 2006) supports fostering a discussion about IPV offenders who are goal-seeking and searching to find meaning in their lives (Langlands, Ward & Gilchrist, this volume). Thus, offenders can construct a dialogue around their strengths and successes (see chapter 3, this volume), or can work toward developing positive emotions (see chapter 7, this volume) or find a new sense of purpose for their lives (see chapter 8, this volume).

Taken together, this presents a future vision that promotes consideration of a *dual language* for working with IPV offenders. Indeed, it can be "both/and," nothing is absolute, and yes the dangers and risks are real, but there are also redeeming qualities to be found in many IPV offenders. Incorporating a *dual language* of thinking around batterer intervention creates a conversational tone, with a moveable foreground and background. Based on their skill and level of knowledge, practitioners can multitask; they are able to focus on the dangers or risks of "how close are you to losing it?" or "how depressed are you?" (e.g., foreground), yet inquire and be mindful about what strengths are present, "can you remember a time when you showed control in the face of all this stress?" or "how have you managed to overcome these feelings before?" (e.g., background). Both can be attended to simultaneously. Each can be accessible for use in programming, each can take prominence when needed, each values the practitioners' skills and knowledge about the complexities of intimate relationships, and each equally identifies with the importance of safety for everyone involved. A *dual language* in BIP work also has the advantage of moving interventions beyond being value-laden (see Augusta-Scott, this volume) and judgmental (Milner, 2004). Confrontation, education, and resocializing need not be the focal point of work that leads toward change.

Dual Language Builds Strengths

Dual language may help practitioners consider shifting some of their emphasis from "what's wrong with you?" and "here's what you need to learn in group" to include conversations that are somewhat broader, such as "what's going well for you in what areas of your life?" and "how might this help you to end your abusive behavior as you come to group?" Altering one's work does not mean leaving behind the cultural context of IPV offenders and their treatment needs, ignoring danger, minimizing any mental illness or substance issues, and so forth. Certainly, each of the chapters in this text is cognizant of this while including ample support for the inclusion of strengths into assessments and/or interventions. Thus, each chapter has been able to attend to "other" multiple resources by supplanting their focus while documenting such attributes as assets and competencies.

CHANGING BATTERER INTERVENTION

In addition to changing the language used about and with IPV offenders, the need to change the overall approach to work with this population is apparent. These changes include building strengths by increasing the practice depth, addressing dual language, and incorporating strengths-based outcomes into research. Building strengths in batterer intervention programming is a natural extension of the social service profession's move toward wellness and competence (e.g., Cowen, 1994, Joseph & Worsley, 2005; Seligman & Csikszentmihalyi, 2000). To be more specific, the broaden-and-build chapter (this volume) highlights how building positive emotions can bolster resilience, which can spiral one's good psychological coping upwards (see also, Fredrickson, 2002, 2003, 2004, 2006). If a person feels good internally, the possibility of examining and broadening individual behaviors is also likely to increase (Frederickson, 2002, 2003, 2004, 2006). It is more probable, then, that men will be willing to engage in unpacking areas of personal resilience as part of their work in their intervention program. To build on these themes, practitioner skills need to be expanded to support practice depth, encourage building relationships, and improve practice outcomes.

Supporting Practice Depth

Building strengths into intervention with IPV offenders has applications for expanding practitioner skills toward a practice depth that goes beyond relying on methods found in the manualized approaches and singular intervention models. Although the concept of practice depth comes from the child protection literature (e.g., Chapman & Field, 2007; Ferguson, 2004; Scott, 2006), it has relevance toward constructive programming with IPV offender populations as well. In short, practice depth is "usually characterized by reflective analysis, sound decision making and demonstration of comprehensive professional knowledge and skill" (Chapman & Field, 2007, p. 23).

To aid in understanding the ideas inherent in practice depth, Exhibit 10.1 has been adapted for use with IPV offender intervention. In this figure, three levels of practice are depicted, each having a wider range of importance. The first level, *conveyor belt practice,* is characterized by event-driven intervention and efficient, short, risk factor focused assessment. The client is then moved (such as on a conveyor belt) into a standardized program. At this first level, little emphasis is given to cultural-specific issues and the role of "therapy" is not considered part of the experience. The second level, *pragmatic practice,* is characterized as continuing compliance with policy and practice guidelines. The difference is that the level of engagement with IPV offenders is considered moderate and interaction with other agencies occurs at a level considered sufficient to manage the work at hand. Case management is a focus of *pragmatic practice* but the relationship is not considered therapy. The third level of practice, *reflective practice,* is therapeutic, as it includes understanding risks while also engaging with the IPV offending client in a positive, active, and responsive manner. At this level, there is a good understanding of the larger biopsychosocial issues impacting IPV (Corvo, Dutton & Chen, 2008). Interventions then are based on quality practice decision making, tailored to the needs around the IPV offender's specific situation and issues.

Exhibit 10.1

UNDERSTANDING PRACTICE DEPTH*

PRACTICE DEPTH

Level 1, *Conveyor belt practice* (Ferguson, 2004), is characterized by event-driven efficient assessment. It is front end focused and may be risk informed. Often moves IPV offender quickly into one-sized treatment programs that follow state standard policies and use standardized curricula. Safety is a priority. Little focus is placed on "therapeutic needs."

Level 2, *Pragmatic practice,* is characterized by an efficient throughput of work, usually case management, and a moderate engagement with the IPV offender and outside agencies. Compliance with policy and practice guidelines is important. Safety is a priority.

Level 3, *Reflective practice,* is characterized by quality practice decision-making and intervention (e.g., triaging), purposeful positive engagement with offenders, and responsiveness to their needs. The IPV offender is helped to become specific and concrete about behavior change. Supports and resources in the community (such as coordinated response) are mobilized. Critical evaluation of outcomes is made. Safety is a priority for partners but is also critical in IPV offenders accounting for their own behaviors.

*Adapted with permission from Chapman & Field (2007)

Within this framework, it is likely that much of the current batterer intervention programming is conducted at the first and second levels of practice. Most intervention is event-driven, mandated by the criminal justice system and front-end focused with the priority of risk factor reduction. The IPV offender is then moved (conveyor belt fashion) into a mandated, manualized, one-sized-fits-all group, most of which follows Duluth model-like protocols (e.g., Gondolf, 2002; Jackson, Feder, Forde, Davis, Maxwell & Taylor, 2003), where the goals of treatment are defined by state standards (Austin & Danwort, 1999; Dankwort & Austin, 1999). The end results of these programs are either (a) completion and closure or (b) referral back to the courts because of program noncompliance. In some ways, *conveyor belt practice* may be considered to be "more of the same." For example, Dalton's (2007) survey of batterer programs found that treatment tracks (matching clients to treatments) amounted to keeping IPV offenders in groups for longer periods of time, thus, the belt keeps moving in a similar manner.

Advancing the domestic violence field toward strengths-based intervention models will require domestic violence professionals to move to the *reflective practice* level with IPV offenders. *Reflective practice* acknowledges that treatment success relies less on the need to educate and more on facilitator-client factors around building motivation such as that described by motivational interviewing (e.g., Dia, Simmons, Oliver & Cooper, this volume; Easton, Swan & Sinha, 2000; Kistenmacher & Weiss, 2008; Musser, Semiantin, Taft & Murphy, 2008; Taft, Murphy, Elliott & Morrel, 2001). Indeed, all of the chapters in this text point in the direction where *reflective practice* merges with batterer intervention. This merger means engaging IPV offenders with a focus on collaboration, understanding the broader circumstances of their situation, being specific and detailed about change, and pausing to consider the best possible decision about treatment instead of moving a client directly into a group. To accomplish this, a heightened degree of professional skills are required. In their chapter on strengths-focused CBT, Eckardt and Schram (chapter 6, this volume) discuss interventions aimed at changes that are not solely therapist-delivered but rather rely on a two-person process, with each person contributing and developing the intervention. This requires more than a short intake or phone interview, necessitating thoughtful steps on the part of the professional to gather information that will be important, useful, and hopefully generate interest in participation. Solution focused brief therapy (SFBT) approaches chart an uncharacteristic approach to assessment, yet one that includes drawing on professional capacity and skill to start the process of change (e.g., Lee, Sebold & Uken, 2003b; Lee, Uken & Sebold, this volume, 2004, 2007; Uken, Lee & Sebold, 2007). In the SFBT chapter, IPV offenders are asked (a) to develop goals for themselves instead of being asked about their history of violence, and (b) what strengths and resources they have. Likewise, narrative therapy is less interested in a prescribed view of the problem of violence, and so takes time to negotiate what the definition of the problem is from the male's perspective (e.g., Augusta-Scott, this volume, 2008; Augusta-Scott & Dankwort, 2002).

Developing Practice Depth

From the ideas inherent in practice depth, the importance of developing skills to attain it develops. This is especially important when working with IPV offenders who are generally not happy about being in treatment, thus initially reluctant to participate. The 4 skill areas Trotter (2002) proposes for child welfare workers may be of value in developing these skills within BIP work. Exhibit 10.2 illustrates these skills, including (a) role clarification, (b) the collaborative problem-solving process, (c) the reinforcement of pro-social skills and actions, and (d) the development of relationship skills (Trotter, 2002).

To some extent, the chapters in this text encapsulate the ideas of Trotter (2002). The core constructs and assumptions of strengths outlined in chapter 2 (this volume) and what follows form the basis for building the strengths-based practice skills, similar to those outlined in Exhibit 10.2. In this process, decision making with IPV offenders becomes more transparent. Assumptions about needs or strengths mean change is not necessarily top-down (e.g., facilitator or curriculum setting an education agenda). IPV offenders know what to expect because they have a stake in being accountable for their own solutions and changes. If there is a need for tailored treatment, it includes not only what's going wrong (e.g., problems and/or mental health issues) but also what's going right (e.g., including strengths).

Building Relationships

The emphasis on building a relationship with IPV offenders should be seen as a natural extension of the strengths approach. It is important to acknowledge there is no *one correct way* to build relationships, and each strengths model presents its own unique approach. As has been discussed throughout this text, the idea and importance of relationships is critical and cannot be left out. Although rarely a consideration in the professional IPV field, a substantial body of evidence highlights the effect of positive human relationships on therapeutic outcome (for summary review see Norcross & Lambert, 2006). The impact of incorporating these ideas into

Exhibit 10.2

DEVELOPING PRACTICE DEPTH SKILLS*

Role Clarification
- Open, honest, and respectful discussion about the intervention
- The dual role of the worker (Skeem, Louden, Polaschek & Camp, 2007): blending caring with control
- The man's expectation of the group facilitator
- The group facilitator's expectations for the man to develop his own goal toward change

Collaborative Problem-Solving Process
- How does partnership (Turnell, 2007) develop as a way of leading to group success?
- Work to understand the man's definition of the problem (rather than the facilitator's)
- Goals created by men and purposeful strategies to achieve success are addressed
- Men identify the personal, social issues impacting behavior that are helpful or are in need

Reinforcing Positive Pro-Social Skills
- Notice all behaviors in (expressing emotions, working on new patterns of thought) and out of (parenting, drug/alcohol use) group that reflect competence and resourcefulness

Relationship Skill Building
- Facilitator skills are developed to build the relationship
- The development of mutual respect
- Offender must perceive fairness on the part of the facilitator

*Adapted from Trotter, 2002

batterer programming is likely to be that (a) the relationships with IPV offenders will have a sizeable contribution to positive outcomes and (b) a dual role between the type of intervention and facilitator characteristics will be created. Taken together, building professional relationships over and beyond an emphasis on just the technical application should be a central consideration as the field moves forward.

As strengths and relationship building in the preceding chapters have been unpacked, an important implication unfolds. That is, developing relationships with people who are offenders can never be taken for granted. Relationship building is not a simplistic, Pollyannaish, do-gooder, bleeding-heart process where anything goes (such as "if I like you enough, I'm sure you'll like yourself and change"). Instead, as Lee, Uken, and Sebold have suggested (see chapter 3, this volume), helping people (especially those who are violent or angry) move toward accountability is hard work. It is serious work, and sometimes relationship building doesn't happen. At the same time, it should be attempted and never be taken lightly.

The Dual Relationship Dilemma

Building on strengths and resources by incorporating practice depth and relationship building requires a balanced perspective. To this end, the dual relationship dilemma inherent in building a therapeutic, strengths-based relationship with the IPV offending client while also meeting the social control aspects of the criminal justice system needs to be addressed. Although this dual relationship dilemma is generally absent in the IPV literature, all professionals who work with family violence and especially those IPV offenders mandated for treatment have some awareness of the dual relationship dilemma. Domestic violence professionals must reconcile the role of a caring, interested problem solver with that of a potentially controlling, limit-setting agent of the court. The limitations of mixing therapeutic treatment and punitive social control must be recognized (e.g., Lee, Seebold & Uken, 2003a, 2003b; Lee, Uken & Seebold, 2004). However, the family violence field has not progressed to a point that the social control aspect of intervention can or should be excluded. Thus, building relationship alliances with IPV offenders mandated to BIP treatment will always be qualitatively different from relationship building in more traditional therapeutic settings. The duality of these opposing roles leads to questions about how to best reconcile the conflicts. The role of procedural justice and relationship building in probation settings are next considered.

Concepts of Procedural Justice. Procedural justice is one area of discussion that may be helpful in addressing the dual relationship inherent in working strengths-based ideas into aspects of social control. The concept of procedural justice was developed by Thibault and Walker (1975) as a way to look at the process of how legal issues are handled and managed rather than focusing solely on their outcome. Simply defined, procedural justice is the perceived fairness of processes and procedures used to make decisions. Over the years, the notion of procedural justice has been found to be useful with victims of domestic violence and their satisfaction with case adjudications (e.g., Gover, Brank & MacDonald, 2007; Wemmers & Cousineau, 2005). In one example of use with IPV offenders, Paternoster, Bachman, Noster, and Sherman (1997) found that when offenders view their legal sanctions as fair, they are more likely to comply with decisions.

The issue of procedural justice within batterer intervention leads to the question "what does fair treatment consist of and how might it be applicable to a strengths approach?" A cursory look at the literature reveals a number of characteristics that include "fairness" when procedural justice is put into a working context. These include but are not limited to (a) transparency about what can and cannot happen, (b) respectful dialogue about decision making, (c) participatory decision making, and (d) control blended with regard and caring (e.g., Gover, Brank & MacDonald, 2007; MacCoun, 2005; Paternoster, Bachman, Noster & Sherman, 1997; Wemmers & Cousineau, 2005). Herein lies the process; it seems fairness as procedural justice combined with practitioner skills may provide more balance toward those IPV offenders genuinely and honestly taking accountability for their behavior. Cooperation and compliance seem likely when an IPV offender perceives the domestic violence professional's attempt to be fair, just, and respectful. A position of fairness toward IPV offenders seems impossible without assuming that the recipient has some capacity to be a part of the process. Put another way, if the relationship with the IPV offender is based on being authoritarian, demanding and confronting, it seems unlikely fairness combined with strengths will have a place.

Probationers Mandated for Psychiatric Treatment. The second area having a strengths-based application for addressing the dual relationship inherent in batterer intervention comes from a series of studies, by Skeem and colleagues (e.g., Skeem, Emke-Francis & Eno Louden, 2006; Skeem, Encandela & Eno Loden, 2003; Skeem, Eno Louden, Polaschek & Camp, 2007), of the dual-role relationships of probationers mandated for psychiatric treatment. Results of these studies include three important ideas relevant to the current discussion. First, relationship quality in mandated treatment involves support, trust, and openness. Second, authoritative (not authoritarian) positioning makes a difference in the probationer's following through. In addition, when fairness is combined with a perception of benevolence and caring, the dual-role relationship benefits. Third, heightened issues of control between parties exist when behavior toward probationers is perceived as indifferent. Incorporating these findings into batterer programming involves taking a position of benevolence with support in the face of being authoritative. Doing so requires a relationship-building effort that is professional but that also has the capacity to focus on the assets and competencies of IPV offenders.

INCORPORATING STRENGTHS-BASED OUTCOMES

The final comments in closing this text and looking forward relate to building strengths-based outcomes into research and evaluation with IPV offenders. In a short summary of evidence in mental health practice, Stuart and Lilienfeld (2007) noted that professionals can extract much information about what is helpful in treatment while also gathering invaluable information about what is harmful. Likewise, Lilienfeld (2007) operationalized and identified a number of psychological treatments that have proven harmful to clients or their loved ones. In this work, he stated the evidence with respect to court-mandated treatments for spouse abusers, although "preliminary" (Lilienfeld, 2007, p. 58), i.e., that these treatments may be harmful to some individuals. Although no firm conclusions about batterer programming harm were made (Lilienfeld, 2007), the fact that mention was made of the potential for harm may be a call to reexamine what is already known about the limitations of current approaches to BIPs. Further, it may also be an opportunity to examine how strengths could play a role in preventing BIPs from doing harm.

Focus of Current Research

At present there is a great deal of research into issues surrounding BIPs, including (but not limited to) program evaluations, method studies, descriptive studies, and studies focusing on specific aspects of intervention. Although space prohibits a detailed discussion, summaries about useful research has not been lost. Authors, including Corvo, Dutton, and Chen (2008), Dutton (2008), Hamberger (2008a, 2008b), Gondolf (2002), Jackson et al. (2003), and many others, continue to be mindful of the need to press for better standards of evaluation around methodology, sample size, design, etc., and greater sophistication of analyses for ever-specialized treatment needs that can "tease out the constellation of issues" (Corvo, Dutton & Chen, 2008, p. 124).

Promising Areas to Be Pursued

At the same time, building a strengths perspective into the family violence research agenda is likely to pose a real challenge. At the moment there is a general absence of research that looks at the relationship of strengths in the context of ending violence. Also, to some extent the evaluation research tends to be largely defined by a field focused on deficit-based outcomes. Thus, the looming question perhaps is whether there is any real interest in giving attention to IPV offenders' strengths, compared to evaluating pathology. Because standardized tools in the IPV field look at outcomes using measures of pathology, anger, depression, distress, and so forth, it would then be an easy transition to also measure strengths, competencies, or personal resources. Doing so will develop a broader understanding of IPV offenders and what is useful in helping them end their violent and abusive behavior. To start this process, it may be beneficial to consider three specific areas of strengths-based research not generally associated with family violence.

The first area of strengths-based research that should be considered comes from the positive psychology research of virtue and character. Seligman and colleagues have defined six broad virtues thought to have the most value, including wisdom, courage, humanity, justice, temperance, and transcendence (e.g., Dahlsgaard, Peterson & Seligman, 2005; Peterson & Seligman, 2004; Seligman 2002). Many positive psychologists believe that good character is a function of these six virtues. However, the problem with this paradigm is that these virtues are unique to each individual, thus subjective in nature. To illustrate, the virtue *courage* can mean different things in different contexts, such as physical bravery in combat or moral integrity in politics. In order to facilitate the definition, cultivation, and measurement of virtue and character, Seligman (2002) identified a total of twenty-four strengths under the six virtues. Furthering these constructs, Peterson and Seligman (2004) created the *Values in Action* (VIA) *Classification of Strengths* included in Exhibit 10.3 and the corresponding *VIA Inventory of Strengths Survey*, a 240-item instrument designed to identify a person's signature strengths. Administered in web and paper format, over 1 million people worldwide have completed this inventory, which is applicable to a wide variety of settings (Linley et al., 2007; Peterson, 2006; Peterson & Seligman, 2004; Seligman, Park & Peterson, 2004). By incorporating these ideas into outcome

Exhibit 10.3

VALUES IN ACTION CLASSIFICATION OF CHARACTER STRENGTHS

The following is a list of virtues and character strengths defined by Peterson, Seligman, and Colleagues*

1. **Wisdom and knowledge**—Cognitive strengths that entail the acquisition and use of knowledge.

   Creativity: Thinking of novel and productive ways to do things; includes artistic achievement but is not limited to it.

   Curiosity: Taking an interest in all ongoing experience; finding all subjects and topics fascinating; exploring and discovering.

   Judgment/critical thinking: Thinking things through and examining them from all sides; not jumping to conclusions; being able to change your mind in light of evidence; weighing all evidence fairly.

   Love of learning: Mastering new skills, topics, and bodies of knowledge, whether on your own or formally. Obviously related to the strength of curiosity but goes beyond it to describe the tendency to add systematically to what you know.

   Perspective: Being able to provide wise counsel to others; having ways of looking at the world that make sense to the self and to other people.

2. **Courage**—Emotional strengths that involve the exercise of will to accomplish goals in the face of opposition, external or internal.

   Bravery: Not shrinking from threat, challenge, difficulty, or pain; speaking up for what is right even if there is opposition; acting on convictions even if unpopular; includes physical bravery but is not limited to it.

   Industry/perseverance: Finishing what you start; persisting in a course of action in spite of obstacles; "getting it out the door"; taking pleasure in completing tasks.

   Authenticity: Speaking the truth but more broadly presenting yourself in a genuine way; being without pretense; taking responsibility for your feelings and actions.

*Reprinted with permission (Peterson & Seligman, 2004). Do not reprint without permission of the authors.

Exhibit 10.3

VALUES IN ACTION CLASSIFICATION OF CHARACTER STRENGTHS *(CONTINUED)*

Zest: Approaching life with excitement and energy; not doing things halfway or halfheartedly; living life as an adventure; feeling alive and activated.

3. **Love**—Interpersonal strengths that involve "tending" and "befriending" others (Taylor et al., 2000).

   Intimacy: Valuing close relations with others, in particular those in which sharing and caring are reciprocated; being close to people.

   Kindness: Doing favors and good deeds for others; helping them; taking care of them.

   Social intelligence: Being aware of the motives and feelings of other people and the self; knowing what to do to fit in to different social situations; knowing what makes other people tick.

4. **Justice**—Civic strengths that underlie healthy community life.

   Citizenship/teamwork: Working well as member of a group or team; being loyal to the group; doing your share.

   Fairness: Treating all people the same according to notions of fairness and justice; not letting personal feelings bias decisions about others; giving everyone a fair chance.

   Leadership: Encouraging a group of which you are a member to get things done and at the same time maintain good relations within the group; organizing group activities and seeing that they happen.

5. **Temperance**—Strengths that protect against excess.

   Forgiveness/mercy: Forgiving those who have done wrong; giving people a second chance; not being vengeful.

   Modesty/humility: Letting your accomplishments speak for themselves; not seeking the spotlight; not regarding yourself as more special than you are.

   Prudence: Being careful about your choices; not taking undue risks; not saying or doing things that might later be regretted.

   Self-control/self-regulation: Regulating what you feel and do; being disciplined; controlling your appetites and emotions.

Exhibit 10.3

6. **Transcendence**—Strengths that forge connections to the larger universe and provide meaning.

Awe/appreciation of beauty and excellence: Noticing and appreciating beauty, excellence, and/or skilled performance in all domains of life, from nature, to art, to mathematics, to science, to everyday experience.

Gratitude: Being aware of and thankful for the good things that happen; taking time to express thanks.

Hope: Expecting the best in the future and working to achieve it; believing that a good future is something that can be brought about.

Playfulness: Liking to laugh and tease; bringing smiles to other people; seeing the light side; making (not necessarily telling) jokes.

Spirituality: Having coherent beliefs about the higher purpose and meaning of the universe; knowing where you fit within the larger scheme; having beliefs about the meaning of life that shape conduct and provide comfort.

research with offenders, family violence researchers can build on the already strong research foundation of positive psychology while exploring ways that are not currently incorporated into research with IPV offenders.

A second area for strengths-based outcome research extends from the field of psychological well-being. Well-being is the subjective state of being happy, healthy, and prosperous (e.g., Ryff, 1989a, 1989b). However, as is the case with the concepts of character and virtues, operationalizing and measuring well-being is difficult. To this end, Ryff (1989a, 1989b) made this subjective term easier to measure by partitioning psychological well-being into six dimensions: self-acceptance, positive relations with others, autonomy, environmental mastery, purpose in life, and personal growth (Exhibit 10.4). Ryff's early work and more recent studies (e.g., Chrouser Ahrens & Ryff, 2006; Ryff & Keyes, 1995; Ryff & Singer, 2002, 1998) have combined to demonstrate a link between positive functioning and well-being.

Exhibit 10.4

DEFINITIONS OF THEORY-GUIDED DIMENSIONS OF WELL-BEING*

Self-Acceptance

High Scorer: Possesses a positive attitude toward the self; acknowledges and accepts multiple aspects of self, including good and bad qualities; feels positive about past life.

Low Scorer: Feels dissatisfied with self; is disappointed with what has occurred in past life; is troubled about certain personal qualities; wishes to be different than what he or she is.

Positive Relations with Others

High Scorer: Has warm, satisfying, trusting relationships with others; is concerned about the welfare of others; capable of strong empathy, affection, and intimacy; understands the give-and-take of human relationships.

Low Scorer: Has few close, trusting relationships with others; finds it difficult to be warm, open, and concerned about others; is isolated and frustrated in interpersonal relationships; is not willing to make compromises to sustain important ties with others.

Autonomy

High Scorer: Is self-determining and independent; is able to resist social pressures to think and act in certain ways; regulates behavior from within; evaluates self by personal standards.

Low Scorer: Is concerned about the expectations and evaluations of others; relies on the judgments of others to make important decisions; conforms to social pressures to think and act in certain ways.

Environmental Mastery

High Scorer: Has a sense of mastery and competence in managing the environment; controls a complex array of external activities; makes effective use of surrounding opportunities; is able to choose or create contexts suitable to personal needs and values.

*Reprinted with permission (Ryff & Singer, 2002). Do not reprint without permission of the author.

Exhibit 10.4

Low Scorer: Has difficulty managing everyday affairs; feels unable to change or improve surrounding context; is unaware of surrounding opportunities; lacks a sense of control over the external world.

Purpose in Life

High Scorer: Has goals in life and a sense of directedness; feels there is meaning to present and past lives; holds beliefs that give life purpose; has aims and objectives for living.

Low Scorer: Lacks a sense of meaning in life; has few goals or aims; lacks a sense of direction; does not see purpose in past life; has no outlooks or beliefs that give life meaning.

Personal Growth

High Scorer: Has a feeling of continued development; sees self as growing and expanding; is open to new experiences; has sense of realizing his or her potential; sees improvement in self and behavior over time; is changing in ways that reflect more self-knowledge and effectiveness.

Low Scorer: Has a sense of personal stagnation; lacks sense of improvement or expansion over time; feels bored and uninterested with life; feels unable to develop new attitudes or behaviors.

Incorporating these ideas into research with IPV offenders is likely to produce similar results.

A third promising area for strengths-based research with IPV offenders falls under the vast and accumulated knowledge base of subjective well-being. Subjective well-being is defined as "a person's cognitive and affective evaluations of his or her life" (Diener, Lucas & Oishi, 2002, p. 63). In operationalizing this concept, the *Satisfaction with Life Scale—SWLS* (Diener, Emmons, Larsen & Griffin, 1985; Pavot & Diener, 2004; see also chapter 9, this volume) is a five-item questionnaire that assesses global judgments about one's life. The statements are intended to represent important aspects of a person's life that may be unpacked through further questioning. As with the two previous strength-markers, the SWLS has wide applicability across a range of cultures, languages, and intervention settings (Diener, 2008).

Moving Research Ahead

Admittedly, strengths-based research is in its infancy. Despite this, obstacles have been overcome, making it a sound science (for review of methods see Ong & van Dulmen, 2007). Currently, there is more confidence than ever that areas of strengths-based research, including (a) values and character, (b) psychological well-being, and (c) subjective well-being meet the standards of research rigor, including operational definition, control of the intervention, quantification, and statistical significance. Thus, as Kazdin (2008) recommended for clinical psychology, there are three possible ways in which the use of strengths-based outcomes could be built into BIP research. First, determine what is at the heart of change. Building strengths models as part of one's methodology may lead to unpacking the mechanisms of change in IPV offenders. For example, does change measured as a consequence of offender participation in group have anything to do with the facilitator or group-participant relationship? How does enhancing character strengths lead to or predict a change to nonviolence? Second, know how your moderators lead to change. In this case, how might moderators (characteristics of the person, group facilitator, or context) translate to the work of better programming for men? Would group facilitators operating from strengths-based assumptions find that men respond with more motivation or self-interest? Or, would strengths-based interventions perhaps predict successful change when used in conjunction with traditional approaches? Would using strengths-based evaluation tools be useful in different cultural contexts? Third, develop qualitative research. In what way could strengths outcomes be better served through qualitative research? How does developing the subjective experience improve outcomes? These are just some of the many areas and questions that need to be pursued as the field looks forward to understanding strengths and incorporating strengths into practice.

LOOKING FORWARD

In the preface of this text the authors asked the reader "to imagine" the possibility of incorporating strengths into batterer intervention programming. Is there room for a small paradigm shift in thinking about what we currently do? To answer this, the editors of this text set a goal of examining a rationale for this proposal and along the way a group of authors joined in to put forward another direction. Although this direction is somewhat new to the BIP field, an optimistic outlook exists; there is room for strengths-based models of practice within the family violence profession and with IPV offenders. The task in proposing this text has been to be constructive about moving the field of practice forward. The direction is full of optimism with respect to the goal of helping IPV offenders continue to be accountable and end violence against their partners.

In conclusion, our first question leads to more questions. Have we opened the door for incorporating strengths into batterer programming? We think there are possibilities. If the domestic violence profession incorporates strengths into practice, we will move beyond the current approach. As members of a profession, we need to decide whether the strengths and competencies of people who participate in batterer intervention programs really matter when it comes to ending violence. Before we do anything else, let's ask each client.

REFERENCES

Augusta-Scott, T. (2008). *Narrative therapy: Abuse intervention program. A program to foster respectful relationships. A group facilitator's manual.* Nova Scotia: Bridges—a domestic violence counseling, research and training institute.

Augusta-Scott, T., & Dankwort, J. (2002). Partner abuse group intervention: Lessons from education and narrative therapy approaches. *Journal of Interpersonal Violence,* 17, 783–805.

Austin, J.B., & Dankwort, J. (1999). Standard for batterer programs: A review and analysis. *Journal of Interpersonal Violence,* 14, 152–168.

Chapman, M., & Field, J. (2007). Strengthening our engagement with families and understanding practice depth. *Social Work Now,* December, 21–28.

Chrouser Ahrens, C.J., & Ryff, C.D. (2006). Multiple Roles and well being: Sociodemographic and psychological moderators. *Sex Roles,* 55, 801–815.

Corvo, K., Dutton, D., & Chen, Y.W. (2008). Toward evidence-based practice with domestic violence perpetrators. *Journal of Aggression, Maltreatment, & Trauma,* 16, 111–130.

Cowen, E.L. (1994). The enhancement of psychological wellness: Challenges and opportunities. *American Journal of Community Psychology,* 22, 149–179.

Dahlsgaard, K., Peterson, C., & Seligman, M.E.P. (2005). Shared virtue: The convergence of valued human strengths across culture and history. *Review of General Psychology,* 9, 203–213.

Dalton, B. (2007). What's going on out there? A survey of batterer intervention programs. *Journal of Aggression, Maltreatment & Trauma,* 15, 59–74.

Dankwort J., & Austin, J.B. (1999). Standards for batterer intervention programs in Canada: A history and review. *Journal of Community Mental Health,* 18, 19–38.

Diener, E., Emmons, R.A., Larsen, R.J., & Griffen, S. (1985). The satisfaction with life scale. *Journal of Personality Assessment,* 49, 71–75.

Diener, E., Lucas, R.E., & Oishi S. (2002). Subjective well-being: The science of happiness and life satisfaction. In C.R. Snyder & S.J. Lopez (Eds.). *Handbook of positive psychology* (pp. 63–73). New York: Oxford.

Diener, E. (2008). Index of notable publications.Retrieved October 18, 2008 from http://www.psych.uiuc.edu/~ediener/ .

Duckworth, A.L., Steen, T.A., & Seligman, M.E.P. (2005). Positive psychology in clinical practice. *Annual Review of Clinical Psychology*, 1, 629–651.

Dutton, D.G. (2008). My back pages: reflections on thirty years of domestic violence research. *Trauma, Violence, and Abuse*, 9, 131–143.

Easton, C., Swan, S., & Sinha, R. (2000). Motivation to change substance use among offenders of domestic violence. *Journal of Substance Abuse Treatment*, 19, 1–5.

Eisikovits, Z., Enosh, G., & Edleson, J.L. (1996). The future of intervention in woman battering: common themes and emerging directions. In J.L. Edleson & Z. Eisikovits (Eds.), Future interventions with battered women and their families: Visions for policy practice and research (pp. 216–223). Thousand Oaks, CA: Sage.

Ferguson, H. (2004). *Protecting children in time; Child abuse, child protection and the consequences of modernity*. New York: Palgrave.

Fredrickson, B.L. (2002). Positive emotions. In In C.R. Snyder & S.J. Lopez (Eds.). *Handbook of Positive Psychology* (pp. 120–134). New York: Oxford.

Fredrickson, B.L. (2003). The value of positive emotions. *American Scientist*, 91, 330–335.

Fredrickson, B.L. (2004). Gratitude, like other positive emotions, broadens and builds. In Emmons, R.A. & M.E. McCullough (Eds.) *The psychology of gratitude*. (pp. 145–166). New York: Oxford University Press.

Fredrickson, B.L. (2006). Unpacking positive emotions: Investigating the seeds of human flourishing. *Journal of Positive Psychology*, 1, 57–60.

Gergen, K.J. (1985). The social constructionist movement in modern psychology. *American Psychologist*, 40, 266–275.

Gondolf, E.W. (2002). *Batterer intervention systems: Issues outcomes and recommendations*. Thousand Oaks California: Sage.

Gover, A.R., Brank, E.M., & MacDonald, J.M. (2007). A specialized domestic violence court in South Carolina: An example of procedural justice for victims and defendants. *Violence Against Women*, 13, 603–626.

Jackson, S., Feder, L., Forde, D.R., Davis, R.C., Maxwell, C.D., & Taylor, B.G. (June 2003). Batterer intervention programs: Where do we go from here? *Special NIJ Report*, Washington DC; National Institute of Justice, U.S. Department of Justice.

Joseph, S., & Worsley, R. (2005). *Person-centered psychopathology: A positive psychology of mental health*. Ross-on-Wye, UK: PCCS Books.

Hamberger, L.K. (2008a). Twenty-five years of change in working with partner abusers-part 1: Observations from the trenches about community and system-level changes. *Journal of Aggression, Maltreatment, & Trauma*, 16, 355–375.

Hamberger, L.K. (2008b). Twenty-five years of change in working with partner abusers-part II: Observations from the trenches about changes in understanding of abusers and abuser treatment. *Journal of Aggression, Maltreatment, & Trauma*, 17, 1–22.

Kazdin, A.E. (2008). Evidence based treatment and practice: New opportunities to bridge clinical research and practice, enhance the knowledge base and improve patient care. *American Psychologist*, 63, 146–159.

Kistenmacher, B.R., & Weiss, R.L. (2008). Motivational interviewing as a mechanism for change in men who batter: A randomized control trial. *Violence and Victims, 5,* 558–570.

Lee, M.Y., Sebold, J., & Uken, A. (2003a). *Solution-focused treatment of domestic violence offenders: Accountability for change.* New York: Oxford University Press.

Lee, M.Y., Sebold, J., & Uken, A. (2003b). Brief solution-focused group treatment with domestic violence offenders: Listen to the narratives of participants and their partners. *Journal of Brief Therapy, 2,* 3–26.

Lee. M.Y., Uken. A., Sebold, J. (2004). Accountability for solutions: Solution-focused treatment with domestic violence offenders. *Families in Society, 85,* 463–476.

Lee. M.Y., Uken. A., Sebold, J. (2007). Role of self-determined goals in predicting recidivism in domestic violence offenders. *Research on Social Work Practice, 17,* 30–41.

Lilienfeld, S.O. (2007). Psychological treatments that cause harm. *Perspectives on Psychological Science, 2,* 53–70.

Linley, P.A., Maltby, J., Wood, A.M., Joseph, S., Harrington, S., Peterson, C., Park, N., & Seligman, M.E.P. (2007). Character strengths in the United Kingdom: The VIA Inventory of Strengths. *Personality and Individual Differences, 43,* 341–351.

MacCoun, R.J. (2005). Voice, control, and belonging: The double-edged sword of procedural fairness. *Annual Review of Law and Social Science, 1,* 171–201.

McNamee, S. (2004). Therapy as social construction: Back to basics and forward toward challenging issues. In T. Strong and D. Pare (Eds.). *Furthering talk: Advances in discursive therapies* (pp. 253–270). New York: Kluwer Academic/Plenum Press.

Milner, J. (2004). From 'disappearing to demonized': The effects on men and women of professional interventions based on challenging men who are violent. *Critical Social Policy, 24,* 79–101.

Musser, P.H., Semiantin, J.N., Taft, C.T., & Murphy, C.M. (2008). Motivational interviewing as a pregroup intervention for partner violent men. *Violence and Victims, 23,* 539–557.

Norcross, J.C., & Lambert, M.J. (2006). The therapy relationship. In J.C. Norcross, L.E. Beutler, & R.F. Levant. (Eds.). *Evidence-based practices in mental health: Debate and dialogue on the fundamental questions* (pp. 208–218). Washington, DC: APA.

Ong A.D., & van Dulmen, M.H.M. (2007). *Oxford handbook of methods in positive psychology.* New York, Oxford.

Paternoster, R., Bachman, R., Brame, R., & Sherman, L.W. (1997). Do fair procedures matter? The effect of procedural justice on spouse assault. *Law & Society Review, 31,* 163–204.

Pavot, W., & Diener, E. (2004). Findings on subjective well-being: Applications to public police, clinical interventions, and education. In In P.A. Linley and S.A. Joseph (Eds.), *Positive psychology in practice* (pp. 679–692). Hoboken, NJ: Wiley.

Peterson, C. (2006). The Values in Action (VIA) Classification of Strengths. In M. Csikszentmihalyi & I.S. Csikszentmihalyi (Eds.). *A life worth living: Contributions to positive psychology,* (pp. 29–48). New York: Oxford.

Peterson, C., & Seligman, M.E.P. (2004). *Character strengths and virtues: A classification and handbook.* Washington, DC: American Psychological Association.

Ryff, C.D. (1989a). Beyond Ponce de Leon and life satisfaction: New directions in quest of successful aging. *International Journal of Behavioral Development, 12,* 35–55.

Ryff, C.D. (1989b). Happiness is everything or is it? Explorations on the meaning of psychological well-being? *Journal of Personality and Social Psychology*, 57, 1069–1081.

Ryff, C.D., & Keyes, C.L.M. (1995). The structure of psychological well-being revisited. *Journal of Personality and Social Psychology*, 69, 719–727.

Ryff, C.D., & Singer, B.H. (1998). The contours of positive human health. *Psychological Inquiry*, 9, 1–28.

Ryff, C.D., & Singer, B. (2002). From social structure to biology: Integrative science in pursuit of human health and well being. In C.R. Snyder & S.J. Lopez (Eds.). *Handbook of positive psychology* (pp. 541–555). New York: Oxford.

Saleebey, D. (2006). *The strengths perspective in social work practice*. (4th ed.). New York: Pearson.

Seligman, M.E.P. (2002). *Authentic happiness: Using the new positive psychology to realize Your potential for lasting fulfillment*. New York, Free Press.

Seligman, M.E.P., & Csikszentmihalyi, M. (2000). Positive psychology: An introduction. *American Psychologist*, 55, 5–14.

Seligman, M.E.P., Park, N., & Peterson, C. (2004). The Values In Action (VIA) classification of character strengths. *Ricerche di Psicologia*, 27, 63–78.

Scott, D. (2006). Towards a public health model of child protection in Australia. *Communities, Families, and Children in Australia*, 1, 9–18.

Skeem, J.L., Emke-Francis, P., & Eno Louden, J. (2006). Probation, mental health, and mandated treatment: A national survey. *Criminal Justice and Behavior*, 33, 158–184.

Skeem, J.L., Encandela, J., & Eno Louden, J. (2003). Perspectives on probation and mandated mental health treatment in specialized and traditional probation departments. *Behavioral Sciences & the Law*, 21, 429–458.

Skeem, J.L., Eno Louden J, Polaschek, D., & Camp, J. (2007). Assessing relationship quality in mandated community treatment: Blending care with control. *Psychological Assessment*, 19, 397–410.

Stuart, R.B., & Lilienfeld, S.O. (2007). The evidence missing from evidence-based practice. *American Psychologist*, 62, 615–616.

Taylor, S.E., Klein, L.C., Lewis, B.P., Gruenewald, T.L., Gurung, R.A.R., & Updegraff, J.A. (2000). Biobehavioral responses to stress in females: Tend-and-befriend, not fight-or-flight. *Psychological review*, 107, 422–429.

Taft, C.T., Murphy, C.M., Elliott, J.D., & Morrel T.M. (2001). Attendance enhancing procedures in group counseling for domestic abusers. *Journal of Counseling Psychology*, 48, 51–60.

Trotter, C. (2002). Worker skill and client outcome in child protection. *Child Abuse Review*, 11, 38–50.

Uken, A., Lee, M.Y., Sebold, J. (2007). The Plumas project: Solution-Focused treatment of domestic violence offenders. In P. DeJong & I.K. Berg, *Interviewing for solutions* (3rd ed.) (pp. 313–323). Pacific Cove, CA: Brooks/Cole.

Wemmers, J., & Cousineau, M.M. (2005). Victim needs and conjugal violence: Do victims want decision-making power? *Conflict Resolution Quarterly*, 22, 493–508.

Index